EARLY INTERVENTION FOR READING DIFFICULTIES

SOLVING PROBLEMS IN THE TEACHING OF LITERACY

Cathy Collins Block, Series Editor

Recent Volumes

Early Intervention for Reading Difficulties

THE INTERACTIVE STRATEGIES APPROACH

DONNA M. SCANLON
KIMBERLY L. ANDERSON
JOAN M. SWEENEY

THE GUILFORD PRESS
New York   London

© 2010 The Guilford Press
A Division of Guilford Publications, Inc.
72 Spring Street, New York, NY 10012
www.guilford.com

Printed in the United States of America

This book is printed on acid-free paper.

Last digit is print number: 9 8 7 6 5 4 3 2

Library of Congress Cataloging-in-Publication Data

Scanlon, Donna M.
   Early intervention for reading difficulties: the interactive strategies approach / by Donna
M. Scanlon, Kimberly L. Anderson, and Joan M. Sweeney.
       p. cm.—(Solving problems in the teaching of literacy)
   Includes bibliographical references and index.
   ISBN 978-1-60623-853-0 (pbk.: alk. paper)—ISBN 978-1-60623-854-7 (cloth: alk.
paper)
   1. Reading—Remedial teaching. I. Anderson, Kimberly L. II. Sweeney, Joan M.
III. Title.
   LB1050.5.S228 2010
   372.43—dc22
                                                              2010012458

About the Authors

Donna M. Scanlon, PhD, is Professor in the Reading Department at the University at Albany, State University of New York. Dr. Scanlon has spent most of her career studying children's reading difficulties. Her studies have focused on the relationships between instructional characteristics and success in learning to read and on developing and evaluating approaches to preventing early reading difficulties. Findings from studies that she and her colleagues conducted have contributed to the emergence of response to intervention as a process for preventing reading difficulties and avoiding inappropriate and inaccurate learning disability classifications. Most recently, Dr. Scanlon's work has focused on the development of teacher knowledge and teaching skill among both preservice and inservice teachers for the purpose of helping teachers to prevent reading difficulties.

Kimberly L. Anderson, PhD, is a research associate in the Child Research and Study Center at the University at Albany, State University of New York, and an adjunct instructor in the University's Reading Department. Dr. Anderson has contributed to the Center's research on the interactive strategies approach (ISA) by serving as an intervention teacher; by providing professional development for teachers learning to implement the ISA in the early primary grades in both classroom and intervention settings; and, most recently, by collaborating with preservice educators from institutions across New York on enhancing preservice teacher knowledge related to literacy instruction. She worked for many years as a school psychologist at the elementary level and has spent several years as a reading teacher at the primary level, utilizing the ISA to provide small-group intervention to kindergartners and first-grade students.

Joan M. Sweeney, MSEd, is a reading teacher in the North Colonie Central School District in Latham, New York. Previously, she was a research associate in the Child Research and Study Center at the University at Albany, State University of New York, where she provided intervention for struggling readers, supervised intervention teachers, and coached classroom teachers utilizing the ISA to support children's literacy development.

Preface

Early Intervention for Reading Difficulties: The Interactive Strategies Approach
is intended to help teachers develop the knowledge and skills to effectively teach
primary-grade children who experience difficulty with learning to read and older
children who have serious reading difficulties. The book describes the interactive
strategies approach (ISA, Vellutino & Scanlon, 2002), an instructional approach
developed and tested in a series of large-scale studies that investigated ways to prevent early reading difficulties. These studies revealed that teachers utilizing the ISA
in classroom, small-group, and/or one-to-one intervention settings with beginning
and struggling readers were able to substantially reduce the number of children
who demonstrated early reading difficulties.

In fact, the ISA studies contributed to the body of research that ultimately
became the rationale for the response-to-intervention (RTI) approach to preventing reading difficulties and determining whether a child should be considered
learning disabled. That is, research utilizing the ISA and studies conducted by several other research groups have demonstrated that many children who are at risk
for or who experience early reading difficulties make accelerated progress when
provided with comprehensive and appropriately intensified early literacy instruction, whereas many of their peers who do not receive such intensified instruction
ultimately qualify as learning disabled in reading. From an RTI perspective, it is
now widely believed that children should not be considered for a learning disability designation until it is clear that high-quality and intensified instruction is ineffective in accelerating their learning to the point where they can meet grade-level
expectations.

Numerous books and articles have been written in support of schools' efforts to implement RTI for both prevention and decision-making purposes. They explain the basic logic of RTI and the approaches that may be used to monitor children's progress and suggest procedures for documenting progress and making decisions about future instructional settings. However, comparatively little has been written about the instruction itself—which is rather surprising given that instruction is widely recognized to be the most "active ingredient" in implementing an RTI model. Our major goal in writing this book is to help teachers effectively identify the sources of children's difficulties so they can plan and deliver instruction that will help accelerate children's progress.

Most of the book is squarely focused on instruction for early literacy learners, particularly students who struggle. In Part I, "A Comprehensive Approach to Early Intervention," Chapter 1 describes the ISA in general terms and gives an overview of the studies that demonstrate its effectiveness in preventing early reading difficulties. It discusses the ways in which the ISA differs from other approaches to early literacy instruction and how the ISA might be implemented in an RTI context. Finally, the chapter explicates the need for comprehensive literacy instruction, briefly notes the factors that place children at risk for literacy learning difficulties, and lists instructional goals around which the ISA is organized.

Chapter 2 discusses how both the instructional goals and the general instructional premises of the ISA may be incorporated into language arts instruction at the classroom level. A major theme of this chapter is that instruction should be responsive to the broad spectrum of students in a typical classroom. To this end, we suggest that language arts instruction include a combination of whole-class, small-group, and one-to-one instruction. Whereas small, ability-based groupings are at the heart of responsive instruction at the classroom level, we argue that a diversity of learners must be considered in all aspects of language arts instruction.

Chapter 3 addresses motivation, the first of the ISA's instructional goals. In our work with teachers relative to the ISA, we have always identified motivation to read and write as the first and most important goal of early literacy instruction, particularly for children who begin their schooling with comparatively limited early literacy skills. We discuss the need to be attentive to motivational factors that impact reading development because these factors have a powerful influence on success (or lack thereof). Attention to motivational issues, particularly the development of intrinsic motivation and a sense of competence relative to literacy, should pervade interactions with early literacy learners.

Parts II through IV are organized around instructional goals to encourage teachers to view instruction in a goal-oriented way. Chapters in these parts feature checklists of subgoals, skills, strategies, and attitudes or approaches to literacy learning with which teachers can track the performance of their students and plan instruction. The use of the checklists is based on the premise that virtually every instructional interaction gives teachers the opportunity to evaluate and document children's learning and, thereby, to guide their planning of future instruction.

Part II, "Learning the Alphabetic Code," focuses on the development of alphabetic knowledge and the understanding of how printed language relates to spoken language. Chapters 4 through 9 detail the development of print conventions, letter–name knowledge, letter–sound knowledge, the alphabetic principle, and the use of larger orthographic units. The development of accuracy and automaticity with these foundational skills allows the developing reader to become an effective word learner.

Part III, "Word Learning," focuses on the development of sight vocabulary (i.e., words that can be identified automatically) through explicit teaching of high-frequency words and through the application of word-learning strategies that enable readers to effectively identify unfamiliar words and, ultimately, to learn them to the point where they become part of the reader's sight vocabulary. We emphasize teaching children to use both the letters in the unknown word and the semantic and syntactic context in which it occurs in the process of word solving. In Chapter 10, extensive discussion is devoted to providing explicit instruction in the use of a specific set of word identification strategies to facilitate word solving in context that, in turn, leads to word learning. We stress helping children to become independent word solvers so that their reading skills improve each time they read to the point where they will ultimately be able to devote most or all of their cognitive resources to understanding the meaning of the text rather than to the process of word solving. Chapter 11 discusses ways to build skill with high-frequency words.

Part IV, "Meaning Construction," focuses on the purpose of reading: meaning making, or making sense of what is read. Comprehension requires not only the ability to read the words, but also language skills and general (background) knowledge—both of which are major topics in this part. Chapters 12 and 13 describe methods that support the development of language skills, especially knowledge of word meanings, and methods of fostering the development of knowledge and active engagement with the meaning of text, all of which are critical to the comprehension of texts.

Last, Part V, "Implementing Intensified Instruction," returns to the RTI approach and discusses how small-group and one-to-one instruction might be organized and implemented within and beyond the classroom. We emphasize the need to provide more intensive instruction for children who experience the greatest difficulties and encourage teachers to coordinate instruction across instructional settings so that children who receive instruction beyond the classroom are not being asked to learn more than their classroom peers. Chapter 14 integrates the information discussed relative to each of the major instructional goals into a cohesive plan for small-group and one-to-one instruction. We detail the lesson structure used in the ISA and the thinking, planning, instruction, record keeping, and reflection components of small-group and one-to-one lessons.

In Chapter 15, we describe a general structure for RTI and propose a four-tiered RTI model for struggling literacy learners in the early primary grades. We offer suggestions about the multiple decisions that schools face as they plan and implement an RTI process. Finally, we continue to spotlight the importance of ensuring that instruction in the context of RTI is of high quality, is responsive to the needs of the children who have entered the RTI process, and is coherent across the settings in which instruction is offered.

ACKNOWLEDGMENTS

This text evolved over the course of nearly 20 years of research focused on preventing reading difficulties among young children. Major work on the text occurred in the context of research supported by grants from the National Institute of Child Health and Human Development (Grant Number: R01 HD42350) and the Institute of Education Sciences at the United States Department of Education (Grant Number: R305W060024).

The number of people who should be recognized for their contributions to the research and thinking reflected in this text is immense. We are especially indebted to the children and teachers who participated in the research and allowed us to study their learning and development and to the school administrators and administrative support staff who facilitated our work.

Our thanks also go to our colleagues and friends who sharpened our thinking about early literacy development and helped us to figure out how to share our thinking with preservice and inservice teachers. The following people played particularly prominent roles: Frank Vellutino, Lynn Gelzheiser, Laura Hallgren-Flynn, Peter Johnston, and Virginia Goatley. We also wish to thank Peggy Connors, Andrea Daley, Deb Rutnik, Danielle Snyder, and Laura Jackson for serving as "model" ISA teachers. Several of the descriptions of instructional interactions are derived from videos of their teaching.

With respect to the conduct of the research, we wish to thank Diane Fanuele for so ably managing the copious amounts of data the studies have generated. Finally, we express our sincere gratitude to Sheila Small, the research coordinator at the Child Research and Study Center at the University at Albany. Her dedication to ensuring high-quality and timely data collection and her incredible ability to build and maintain strong relationships with participating schools contributed immeasurably to the research on early literacy development which is the foundation for the instructional practices described in this book.

Special thanks are also due to Molly Jaffe Douglas who contributed most of the artwork.

DONNA M. SCANLON
KIMBERLY L. ANDERSON
JOAN M. SWEENEY

Contents

PART I

A COMPREHENSIVE APPROACH TO EARLY INTERVENTION

CHAPTER 1

The Interactive Strategies Approach

Children vary considerably in the ease with which they learn to read. Some learn with fairly little instructional guidance, whereas others find it to be a nearly impossible undertaking given the instruction traditionally offered in schools. A substantial body of research that has accumulated over the last two decades indicates that most early reading difficulties can be prevented through the implementation of appropriately targeted and intensified instructional interventions (e.g., Brown, Denton, Kelly, Outhred, & McNaught, 1999; Center, Wheldal, Freeman, Outhred, & McNaught, 1995; Mathes et al., 2005; Gomez-Bellenge, Rogers, & Fullerton, 2003; O'Connor, 2000; O'Connor, Harty, & Fulmer, 2005; Scanlon, Vellutino, Small, Fanuele, & Sweeney, 2005; Scanlon, Gelzheiser, Vellutino, Schatschneider, & Sweeney, 2008; Torgesen et al., 2001; Vaughn, Linan-Thompson, & Hickman, 2003; Vellutino et al., 1996; Wanzek & Vaughn, 2008).

This book describes one approach to early literacy instruction and intervention—the interactive strategies approach (ISA; Vellutino & Scanlon, 2002)—which was developed and tested over the course of three major longitudinal studies that focused on reducing the number of children who experienced serious reading difficulties in the early primary grades. These studies have demonstrated that instruction based on the ISA has a positive impact on student achievement when implemented by classroom teachers and when implemented in small-group and one to one intervention settings beyond the classroom. Before describing these studies, however, we first provide a brief introduction to the ISA.

Research-Based Instruction

At a time when schools are called upon to implement research-based instructional practices, it is important to consider the distinction between "research-based" approaches and "research-tested" approaches. Many instructional approaches that are identified as research-based are simply that—based on research. The *research-based* label can be attached to a product/program if the developer(s) have simply familiarized themselves with the research and then based their program on what was learned in that research. The What Works Clearinghouse (WWC), which is sponsored by the Institute of Education Sciences at the U.S. Department of Education (*ies.ed.gov/ncee/wwc*), reviews the scientific evidence on education programs, including beginning reading programs, to evaluate their effectiveness and serves as an unbiased source of information relative to research-tested educational products. Although there are many programs and approaches that have yet to be evaluated by the WWC (including the ISA), this website offers a valuable resource for schools as they contemplate investments in instructional materials and programs.

CHARACTERISTICS OF THE ISA

The ISA is an *approach* to early literacy instruction, not a program. It is not tied to particular instructional materials, nor does it provide highly scripted instructional interactions. Rather, the ISA offers a way to conceptualize early literacy development and to support children as they learn to read and write. We view teachers as professionals who use their knowledge of their students' skills and abilities in combination with knowledge of their curriculum and the process of literacy development more generally to plan and deliver effective literacy instruction. Although we do make some suggestions for instructional materials that are illustrative of the types of materials we encourage teachers to use, we also offer ideas for how teachers might evaluate and utilize the materials they have on hand to more effectively meet the needs of their students—particularly those who find learning to read challenging. Our primary goal in this book is to help teachers more thoroughly understand early literacy development and to effectively respond to, plan for, and teach the children who find reading challenging. The ISA places particular emphasis on meeting the needs of children who struggle at the early stages of learning to read through careful analysis of their literacy skills and provision of instruction that is responsive to their current capabilities. In order to provide such responsive instruction, teachers need to become highly knowledgeable about early literacy, how it develops, and how to respond to literacy learning difficulties. Therefore, the development of teacher knowledge related to early literacy development is a major focus of the ISA and, thus, a major focus of this book.

The name of the approach conveys the importance placed on helping children become strategic in their reading and writing endeavors. From our perspective, the goal of instruction should be to teach foundational skills and strategies that children will learn to use independently, flexibly, and interactively while reading and writing. Through this active and thoughtful engagement in reading, children will grow as readers. Thus, the goal of instruction is to help children develop a *self-teaching mechanism* (Share, 1995) that enables them to become stronger readers through engagement in reading. To facilitate self-teaching, instruction should provide children with guided practice in reading and writing in contexts that are motivating and rewarding and using materials that are interesting, personally meaningful, and manageable (meaning, not too difficult).

The logic behind the ISA stems from what we know about the development of certain reading-related skills and the young child's ability to comprehend written text—which is, after all, the only reason for reading. For children in the primary grades, the ability to comprehend written material is largely dependent upon their ability to accurately and quickly identify the words in the text. This is true partly because many of the materials that early primary-grade children read are not very challenging conceptually. Of course, when children do encounter reading materials that are conceptually challenging, fast and accurate identification of the majority of words in the text is still an important determinant of comprehension. However, the child's general world knowledge, vocabulary, and active thinking about the meaning of the text are also important determinants of comprehension.

In order to facilitate teachers' thinking and planning around the needs of their literacy learners, much of this book is organized around a set of instructional goals that can be addressed in a variety of settings (e.g., whole class, small group, one to one) and activities (e.g., read-aloud, shared reading, writing). The purpose of organizing instruction around a goal structure is to encourage teachers to be mindful of what they are trying to accomplish with their students in each instructional activity and thus to avoid engaging children in instructional activities that do not move them forward relative to their literacy learning goals.

In any given primary classroom, there is likely to be considerable diversity in the literacy skills and abilities of the children. Classroom teachers using the ISA are encouraged to be mindful of this diversity as they plan and deliver whole-class and small-group literacy instruction. To address the needs of the children who struggle the most with literacy acquisition, classroom teachers are encouraged to provide small-group reading instruction on a daily basis, with lessons planned to specifically meet the needs of the children in the group. For children who qualify for intervention beyond the classroom, intervention teachers are similarly encouraged to provide instruction that is responsive to the children's current capabilities. Further, instruction in these settings should be supportive of the children's classroom language arts program as well, so that the children are better prepared to profit from classroom instruction.

What's Different about the ISA?

In discussing the ISA, we are often asked to indicate how it differs from other approaches to early literacy instruction. If teachers who were experienced in using the ISA were asked this question, they would, most likely, talk about the approach to helping young children learn how to effectively puzzle through unfamiliar words encountered while reading. In the ISA children are explicitly taught word-solving strategies and are coached in their use. The goal is for the children to become so effective and independent in word solving that they essentially have a self-teaching mechanism (Share, 1995) that enables them to learn to read the huge number of words that proficient readers ultimately know.

If we were asked the same question, we would agree with the teachers that the approach to teaching word-solving strategies is the most obvious difference between the ISA and other comprehensive approaches. However, we would add that the approach to teaching about the alphabetic code, for the purpose of facilitating word learning, is more thorough than many other approaches and more attentive to the need for children to learn to be flexible in their decoding attempts due to the irregular nature of English spellings. We would also argue that the attention given to enhancing children's vocabulary and world knowledge and to the impact of these knowledge sources on both oral reading and comprehension distinguishes the ISA from many other approaches to early literacy instruction. Finally, we would add that, unlike many other approaches to early literacy instruction, the foundational principles on which the ISA is built are applicable across both classroom and intervention settings and, in fact, the ISA has been researched and proven effective in whole-class, small-group, and one-to-one instructional settings.

STUDIES OF THE ISA

In the first study (Vellutino et al., 1996), an early version of the ISA was developed and implemented in the context of one-to-one tutoring for struggling first-grade readers. Participating children were randomly assigned to receive ISA-based tutoring or the instruction normally offered in their schools. Children who participated in the ISA tutoring were substantially less likely to experience long-term reading difficulties than were children in the comparison group.

The second study (Scanlon et al., 2005) was undertaken to address the dual concerns that intensive one-to-one intervention was too costly for schools to sustain on a large scale and that, even when children were provided with intensive one-to-one intervention in first grade, some continued to experience significant reading difficulties. To address these concerns, we attempted to reduce the number of children who would qualify for intensive intervention in first grade by identifying children who were at risk of literacy learning difficulties at kindergarten entry and instituting intervention in a small-group context during the kindergarten year. The logic was that beginning intervention in kindergarten would prevent early limitations in literacy skills from growing and becoming debilitating. It was antici-pated that this intervention would reduce the number of children who qualified for more intensive intervention in first grade and would reduce the severity of difficul-ties among children who continued to struggle despite kindergarten intervention. Random assignment to treatment conditions was, once again, utilized. The results indicated that participating in the ISA kindergarten intervention reduced the num-ber of children who qualified as poor readers in first grade. Further, for children who did qualify as poor readers in first grade, those who had participated in the ISA-based kindergarten intervention were less likely to demonstrate severe reading difficulties at the end of first grade than were children who had not participated in the ISA-based intervention in kindergarten. Thus, the effects of the kindergarten intervention were evident a full year after the children had left kindergarten, and this was true regardless of the type of intervention they received in first grade. It is also important to note that, in one combination of conditions, more than half of the children who qualified for intervention at the beginning of first grade (by scoring below the 15th percentile on a standardized measure of early literacy skills) made strong gains during first grade and scored above the 50th percentile at the end of the year. Thus, for children who did not respond well to an initial attempt to intervene, a second round of intervention that was more intensive and more specifically targeted on meeting their individual needs was effective in accelerating their reading growth.

The third major study of the ISA (Scanlon et al., 2008; Scanlon, Gelzheiser, Anderson, Vellutino & Schatschneider, in preparation) involved implementing the ISA in one of three ways at both the kindergarten and first-grade levels. One approach to implementation involved providing small-group and one-to-one inter-ventions for children, much like what was done in the Scanlon et al. 2005 study. The second approach involved providing ISA-based professional development for classroom teachers that entailed engaging the teachers in a summer workshop that paralleled the training provided for intervention teachers and, thereafter, provid-ing in-school consultation on the implementation of the approach. The third type of implementation involved both direct interventions for children and professional development for their classroom teachers. All three approaches were effective in reducing the incidence of reading difficulties by the end of both kindergarten and first grade. However, the anticipated benefit of the condition in which both inter-vention and professional development were provided did not materialize. School personnel, upon hearing of this surprising outcome, suggested that it may have been the result of classroom teachers feeling that they did not need to attend to the needs of the students in ISA-based intervention because their needs were being met by the intervention program. This, of course, is not the purpose of intervention programs. We have no way to evaluate this possibility. However, it does give us reason to strongly caution schools that are implementing interventions on behalf of struggling readers to be certain that the interventions are an add-on to, rather than a replacement for, the instruction that would normally be available in the classroom.

THE ISA AND RESPONSE TO INTERVENTION

As a result of the extensive research on the effectiveness of instructional enhancements in preventing long-term reading difficulties, including research on the ISA, there has been a major conceptual shift in thinking about how schools and teachers should respond to children who demonstrate reading difficulties. Whereas in the past, children who were judged to be otherwise "normal" but who lagged seriously behind their peers in the development of reading skill were often identified as learning disabled (or reading disabled), it is now widely recognized that an individual's ability to read is the result of a complex interaction between the underlying characteristics of the child and his or her prior experiences and the amount, type, and quality of the instruction that she receives. While it is certainly acknowledged that some children need more instructional guidance to learn to read and that some, in fact, need very intensive and individualized support, it is now recognized that nearly all children who are not hampered by severe intellectual, perceptual, or emotional limitations can learn to read. As a result of this shift in thinking, a new process for determining whether a child should be identified as learning disabled has been made available to schools through federal legislation passed in 2004. The Individuals with Disabilities Education Improvement Act (IDEIA) encourages schools to identify children who are at risk of experiencing learning difficulties early in their schooling and to begin interventions in an effort to ameliorate their difficulties. Further, information about the child's response to instruction is used in determining whether she should ultimately be identified as learning disabled. This process is widely referred to as *response to intervention* (RTI; National Association of State Directors of Special Education, 2005). An important advantage of an RTI process is that it has the potential to prevent children from experiencing long-term learning difficulties because efforts to intervene are instituted before learning gaps have a chance to grow and become disabling. As a result, the process has the potential to reduce the number of children who may be inaccurately identified as learning disabled due to inadequate instructional experiences.

At this time, the most widely recognized model of RTI utilizes a tiered approach to implementation. This approach (as described by Fuchs & Fuchs, 2006) entails (1) universal screening of all children, (2) identification of children who appear to be at risk of not meeting grade-level expectations and closely monitoring their progress, and (3) gradually increasing the amount and/or intensity of instructional support offered to children who do not show the gains needed to meet grade-level expectations. While there appear to be as many models of RTI implementation as there are research groups exploring the RTI process (Scanlon, in press), most models involve three or four tiers of intervention, with Tier 1 encompassing instruction and intervention provided by the classroom teacher, Tier 2 involving more intensive and expert intervention provided beyond the classroom, and Tiers 3 and 4 providing even more intensive intervention and/or special education services, depending on the model. (The model that we advocate, which is discussed briefly in the next chapter and in greater detail in Chapter 15, involves four tiers and begins early in kindergarten and continues through at least the end of first grade.)

Since passage of the IDEIA legislation in 2004 and the issuance of the accompanying regulations (Yell, Shriner, & Katsiyannis, 2006), much has been written about the RTI process. Most of the practitioner-oriented literature has focused on the broad frameworks for RTI approaches and on the demands of the record keeping needed to document interventions and progress. Remarkably little has been written about the instruction that is offered to children who are at risk of experiencing long-term difficulties. In fact, instructional recommendations are often limited to advice to adopt research-based programs and to implement them with fidelity (e.g., Brown-Chidsey & Steege, 2005; Mellard & Johnson, 2008). However, research on instructional effectiveness suggests that it is what the teacher does rather than the program she uses that is the most important determinant of children's achievement (Bond & Dykstra 1967; Duffy & Hoffman, 1999; Nye, Konstantopolous, & Hedges, 2004; Scanlon et al., 2008; Tivnan & Hemphill, 2005). Therefore, in the ISA, as noted above, we focus on the development of teacher knowledge related to early literacy development and instruction so as to enable teachers to provide effective early literacy instruction across instructional contexts and materials. We argue that the nature and quality of instruction are the most important determinants of a child's response to intervention. Further, we argue that, to be optimally effective, the instruction offered across instructional settings and contexts (i.e., the different tiers of intervention) should be responsive to the children's needs and be coherent and mutually reinforcing. This position is based on both empirical and logical grounds. Empirically, Borman, Wong, Hedges, and D'Agostino (2001) found that a greater degree of curricular congruence across instructional settings was associated with stronger reading outcomes in the early primary grades. On logical grounds, if our goal is to enable children to benefit from and succeed in the classroom language arts program, it seems that alignment of instruction across classroom and intervention settings would be the most prudent approach. Of course, if the classroom language arts program is weak and/or inappropriate for the children who qualify for intervention, modifications to the classroom program would be an important (first) step in enhancing the quality of instruction that is offered.

READING IS A COMPLICATED PROCESS AND REQUIRES COMPREHENSIVE INSTRUCTION

Reading is a complex process that requires the analysis, coordination, and interpretation of a variety of sources of information. In order to effectively meet the needs of literacy learners, especially those who struggle, instruction needs to take account of this complexity. Consider, for example, what is involved in reading and understanding the simple text below:

Matt was going to Sara's party. Sara likes kites. Matt can bring her a kite.

To understand this text, the reader obviously needs to be able to (1) read the words, (2) retrieve the words' meanings, (3) put the words together to form meaningful ideas, and (4) assemble a larger model of what the text is about. Because difficulties with any of these processes can result in reading difficulties, all of these important processes need to be considered when designing instruction to help children learn to read.

Because teachers are proficient readers and perform many, if not all, of these processes effortlessly, they are sometimes surprised by, and insensitive to, the complexity of the processes. By becoming more attuned to these complexities, teachers can become better able to provide instruction and guidance to students who are learning to read. To help teachers gain these insights, we begin with an (incomplete) analysis of what a reader might do while reading the text about Sara's party.

Read the Words

All of the words in this text are known to proficient readers. They can identify them automatically with little or no conscious thought. As a result, readers can devote most, if not all, of their thinking to making sense of the text. For beginning or struggling readers, however, some of the words will be somewhat or very unfamiliar and they *will* have to devote thought to figuring out the words. Their success in doing so will depend on several things, including what they understand about how the alphabetic code works (i.e., how the printed letters represent the sounds in spoken words) and their ability to make use of other sources of information, such as the context in which the word occurs. For example, if students attempted to "sound out" the word *was*, it would rhyme with *pass* rather than with *fuzz*! Using the context of the sentence in combination with the information provided by the letters in the word, beginning readers would be more likely to figure out the word.

Retrieve the Words' Meaning(s)

The meanings of words are usually accessed quite automatically while reading *if* the words are in readers' vocabulary. So, for example, readers who know what a kite is will activate that knowledge when reading the word *kites*. In fact, having knowledge of kites will allow readers to confirm that the printed word is, in fact, pronounced as *kites* rather than as *kit-es* or *kite-es*. For a word such as *can*, which has more than one common meaning (the container vs. the ability to do something), proficient readers generally become aware of only the meaning of the word that is signaled by the context.

Assemble Words to Form Idea Units

As noted, the context in which a word occurs helps readers identify the word, and for words with more than one meaning, helps readers to select the intended meaning of the word. One of the ways that context operates is through readers' knowledge of spoken language and the implicit rules regarding which words can follow one another. For example, the verb meaning of *can* is selected in the sentence *Matt can bring her a kite*, partly because, within a sentence in English, a noun is more often followed by a verb than by another noun. Moreover, if in this sentence the proper noun *Matt* were to be followed by another proper noun (like *Jack*), there would be a comma between the two proper nouns—another signal to which proficient readers attend unconsciously.

Even when none of the words has multiple meanings, a hallmark of proficient reading (and listening) is that readers/listeners process the words in meaningful units or phrases. A meaningful unit might be a sentence, if it is short enough, or it might be only a part of a sentence—but the part would comprise a unit of meaning. For example, the sentence *Sara likes kites* might be processed as one meaningful unit because it is only three words long and presents a fairly simple idea. However, the longer sentence *Matt was going to Sara's party* might be processed as two meaningful units (e.g., *Matt was going [somewhere]* and *to Sara's party*). Exactly how a sentence would be processed would depend on a variety of factors, including how familiar readers/listeners are with the general topic, how easily they can access the meanings of the individual words, how easily they can identify the individual words, and so on.

Assemble a Larger Model of the Text

By this point, readers of this chapter are likely to be growing weary of thinking about all of the things that proficient readers do while reading just three fairly simple sentences. However, so far, the discussion has hardly touched upon the major purpose of reading and what is, perhaps, the most complicated part of the process: to understand, interpret, and/or react to what is stated in the text. In order to fulfill this purpose, readers must relate the idea units to one another to form a conceptual understanding of the text that spans the sentences and taps readers' knowledge in ways that facilitate comprehension. That is, while reading a text, readers "read" more than what is actually on the page; how they understand the text depends on what they already know about the topic. So, for example, if they know something about birthday parties, readers may infer that Sara's party is a birthday party because that is the kind of party to which one might bring a toy for a present. Readers are also likely to make some inference about Sara's age because it is less likely that one would bring a kite to a very young child or to an elderly adult. A discussion of the extent of thinking and inferring that might go on relative to this little bit of text could be quite extensive. Many readers, for example, construct a visual image of the two characters, including what they are wearing, what color hair they have, etc. The print on the page stimulates readers to think and visualize. For fully engaged and proficient readers, the thinking generally goes far beyond what is literally stated on the page.

The discussion above is not intended to make teachers feel overwhelmed by what needs to be taught (although this would be a reasonable reaction). Rather, the purpose is to help teachers more fully appreciate the complexity of the processes involved in reading and to develop insights into aspects of the process that may need explicit instructional attention. In what follows, we present information on how to support children's development as they are learning to read. Early in reading development, learning to read the words is a major hurdle, and so we focus a good deal of the discussion on this critical step. However, as the analysis above emphasizes, reading the words is only a part of the process. Early literacy instruction needs to attend to all aspects of the process. Teachers need to provide instruction that helps children develop knowledge of word meanings and the background knowledge that will enable them to do the kind of inferencing and reading between the lines that proficient readers do quite effortlessly. Teachers of beginning readers also need to ensure that the children understand that the purpose of print is to communicate, because only when readers understand that there is a message in the print will they engage in thinking beyond the initially challenging step of figuring out the words.

CHILDREN WHO STRUGGLE WITH LITERACY ACQUISITION

We have known for many years that children who lag behind their peers in early reading development are at high risk of experiencing prolonged reading difficulties (Francis, Shaywitz, & Steubing, 1996; Juel, 1988; Phillips, Norris, Osmond, & Maynard, 2002; Rayner, Foorman, Perfetti, Pesetsky, & Seidenberg, 2002) and, ultimately, of being identified as learning (or reading) disabled. Research comparing children who struggle with reading and those who learn to read with ease has identified critical areas that differentiate the two groups. Much of that research has been comprehensively summarized in a book, *Preventing Reading Difficulties* (Snow, Burns, & Griffiin, 1998), and in a more recent article by Vellutino, Fletcher, Snowling, and Scanlon (2004). Similar findings emerged in the National Early Literacy Panel report (2008). Based on this body of research, there is a developing consensus about the areas of difficulty that affect struggling readers and about the role of instruction in preventing reading difficulties. We briefly summarize this research below and periodically revisit it in relevant sections of this text.

Phonological Processing Difficulties

The research evidence on reading difficulties reveals that the most common area of difficulty among children who are identified as struggling readers at the early stages of learning to read is phonological processing (Snow et al., 1998). Because there is also strong evidence that the phonological processing skills of struggling readers can be improved through instruction and practice (e.g., Ball & Blachman, 1991; Blachman, 1991; Scanlon et al., 2005; Tangel & Blachman, 1992, 1995; Vellutino et al., 1996), we focus much of this book on ways to promote the development of phonological processing skills, including the ability to attend to the individual sounds in spoken words and to use the relationships between letters and their sounds to figure out the pronunciation of printed words. However, this focus should not be interpreted as suggesting that all early literacy instruction should emphasize phonological components. Indeed, many children appear to become proficient in the phonological domain with relatively little explicit guidance. Instruction that is too heavily focused on phonological skills may do little to further the development of these children.

Limitations in Language and General Knowledge

Research has demonstrated that vocabulary knowledge at the preschool and early primary level is a strong predictor of reading comprehension in late elementary grades and throughout schooling (Scarborough, 2001; Storch & Whitehurst, 2002). That is, in general, children who know the meanings of fewer words when they are young are likely to have difficulty comprehending the things they read when they are older (Cunningham & Stanovich, 1997). There is also evidence that classroom instruction can influence vocabulary knowledge. For example, Dickinson (2001) reports that, at least in preschool settings, the amount and quality of the language used by the children's teachers, the kinds of verbal interactions that occur in the classroom, and, more specifically, the types of interchanges that occur during read-alouds influence the development of oral language and vocabulary. In other words, early childhood teachers, in their instructional interactions with children, have the potential to positively impact language skills that are *critical* to future success in the comprehension of text. Whitehurst and Lonigan (1998) have provided similar findings with regard to book interactions between parents and their young children.

Reading comprehension is also influenced by the general knowledge possessed by readers. That is, what one already knows about a topic influences the acquisition of new information about that topic (Bransford & Johnson, 1972; Cain, Oakhill, Barnes, & Bryant, 2001; Neuman, 2006). Children who have had limited opportunities to develop the knowledge base that is expected in U.S. schools are at a serious learning disadvantage as they progress through the elementary grades because they are expected to build on a knowledge base that is shaky or even nonexistent. ISA teachers are encouraged to use children's books—both books that are read to children and books that the children read themselves—as a major resource for the development of language and general knowledge. We contend that early literacy instruction for all children, but particularly for children who demonstrate difficulties, needs to lead children to expect that the texts they listen to and read will make sense (Perfetti, Landi, & Oakhill, 2005). Without this expectation, we are allowing children to become passive comprehenders—that is, children who do not take an active role in making sense of the texts they read. To this end, we urge teachers to model and foster children's engagement with text meaning during interactive read-alouds from the very beginning.

INSTRUCTIONAL GOALS IN THE ISA

Taking into account the multiple factors that influence an individual's ability to comprehend written texts, the ISA is organized around a set of instructional goals. Teachers are encouraged to view instruction as a goal-oriented activity wherein they work to help children achieve identified goals, using a variety of instructional formats and materials. The goals range from the relatively simple and straightforward (e.g., developing letter-name knowledge) to those that are quite complex and involved (e.g., helping children become strategic and active readers). Subsequent chapters in this book are devoted to discussing each of the goals in detail. As we discuss each goal, we highlight the importance of being able to view literacy and literacy-related skills from the perspective of a young child who is a relative novice when it comes to understanding the intricacies of written language and how it relates to spoken language. Often in our formal and informal observations of teachers working with young children and in our own work with young children who are struggling to learn about written language, we are struck by how difficult it is for highly literate people to take a step back and understand the complexity of reading and writing processes from the perspective of a child who is just beginning to experience print. This is a theme to which we return frequently in discussing the ISA goals because one of our major purposes in this book is to help teachers develop greater expertise in identifying and responding to the difficulties experienced by struggling readers. Understanding the source of a child's confusion is an important step in responding to that confusion.

We review the relevant research for each goal and discuss how the goal relates to reading and writing processes more generally. We also discuss and provide sample instructional activities that can be used to help children achieve the goal, and where relevant, we discuss more and less challenging aspects of particular activities—often presenting a sequence of objectives within given goals. We discuss informal assessment tools for many of the goals and the need to use assessment to guide grouping decisions and instructional planning. Each of the goals is briefly described below.

Motivation to Read and Write

> The child will develop the belief that reading and writing are enjoyable and informative activities that are not beyond his or her capabilities.

In discussing this goal, we focus on a variety of factors that contributes to motivation, such as ensuring that children face an appropriate level of challenge in literacy tasks, expressing enthusiasm for reading and writing activities, actively engaging children in thinking about and responding to texts, making read-alouds an important and interactive part of the day, and construing reading and writing as privileges rather than as jobs (e.g., "You *get* to finish your book before recess" rather than "You *have* to finish your book before recess").

Alphabetics

> The child will understand the relationships between printed and spoken language and will be able to use these relationships in reading and writing.

This is an overarching goal that includes several individual goals related to the development of skill in using the alphabetic code. Each of the alphabetics goals is identified and described below.

Purposes and Conventions of Print

> The child will understand that the purpose of print is to communicate. The child will also understand the most basic print conventions, such as the left-to-right and top-to-bottom sequencing of print, where to begin reading a book, the concepts of letter and word, etc.

We provide a brief discussion of the confusion some children experience related to purposes of print and to the conventions regarding how print is organized on the page.

Phonological Awareness

> The child will have a conceptual grasp of the fact that words are made up of somewhat separable sound segments. Further, the child will be able to say individual sounds in words spoken by the teacher and blend separate sounds to form whole words.

In addressing this goal, we attempt to attune teachers to the phonemes in spoken language. Many highly literate adults are confused about how to segment words in which there are more letters than sounds (e.g., *through*) or more sounds than letters (e.g., *box*). We discuss various approaches to developing phonemic awareness, with a particular emphasis on blending and segmenting. We also discuss the relative difficulty of analyzing words into different units (onsets and rimes vs. individual phonemes) and discuss the features of phonemes that make them more and less challenging for children to attend to and/or manipulate (e.g., continuant consonants vs. stop consonants, consonants that differ only in one critical feature [e.g., voicing]).

Letter Naming

> The child will be able to name, rapidly and accurately, all 26 letters of the alphabet, both upper- and lower-case versions.

In discussing this goal, we begin to address fluency with foundational skills as an important contributor to reading comprehension. We stress that automaticity (speed) with letter identification is important in order to free up cognitive resources for higher-level skills. To promote fluency with letter identification, we stress the importance of having children say the letter names frequently during the course of the various activities used to promote letter-name knowledge.

We also discuss young children's tendency to rely on the names of the letters as an aid to remembering their sounds. For example, the sound for the letter *b* is the first phoneme in its name (/b/).[1] Thus, for many letters, if children know the name of the letter, it will be easier for them to remember the sound of the letter.

Letter–Sound Association

> The child will be able to associate the most common sounds of individual letters with their printed representations.

For this goal we continue to focus on the relationship between letter names and letter sounds, how to take advantage of that relationship, and how to address the confusions that arise for those letters where the relationship does not hold. We discuss the utility of using key words to help children remember letter–sound correspondences, of using the same key words across instructional settings and grade levels, and of explicitly teaching children how to use the key words when reading and writing.

The Alphabetic Principle and the Alphabetic Code

> The child will understand that the letters in printed words represent the sounds in spoken words and will understand how to use the alphabetic code to read and spell words.

This goal is divided into two parts that focus on early and later development of skill in using the alphabetic code in reading and writing. In the early-development section we describe instruction designed to help children acquire a conceptual understanding of the alphabetic principle; that is, the fact that the letters in printed

---

[1] To denote the sound of a letter, we follow the convention of enclosing the letter in slashes.

words represent the sounds in spoken words. In the later-development section we discuss ways to increase skill with decoding and encoding by teaching children about consonant digraphs, consonant blends, short and long vowels, and vowel digraphs. In working on this goal, we stress the benefits of guiding children to be strategic as they apply their developing knowledge of the alphabetic code in authentic (real) reading and writing situations.

Larger Orthographic Units and Multisyllabic Words

The child will develop the ability to use a variety of larger orthographic units (word families/phonograms, prefixes, suffixes, etc.) to read and spell words.

For this goal, we discuss teaching children how to use larger units of print to read and spell. This instruction largely involves helping children become sensitive to recurrent patterns, aware of clues to syllable boundaries, and learn how to apply this knowledge when puzzling through unfamiliar words.

Word Learning

The child will learn to effortlessly identify a large number of words.

This major goal is addressed via two subgoals, each of which focuses on a different vehicle for word learning. Although the term *sight vocabulary* is sometimes used to refer to high-frequency words or irregular words, we use the term to refer to all words than can be identified effortlessly "at sight."

Strategic Word Learning

The child will develop flexibility and independence in applying code-based and meaning-based strategies to identify and learn unfamiliar words encountered in text.

Strategic word learning is a central goal of the ISA, as having the ability to puzzle through and accurately identify unfamiliar words provides children with a powerful mechanism by which to expand their sight vocabulary and thereby their ability to read. We emphasize the need for children to use both code-based and meaning-based strategies in interactive and confirmatory ways.

High-Frequency Words

The child will be able to read the most frequently occurring words accurately and quickly.

While many of the words that become part of a child's sight vocabulary are learned during the course of strategic reading, some words warrant special instructional attention. These are words that occur frequently in print and are somewhat more difficult to learn due to their irregular spellings and/or abstract nature. Teachers are encouraged to explicitly teach and provide practice with such words. We discuss game-like drill activities that motivate children to practice the high-frequency words and texts that provide additional practice.

Meaning Construction

> The child will have the language skills and knowledge base needed to enable him or her to derive and construct the meaning from the texts that are read.

Comprehension is the goal of reading. Because children who are identified as struggling readers in the early primary grades are generally labeled thusly on the basis of their difficulties with the alphabetic coding and word-learning aspects of reading, the importance of attending to meaning construction is sometimes overlooked. Instruction specifically focused on enhancing comprehension is addressed through discussion of two goals: vocabulary and language development and comprehension and knowledge.

Vocabulary and Oral Language Development

> The child will learn the meanings of new words encountered in instructional interactions and will be able to use the words conversationally. Further, the child's ability to understand and use more complex grammatical structures will improve.

Reading is a language skill. Children need to develop the vocabulary and other language skills upon which reading comprehension depends. ISA teachers are encouraged to be alert to vocabulary and syntactic challenges throughout their instructional interactions. The opportunities for the development of vocabulary and syntactic knowledge provided by interactive read-alouds are a major focus relative to this goal. However, teachers are also alerted to the fact that children frequently encounter unfamiliar words in their own reading and that word identification difficulties are sometimes due to the fact that they do not know the meaning of words they encounter and, as a result, cannot decide (or confirm) that a word has been accurately decoded.

In developing word consciousness in teachers, we rely heavily on the work of Beck, McKeown, and Kucan (2002) to structure teachers' thinking about which words to select for instruction, how instruction should proceed, and the importance of using targeted words repeatedly, in a variety of contexts, and over an extended period of time. Teachers are also encouraged to provide children with ample opportunity to engage in extended conversations with adults and peers to promote the development of oral language skills.

Comprehension and General Knowledge

The child will develop the foundational knowledge and comprehension skills and strategies that will enhance his or her ability to construct the meaning of, and learn from, texts heard or read.

For children in the early primary grades, the development of active engagement in meaning construction is discussed in the context of read-alouds and supported reading. We encourage teachers to model comprehension strategies and to engage children in conversations that require the use of those strategies (e.g., "I think he's going to get a puppy for his birthday. What do you think he's going to get? Why?"). To help build the critical knowledge base upon which comprehension depends, we encourage teachers to read informational books to the children as often as possible. As children begin to read texts on their own, teachers are encouraged to engage children in discussions of what they are reading, as we have encountered many children who read quite fluently but have little recollection of what they read.

GENERAL PRINCIPLES FOR PREVENTING READING DIFFICULTIES

One of the main purposes of early intervention efforts is to prevent early differences in literacy skills from growing and becoming disabling. Although the specific content of what is taught is an important factor in the success of interventions, there are equally important general principles of instruction that can help maximize the impact of the instruction offered.

Teach Children to Be Effective and Independent Problem Solvers

Vygotsky (1978) was a developmental theorist who believed that much of what children learn as they grow and develop is the result of extended interactions with adults or more expert "others." Vygotsky argued that the skills that children acquire reflect the internalization of problem solving that they have initially done in collaboration with adults, who have provided *careful verbal guidance to direct and guide children's thinking.* The theory is that children internalize the verbal guidance initially provided by their teachers in such a way that it becomes a form of inner speech that influences children's thinking when they encounter similar problems.

If we assume that adults' speech (and through it, adults' thinking) is, on some level, internalized by children, then it becomes important to carefully consider our instructional language and to try to take the perspective of the children relative to our language. Do we use terms or expressions that may not hold the same meaning to the children? It is all too easy to inadvertently use terminology that carries no meaning or a different meaning for children who struggle with literacy acquisition.

For example, for some beginning kindergartners, a *letter* is something that comes in the mail, not a little squiggle that is associated with a sound and a meaning. It is remarkably easy to wrongly assume that children know or understand things; as a result, an instructional episode may be quite confusing to them. Virtually every teacher has had this experience.

It is also important to give children the opportunity to see how to use the problem-solving processes we teach. Since problem solving is a thinking process, the only way the children can "see" the process is if we think out loud so that they can vicariously experience the process. The instructional jargon for this approach to instruction is called *think-aloud,* and it is an important component of instruction designed to develop strategic thinking. When we think out loud for the children, we are essentially guiding the development of their thinking.

Vygotsky (1978) also argued that the most effective instruction focuses on skills and abilities that are somewhat challenging for a child to handle independently but that are easy enough for the child to handle when assistance is offered at key points. The disparity between what children are able to do with and without assistance is referred to as the *zone of proximal development.* From a Vygotskian perspective, the role of a teacher is that of a skilled collaborator. In this role, teachers must be:

- Adept at evaluating children's current level of competence and deciding what they are ready to learn next.
- Facile at modifying the demands of the task so that it suits the needs of each child.

Based on Vygotsky's theory, Wood, Bruner, and Ross (1976) developed the concept of *scaffolding* as an analogy for the role that skilled collaborators play in supporting a child's learning. Scaffolding involves the provision of various types of support that allow children to successfully accomplish a task that is too challenging for them to accomplish on their own. The scaffolding technique also involves the gradual *reduction* of support as a student demonstrates the ability to regulate his or her own thinking and problem solving. In order to do the types of assessment, modification, and scaffolding suggested above, it is necessary for teachers to have a firm grasp of the developmental progression of the skills they are helping students develop.

Tracking Student Progress

Because knowing what children are already able to do is so essential for knowing what they are ready to learn next, it is important for teachers to keep records of their students' skills and strategies. To this end, for most aspects of literacy development that are discussed in this book, we provide skill and strategy checklists to facilitate record keeping and, most importantly, to support teachers as they plan instruction.

Because teachers usually use such record-keeping devices in the context of working with small groups of children, each checklist provides space for teachers to record information on up to five children. We refer to these checklists as "snapshots" because they allow teachers to get a quick look at the skills of a particular group of children as they plan their instruction. Each snapshot is discussed in some detail in the relevant sections of the book.

Many of the snapshots call for the teacher to rate children's skills and strategies using a 3-point scale: *beginning*, *developing*, and *proficient*. Such ratings are appropriate for what Paris (2005) refers to as constrained skills—skills that are learned over a relatively short time span and that are mastered by most students. As illustrated below, to make the record keeping as efficient as possible, teachers are encouraged to use slashes to denote their judgment of individual children's standing relative to particular skills and strategies. However, some teachers prefer to use the letter codes.

☐ *B—Beginning* indicates that instruction has addressed the objective but that the child has only a preliminary understanding or capability with regard to that particular objective.

☒ *D—Developing* indicates that the child has some understanding of the objective but does not reliably demonstrate that understanding or capability or is not yet automatic (fluent) with the skill.

☒ *P—Proficient* indicates that the child reliably and automatically demonstrates the understanding or capability.

In other instances, the snapshots call for teachers to indicate whether individual children's capabilities in given areas are *well developed*, *appropriately developed*, or *need development*. Essentially, this rating reflects the teacher's judgment as to whether or not this is an aspect of literacy development that requires greater instructional emphasis.

Ensure That Students Are Actively Engaged in Learning

The more reading and writing children do and the more they practice the underlying skills that are foundational for reading and writing, the more quickly they become proficient. This is true when children actually engage in the cognitive processes required to read and write. Unfortunately, children sometimes find ways of avoiding the thinking parts of instructional activities. For example, in a choral reading situation, when the entire class or group is engaged in reading the same text, some of the children may not be looking at the words and thinking about them. Rather, they may be simply gazing in the right direction and saying the words just slightly after their friends say them. These children may look engaged, but they are not. They need the opportunity to read text to the teacher or to a friend in order to fully engage in the necessary thinking processes.

Similar types of disengagement can arise when a teacher calls on one child *before* asking a question. For example, if the teacher is engaging the children in a shared writing activity and wants to know what letter to use at the beginning of the word *dog*, she might call on one child, saying, for example, "Jake, what letter do I need at the beginning of the word *dog*?" As soon as the teacher says Jake's name, some of the children in the group may disengage, knowing that they will not be expected to answer. If, on the other hand, the teacher asks the question without immediately calling on an individual, more of the children are likely to engage in the thinking. Better still, if the children all have whiteboards or chalkboards on which to write, they could all engage in the task. The teacher might say, "Write down the letter you think I need at the beginning of the word *dog*." This allows every student to respond; as a result, they are *all* likely to benefit from the instructional interaction. We strongly encourage teachers to incorporate opportunities for every student to respond during the course of instruction.

> **KEEP IN MIND** In developing instructional activities, an important question to ask is "What are the children likely to be thinking about/focusing on during the activity?" If the conclusion is that they are unlikely to be focused on the skill or concept (the goal) that the activity was designed to support, the activity should be redesigned.

Another consideration relative to the relationship between engagement and learning is the fact that children sometimes become overly involved in the hands-on (e.g., cutting, gluing, coloring) aspects of instructional activities and are not really thinking about the skill or concept that the task was designed to support. It is important to make clear to the children why they are doing specific things and what they can do during the hands-on aspects of the activity to support their learning. For example, if children are learning the sound of the letter *m* and gluing macaroni to a cut-out of an *M*, while they are doing this, they might be encouraged to think of other words that have the /mmm/ sound that is heard at the beginning of the word *macaroni* and to share their ideas with other children at the table. Without providing children with guidance in how to think about the instructional activity, at least some are apt to devote most of their thinking to the gluing and fine-motor activity or to thinking about the food with which they are working. Similarly, if children are practicing their spelling words by writing them several times, it would be helpful for them to say each letter as they write it and then say the word each time it is completed. It would also help if they tried to write the word from memory each time and then checked it against a model. Otherwise, the spelling practice may become nothing more than an unengaged copying task.

The general point with regard to engagement is that teachers need to guide how children think about instructional activities so that the activities actually move the children forward in literacy acquisition.

Set High Expectations for All Children

At various points in the history of education, people have believed that some children were just destined to have great difficulty learning to read and/or write and that there was little to be done to help them overcome their difficulties. Research has demonstrated that students tend to live up to the expectations we have for them (Smith, Jussim, & Eccles, 1999). Thus, a belief that a child is unlikely to make progress has the clear potential to slow the progress made by that child. Conversely, the expectation that a child will succeed academically increases the likelihood that she will do so. In fact, research conducted in "beat-the-odds" schools, where children succeed at much higher levels than might be expected given their socioeconomic circumstances, indicates that a common characteristic of such schools was that all school staff held high expectations for all of the children (Taylor, Pearson, Clark, & Walpole, 2000).

What Does "Ready to Learn" Mean?

For many years there was a commonly held belief that children needed to be developmentally ready to learn to read. Exactly what people meant by "being ready" varied, but it was certainly tied to the child's age and, in some cases, physical development. For example, some thought that children should not be taught to read until they had lost their first tooth!

What we mean when we use the phrase *ready to learn* is that the child has the prerequisite conceptual understandings and skills to allow him or her to benefit from instruction in a certain area. Every child is ready to learn something. Our job as educators is to figure out *what* the child is ready to learn, not *whether* the child is ready to learn.

The research on the success of early literacy interventions makes it easier to hold high expectations for children who initially demonstrate limited literacy skills. Every child is expected to do well in reading and writing development, and, if the child is not progressing, we are more inclined to examine the instruction than to examine the child to determine what has gone wrong. In other words, instruction is now considered to be a much more powerful influence on a child's reading and writing development than it once was. Children do learn what we teach them, as long as we teach them what they are ready to learn. The challenge, of course, is that the children in any given classroom generally are not all ready to learn the same things. Nevertheless, they are all expected to attain the same grade-level standards. This is why different amounts and intensities of instruction and intervention are so important to promoting literacy success. In a classroom setting, working with small, flexible, skills-based groups for a substantial portion of the language arts block offers the greatest opportunity for the teacher to meet this challenge. Similarly focused small-group and one-to-one instructional contexts enable intervention teachers to respond to the needs of the children who are more challenging to teach.

Interface Support Services with the Classroom Program

For children who are receiving intervention services beyond the classroom, it is important that the instruction in all settings works toward mutually supportive ends. To the greatest extent possible, intervention teachers should support and reinforce the content of the classroom program. For example, at the kindergarten level, if instruction about the alphabet is sequenced in a particular way, it makes sense to sequence alphabet instruction in intervention settings to parallel the classroom sequence. Similarly, if key words are used in the classroom to support the learning of letter sounds, supplementary instruction should use the same key words. Likewise, it is helpful to determine which high-frequency words children are expected to know by the end of a given grade level and to make these words a priority for instruction. Additionally, some of the reading materials used in intervention settings should come from the classroom program. Such a purposeful selection gives the children the opportunity to interact with these materials in a way that they may not experience in the larger classroom context. Many more opportunities to build congruence could be cited. By increasing the congruence between classroom and supplementary instruction, we hope to increase the instructional impact of both the classroom program and the intervention program. The children who struggle in the classroom program will be better prepared for subsequent instruction in that program if they have reviewed some of the material in another context.

Plan for Success

In all instructional interactions, teachers should make every effort to structure the activities so that the children experience success and the rewarding feelings that go along with it. Teachers should look for opportunities to provide genuine praise to children for their efforts. Conversely, teachers should avoid making negative and discouraging comments. Although a teacher may sometimes feel frustrated that she has yet to find a way to help a particular child accomplish a particular objective, communicating this frustration will only serve to make the child feel that the situation may be hopeless. If the child is not progressing in a certain area, it is important to try to determine the source of the problem. Perhaps the level of difficulty needs to be reduced. Perhaps the child is misconstruing the task. Perhaps the teacher is using terminology for certain concepts that is different from the terminology to which the child is accustomed. It is particularly important for teachers who are providing supplementary instruction to be aware of the terminology used in the children's classrooms. For example, whereas adults and most older children readily recognize the equivalence of terms such as *upper-case* and *capital*, young children often do not. Attending to potential stumbling blocks such as task difficulty or confusion regarding terminology before they occur will help to ensure that children experience success and continually move forward in their literacy development.

ORGANIZATION OF THE BOOK

The remainder of this book is largely organized around the instructional goals for young children detailed earlier and the instructional methods for helping children to achieve those goals. However, first we devote a chapter to describing what a typical week and a typical day of language arts instruction might look like in a kindergarten or first-grade classroom, our purpose being to provide a framework for considering how the goals would be addressed in the context of language arts instruction. Next is a chapter on academic motivation as it relates to literacy learning and particularly to those who struggle with literacy acquisition. Thereafter, we devote a section to the development of alphabetic skills and the knowledge bases (i.e., phonemic awareness and print concepts) that contribute to the development of skill with the alphabetic code. Next we provide a section devoted to word learning, with separate chapters discussing the different ways in which sight vocabulary is developed—through strategic word solving while reading and via explicit instruction and practice with high-frequency words. In the meaning construction section that follows, we discuss the language, background knowledge, and engagement factors that influence readers' ability to comprehend the things they read, and we suggest ways of supporting the development of these important contributors to comprehension. The final two chapters are devoted to a more thorough discussion of ISA-based interventions for the children who struggle the most and to a proposed model for RTI.

CHAPTER 2

Responsive Classroom Instruction

Within an RTI process, effective and differentiated classroom instruction is a crucial component of efforts to address the needs of children who appear to be at risk of experiencing literacy learning difficulties. In the RTI model that we propose, classroom instruction takes account of the diversity of student skills during the course of whole-class, small-group, and one-to-one instruction. Further, to better address the specific needs of the children who are identified as at risk, classroom teachers plan small-group instruction such that they have the opportunity to teach the children who are at greatest risk more intensively than the children who are not identified as being at risk. Intensification can be accomplished in a number of ways. For example, teachers might arrange their weekly schedule so that they can meet with the at-risk group(s) on a daily basis, while working with the children who are not at risk somewhat less frequently. In addition, group size would, ideally, be smaller for the at-risk children than for the children who are not at risk. Children with the most extreme needs—that is, those who make limited progress when provided with intensified classroom instruction—would receive additional intervention beyond the classroom either in the context of small-group (Tier 2) or one-to-one instruction (Tier 3). These more intensive forms of intervention are discussed later in the chapter. We first focus on instruction provided by the classroom teacher for the full spectrum of students.

CLASSROOM INSTRUCTION IN AN RTI CONTEXT

In a typical primary-grade classroom, children will have a variety of skills and be at different performance levels with regard to reading and writing. In fact, estimates suggest that in a typical classroom, the reading levels of the children can range three grade levels or more (Chorzempa & Graham, 2006). Instructional plans need to consider the current literacy status of all the children in the class. Once this information is established, a teacher with a clear understanding of the instructional goals will be better able to address students' literacy development via instructional formats that include whole-class, small-group, and one-to-one instruction. Although it is not possible to specify the ideal mix of formats, it is clear that a mix is ideal. Several research groups have provided evidence that children, particularly those who struggle, make better progress in classroom programs and intervention settings in which they are grouped by reading level for supported reading lessons and are given the opportunity to read texts that provide some, but not too much, challenge (e.g., Ehri, Dreyer, Flugman, & Gross, 2007; Fisher & Berliner, 1985; Scanlon et al., 2008; Taylor et al., 2000; see also, Allington, 2009).

Whole-Class Instruction

Instruction offered to the entire class is appropriate for many components of language arts instruction, including read-alouds, shared reading, shared writing, and oral language activities. Whole-class instruction provides the opportunity to involve all of the children in activities that (1) foster active engagement with text, (2) illustrate the use of word identification strategies, (3) build foundational skills such as knowledge of how the alphabet works, and (4) help to build oral language and general knowledge. However, even during whole-class instruction, teachers need to be mindful of, and plan for, the variety of skill levels in the class. So, for example, during a shared writing activity when the teacher writes in collaboration with the students, a first-grade teacher might:

- Engage all of the children in the composition of the message.
- Model and engage the children in stretching and segmenting some of the words to meet the needs of children who have yet to become fully phonemically aware.
- Encourage the children to refer to the class word wall for the spelling of recently taught high-frequency words.
- Explicitly discuss and model the formation of a few of the letters as she writes them.
- Discuss spelling and print conventions for children who are at different points along the developmental continuum (perhaps directing attention to the key-word chart for the spelling of the short-*a* sound for the children at

an earlier point of development and discussing the *-tion* spelling unit for children who are further along).

The point is, in whole-class instruction, the teacher should plan to provide multilevel instruction that keeps all children engaged and moving forward.

Small-Group Instruction

Small-group configurations generally involve grouping children by instructional level, by the need for instruction on particular skills or strategies, and/or by interest (e.g., a group interested in a particular topic or book). All of these approaches to grouping may occur in any given classroom. For purposes of primary reading instruction, however, it is important that the children receive their supported reading lessons in small groups formed on the basis of their current reading levels.

Supported Reading

We use the term *supported reading* rather than *guided reading* in order to distinguish small-group reading instruction provided in the ISA from guided reading as described by Fountas and Pinnell (1996), as the two approaches differ in several important ways. For example, the ISA places heavier emphasis on explicit and systematic instruction related to the alphabetic code, and in most lessons, new decoding elements are taught and practiced in preparation for reading a book in which words that include that decoding element will be encountered. In guided reading, the decoding skills that are taught are drawn from the text, based on the challenges the children encounter while reading, and become the focus of instruction after the children have read the text. Further, in the ISA, children are taught a small number of specific word-solving strategies and are explicitly taught how to utilize them in interactive and confirmatory ways upon encountering unfamiliar words in context. Independence in the use of these strategies is an important instructional objective. In guided reading, teacher prompting is used to guide children's word-solving attempts, but the children are not given a specific listing of strategies.

Small-group formats are more effective in accelerating children's progress because they allow the teacher to differentiate instruction such that the texts that the children read provide an appropriate level of challenge and the focus of skill and strategy instruction is targeted so as to bring the children just a bit further along relative to what they are currently able to do. Further, small-group instruction allows the teacher to more effectively monitor what the children understand about reading and writing and to determine what they are ready to learn next. The group snapshots provided in the upcoming chapters are intended to help teachers keep abreast of the skills and strategies of the children who have been grouped together and to allow teachers to consider whether children who are in a given group are appropriately placed by examining similarities and differences in profiles within and across groups.

One-to-One Instruction

Virtually every classroom teacher in the primary grades offers some one-to-one instruction (sometimes referred to as side-by-side instruction). Such instruction is provided in contexts in which the teacher confers with individual children about their reading, writing, and other academic work. In the context of both whole-class and small-group instruction, teachers often provide children with the opportunity to work independently for periods of time. For example, children might be asked to discuss with a partner how they think a particular book will end or to write a journal entry relating to the same question. During such activities, the teacher can be attentive to individual children to make sure that they are engaged in productive ways and be alert for opportunities to guide their thinking relative to the instructional activity in which they are involved. The problem-solving skills and strategies that teachers address in these one-to-one interactions will vary considerably from child to child.

DEVELOPING A LANGUAGE ARTS PROGRAM
FOR READERS AT MULTIPLE LEVELS

Language arts instruction at the primary level typically comprises several fairly distinct components, which, together, address the instructional goals discussed in Chapters 3 through 13. Table 2.1 lists the goals and the components of instruction during which the goals might be addressed. The checkmarks in the boxes indicate which goals might be addressed within the various components of language arts instruction. The purpose of this chart is to demonstrate that multiple goals can and should be addressed in each component of language arts instruction.

In a typical classroom a substantial proportion of the language arts program is delivered to the whole class at once. To plan for the full spectrum of students who will participate and to engage all of them productively, teachers need to be knowledgeable about the abilities and understandings of all of the children and to rely on this information as they interact instructionally with individual students within the larger context. For example, at the beginning of first grade, students are likely to be at very different places in terms of their literacy development. For purposes of discussion, we describe four different "types" of students that might be in a single early primary class. However, before doing so, it is important to emphasize that literacy development is a fluid and multidimensional process and that children do not necessarily fit neatly into a given type. Of the many different dimensions along which a literacy learner might be described and considered, for current purposes we focus primarily on the dimensions related to the development

TABLE 2.1. Intersection of the Goals of Instruction and the Components of Language Arts Instruction

Language arts components	Instructional groupings	Motivation	Print concepts	Alphabetics		Word learning		Meaning construction	
				Phonological analysis	Alphabetic coding skills (letter names, sounds, alphabetic principle, etc.)	Strategic word identification	High-frequency sight words	Language and vocabulary development	Knowledge and comprehension
Read-aloud	WC, SG, and I	✓		✓	✓	✓		✓	✓
Shared reading	WC, SG, and I	✓	✓	✓	✓	✓	✓	✓	✓
Independent and buddy reading	WC, SG, and I	✓	✓	✓	✓	✓	✓	✓	✓
Writing/composition	WC, SG, and I	✓	✓	✓	✓	✓	✓	✓	✓
Oral language	WC, SG, and I	✓		✓	✓	✓		✓	✓
Foundational skills	WC, SG, and I	✓	✓	✓	✓	✓	✓	✓	✓
Supported reading group	SG and I	✓	✓	✓	✓	✓	✓	✓	✓

Note. WC, whole class; SG, small group; I, individual. Adapted from Scanlon and Anderson (2010). Copyright 2010 by the International Reading Association. Adapted by permission.

of the ability to read the words in connected text. In doing so, we do not wish to diminish the importance of general language and vocabulary knowledge nor the importance of background knowledge in contributing to children's ability to comprehend the texts they read. However, because at early stages of development, the latter characteristics are often unrelated to the child's abilities to read the words in the text (see Paris & Paris, 2007) and because most of the research on reading difficulties suggests that most early reading difficulties are due to difficulties with figuring out how to read printed words, we develop our characterization around those early, foundational skills. Our characterization draws heavily on, but is not totally consistent with, the work of Ehri (2005).

Emergent Readers

Emergent readers have very limited understanding of the role played by print in the reading process. Emergent readers may know the names of few, if any, letters and have limited understanding of the role of the most basic print conventions. When they attempt to read emergent-level books, they rely primarily on the pictures and their memory of the text if it has been read to them previously. They may or may not understand many other aspects of reading, such as that books tell stories and/ or are sources of useful and interesting information.

Developing Readers

Developing readers have begun to learn something about the alphabet and the alphabetic principle. They may know the names of most of the letters and the sounds of many of them. When attempting to identify printed words, developing readers tend to rely on a combination of the alphabetic code and the context in which the word occurs, with the relative weight placed on one source of information, changing gradually from heavy reliance on context to greater reliance on the code. Developing readers may be able to identify many of the most frequently occurring words with relatively little effort.

Maturing Readers

Maturing readers are effective word learners who use both code-based and meaning-based strategies fairly efficiently to puzzle through unfamiliar words. However, their need to word-solve is still apparent, as evidenced by either multiple attempts at the pronunciation of the occasional word (during oral reading) or by hesitation over a word followed by accurate identification. Because maturing readers are effective word solvers, their sight vocabulary grows rapidly (when they engage in reading, of course). Further, when reading texts that do not contain too many unfamiliar words, they tend to sound quite fluent as they read.

Proficient Readers

Proficient readers are able to quickly analyze and identify unfamiliar words, even those that are composed of multiple syllables. Part of their efficiency is due to the fact that they have stored many larger orthographic units (e.g., *-tion, re-, -ly, -ing*) in memory. Thus, although they do not necessarily know all of the words, they figure them out so quickly that they sound fluent. Proficient readers are able to devote virtually all of their thinking to interpreting and responding to the texts as they read.

In the primary grades a classroom might be comprised of all four types of readers—as well as readers at all the intermediate points between the types described. However, at each grade level and at different points in the year, the mix of children is likely to be different. Thus, early in kindergarten most children are likely to be emerging or developing readers, whereas at the beginning of first grade most are likely to be developing readers, a few might be described as maturing, and a very few as either emergent or proficient. By the beginning of second grade we would expect the balance to shift again, with a few being described as developing readers, most looking like maturing readers, and several likely to be proficient. Regardless of the distribution of students along the continuum, the classroom teacher is responsible for providing instruction that moves all students forward.

While small-group instruction is one of the most effective ways of addressing the diversity of skill levels found in typical primary-grade classrooms, many instructional needs of the children in a class can be addressed through whole-class instruction. Since whole-class instruction influences the development of all children, it could be argued that, for some goals, it is a more efficient form of instruction.

A WEEK AND A DAY IN FIRST GRADE

In this section we discuss the balancing act that teachers face in planning and delivering language arts instruction for a classroom full of students who differ substantially in their literacy skills. We illustrate how small-group instruction might fit into the context of the broader language arts program and into the context of the instructional day. As an example we provide a possible first-grade weekly schedule and discuss each component of the day. The schedule itself is outlined in Figure 2.1. We discuss each of the components on the schedule that is specifically related to literacy development.

Attendance, Lunch Count, Book Browsing, and Writing

The day begins with a 10- to 15-minute period during which the children have time to put their belongings away, socialize a bit, sign in for attendance and lunch purposes, and do a little reading or writing if time permits. They may read one or more books that were read previously, browse a book previously read by the teacher, explore the classroom library, and so forth. Many teachers also offer the children the opportunity to do some writing during this segment of the day. They might write notes or letters to friends, write in their journals, or document observations related to an ongoing science project, for example. During this period, the teacher has time to attend to necessary paperwork, including notes from parents, and to greet individual children and make them feel welcome.

Morning Meeting

Many teachers have a brief morning meeting in which they bring the whole class together and outline the day. Teachers use this period in many different ways to address literacy and other academic goals. For example, some teachers focus the children's attention on a large calendar to help the children learn to read numbers, or the names of the days of the week, or the letters in the name of the month. They might also use it to teach and reinforce certain science concepts by, for example, engaging the children in observing and recording characteristics of the weather and placing symbols for rainy, sunny, snowy, or cloudy on the calendar each day.

	Monday	Tuesday	Wednesday	Thursday	Friday
8:15–8:30	Attendance, lunch count, book browsing, and writing	Attendance, lunch count, book browsing, and writing	Attendance, lunch count, book browsing, and writing	Attendance, lunch count, book browsing, and writing	Attendance, lunch count, book browsing, and writing
8:30–8:40	Morning meeting	Morning meeting	Morning meeting	Morning meeting	Morning meeting
8:40–8:55	Shared reading	Shared reading	Shared reading	Shared reading	Shared reading
8:55–9:10	Introduction of center activities	Introduction of center activities	Introduction of center activities	Introduction of center activities	Introduction of center activities
9:10–9:35	Group 1	Group 4	Group 3	Group 1	Group 2
9:40–10:05	Group 2	Group 1	Group 4	Group 2	Group 1
10:10–10:35	Group 3	Group 2	Group 1	Group 3	Group 4
10:35–10:50	Snack and discussion	Snack and discussion	Snack and discussion	Snack and discussion	Snack and discussion
10:50–11:20	Read-aloud	Read-aloud	Read-aloud	Read-aloud	Read-aloud
11:20–11:50	Writing and composition	Writing and composition	Writing and composition	Writing and composition	Writing and composition
11:50–12:35	Lunch and recess	Lunch and recess	Lunch and recess	Lunch and recess	Lunch and recess
12:35–1:15	Special	Special	Special	Special	Special
1:20–2:05	Math	Math	Math	Math	Math
2:05–2:20	Wrap-up and reflection	Wrap-up and reflection	Wrap-up and reflection	Wrap-up and reflection	Wrap-up and reflection

FIGURE 2.1. Sample daily schedule for first grade. Although it is not explicitly blocked out on the schedule, it is understood that a focus on science and social studies content is a critical aspect of primary-grade instruction. We strongly encourage teachers to integrate content-area subject matter into the various instructional components described above, particularly shared reading, center activities, read-aloud, and writing/composition. When necessary, teachers might opt to use one of the writing/composition or math blocks for introducing a new unit or theme, then continue with the remainder of the schedule as usual.

Shared Reading

During shared reading, the teacher and the class read a text in which the print is large enough for all of the children to see comfortably and the teacher explicitly directs their attention to the print by pointing to the words as she reads. Shared reading often occurs immediately after the morning meeting and may, in fact, blend in with the morning meeting. For example, one of the texts used for shared reading may be a teacher-prepared passage on chart paper that describes the schedule for the day (e.g., what the special is, whose birthday it is, plans for a field trip) for the class to read together. Alternatively, the teacher may use a big book or poem for shared reading. Often teachers use such a text to introduce, review, and/or practice high-frequency words and/or specific decoding elements that have been taught.

Many of the big books used for shared reading are at a level of challenge that would make them accessible to most children following a few experiences with shared reading of the book. Many publishers provide instructional materials that include a big book and accompanying child-size versions of the text.

Teachers implementing the ISA use shared reading as an opportunity to model and engage children in the use of word-solving strategies. Periodically, while sharing the reading, the teacher stops at a word that lends itself to being identified by using particular strategies. Modeling and discussing with the class how to puzzle through the word, the teacher notes the usefulness of the strategies once the word is identified. Teachers often post a large print version of the strategies list (see Chapter 10) so that it can be seen by all of the children. Many teachers leave the materials used during shared reading available for the children to use during center time or as a free-choice activity. Young children often delight in playing teacher and will enthusiastically gather together some friends to serve as students as they take on the role.

As teachers plan and deliver a whole-class shared reading lesson, they need to think about the full spectrum of students that will participate in the lesson and attempt to engage all students productively. This, of course, requires that the teacher do different things for different students in the class. In Table 2.2 we describe how a shared reading lesson might vary for children at different points along the developmental continuum. The table presents each of the instructional goals that teachers might address in the lesson and provides a brief glimpse of what teachers might do (or plan to do) for children at different points along the continuum. Typically, of course, the students in a given class will not be distributed evenly along the continuum. Therefore, teachers should distribute their time and focus in accord with the composition of their class. That is, if most of the children are emergent readers, the instructional interaction related to alphabetics would focus on basic print concepts and the identity of individual letters that the children are learning. If, on the other hand, most of the children are developing readers, most of the instructional interaction related to alphabetics would focus on engaging the children in puzzling through single-syllable words. As noted in Table 2.2, instructional interactions during shared reading will, of course, focus on much more than alphabetics.

Introduction of Center Activities

Centers are intended to provide the opportunity for children to work productively toward academic goals when the teacher is working with other children in a small-group context. While it may not be necessary to set aside time to intro-

(text continues on p. 38)

TABLE 2.2. Teacher Thinking before and during Shared Reading, Related to the Goals and to Children at Various Points in Development

Goal	Emergent	Developing	Maturing	Proficient
Motivation	Encourage enjoyment and engagement with text.			
Alphabetics Purposes and conventions of print	Model and discuss print conventions, such as the right-to-left and top-to-bottom directionality of print.	Model and discuss print conventions such as the use of spaces to demarcate words and some of the most frequent punctuation (capitalize the first word, use of periods and question marks).	Model and discuss more advanced print conventions, such as print size, exclamation points, and quotation marks.	Model and discuss commas, colons, semicolons, etc.
Phonological awareness	Occasionally select texts characterized by rhyme and alliteration to help heighten children's sensitivity to sounds.	Occasionally select texts characterized by rhyme and alliteration to help heighten children's sensitivity to sounds.	Goal accomplished.	Goal accomplished.
Letter names	Draw children's attention to the letters they are learning the names of, invite them to find letters that have recently been introduced (recognition), or to name letters that they are expected to know (identification).	Build fluency with letter identification by occasionally inviting children to name all of the letters in particular words.	Goal accomplished.	Goal accomplished.

(cont.)

35

TABLE 2.2. *(cont.)*

Goal	Emergent	Developing	Maturing	Proficient
Alphabetics (cont.)				
Letter sounds	Not a focus at this time.	Emphasize the sound of some letters as words are articulated or ask children to provide the sound for a particular letter encountered in the text ("This word starts with *S*; what sound will this word start with?"). Occasionally model use of the key-word chart when discussing letter sounds.	Encourage children to participate in puzzling through words to enhance fluency with letter sounds.	Goal accomplished.
Alphabetic principle and alphabetic code	Not a focus at this time.	Occasionally draw children's attention to the beginning and perhaps ending letters in words as they are reading. A bit later, draw attention to both beginning and ending sounds.	Draw attention to all of the letters in one-syllable words—particularly in regularly spelled words.	Goal accomplished.
Larger orthographic units	Not a focus at this time.	Draw children's attention to examples of words from word families that have been taught.	Model and engage students in approaches to puzzling through words with multiple syllables.	Goal accomplished.

Word learning				
Strategic word learning	Model the use of picture cues when reading highly predictable text.	Guide word solving by occasionally modeling the use of context in combination with partial alphabetic information—beginning letters and, later, final letters. Revisit some of the word-learning strategies that were used while reading, after reading, and discussing the entire text.	Occasionally draw children's attention to more detailed alphabetic information and to larger orthographic units and illustrate how to use that information in combination with context in order to solve unfamiliar words.	Occasionally draw children's attention to larger orthographic units (word families, prefixes, suffixes, and other recurrent spelling patterns) and illustrate how these units can be used in combination with context to facilitate identification of unfamiliar words.
High-frequency words	Point out any high-frequency words that are being taught and provide the opportunity to do a word hunt after the text has been read and discussed.	Point out the high-frequency words that the children have been learning. After the entire text has been read and discussed, occasionally give children the opportunity to do a word hunt for words they know or are learning.	Occasionally fade voice while leading the choral reading so that children have the opportunity to retrieve learned high-frequency words from memory.	Goal accomplished.
Meaning construction				
Vocabulary and oral language	Explain the meanings of unfamiliar words and syntactic structures as they come up in the text. Teach or revisit meanings of a few words in follow-up activities.			
Comprehension and world knowledge	Engage children in actively thinking about the meaning of the text before, during, and after reading it with them. Facilitate the process of making connections between what the children already know and what they encounter in the text.			

duce center activities every day, it is important to be sure that there is time in the schedule to do so if necessary. Several suggestions for literacy-focused center activities are described later in the text. In addition, centers focused on math, science, social studies, and art—either integrated with the literacy activities or as separate activities—should be included. In considering the daily schedule, notice that there is a permeable (dashed) line between the "shared reading" segment and the "introduction of center activities" segment in Figure 2.1. As it is often necessary to allocate more time to introduce more complicated centers and projects, this permeable line suggests this need for flexibility. For example, in preparing children to learn in a center that is cross-curricular (e.g., involves science and/or math and reading and writing), such as studying the life cycle of a plant, the teacher might utilize the entire 30-minute block to familiarize the children with center activities and expectations.

Small Literacy Groups

Small-group literacy instruction provides the classroom teacher with the greatest opportunity to differentiate instruction and to better meet the needs of children who are at different points in development. This format is a critical component of language arts instruction and requires careful planning and organization to realize its full potential. In order to discuss small-group instruction in detail while not "breaking the flow" of our description of the daily schedule, we have postponed a full discussion to a later segment of this chapter.

Snack and Discussion

Snack time can be used to support the development of children's language skills by incorporating activities such as *describe and guess,* which is a bit like *show and tell* but which requires the use of more sophisticated language (see Chapter 12). This is also a time for the teacher to model and encourage social but unstructured conversations among children. If the teacher explicitly models conversations by joining different groups of children, over time, the children are likely to begin to emulate the conversational conventions that the teacher demonstrates.

Read-Aloud

A read-aloud involves the teacher reading a book or other text without the expectation that the children will attend to the print. Reading aloud to children and engaging them in discussion of the text before, during, and after they read provides a powerful vehicle for:

- Expanding their vocabulary and syntactic skills.
- Developing knowledge and vocabulary related to the science and social

studies content that is covered in primary-grade classrooms, particularly if several books on the same or related themes are read.

- Modeling and engaging the children in active processing of the text.
- Increasing motivation for and interest in reading.

Further, in the early primary grades, books used for read-aloud can help to promote the development of phonemic awareness if they contain rhyme or alliteration. And, alphabet books help develop knowledge of letter names and letter sounds since, in most such books, the letter that is the focus of each page is large enough for children to see even when the rest of the words are not.

Many times the books teachers select for reading aloud are related to a classroom theme (e.g., seasons, oceans, early settlers). Reading several books related to a common theme helps children to develop more thorough knowledge and vocabulary related to that theme and enables the teacher to integrate science and social studies content areas into the language arts curriculum.

Teachers might also organize book selection around author or genre studies. Reading and discussing several books by the same author helps children learn about the authors' craft and contributes to their writing development by highlighting characteristics and tactics of different authors. Genre studies (biography, fairy tales, memoirs, etc.) help children develop schemas for the different genres. When children understand the characteristics of a particular genre, they are likely to use that knowledge to guide their interpretation of texts. For example, knowledge that a folk tale generally is intended to teach a lesson puts the reader on the alert to look for the lesson the tale is trying to teach. Thus, the genre itself gives the reader a purpose for reading. Moreover, engaging children in noticing characteristics of various genres and writing styles provides them with models that they may want to emulate in their own writing.

As for other components of instruction offered in a whole-class format, it is important to try to engage the entire class and to give some forethought to how a particular text might be used to support progress toward the various instructional goals. Moreover, particularly for children who have been identified as at risk, those who have limited experience with being read to, and/or those who find it difficult to attend to text in the context of whole-class instruction, it is also productive to read aloud in small-group or one-to-one situations. Classroom volunteers can be particularly helpful in providing additional opportunities for children to listen and respond to books. Of course, volunteers may need guidance in how to effectively engage children in read-alouds.

It should be noted that although the packed daily schedule presented in Figure 2.1 could suggest that there is no time allocated to science and social studies, this is not the case. When the class is focusing on particular themes or topics in science or social studies, books related to those themes should be selected for shared reading or read aloud; those themes could also be carried forward in the writing/composition block. Further, as noted previously, one or more of the centers offered during small-group time could be devoted to providing the children with additional opportunities to engage with that content.

Writing and Composition

Different kinds of writing activities should be routinely included in work with beginning readers. In one, the teacher does the writing with assistance from the child(ren). In the other, the children do the writing with assistance from the teacher. In addition, children should explore writing independently in the context of open-ended writing opportunities in the classroom (e.g., journal writing, observation logs).

In the sample schedule, writing and composition immediately follows read-aloud largely because teachers sometimes want their students to incorporate, in their own writing, elements of what was discussed during the read-aloud. So, for example, early in first grade, the teacher might ask the children to draw a picture of the portion of the text that interested them the most (or surprised or bothered them the most) and to write a caption for the picture. As children progress as readers and writers, they might engage in a variety of writing types. For example, the children might be asked to:

- Collaborate in developing a class book that tells further adventures of a character they learned about during a read-aloud.
- Write a letter to an author inquiring about reasons for certain decisions that he made in writing the text.
- Write a new ending for a story that was read.
- Keep a journal telling what they have learned related to a particular theme they have been pursuing through read-alouds.
- Model their writing after a particular genre or author's style.
- Write a letter to a friend telling the friend why he would probably like a particular book.

Whether the writing is focused on reacting to a specific text or is of a more creative nature, the writing/composition portion of the day often begins with a mini-lesson in which the teacher models and discusses certain aspects of the writing process. In the early primary grades, teachers often focus on both the mechanics of writing (letter formation, spacing between words, punctuation, sound spelling, conventional spelling, etc.) and on the construction of meaning (formulating the intended message, considering wording, revising for clarity, etc.). Mini-lessons often take the form of shared writing during which the children have the opportunity to observe as the teacher writes, modeling her thinking and engaging the children in as much of the problem solving as they are able to do (e.g., thinking about how to word a statement, stretching the words to analyze the sounds, thinking of the letters needed to represent the sounds, and so on).

Once the children begin to write, the teacher circulates for a period of time, providing guidance and encouragement in the form of mini-conferences. Alternatively, teachers sometimes choose to create temporary groups to teach specific writing conventions and strategies during writing time. Thus, the teacher might meet with one group of children one day and a different group of children the next. While the teacher is meeting with groups, the remaining children continue to work on their own compositions and/or engage in conferences with their peers. Some time is set aside at least a couple of times each week for individual children to share their writing with classmates.

In planning and delivering writing instruction, teachers engage in the same sort of thinking about the instructional goals and the competencies of their students as was detailed in Table 2.2.

SMALL-GROUP LITERACY INSTRUCTION

In order to be able to work fairly productively with children at various points in the development of language arts skills, teachers need to plan and organize instruction carefully. As noted above, providing small-group instruction is particularly important for primary reading instruction and, therefore, should be a daily occurrence once the school year gets underway. Initially, however, in preparation for small-group instruction teachers need to (1) identify which children will be grouped for instruction, and (2) prepare children to work productively when they are not directly engaged with the teacher.

Grouping for Supported Small-Group Literacy Instruction

The process by which teachers might form groups for supported small-group instruction varies considerably depending upon the children's grade level, the instructional program in use, and the point in the school year. For example, early in the school year in kindergarten, groups may be formed on the basis of the children's knowledge of alphabetics (including their phonological awareness and letter-name and letter–sound knowledge). Children who demonstrate similar levels of skill would be grouped together. As the school year progresses, however, the teacher might regroup children based on ongoing observations of what the children know and are able to do, perhaps using checklists such as the snapshots described in subsequent chapters.

As the children advance, their ability to read leveled texts or their ability to read texts in the core reading series may serve as the basis for forming instructional groups. Young children who are learning to read in a particular curriculum are likely to learn the things that are emphasized in that curriculum, so assessment should certainly evaluate the extent to which children have learned what has been taught (i.e., specific decoding principles, high-frequency words, specific strategies for word solving). As children progress as readers and as they read more and more texts, their abilities will broaden and likely be progressively less dependent on the particular curriculum. At this point, assessment for the purpose of forming instructional groups (and informing instruction) can use more general (less curriculum-specific) measures of reading.

> **KEEP IN MIND** Regardless of the approach used to forming instructional groups, it is important to consider the groups to be temporary and flexible. Children's reading progress typically does not proceed at a fixed rate, particularly when efforts to intervene are in place.

As an alternative, instructional groups might be formed on the basis of periodic administrations of more formal assessments that can be used for the purpose of documenting progress. However, depending on the assessment used, multiple administrations can be time-consuming and may add little to inform grouping decisions or instructional planning. It is the child's performance on a day-to-day basis that is particularly important rather than the child's performance at a single point in time. This last point should not, of course, be taken as a rationale for doing away, altogether, with systematic data collection; such data are needed for the purpose of documenting growth. Rather, the point is that teachers who are well informed about early literacy development, who are working closely and thoughtfully with children in small-group settings, and are systematically documenting children's performance during ongoing instructional interactions will likely know more about the students' abilities than can be learned from more formal assessments.

Preparing Children to Work without the Teacher during Small-Group Time

Ideally, the children in a supported small-group literacy context should receive the undivided attention of the teacher. However, since teachers are generally responsible for the entire class, they need to prepare the children to work effectively and independently when they are involved with their small groups. To accomplish this, many teachers, particularly in the primary grades, report that during the first week or two of school, they do not actually work with small groups but rather invest time in teaching children the routines and procedures that will eventually govern their independent work once they begin to meet with groups. Teachers typically develop a number of centers or stations in the classroom where individuals or groups of children engage in practice and reinforcement activities for particular academic skills and/or in activities that provide the opportunity for new learning/ knowledge building. For example, a teacher might develop a listening center where the children listen to recordings of information books, or a computer center where the children watch videos relating to the science or social studies content about which the class is learning.

Planning, Planning, Planning

The activities in which the children engage should be so well planned and so well described to them that little or no teacher support is required once the children have learned what to do at each center. All of the necessary materials should be readily available and accessible to the children. For centers that focus on the development of early literacy skills, such as knowledge of high-frequency words or the development of skill with the alphabetic code, the activities should lend themselves to some degree of differentiation. Thus, each child might have a folder at the center that contains items that are matched to his current skill level.

Another aspect of planning is deciding which children will be placed together at each center. In our opinion, centers work best when children at various points of development interact. This way the children who are a bit further along can assist children who are less so, and both are likely to benefit from the interaction.

Setting Reasonable Expectations

It is unlikely that young children will be able to sustain productive engagement with the same activity for prolonged periods of time. Therefore, the activities designed for each center should generally require no more than 15–20 minutes to complete, and at least some of the centers should encourage the children to talk with their friends as they engage in learning activities—this conversational aspect will help to promote language development and to deepen the children's learning by providing them with the opportunity to gain another child's perspective. For example, in the listening center, the book to which the children listen might be marked with sticky notes that signal them to stop and discuss (1) their predictions, (2) how what happened in the story/text compared to their predictions, (3) what they are wondering about, and (4) how they would feel in a similar situation.

To ensure quiet, productive activity as transition times approach, it is important to have appealing but simple activities for the children to engage in once they have completed the major center activity. For example, there might be options such as playing games with high-frequency words or decoding elements or book browsing.

Teaching for Self-Regulation

In order to provide the teacher with the focused time needed to give instruction in small-group contexts, children need to learn to work productively and independently when they are not directly engaged with the teacher. This independence requires them to regulate their own behaviors and to solve small problems without seeking assistance. Self-regulation develops more readily when it is guided by the teacher—that is, when the means of self-regulation are directly taught (explained and modeled) and when attempts at self-regulation are explicitly noticed and publicly valued.

To establish the desired self-regulation, the teacher might spend the first week or two of school demonstrating what to do in the centers, discussing what to do if problems arise, monitoring and guiding the children's problem-solving skills while engaged in the centers, and explicitly praising evidence of self-regulation and engagement (e.g., "I love the way that Alex found his folder and got busy with writing and checking his spelling words right away;" "I see that Kayla and Olivia are already very interested in their book in the listening center!"). As the children begin to show some independence in utilizing the centers, the teacher should begin to work with the small groups, initially for relatively short periods of time and working up to the full amount of time planned by the end of the third or fourth week, or so, of school.

"Eyes in the Front of Her Head"

While effective primary-grade teachers are often described as "having eyes in the back of their heads" because they seem to know what's going on in all parts of their classrooms at all times, it is more likely that their "with-it-ness" is due to careful planning and positioning: They anticipate potential difficulties in the classroom and try to prevent them. Moreover, when they organize for small-group instruction, they position themselves so that they can see the entire classroom and monitor the children who are not in the group with which they are working.

Assistants in the Classroom

The foregoing discussion has assumed that the classroom teacher is the lone adult in the room. However, if additional adult resources are available, instruction has the potential to be even more productive. For example, if a classroom aide is available during the period in which the teacher is providing small-group instruction, the aide can monitor and support the children who are engaged in center activities. If more than one additional adult is available, those adults can be pressed into service in providing guided practice opportunities for the children. For example, they might listen to individual children reread and discuss books that were previously read with the teacher, or they might do small-group interactive read-alouds. To be optimally effective in either of these roles, the assistants/volunteers will typically benefit from some orientation and guidance concerning the goals of these activities and how they might support children in achieving those goals.

Teaching Small Groups

In the schedule presented in Figure 2.1, it is assumed that the teacher has four different groups of children with whom she works during the course of a week. Group 1 is at the earliest point in development and would consist largely or exclusively of children who have been identified as being at risk; the schedule allows the teacher to work with these children 5 days a week. Group 2 comprises children who are somewhat more advanced in terms of their early literacy skills but are not yet at grade level. Some of these children may have been identified as at risk but may be showing sufficient growth such that they do not need the level of intensity provided for the children in Group 1. The schedule allows the teacher to meet with students in Group 2 on 4 days of the week. Groups 3 and 4 consist of children who are at grade level and somewhat above grade level, respectively. Because these children are predicted to readily meet or exceed grade-level expectations by the end of the year, the teacher needs to meet with them less frequently and/or less intensively to support their development. In the schedule there is time for the teacher to meet with each of these groups three times per week. An alternative for Groups 3 and 4 might be to meet with them 5 days per week but for abbreviated lessons on 2 of the days. Thus, in the schedule depicted in Figure 2.1, the teacher might opt to meet with Group 3 and Group 4 students on both Thursday and Friday, with the time set aside for that block divided between the two groups.

As depicted in the sample schedule, the teacher meets with different groups in different time slots each day. The rationale for this is twofold. First, because children are likely to move back and forth between and among groups as their literacy skills develop, having the groups meet in a different order on each day may help to avoid having the children develop a strong sense of which group is the "top" and "bottom" reading group. Given that identifying oneself as being in the bottom reading group can have a serious negative impact on one's sense of efficacy, it is clearly desirable for the children to perceive the groups as fluid (and for the groups to *be* fluid, of course). Secondly, having the groups meet at a different time each day will help to ensure that the students in each group have the opportunity to receive their small-group literacy instruction when they are relatively fresh.

The instruction provided during small-group time should be guided by the skills and performance levels of the children in the group. Children who are performing at levels substantially below grade level (Group 1 in the current scenario) are obviously ready to learn very different things than children who are performing substantially above grade level. For example, the children in Group 1 may be limited in their phonemic awareness, knowledge of the alphabet, and understanding of print conventions. Thus, these skills will need to be explicitly addressed in the small-group context, at least early in the year. Children in Groups 3 and 4, on the other hand, probably have these skills fairly well established, and, as a result, most of their small-group time can focus on engaging them in reading and responding to books and other texts.

In the ISA, the typical components of a small-group lesson include the following:

- Rereading a book from a previous lesson.
- Alphabetics, including isolated phonemic analysis instruction for children with very limited skill.
- Reading a new book.
- Writing.
- Practicing high-frequency words.

Table 2.3 provides an outline of what small-group lessons might look like at the beginning of first grade for children in the four groups described above. When specific instructional activities are noted (e.g., onset–rime blending, singing the alphabet), these are meant as examples only. Different activities (e.g., sorting pictures by ending sound, filling in missing letters on an alphabet strip), based on students' developing skills, would be selected on different days. For purposes of illustration, Group 1 is assumed to be at an emergent level, and Groups 2, 3, and 4 are considered to be at various points along the continuum that might be considered "developing." If there are maturing or proficient readers in the class, the teacher might need to consider adding a group and/or arranging for these children to join a second-grade group taught by another teacher. (Please note that the group designations in Table 2.3 are different from the emergent, developing, maturing and proficient designations illustrated in Table 2.2). At the beginning of first grade it is unlikely that many children would have the skills of a mature or proficient reader. However, the range of skills within the "developing" designation is likely to be broad enough to warrant separating children into groups for reading instruction.

INTERVENTIONS BEYOND THE CLASSROOM

Where Does Time for Intervention Fit In?

For at-risk children who do not appear to be making sufficient progress to overcome their difficulties with classroom instruction alone, it can be more than a bit of a challenge to find time in the day to provide *additional* intervention services. However, if it is determined that a child needs more instructional support than what can be provided within the classroom program, that support needs to be provided in addition to the supported small-group reading provided in the classroom. Only then can intensification of instructional experiences be achieved. In the sample schedule provided in Figure 2.1, the ideal time for additional intervention would be during the times when the classroom teacher is engaged in providing small-group instruction to children in groups other than the one to which the child belongs. Because children would probably benefit from a bit of a break between

(text continues on p. 50)

TABLE 2.3. Small-Group Lesson: Four Different Groups

Lesson components		Group 1	Group 2	Group 3	Group 4
Rereading	All groups	Each child individually reads one or two books from a prior small-group session. Children are allowed to choose their books from a selection provided by the teacher. The teacher listens in and provides guidance to individual children.			
	Separate groups	Teacher attends to print concepts and conventions.	Teacher attends to voice–print match, use of initial letter cue, and context.	Teacher attends to confirmatory use of print (including single letters and larger orthographic units) and context for word solving.	Teacher attends to confirmatory use of print (including single letters and larger orthographic units) and context for word solving.
Phonemic analysis	Separate groups	Teacher engages children in onset–rime blending.	Teacher engages children in phoneme segmentation using sound boxes.	Not needed.	Not needed.
Alphabet knowledge	All groups	Teacher plans to teach a specific decoding skill that can be applied in the new book that the children will read.			
	Separate groups	Sing whole alphabet a few times while pointing to letters. Then focus on learning the names of two letters that occur frequently in the new book for the day.	Focus on letter–sound correspondence for consonants that occur frequently in the new book for the day and/ or on a new word family that will appear in the book. For word families, practice should incorporate one or more previously taught word families.	Depending on the characteristics of the book to be read, the teacher may teach and/or review word families or other decoding elements that will enable children to successfully puzzle through unfamiliar words that will appear in the day's book.	

(cont.)

TABLE 2.3. (cont.)

Lesson components		Group 1	Group 2	Group 3	Group 4
Reading new books	All groups	Teacher prepares the children to successfully read the book selected for the group. Part of the preparation occurs in the alphabet knowledge segment of the lesson (see above). Additional preparation may include (1) teaching a new word identification strategy that can be applied in the new book and/or reviewing strategies that have already been taught; (2) teaching one or more high-frequency words that will occur in the text and which the children are unlikely to be able to identify, given their current decoding skills and the contextual support for word identification provided by the text; and/or (3) providing a book introduction that is sufficiently detailed as to allow the children to be successful in the text but not so detailed as to limit the children's opportunities to be strategic. Each child will have the opportunity to read the entire book at least once during the small-group session. The teacher provides the level of support that is appropriate. For groups that are moving quickly, two books may be read during this segment of the lesson.		
	Separate groups	Text selection: Use texts in which there is a reliable and repetitive language pattern and a close correspondence between the pictures and the text. Texts that support the development of letter recognition and identification are preferred.	Text selection: Use texts that make some use of repetitive language and provide the opportunity for the children to effectively use initial letters in combination with context to puzzle through unfamiliar words. Texts specifically designed to promote the development of high-frequency sight vocabulary might also be used.	Text selection: Dependent on the instructional materials in use.	
High-frequency words	Separate groups	Children rely on nonalphabetic features for word learning until they learn about the	To begin to learn high-frequency words, children need to attend to the letters in the	High-frequency words serve as an important anchor for children in puzzling through texts at their level. Helping children to become automatic in identifying words they have encountered in	

		alphabet. Word learning is very idiosyncratic. Only words in which the children can identify all of the letters should be taught and only words which occur in an emergent level text.	words. Texts in which the high-frequency words occur in slightly different contexts will facilitate this learning.	text will allow them to be more effectively strategic in puzzling through less familiar words. A variety of game-like activities, such as sticky-note bingo, can be used to support the development of fluency with high-frequency words.
Writing	All groups	Shared writing conducted in whole-class contexts provides the teacher with the opportunity to demonstrate various aspects of the writing process. In small groups, children should be involved in both shared and supported writing, with the teacher specifically focusing on what the children are ready to learn. In small-group and intervention lessons, writing may occur following the reading of either book and typically (but not always) involves writing a response to the book that was read. To maximize the use of the time available to write, the teacher often provides a fairly specific writing prompt.		
	Separate groups	Teachers need to focus on print concepts and the formation of individual letters. They may serve as scribes in the composition process. Teachers often model, and engage children in analyzing, the phonological components of words to be written.	Teachers model and engage children in composing messages and analyzing the phonemes in individual words. Particular emphasis is placed on analyzing and spelling the beginning sounds in words. Children are encouraged to use the key-word chart to remind them of letter–sound relationships and to refer to the "Words I Know" chart for the spellings of known high-frequency words.	Teachers model and engage children in more thorough sound analysis and spelling of words. Children are encouraged to refer to available resources to support their spelling, including the book they are responding to and the key word, "Words I Know," and phonogram charts.

their small-group classroom instruction and their intervention lesson, it may be ideal to allow them 15–25 minutes of center time between the two lessons. If the intervention teachers cannot accommodate to the rotating schedule suggested, of course, the time slots for individual groups would need to be stabilized.

What Do/Should Intervention Lessons Look Like?

Early research on the ISA focused solely on providing interventions beyond the classroom (Vellutino et al., 1996; Scanlon et al., 2005). The classroom application of the approach was based on the success of the interventions and the belief that classroom teachers would benefit from having the knowledge and insights into literacy development that we had been developing with the intervention teachers with whom we worked. Therefore, from our perspective, Tier 2 and Tier 3 interventions should look very much like high-quality, supported, small-group literacy lessons that would be provided in the classroom. Ideally, however, the group size in intervention settings beyond the classroom would be smaller than the group sizes that are possible/necessary at the classroom level. This smaller size would allow the intervention teacher to individualize instruction a bit more than the classroom teacher is typically able to do. As we stress at several points throughout this book, in order to maximize the effectiveness of literacy instruction for children in intervention, it is important to ensure that the instruction offered in the classroom and instruction offered in intervention settings are mutually supportive. We address this topic in several ways in upcoming chapters that focus on the instructional goals of the ISA. We feel that when classroom and intervention teachers share a common set of instructional goals and continually reflect on ways to address those goals, the instruction they offer is more likely to be effective in supporting children's literacy development.

CHAPTER 3

Motivation to Read and Write

MOTIVATION GOAL

The child will develop the belief that reading and writing are enjoyable and informative activities which are not beyond her capabilities.

Motivation is what gets one going, keeps one engaged, and moves one forward in any task that requires effort. If students are not motivated to learn to read and write, instruction will have limited impact. Most young children begin school eager to learn to read and write and fully expecting that they will successfully learn to do so (McKenna, Kear, & Ellsworth, 1995). Unfortunately, when children encounter difficulties with learning, their enthusiasm is likely to wane, their beliefs about themselves as learners are likely to change, and they may come to view literate activities as work rather than as enjoyable and informative undertakings. Indeed, children who struggle with becoming literate often try to avoid reading and writing; as a result, they do less of it and make less progress. The challenge for teachers, then, is to try to avoid this downward spiral.

In this chapter we discuss things that teachers can do that may maintain and enhance children's initial enthusiasm and help them to adopt belief systems that promote active and joyful engagement in literate activities. Here we discuss early literacy instruction from a motivational perspective. The topics to be discussed include:

- The importance of engaging children in reading and listening to interesting texts and reacting to them.
- Helping children develop a sense of competence and confidence in their literacy skills by:
  - Ensuring that the texts they encounter, particularly those they read and write, are not too challenging.
  - Helping them to develop effective approaches to solving problems they encounter with both word reading and comprehension.
  - Scaffolding their reading—providing just enough support to allow them to succeed but not so much support that they do not learn how to engage independently.
- Helping the children to value literacy for its own sake rather than viewing it as "work" for which they should be rewarded.
- Helping children to notice their successes and to attribute their success to things that are under their control—such as the amount of effort they expend and the strategic problem solving they do—rather than factors that are beyond their control.

PROMOTING INTEREST IN BOOKS

Teachers often identify "developing a love of reading" as one of their major instructional goals (Nolen, 2001). Clearly, children are more likely to love reading if they love the books that they read or hear and if they enjoy the interactions that occur around these books. In the early primary grades (and before) reading aloud to children provides an important context for developing this love. Children who have had a lot of positive experiences with being read to are likely to already love being read to and will continue to enjoy it and profit from it during the primary-grade years (and beyond). However, many children who struggle at the early stages of literacy development have not had the hundreds (or thousands) of hours of book experience we would like. Therefore, they may not yet know about the pleasure that books can provide. For these children it will be especially helpful to engage them in listening and reacting to books that are of particular interest to them. Thus, a teacher might make a point of choosing to read a book on certain cultural traditions, or certain animals, or certain family dynamics, etc., because she knows that those topics will be of particular interest to one or more of the students. Letting children know that a book was selected for them, because of their particular interests, will help them to understand that books can be special to them as individuals—a very motivating thought!

Website Resource

We have recently become aware of a website (*kansas.bookconnect.com*) that may help teachers (and parents) find books on particular topics of interest for their children. The site allows searches based on major topics (e.g., animals, holidays, science, people) and subtopics within those topics (e.g., polar bears, Cinco de Mayo, habitats, U.S. presidents). Further, particular interest levels can be designated (e.g., kindergarten through third, fourth through sixth), as can book levels as indicated by grade and month in school (e.g., a book at level 1.8 would be a book that an average child in the eighth month of first grade should be able to read fairly independently).[1] This website, at least at this time, offers open access.

Interactive Read-Alouds

We discuss the value of interactive read-alouds in several of the upcoming chapters because they are valuable in many ways. In this chapter we focus on the role of interactive read-alouds in promoting motivation to read and write. Books read during interactive read-alouds are often more challenging than books that the children would be able to read on their own, and the reader generally does not direct the children's attention to the print very much, if at all. When reading books with pictures, the reader does, of course, encourage the children to attend to the pictures both to enhance their understanding of the text and to enhance their aesthetic experience. What makes an interactive read-aloud *interactive* is that the children and the reader engage in conversation about the book, and the conversation is not entirely controlled or initiated by the reader. Thus, ideally, in an interactive read-aloud the children are free to offer their observations, ask and answer questions, make predictions, and generally react to the story fairly freely. The reader also shares her thinking and draws children's attention to various aspects of the text, depending on the purposes for reading that particular text.

At the most obvious level, reading aloud to children helps to build motivation to read because listening to books that capture their imagination or offer information that interests them is just plain enjoyable for children. They get "hooked" and are apt to want to listen to more books on the same or similar topics and/or by the same author. Reading aloud to children can also promote an interest in writing, particularly when children are helped to notice and appreciate what an author does when she writes. For example, while children often readily become involved in the storyline of a book, they are often surprised when, on occasion, the reader steps back a bit to help them think about the author's craft. For instance, the reader

---

[1] It is important to note that there are a number of ways in which books are "leveled" for readability and that the leveling systems generally do not totally agree with one another. We are not necessarily endorsing the leveling system utilized by this website.

might point out how the author makes the audience feel particular ways by the words she chooses.

While a teacher may, and typically should, have multiple reasons for selecting a particular book to use for an interactive read-aloud, developing a love of reading and writing should always be an important purpose. Thus, *the first encounter with a book should always be focused on stimulating enjoyment and comprehension of the text*. The box below provides some suggestions for making interactive read-alouds fun and motivating experiences.

Interactive Read-Alouds from a Motivational Perspective

Be enthusiastic. The teacher should show enthusiasm for and interest in the reading materials in use.

Collaborate—don't test. Interactions concerning a text should have a collaborative rather than a test-like tone. The teacher should avoid asking questions for which she already knows the answer. There is no reason to ask such questions other than to "test" the children's understanding. Rather, teachers should offer their own thinking about the text and invite children to share theirs. Both the teacher and the children should ask genuine questions, analyze, interpret, and react to the text. Teachers should avoid the use of evaluative language. For example, rather than asking whether a prediction was right or wrong, the teacher might ask whether the prediction *matched the author's thinking*.

Discuss the illustrations. The teacher should occasionally provide opportunities for the children to enjoy and discuss the illustrations and to use the illustrations to inform their understanding of the text. For example, children might use an illustration to determine how a character was feeling (by considering the character's facial expression) or to infer what time of year the story takes place (by noticing what the characters are wearing or what the environment looks like). Then, the teacher would read and the children would listen to find out if their interpretations are supported by information in the text.

Encourage personal reactions to the story. Encourage the children to discuss how they might have reacted and/or felt in a situation similar to that depicted in the story. The teacher should also share her personal reactions to the story (but should not dominate the conversation).

Edit or modify the story. Occasionally rewrite a portion of the story in a way that the children suggest. For example, in the book *The Velveteen Rabbit* (Williams, 1922) the children might like to add a page or two telling how the boy got a new rabbit.

Act out portions of the story. It is often fun for children to act out some or all aspects of a story they have heard. Such activities engage the children in (sometimes passionate) discussions of the sequence of story events. Providing a few props (e.g., items of clothing befitting the main characters) can be particularly motivating. Also providing a copy of the text for children to refer to as they plan their reenactment will help them to view books as valuable resources (Welsch, 2008).

DEVELOPING A SENSE OF CONFIDENCE AND COMPETENCE

Several factors can influence the development of confidence and a sense of competence for beginning and struggling readers. We discuss three particularly important factors in this section: keeping the challenge at a moderate level, helping children develop effective approaches to problem solving, and providing just enough support in problem-solving situations.

Moderate Degree of Challenge

As Schultheiss and Brunstein (2005) report, successful experiences lead to hopefulness and an inclination to seek further opportunities to solve similar problems, whereas repeated experiences with failure lead to expectations of further failure and therefore lead one away from engagement. This is one of the reasons that RTI has the potential to be so powerful: It encourages schools to organize instruction that meets students' needs sooner, and the smaller instructional groupings allow for greater individualization with regard to instructional materials.

When children are frequently asked to read texts that are too difficult for them, as texts for struggling readers often are, they are likely to try to find ways to avoid the whole enterprise. They might, for example, try to engage the teacher and/or peers in conversation, or they might find multiple excuses to move around the classroom (to use the rest room, to sharpen a pencil, to get a drink of water, etc.) or indicate that they are tired and put their heads down on the table.

In upcoming chapters we revisit the issue of text challenge in various ways. For now, the "take-away message" is that the level of challenge that children encounter when they attempt to read affects their sense of competence for reading and their motivation to read more generally.

Developing Effective Approaches to Problem Solving

Instruction that focuses on the development of word identification strategies has the potential to contribute to children's sense of competence[2] as readers because it gives them the tools to figure out unfamiliar words that they encounter in text—one of the most challenging parts of the reading process for many beginning and struggling readers. Here we address aspects of instructional and interpersonal interactions around word solving that can influence the child's willingness to engage in the process. This willingness (or motivation) is important because, if readers believe that they will be able to figure out the unfamiliar words they encounter, they are much more likely to expend the effort that it might take to do so.

---

[2] A sense of competence is sometimes referred to as *self-efficacy*, which Bandura (1997) defines as learners' perceived capabilities for learning or performing actions at designated levels.

For most individuals, a sense of competence develops through successful experiences with a particular activity and recognition of that success. With regard to word solving, we have found it useful to explicitly teach several word identification strategies and to provide the children with guidance and practice in using them in interactive and confirmatory ways, ultimately helping them become spontaneous and independent in the use of their problem-solving skills and to recognize their own ability. For example, the teacher might say, "I saw you make that first sound and then read past that puzzling word to get a better idea of what word would make sense. You are really thinking like a reader!" or "I see you checking your key-word chart to help you remember the sound of that letter! That's what readers do when they need to!" Both of these comments focus on the problem-solving process, provide the reader with a vote of confidence in her word-solving skills and, therefore, help her build a sense of competence.

In addition to explicit discussion of word-solving strategies, the way in which teachers and peers talk about and react to successes and difficulties with word solving can be very influential in shaping how learners think about the process and their own ability to engage in that process. For example, when a child encounters an unknown word in text and the teacher says "Oh, that's a hard [tricky, challenging] word," it might lead some children to give up on solving the word. As an alternative, the teacher might use the word *puzzling* to describe the unknown word because it more clearly conveys the need to think about what the word might be and to use various sources of information to solve it.

The reactions of peers (and others, such as parents and older siblings) to children's word-solving efforts can also influence their motivation and sense of competence. For example, when someone loses patience with a child's attempts at puzzling through a word and does something that reflects that impatience, it is likely to diminish the child's sense of competence. Reactions that might undermine a child's confidence include providing the word (with an impatient tone of voice) or saying things like "You know that word!" or "You just read that word on the other page!" So too are comments such as "Who can help Alex?", which conveys that, although Alex can't solve a particular word, the teacher fully expects that other children can.

We encourage teachers to put word solving in a positive light by talking about how figuring out a new word is a bit like doing a puzzle: You may need to think about several different things (e.g., the shape of the piece, the color of the piece, the larger picture into which the piece must fit) in order to figure out which piece fits just right. By emphasizing the pleasure of figuring something out, we can put word solving in an entirely different light both for children who may become impatient while waiting for a peer to figure things out and for those who may need a bit more time to puzzle through a word. We do not, of course, wish to suggest that word-solving assistance should never be provided. Indeed, providing thoughtful in-the-moment assistance with word solving is an important aspect of literacy instruction. However, the assistance offered should have the goal of enhancing children's word-solving strategies and their sense that they have the ability to puzzle through unfamiliar words successfully.

Scaffolding Children's Reading

Building a sense of competence for carrying out a complex process such as reading occurs over a protracted period of time and, for some children, requires a substantial amount of teacher guidance. The way in which the teacher provides guidance and the kind of guidance provided can make a difference. A teacher who is too directive may prevent the child from engaging in the kind of problem-solving efforts that will build her ability to problem-solve independently and thereby interfere with the development of a sense of competence. On the other hand, a teacher who offers too little guidance may put children in the position of being overwhelmed and frustrated in their attempts to read; this too will interfere with their development of a sense of competence. Thus, an early literacy teacher needs to do a bit of a balancing act to try to ensure that the support that she offers is "just right."

To do so, the teacher must have insight into how children approach a task so that she can recognize their sources of confusion and help to effectively clear them up. For example, when a child misidentifies a word encountered while reading, the teacher is likely to recognize the error immediately—because the teacher already knows the word. The child, on the other hand, obviously does not already know the word and therefore may not realize that an error has occurred until she gets further along in the sentence or paragraph. The teacher's response to the child in this situation will influence the child's sense of competence and, hence, her motivation to persist. If the teacher jumps right in to correct the child before the context has clued the child to the problem, her sense of competence can be undermined. If, however, the teacher provides the child with the time to notice and potentially correct the error, the child's sense of competence is likely to be enhanced. Tables 3.1 and 3.2 provide some examples to illustrate this point.

TABLE 3.1. Sample Interactions Following a Word Identification Error That _Will_ Promote a Sense of Competence in Reading

Teacher response	Child's possible interpretation
Waits until the child has read far enough along to realize that an error has occurred.	"I'm not sure about that word—but maybe I'll figure it out if I read a little further."
Notices when the child notices a word identification error (e.g., "I hear you slowing down there—are you thinking that something is not quite right?").	"It's OK to slow down and think a bit when something doesn't seem right."
Notices when the child spontaneously corrects a word identification error and encourages the child to reflect on this success (e.g., "I noticed that you went back and changed that word. How did you know that that word was . . . ?").	"I know how to figure out words."

TABLE 3.2. Sample Interactions Following a Word Identification Error That *Will Not* Promote a Sense of Competence in Reading

Teacher response	Child's possible interpretation
Too much support: Identifies the error *before* the child has read far enough to realize that an error has occurred.	"I can't do this on my own" or "I need someone to tell me the words I don't know."
Too little support: Allows the child to keep reading, despite error(s).	"Guessing at the words seems to be OK with my teacher" or "All I have to do is say something and keep going—I'm not sure what I'm supposed to be doing here!"

We discuss the issue of trying to offer just the right amount of support in several places throughout this book. The point here is that appropriate scaffolding makes an important contribution to children's sense of competence.

ATTRIBUTIONS FOR SUCCESS

Motivation researchers have identified two general types of beliefs that students may hold with regard to their academic abilities: fixed versus malleable (Dweck & Molden, 2005). That is, some students believe that their academic abilities are fixed or unchangeable, for example, believing "I'm not good at reading and I will never be." Students who hold this belief may see little reason to expend the effort it might take to improve. Other students appear to believe that academic abilities are malleable (they can be changed). Such students believe that their current status, whatever it may be, is temporary. Children who hold this belief are more likely to maintain motivation in the face of difficulty (Niiya, Crocker, & Bartmess, 2004).

Children in the early primary grades tend to think of their abilities as changeable and under their control. They tend to believe that if they put in enough effort, they can do just about anything (Chapman & Tunmer, 1995; Nicholls, 1978, 1990). They attribute their learning successes to their efforts rather than to innate abilities. Older students, on the other hand, particularly those who struggle with academics, tend to think of their abilities as being unchangeable and not within their control. They do not see their efforts as being an important determinant of their progress. Needless to say, once struggling learners come to believe that there is little they can do to improve their reading ability, their motivation to engage in reading is likely to be substantially diminished. Unfortunately, because of the systems currently in place, schools contribute to this belief system by identifying the children who make the least progress as *learning disabled.*

Thus, an important goal of early intervention for struggling learners is to keep children from adopting beliefs about their abilities that are counterproductive. One way of doing this is to help children become stronger readers—which is the focus of much of this book. However, it is also important to try to keep children from adopting a fixed view of their abilities. To do this, we encourage teachers to explain the roles of practice and effort and to help children reflect on their successes.

The Role of Practice and Effort

In general, the more reading a child does, the easier reading becomes. Although teachers clearly understand this, some children do not. Children who struggle, particularly those who are frequently asked to read texts that are too challenging for them, can come to believe that reading will always be difficult for them—because it always has been. This is a very logical but unfortunate conclusion.

Several of the teachers with whom we have worked have found it useful to explain the practice–progress relationship through the use of analogies that illustrate how effort can serve to make a task that seems very challenging eventually manageable and, ultimately, nearly effortless. For example, for a child who already knows how to ride a bike, a teacher might talk about how hard and frustrating it was to learn, and how easy it is now. Alternatively, for children who have younger siblings, the teacher might talk about how difficult it is initially to learn to walk and/or talk and how easy it is for children in kindergarten and first grade to do those things.

An Anecdote

I (DMS) once observed a little boy who was receiving daily one-to-one tutoring in reading and making very little progress. After observing a lesson and finding nothing clearly amiss in its focus and pace, I had a little chat with the child. I explained to him that Mrs. D (the tutor) really knew how to teach reading and that if he really tried to do the things that Mrs. D asked, it would be much easier to learn to read.

"Really?!?" he said with a note of both disbelief and surprise and eyes opened wide.

"Really!" I said with conviction.

From that point forward, the child made much more rapid progress. The tutor was astounded and so was I. The child's sudden increase in rate of progress might certainly have occurred without this little chat. However, in light of the research discussed in this section (which, at the time, I had not yet read), it seems possible that his enhanced growth may have been due to a new-found belief that he *could* learn to read.

Attending to and Reflecting on Success

While we certainly want children to be willing to expend the effort it will take to grow as readers, simply telling them to try harder is not likely to accomplish this goal. It has long been recognized that one of the most effective ways to elicit desired behaviors from children is to attend to desired behaviors. For example, when a group of kindergartners becomes too noisy during a read-aloud, one of the most effective ways to quiet them down is to notice the children who are engaged in the story in appropriate ways: "I like the way that Mike and Michaela are listening and thinking. . . . "

A similar tact can be taken in supporting individuals around word solving or comprehension monitoring: "I like the way you went back and reread that when it wasn't making sense to you." Further, children can be encouraged to attend to and reflect on their own successes initially by asking them to explain how they solved particular problems ("How did you know that word was . . . ?") and later by asking them to identify and reflect on instances when they were effective problem solvers.

GOAL ORIENTATION: INTRINSIC VERSUS EXTRINSIC MOTIVATION

A child who is intrinsically motivated wants to do/learn/participate in something because it is interesting and valuable to her. On the other hand, a child who is extrinsically motivated engages in activities for the sake of earning social rewards, such as praise or recognition, or physical rewards, such as stickers or some form of token that can be traded for a desired commodity (free time, reduction in homework, etc.). In a very simplified form, a summary of the research on extrinsic versus intrinsic motivation suggests that children who are intrinsically motivated to learn are more likely to succeed at challenging academic tasks (see Schunk, Pintrich, & Meece, 2008), whereas students who need to be extrinsically motivated in order to engage in academically challenging tasks tend to have poorer academic outcomes.

Although students can be both intrinsically and extrinsically motivated, schools tend to be organized around extrinsic motivation systems—grades, rewards, and praise—so many students tend to focus on the external reward. Since research suggests that intrinsic motivation leads to greater long-term learning, the motivational systems that characterize schools need to be carefully considered. McKenna et al. (1995) documented a general decline in motivation for reading among children as they progressed through the elementary years. This decline may well be related to the extrinsic motivational systems that characterize many schools.

Many of the suggestions made earlier in this chapter will help to promote the development of intrinsic motivation. In addition, we encourage teachers to do the following:

• *Treat reading and writing as a privilege (not as work).* When teachers treat reading and writing as jobs that must be accomplished/completed in order to gain access to more preferred activities (e.g., recess or free-choice time in the classroom), children, especially those who struggle with literacy acquisition, are likely to view reading and writing as work. If, on the other hand, teachers convey the idea that reading and writing are pleasurable activities that are valuable in their own right, children are more apt to adopt such a perspective. Think, for a moment, about what we convey to children when we say, "Let's get our (reading or writing) work done so that we can have free time." One translation of this is, "Let's get this unpleasant (reading or writing) work done so that we can have the reward of not having to read or write anymore!" Such a message is clearly not intended. Minor changes in wording can dramatically alter the interpretation of a statement or request. Table 3.3 provides some suggestions for rephrasing to send very different motivational messages.

• *Avoid social comparisons and encourage personal comparisons.* Because children begin their school careers at very different places in development, progress and achievement for each child need to be evaluated using different metrics. For example, a child who begins kindergarten knowing the names of all of the letters of the alphabet is not necessarily a better student than one who knows few letters at the beginning of the school year but learns several during the first few weeks or months of school. However, it is not unusual to find classrooms where student achievement, even on such elementary skills, is publicly posted, apparently with the intention of motivating more students to attain the same level of skill. In such a classroom, a child who begins school with very limited early literacy skills is apt to begin to view herself as inadequate from early on. This self-perception of inadequacy can, ultimately, lead a child to adopt an identity in which she perceives herself as someone who is unable to perform at a level commensurate with her peers. Such a perception is likely to limit the child's willingness to exert the effort needed to grow and develop in literacy. On the other hand, if the same child was given the opportunity to evaluate her performance relative to her previous levels, there is a greater likelihood that the child would experience the motivating feelings that come with advancing skills/accomplishments.

• *Use praise judiciously to encourage intrinsic motivation and a mastery orientation.* What teachers say to children matters tremendously and can have

TABLE 3.3. Motivating and Unmotivating Messages Teachers Might Send

Unmotivating messages	Motivating messages
"We need to read this book today before recess."	"We get to read this book today before recess."
"I want to see what you are going to write next. You need to finish your journal entry before you go to the block area."	"I can't wait to see what you are going to write next. I hope you get to finish your journal entry before you go to the block area."
"Let's see how many of these letters you know."	"Let's see how many of these letters you *already* know."
"Each of you will do a report on dinosaurs."	"You will each have a chance to do a report on a dinosaur that you are especially interested in."

significant impact on how children view themselves as learners. Teachers can convey that academic engagement and performance are primarily for the purpose of pleasing the teacher ("What a good job") or gaining social recognition ("You're so smart!")—both of which are, essentially, forms of extrinsic motivation. On the other hand, teachers can convey that learning and performance are rewarding in their own right ("What an interesting thought!" or "I bet it felt great to figure that out!"). Such responses to student thinking help to promote the development of intrinsic motivation.

DOCUMENTING LITERACY MOTIVATION

To help teachers be mindful of their students' motivational status, we provide a list of motivational characteristics that can be used to periodically rate students (see Figure 3.1). In using this tool, the teacher would list the names of children at the top of each column and then rate each child on each characteristic on the basis of informal observations made during instructional interactions. As depicted in the key for Figure 3.1, we suggest using a 3-point rating scale ranging from a "not at all" rating for a child to an "absolutely" rating for a child. The purpose of these ratings is not to provide an overall score for motivation but to give a snapshot of the motivational status of an instructional group. This enables the teacher to reflect on what may need to be done instructionally when students are observed to lack motivation and/or to hold beliefs that are associated with limitations in motivation.

MOTIVATION AND RTI

Attention to children's motivation for reading and writing is especially important in discussions of RTI. It is widely recognized that individuals who find learning challenging are apt to try to avoid those learning situations (Morgan, Fuchs, Compton, Cordray, & Fuchs, 2008; Stanovich, 1986; Taylor & Adelman, 1999). Children who are involved in the RTI process are, by definition, experiencing difficulty with literacy acquisition. Attention to the motivational aspects of instructional interactions are particularly important for these children.

Group Snapshot—Motivation					
Student Names					
Child is enthusiastic about fictional read-alouds.					
Child is enthusiastic about informational read-alouds.					
Child demonstrates active engagement when being read to.					
Child is enthusiastic about reading.					
Child is enthusiastic about writing.					
Child perceives him- or herself as a capable reader.					
Child perceives him- or herself as a capable writer.					
When encountering difficulty while reading, child appears to believe that he or she has strategies to be successful.					
Child has developed an interest in a particular genre/series of books.					
Child believes that his or her status as a reader is dependent on his or her effort.					
Child understands that reading practice will lead to reading growth.					

Key:
N = Not at all   S = Somewhat   A = Absolutely

FIGURE 3.1. Motivation checklist.

PART II

LEARNING THE ALPHABETIC CODE

INTRODUCTION

In order to learn to read in an alphabetic writing system such as English, individuals need to develop some critical understandings about how the writing system works. First, they must understand that the *purpose of print* is to communicate, and they must understand the basic *conventions of print*, such as that we read from left to right and, generally, from the top to the bottom of the page. They must also recognize that spoken words are comprised of somewhat separable sounds that are strung together, and they must be able to manipulate those sounds. Someone who can analyze and manipulate the sounds in spoken words is said to have achieved *phonemic awareness*. Readers also need to understand that the letters in printed words represent the sounds in spoken words. This association is often referred to as the *alphabetic principle*; understanding the alphabetic principle enables children to learn to use the *alphabetic code*. Clearly, to understand the alphabetic principle and the alphabetic code, one must know something about *letter names* and must be familiar with at least some of the most common sounds associated with the letters (*letter–sound association*). As readers gain skill and experience with an alphabetic language, they learn to process *larger orthographic units* such as prefixes, suffixes, and phonograms (e.g., *ook, ight*). Being able to process these larger units allows readers to be more efficient in identifying unfamiliar words.[1]

---

[1]The progression of skill development we describe for the alphabetic code is largely, although not entirely, consistent with Ehri's (2005) theory of word learning.

Figure II.1 provides a schematic representation of the progression from earlier to later phases of the development of skill with the alphabetic code. On the far left, phonemic awareness and letter identification (letter-name knowledge) are identified as starting points for the developmental sequence. Instructionally, these two skill areas might be addressed separately until the student develops some familiarity with each. As depicted, engaging in reading and writing (in this case, shared reading and writing activities) may help children become phonemically aware, learn the names of printed letters, and simultaneously help them learn about the purposes and conventions of print. Once children know the names of some letters and are beginning to be somewhat phonemically aware, they begin to learn about the relations between printed letters and the sounds they represent. Learning about letter sounds extends children's phonemic awareness and enhances their learning as they engage in reading and writing. These activities, in turn, extend children's knowledge of letter–sound relationships. Thus, the multiple experiences that children have with printed language become mutually supportive and reciprocal in nature.

Over time, skill in phonemic analysis and developing letter-sound knowledge help children to understand the alphabetic principle—the idea that the letters in printed words represent the sounds in spoken words. As children begin to understand this principle, they learn more and more about the alphabetic code. Understanding of the alphabetic principle develops gradually. For most children, it follows a progression from letters and sounds at the beginning of words, to letters and sounds at the end of words, to those in the middle of words—rather than from the beginning, to the middle, to the end, as might seem logical. Letters and sounds at the ends of words are easier to attend to than those in the middle partly because the medial sounds are influenced by (co-articulated with) both the sound that

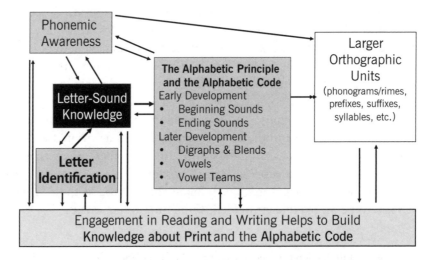

FIGURE II.1. Schematic representation of the development of skill with the alphabetic code.

comes before them and those that come after. (An explanation of co-articulation is provided in the discussion of the development of phonemic awareness in Chapter 5.) Engagement in appropriately challenging reading and writing activities helps to further extend the child's understanding of, and facility with, alphabetic coding. Ultimately, the child will come to recognize larger orthographic units such as phonograms, which are at the center of word families, and prefixes and suffixes. Recognizing these larger chunks helps children identify unfamiliar words more effectively and efficiently. As a result, children are likely to read and write more and build their sight vocabularies more quickly. This larger sight vocabulary, in turn, allows children to read even more effectively and efficiently, which, again, leads to more improvements in overall reading ability.

Most young children who are identified as being at risk in an RTI process demonstrate limitations in the skills that are the focus of Part II, and many will need greater guidance in developing these skills than do children who learn to read with relative ease. We discuss these aspects of learning to read in detail because there is a good deal of research indicating that children who experience difficulty at the early stages of learning to read have substantial difficulty with the decoding part of the process. In fact, it is widely believed that the development of phonemic analysis and phonics skills is a major stumbling block for children who struggle with literacy acquisition. These findings were summarized by Adams in 1990 and more recently by Snow et al. (1998), the National Reading Panel (2000), and Pressley (2006).

Because struggling literacy learners often do need such guidance, schools sometimes implement highly structured and prescribed phonemic awareness and phonics programs to address this need. As noted earlier, one important principle of the ISA is that the instruction offered to struggling readers should be as coherent as possible. Therefore, if schools are considering the adoption of supplementary programs for their struggling learners, we encourage them to examine the alignment between their core instruction and any supplementary phonemic awareness or phonics programs to ensure that the programs are congruent with the core language arts instruction that is offered in their classrooms. Moreover, it is important to ensure that the supplemental instruction is responsive to what the children know and are able to do and that the children understand the utility and application of what they are learning to authentic reading and writing. It is also important to convey the reality that the alphabetic code is not entirely reliable and that children need to learn to be somewhat flexible in their decoding attempts.

Part II focuses on helping teachers become highly knowledgeable about the developmental course of phonemic awareness and phonics skills to enable them to effectively identify what their students are ready to learn and how the various component skills might be most effectively taught in isolation and applied in context. The section comprises several chapters in which we discuss the progression through each step in the developmental sequence in some detail. However, as we become immersed in the details of each process, it is important to keep in mind how all the processes fit together. They are intricately related and are mutually supportive; they are important only to the extent that they support the development of meaningful reading and writing. It is very easy for teachers, whether they teach beginning readers and writers or older children who struggle, to focus primarily on these foundational processes, possibly losing sight of their goal—to help children understand the texts they read. In fact, because this book devotes so much attention to these foundational processes, we fear we might contribute to this tendency to lose sight of the desired outcome: children who read for understanding and enjoyment.

Before moving on, it is important to note that much of the research that has focused our attention on difficulties with the alphabetic code as a major cause of early reading problems has been done on middle-class children in middle-class schools. Neuman (2006) argues that many children, especially children from economically stressed households, experience reading difficulties not because they have difficulty with acquiring facility with the alphabetic code but because their knowledge of word meanings and their world knowledge are limited. As was discussed in Chapter 2 and as is discussed in subsequent chapters, the ability to understand written material is only partly dependent on one's ability to read the words in the text. The reader also needs to understand what the words mean and to have some understanding of the general topic that the text is addressing.

CHAPTER 4

Purposes and Conventions of Print

ALPHABETICS GOAL 1

The child will understand that the purpose of print is to communicate. The child will also understand the basic print conventions, such as the left-to-right and top-to-bottom sequencing of print, where to begin reading, the concepts of letter and word, etc.

Deciding where to place this particular goal was a bit difficult because, as becomes evident below, there are aspects of the print conventions/print awareness notion that are not exclusively related to the development of alphabetic knowledge. However, because it would be extremely difficult, if not impossible, for a child to develop skill with alphabetics if he did not understand the basic purposes and conventions of print, we ultimately concluded that this goal needed to be discussed before presenting the other goals related to the development of alphabetic skills.

THE PURPOSES OF PRINT

Some children are identified as at risk at the beginning of kindergarten largely because they have had very limited prior experience with print. For these children, it is important to frequently discuss and model how print is used for communication. Below are some examples of things that a teacher might do to facilitate an understanding of the communication value of print[1]:

Teacher Writing

While writing a note to a parent or to another teacher, the teacher might explain that she is writing a note to tell that person . . . (a particular thing).

Writing Names on Papers and Belongings

When asking children to write their names on papers or other belongings, the teacher should explain the purpose of doing so (so that everyone knows to whom it belongs).

Reading to Children

- When reading aloud to children, the teacher might periodically explain that, since the author couldn't be there to tell the story, he wrote it down instead.
- The teacher might start by looking at the pictures in the book with the children and explaining that the words on the page(s) tell the story that goes with the pictures.
- With each reading of a book, the teacher might stop at different points and ask the children to say what the author has told them so far or what they think will come next in the story.
- The teacher could also introduce a wordless book (e.g., *Good Dog, Carl* [Day, 1997]) and suggest that they all (the teacher and the children) write a story that goes with the pictures.

Shared Writing

Children should have multiple opportunities to express their thoughts in print.

- At early stages, the teacher might do the writing and record the children's thoughts while the children look on. After reading aloud what a particular child has dictated, the teacher might ask, "Is that what you want it to say?" (If necessary, the teacher and the child might need to collaborate to make the child's intended message clear.)
- The teacher should demonstrate how the writer goes back and reads portions of the text that have already been written so that the writer remembers what he wants to say next.

---

[1]Note that in this section the discussion is limited to the purposes and conventions of print goal. There are many other goals that can be addressed in (shared) reading and writing activities.

- Some teachers engage their students in writing a class letter to parents at the end of each week to tell them about the class's experiences. Once the letter is completed, the teacher leads the class in shared reading of the letter a few times, and a copy of the letter is then sent home with the children or is posted on the class's webpage. The children are encouraged to share the writing piece at home so that parents will know what is happening in school.

Using Print for Record-Keeping Purposes

Even at the early stages of the development of print knowledge, children can either write or use a name card to sign up for activities or express preferences. For example, children can:

- Sign their name on an attendance list or place their name card in the "present" box.
- Sign up for a turn at a specific center.
- Write their lunch preferences on a lunch count list, etc. (Note: Early on, it is helpful to have models to which the children can refer. For example, if pizza is on the lunch menu, a labeled picture of a slice of pizza would be provided.)

CONVENTIONS OF PRINT

Different writing systems have different conventions regarding how print is organized and displayed. Children who are just beginning to learn about the writing system for their particular language sometimes need explicit guidance regarding the conventions of that language. Conventions in the English writing system include such things as these:

- There are special kinds of marks on paper (and other media) that are called letters. By themselves the letters are fairly meaningless, but, when placed next to each other in the correct sequence, they form words.
- The word *word* refers to a unit of meaning.
- Printed words are separated by spaces.
- Print is organized from left to right on a line and from top to bottom on a page.
- Words are organized into larger units of meaning called *sentences*.
- There are other markings in written language (punctuation marks and the use of print size, italics, etc.) that signal intonation and phrasing.

Proficient readers are often so familiar with these conventions that they don't even think about them and so may neglect to explain them to early literacy learners. Whereas children who have been read to frequently and who have had the opportunity to experiment with writing often begin to understand some of these conventions before they start kindergarten, children who have had very limited print experience are sometimes baffled by these arbitrary conventions. For these children, it is important to teach these conventions explicitly. Such explicit teaching about print conventions is also important for children whose primary language has different conventions (e.g., Chinese, Arabic, Korean, Hebrew).

Developing an Understanding of English Print Conventions

Shared Reading

When reading to children, the primary focus should always be on the meaning of the text. In the early primary grades, it is helpful to read large-print texts (e.g., big books, language experience charts, morning messages) with the children every day. During shared reading, it is important for the teacher to do the following:

• Point to the words while reading. The reading should be done with natural intonation and phrasing but at a somewhat slower pace than might be used when reading for other purposes. Slowed reading, coupled with pointing, will give the children the opportunity to observe the left-to-right and top-to-bottom sequencing of print. On occasion it is helpful to mention the "return sweep" one does while reading. That is, when readers get to the right-hand end of a line of print, they return to the left-hand side of the page—but one line down.

• Talk explicitly about important print concepts. For example, the teacher might discuss the number of words in the title of a book, the number of letters in a character's name, etc.

• Occasionally discuss the directionality of print explicitly (e.g., "When we read, we always start on this side") and the purpose of punctuation marks (e.g., "This little dot is called a period. Authors put periods in to tell us when they are done with one idea. When we are reading and we see a period, it tells us to stop for a second and think about what we just read").

• Share the reading with the children by encouraging them to chime in while the adult reads. Repeated readings of the same text will help the children realize that the same page of print sounds essentially the same each time it is read.

• Encourage children to point to the words during shared reading. Once the text is somewhat familiar to the children, giving them the opportunity to point to the words while the group reads the text chorally will help them attend to the sequencing of print.

Activities such as these should not supplant the focus on the meaning of the text.

Shared Writing

In order to promote the understanding of print concepts while writing, the teacher could do the following:

- Explicitly talk about where on the page one starts to write and about the direction one follows when continuing to write.
- Talk about the spacing between letters and words and how the spacing helps the reader/writer to know where one word ends and the next one begins.
- Talk about when upper- and lower-case letters are used.
- Talk about the use and purpose of punctuation marks.

EVALUATING AND DOCUMENTING CHILDREN'S PROGRESS

Skill and strategy checklists are provided for most aspects of literacy instruction discussed in this book. These checklists, referred to as group snapshots, serve dual purposes. They provide an efficient way for teachers to document what children in a particular group know and are able to do with respect to a particular aspect of literacy development, and they support teachers as they plan instruction.

Figure 4.1 presents the group snapshot that might be used to track children's understanding of the purposes and conventions of print. Understanding of the various concepts can be demonstrated during shared reading and writing activities; it is not necessary that the children be able to read and write independently in order to be credited with understanding the purposes and conventions of print. This snapshot is used to document whether the child reliably demonstrates that he understands such conventions as the following:

- *The directionality of print.* In English, print is followed from left to right and from the top to the bottom on a page. Close observation of what the child does while reading and writing will allow the teacher to note the child's understanding of these conventions.
- *The concepts of letter and word.* Partly because some of the earliest words they learn are also letters (*I* and *a*), it can take children a while to fully understand the differences between words and letters. This understanding is usually evaluated through direct questioning. For example, the child might be asked to count the number of letters or words on the page of an emergent-level book.
- *The fact that print is a form of communication.* The child's understanding of this fact can be demonstrated in a variety of ways, such as when a child chooses to write to someone for the purpose of conveying information, or when a child asks to have printed language read to him ("What does that say?").
- *Punctuation has a purpose.* Punctuation is used to convey meaning within and across sentences. In evaluating young children's understanding of the purposes

Group Snapshot—Purposes and Conventions of Print						
Student Names						
Left to right	Reading					
	Writing					
Top to bottom	Reading					
	Writing					
Concept of word	Reading					
	Writing					
Concept of letter	Reading					
	Writing					
Print as communication	Reading					
	Writing					
Purpose/use of punctuation	Reading					
	Writing					
One-to-one match	Reading					
	Writing					

Key:

◻ **B—Beginning** indicates that instruction has addressed the objective but that the child has only a preliminary understanding or capability with regard to that particular objective.

⊠ **D—Developing** indicates that the child has some understanding of the objective but does not reliably demonstrate that understanding or capability or is not yet automatic (fluent) with the skill.

⊠ **P—Proficient** indicates that the child reliably and automatically demonstrates the understanding or capability.

FIGURE 4.1. Group snapshot for purposes and conventions of print.

and uses of punctuation, do not expect them to be proficient in its use (many highly literate adults continue to struggle with aspects of punctuation). Rather, to be considered proficient, the young child should demonstrate that he understands the basics such as that sentences and proper names begin with capital letters, sentences end with a punctuation mark, that different punctuation marks are used for different kinds of sentences, and that the reader's voice reflects the ending punctuation (rising with a question mark, adding emphasis with an exclamation point, etc.).

• *The correspondence between written and spoken words.* Children who are just beginning to learn to read often start by learning to read patterned, predictable, emergent-level books. These books usually have one to four words on a page. Once the child has learned the pattern of the book (e.g., "I see a . . . ") he is able to read the book by repeating the patterned phrase and labeling the accompanying picture. A child who is able to accurately point to each word as he reads it has developed the ability to do one-to-one print-to-speech matching.

CHAPTER 5

Phonological Awareness

ALPHABETICS GOAL 2

The child will have a conceptual grasp of the fact that words are made up of somewhat separable sound segments. Further, the child will be able to say the individual sounds in words spoken by the teacher and blend separate sounds to form whole words.

The development of skill with the alphabetic code requires that children have the insight that spoken words are composed of individual sounds that are connected to letters in written words. Some children develop these insights with relatively little guidance and will not need the type of thoughtful and explicit instruction described in this chapter. However, many children who are identified as at risk will benefit from explicit and responsive phonemic awareness instruction. To enable teachers to be responsive to the skills of their students, we begin by discussing some of the intricacies of phonology and why it can present a challenge for some children.

Terminology

Phoneme—the smallest unit of sound which distinguishes between the meanings of words. For example, *can* and *cane* differ by one phoneme (short *a* vs. long *a*). *Can* and *cane* each have three phonemes.

Phonology—the study of the unconscious rules governing the production of speech sounds.

Phonetics—the study of the way in which speech sounds are articulated (i.e., what parts of the mouth are used in what way to produce particular sounds).

Phonics —the system by which the sounds in spoken language are represented by the letters (or other symbols) in printed language.

Phonological Awareness—the ability to reflect on and manipulate the component sounds of spoken words (e.g., syllables, onsets and rimes, and phonemes).

Phonemic Awareness—a particular type of phonological awareness: the ability to reflect on and manipulate the phonemes in spoken words. Phonemic awareness is the most important type of phonological awareness relative to reading and writing development.

PHONEMIC AWARENESS VERSUS PHONICS

Many people confuse the concepts of phonemic awareness and phonics. Therefore, even though definitions for these terms are provided in the box, a more thorough discussion of the distinction and relationship between them is warranted. In its purest form, phonemic awareness involves the ability to analyze and manipulate the sounds in *spoken* words and has nothing to do with the written representation of words. Phonics, on the other hand, involves the connections between the sounds in spoken words and the letters that represent those sounds in written form. It is possible for a child to be quite phonemically aware but know little or nothing about phonics.

Proficient readers (e.g., teachers) sometimes have difficulty accurately analyzing words at the level of the phoneme when the words have more letters than sounds (e.g., *though*) and when the words have more sounds than letters (e.g., *box*). In working with teachers we have found it useful to engage them in some "consciousness raising" around phonemic analysis, to help them keep the distinction between phonemic awareness and phonics in mind. We do this by engaging them in counting and articulating the individual phonemes in a variety of spoken words. Because we are focusing on spoken rather than written words, we show teachers an array of pictures representing words that might be used in various phonemic analysis activities. We ask them to articulate the sounds in each of the words, and we discuss the features of the words that make them more or less difficult to segment into individual sounds. (Figure 5.1 provides examples.) Teachers need to be

Words and the phonemes that comprise them

Explanation and elaboration

/s/ /u/ /n/

It is relatively easy to articulate the individual sounds in the word *sun* because each of the consonant sounds can be articulated without the addition of a vowel sound (i.e., /ssss/ and /nnnn/). However, some teachers have a habit of adding an unnecessary *schwa* (short-*u*) sound when articulating these sounds (they say "*suh*" rather than /sss/ or "*nuh*" rather than /nnn/). We encourage teachers who are "*schwa*-sayers" to own up to their bad habits and to try to eliminate the *schwa* sound whenever possible.

/f/ /i/ /sh/

The word *fish* has three sounds but four letters. In discussing this word in professional development sessions, there is usually at least one teacher in the group who will argue that a word like *fish* should not be used in phonemic awareness activities because it has a digraph (*sh*). Our response, however, is that /sh/ is a common sound in spoken language and that, since we are not focusing on the written word, there is nothing wrong with using *fish* in phonemic analysis activities.

/n/ /o/ /z/

The last sound in the word *nose* is /z/, but it is represented by the letter *s*. Because it is often difficult for literate people to ignore the spellings of words, teachers illustrating how to say the individual sounds in words will sometimes incorrectly articulate the sounds in accord with the way the word is spelled (/n/-/o/-/s/) rather than the way it sounds (/n/-/o/-/z/). Since maintaining a focus on the sounds is critical when working on phonemic analysis skills, we frequently remind teachers to try to avoid letting the spellings of words interfere with their perception of the sounds that comprise the word. We find ourselves frequently saying "Let the letters go!."

/f/ /o/ /k/ /s/

Fox is another example that illustrates a discrepancy between the letters and the sounds. There are four sounds in *fox* but only three letters. Sometimes in a group of teachers there will be individuals who argue that the last sound in fox is /ks/—but this is, obviously, two sounds. To convince teachers of this, we typically ask them to decide whether the words *fox* and *socks* rhyme. When they realize that they do rhyme, they concede that *fox* has four phonemes.

FIGURE 5.1. Phonemic analysis "consciousness raising" for teachers.

sensitive to the sounds that actually occur in spoken words in order to be effective in guiding children to attend to those sounds. Otherwise, they may provide children with guidance and feedback that only serves to confuse them. This will, of course, be especially problematic for children who are struggling to develop early literacy skills.

WHY IS PHONEMIC AWARENESS IMPORTANT?

Children who understand that spoken words are composed of small units of sound and who can manipulate those units (e.g., hear the sounds /m/ /a/ /t/ and say *mat* or separate *mat* into its component sounds) are generally more successful in the early stages of learning to read than are children who do not understand this concept and cannot, therefore, manipulate those sounds (e.g., Brady, Shankweiler, & Mann, 1983; Bryant, MacLean, Bradley, & Crossland, 1990; Fletcher et al., 1994; Vellutino et al., 1996; Wagner, Torgesen, & Rashotte, 1994). A child who understands that words or syllables are composed of somewhat separable sounds will more readily come to understand that the sounds in spoken words are represented by the letters in printed words. Understanding this relationship between sounds and letters is thought to be one of the fundamental tasks facing the beginning reader and writer (Adams, 1990).

For some children, the realization that speech can be segmented into words, words into syllables, and words or syllables into phonemes (individual sounds) takes a good deal of time to develop. Other children appear to develop this insight into spoken language quite easily and without explicit instruction (Scarborough & Dobrich, 1994; Torgesen, Wagner, & Rashotte, 1994). Generally, children who demonstrate phonemic awareness without having had explicit instruction come from literacy-rich and language-rich backgrounds. However, coming from such a background does not guarantee that a child will develop phonemic awareness easily.

PHONEMIC AWARENESS AND READING PROBLEMS

Children who experience significant difficulty in learning to read tend to have difficulty in developing sensitivity to the phonemes in spoken language. Many researchers believe that this slow development of phonemic sensitivity is an important *cause* of reading difficulties. Numerous studies have found that measures of phonemic awareness, administered in kindergarten, are strong predictors of reading success in first grade and beyond (Torgesen & Burgess, 1998; Yopp, 1988). However, it should also be noted that learning to read helps children become more sensitive to the sound structure of words. Thus, phonemic awareness helps children learn to read and spell, and learning to read and spell helps children to become more phonemically aware. In short, the two processes are reciprocal.

INSTRUCTIONAL INFLUENCES ON THE DEVELOPMENT OF PHONEMIC AWARENESS

Many studies (e.g., Ball & Blachman, 1991; Blachman, Ball, Black, & Tangel, 1994; Bradley & Bryant, 1991; Schneider, Roth, & Ennemoser, 2000) have demonstrated that explicit instruction designed to promote phonemic awareness has a positive effect on the reading and writing performance of the children who receive such training, both in the short term (immediately after training) and in the long term

(1–5 years after training was provided). Further, positive effects have been noted in a variety of instructional groupings (one to one, small group, and whole class). While there is clear evidence for the importance of helping children to become phonemically aware, the National Reading Panel (2000) concluded that training in phonemic awareness alone is not as effective in promoting reading and writing abilities as is training in phonemic awareness that is coupled with explicit instruction in letter–sound correspondences and in the application of the alphabetic principle.

WHY IS IT DIFFICULT FOR SOME CHILDREN TO NOTICE/ATTEND TO PHONEMES?

People who are proficient readers and writers in an alphabetic language often find it difficult to imagine how anyone would have difficulty noticing the phonemes in spoken language. It just seems obvious to them. However, people who are proficient readers and writers in languages that do not use an alphabetic writing system are generally not as phonemically aware. Their languages are no less phonemic than English, but they simply don't notice the phonemes because there is really no need to; the phonemes are not represented in their language's writing system (Read, Zhang, Nie, & Ding, 1986). Thus, it is not surprising that many children with very limited literacy experience will not be phonemically aware. Many such children will begin to develop this insight when their attention is drawn to the sounds in words through their engagement in reading and writing activities and through involvement in learning songs and poems that emphasize sound similarities (e.g., alliteration and rhyme). However, for a variety of reasons some children need much more explicit and focused instruction in order to become aware of the component sounds in spoken words.

Below we describe some factors that may contribute to children's difficulty with attending to the phonemic nature of spoken language:

A Natural Inclination to Focus on the Meaning of a Word Rather Than Its Sounds

Children, like proficient readers in nonalphabetic languages, are naturally inclined to attend to the meanings of words. After all, the concept of a *dog* is much more interesting than the sounds the word contains. If you ask a young child how many sounds are in *dog*, he is apt to say "*woof, woof*" rather than "three."

The Fleeting Nature of Speech Sounds

The sounds in words are rather fleeting. It takes substantially less than a second to articulate the first sound in *ball* or the first sound in *sun*. As a result, it can be hard to draw children's attention to the individual sounds. When attempts are made to do so, they are differentially effective depending on the characteristics of the sound.

Thus, for example, some consonant sounds are classified as *continuant sounds*, which, among other things, means that the sound can be articulated over a protracted period of time without distortion. Examples of continuant sounds include /ssss/, /rrrrr/, /fffff/. However, many consonant sounds are not continuants—which means that they cannot be "stretched" without distortion. These sounds, including those associated with the letters *b, d, g,* and *t,* are referred to as *stop-consonant sounds* because their production requires that the air flow be briefly stopped during articulation. As a result of this stoppage of the airflow, it is impossible to elongate the pronunciation without distorting the sound. Thus, for example, when teachers attempt to draw children's attention to the initial sound in the word *boy,* they are likely to say /buh/ with an emphasis on the /uh/ portion. Children who are not yet attuned to the phonemic qualities of spoken language might well attend to the /uh/, which takes longer to articulate than the /b/, which is fleeting.

The Problem of Coarticulation

Another reason why phonemes are not particularly obvious is that the phonemes in words are hard to separate from one another. For the sake of efficiency, the articulators (the parts of the mouth that move in order to produce the intended sounds) are preparing to say the next sound in a word while they are still finishing up the previous sound. As a result, there is no clear point of demarcation between one sound and the next. The sounds are literally blended together. This blending is referred to as *coarticulation.*

Examples of Coarticulation

To get a better sense of co-articulation, try these exercises:

Say the words *see* and *so* out loud a few times. Are the sounds you hear at the beginnings of those two words the same? Your answer is, of course, yes. Now, say the same words again (*see, so*) but notice the position of your lips as you make the /s/ sound in each word. Is your mouth position the same? Probably not. Typically, when pronouncing the /s/ in *see,* your lips are stretched back a bit in preparation for pronouncing the /E/ (long-*e*) sound. When pronouncing the /s/ in *so,* your lips are more rounded in preparation for pronouncing the /O/ (long-*o*) sound.

Say the words *at* and *ant* out loud. Listen to the vowel sound in each word. Pretend you don't know how the words are spelled. Do the vowels sound the same? Probably not. For most people the two sounds are actually quite different. The /a/ in *ant* is sort of "twangy" as a result of the articulators preparing to produce the /n/ sound. In producing the /n/ sound, air is pushed through the nose. Therefore, while producing the /a/ in *ant* some of the air is pushed through the nose as well. On the other hand, in pronouncing the /a/ in *at,* all of the air is pushed through the mouth. The path of the air changes the sound.

Similarity of Many Phonemes

Because children tend to rely on what their mouth is doing as they articulate sounds, it is sometimes difficult for them to distinguish between two sounds that are articulated in almost the same way (see Figure 5.2). In many cases, the only difference in the articulation of two sounds is in whether or not the vocal chords vibrate. Such sounds are said to differ in *voicing*. For example, the sounds /f/ and /v/ are articulated in the same way *except* that the /v/ sound is voiced (the vocal chords vibrate) whereas the /f/ sound is not voiced.

Many pairs of phonemes in English differ only in voicing. Children often confuse these sounds—particularly in their writing. Children who make these types of substitutions are more phonemically aware than teachers sometimes realize. There are some clear instructional implications related to these potentially confusable sound pairs, such as:

- In planning instruction to promote phonemic awareness, it is important to initially avoid asking the children to discriminate between sounds that are confusable—because this makes the task more difficult. For example, if children were asked to sort groups of pictures by similarities in their beginning sounds, it would be much more challenging to sort a set consisting of *van, fork, fox,* and *vase* than to sort a set consisting of *mat, fork, fox,* and *mop.*
- In responding to children's errors, particularly in early writing, knowing that they've produced a close approximation for the sound will lead to providing different kinds of feedback to them.

ASSESSING PHONOLOGICAL AWARENESS

A checklist for phonological skills appears at the end of this chapter (in Figure 5.11, p. 106). Much of what follows is keyed to this checklist (the numbers in the

Sound pairs that differ only in voicing

Voiced	Unvoiced
/b/	/p/
/d/	/t/
/v/	/f/
/g/	/k/
/j/	/ch/
/z/	/s/

Other confusable pairs

/l/	/r/
/m/	/n/

(Note: Both sounds in each pair are voiced. They are confusable because there is only a slight change in mouth position when articulating one or the other member of the pair.)

FIGURE 5.2. Pairs of phonemes that are easily confused.

checklist and the subheadings in this section correspond). This checklist can be used to guide informal assessment of phonological skills and instructional planning. Before turning to the assessment and instructional activities, however, a brief discussion of the use of written spelling as an index of phonemic awareness is provided because, at least for children who have some understanding of the writing system, an assessment of written spelling is an efficient way to gather preliminary information regarding children's degree of phonemic awareness.

Using Written Spelling to Assess Phonemic Awareness

Although *phonemic awareness* refers to the ability to analyze and manipulate the sounds in *spoken* words, written spelling can be used as an indicator of a child's phonemic analysis skill. For beginning readers/writers to spell words that they have not committed to memory, they need to analyze the sounds (phonemes) that make up the word and then represent those phonemes with letters. Because measures of written spelling can be administered fairly quickly and to several children at once, they are an appropriate first step in analysis of phonemic awareness for children who know something about the writing system.

A child who accurately spells the word *jet* when asked to do so must be fairly phonemically aware. So, too, is the child who spells *jet* with a *g* (*get*) or *jet* with an *a* (*jat*), or *jet* with both a *g* and an *a* (*gat*). Obviously, the latter spellings are at odds with the conventional spelling for *jet*. However, they all show that the child has noticed all of the phonemes in the word. Therefore, that child is sufficiently phonemically aware and does not need explicit instruction in phonemic awareness. (The substitution of *a* for *e* is certainly an indicator that the child does not yet know the conventional spelling of the short-*e* sound, but it also indicates that the child has no difficulty isolating the middle phoneme. The reasons for such spelling errors are discussed in a subsequent chapter.)

A Note about Sound Spelling

Once children have learned something about the alphabetic writing system and before they have learned the conventional (correct) spellings of many words, they often write words by thinking about the sounds they hear in them and then representing those sounds with letters. Several different terms have been used to describe this approach to spelling, including *invented spelling, inventive spelling, kindergarten spelling*, and *temporary spelling*. We prefer the term *sound spelling* because it more clearly conveys to children what they are expected to do when attempting to write words that they don't already know how to spell.

A child who cannot sound-spell simple words may or may not be phonemically aware. Problems with sound spelling may be due to lack of familiarity with the alphabetic code *or* to lack of phonemic awareness *or* both. Thus, poor performance on a measure of sound spelling signals a need for further assessment of the child's phonological skills. Good performance on such a measure signals that the child may not need further explicit instruction in phonemic awareness.

Many teachers find developmental spelling assessments useful for gaining initial insights into children's phonemic analysis and phonics skills. The Primary Spelling Inventory from *Words Their Way* (Bear, Invernizzi, Templeton, & Johnston, 2008) is widely used for this purpose. This assessment is administered much like a traditional spelling test. However, children are asked to spell words that have not been "studied," and the teacher analyzes the elements that are represented in the children's spelling attempts, not just whether or not the words are spelled conventionally. Teachers can use their analyses to make initial judgments about what an individual child already understands about phonemic analysis. For example, if a child represents most or all of the beginning sounds for the dictated words but little else, the teacher can probably conclude that the child does not need phonemic awareness instruction focused on helping her to attend to beginning sounds and that she is probably ready for instruction that focuses attention on the ending sounds in words. Such an assessment would, of course, also provide evidence of the child's understanding of letter–sound correspondences.

Children who show no evidence of phonemic analysis skill in their sound spellings may, nevertheless, be at least somewhat phonemically aware. Further assessment of their skills would need to be conducted in a context in which they are not required to write. Teachers can learn a great deal about children's phonemic analysis skills by using checklists such as the group snapshot presented at the end of this chapter as a systematic guide in evaluating which types of skills the children demonstrate.

GROUPING AND PACING

Some children need little or no explicit instructional guidance in order to become sensitive to the individual phonemes in spoken words (i.e., they may not need to be included in a phonemic awareness group at all). Others need some guidance but then make rapid progress and have no further need for that sort of instruction. Still others need more prolonged engagement in carefully sequenced instructional activities. Initial assessment followed by ongoing monitoring (via anecdotal records or checklists) can help to ensure that instruction is appropriately responsive.

ACTIVITIES FOR PROMOTING (AND ASSESSING) PHONOLOGICAL AWARENESS

Described below are some methods for helping young children become attuned to the sound structure of spoken language. While the activities are presented in somewhat of a list form, this presentation format is used primarily for the sake of clarity. It is anticipated that teachers will draw on different instructional techniques as the need arises and will think of the exercises presented throughout the remainder of the chapter as mutually reinforcing activities.

Some of the instructional activities are sequenced, reflecting research that suggests that there is a clear developmental progression. The progressions described can be used to differentiate instruction for individual children or groups of children. The phonological awareness snapshot is designed to help teachers keep this progression in mind.

I. Sensitivity to Sound Components in Texts

Using the Group Snapshot

In using the phonological awareness group snapshot the goal is to make note of whether a child demonstrates particular skills/knowledge with sufficient ease that you would expect her to be able to do it reliably in the future. As children are engaged in the activities described in this section, the teacher makes note of those children who reliably:

- *Complete the rhyme in known text.* When reading aloud a familiar text to the children, the teacher reads the first portion of a rhyming couplet and then pauses to let the children supply the rhyming word.
- *Identify rhyming words in text.* When the teacher reads a rhyming couplet, the child indicates which two words rhyme.
- *Identify alliterative words in text.* When the teacher reads a portion of text that contains several words that begin with the same sound, the child can identify words that have the same beginning sound.

Reading/Singing/Reciting Stories, Songs, Nursery Rhymes, and Poems

While the activities described in this section are most often used in a whole-class context, they are appropriate to use in small-group and one-to-one instructional settings as well. Too often, in a whole-class setting, the children who are at greatest risk for reading difficulties do not participate fully in language activities. An observer will often notice that when such children do engage, they do so by shadowing (i.e., copying) the responses of the children who are not at risk.

Children who become phonemically aware without explicit guidance tend to spontaneously do the kinds of language play encouraged in the activities described in this section. The goal of the modeling and guided practice described is to encourage children who do not do these kinds of things spontaneously to engage in productive language play.

READ BOOKS THAT PLAY ON THE SOUNDS IN LANGUAGE

Perhaps the easiest and most pleasant way to begin to attune children to the sounds in spoken language is through the use of books, poems, and songs that include rhyme and/or alliteration (many words that have the same beginning sound). There are many such children's books available. Yopp (1995) has developed an annotated bibliography of books that are well suited to this purpose. A more extensive listing of such books is provided by Adams, Foorman, Lundberg, and Beeler (1998). Examples of these books are provided below:

> *There's a Wocket in my Pocket* (Seuss, 1974)
> *"I Can't," Said the Ant* (Cameron, 1961)
> *Six Sleepy Sheep* (Gordon, 1991)
> *Alphabears* (Hague, 1984)
> *All About Arthur* (Carle, 1974)

While the children listen to books, poems, and songs that highlight the sound structure of language, teachers can encourage them to listen for rhyming words and/or words that have the same sound at the beginning. Repeated readings of such texts will give the children more opportunity to become attuned to the sound similarities in the text. If children are having difficulty noticing those similarities, the teacher can emphasize the similar-sounding words as she reads the text.

Yopp (1995) and Adams et al. (1998) suggest several ways in which the word play in books can be extended to engage children in actively considering the sounds in words. For example, the teacher might do the following:

- After the children have heard the text a few times, read it to them again, but stop before reading the second word in a rhyme pattern to allow the children to provide the rhyming word.
- Periodically stop after reading a rhyming couplet and ask the children to identify the rhyming words.
- Comment on certain groups of words that occur in the text, for example, "The author called the little girl 'Rrrrosy Rrrrobin Rrrrross' [Seuss, 1963, p. 42]. What sound do you hear at the beginning of all of those words?"
- Involve the children in creating additional verses that follow similar sound patterns.

KEEP IN MIND Although not directly related to the specific goal of helping children develop phonemic awareness, it is useful to present nursery rhymes, poems, and lyrics in print that is large enough for the children to see.

SING SONGS THAT PLAY ON THE SOUNDS IN WORDS

Because rhyme is a prominent characteristic of many songs, singing and listening to songs will help attune children to the phonemes in spoken language. Songs that engage children in active manipulation of the sounds in words will be most effective in moving the children forward. Manipulating the sounds in words in the ways suggested by the songs below[1] can be fairly challenging for children who are just beginning to become phonemically aware.

"Willoughby, Walloughby. . . . "
"Down by the Bay"
"The Name Game"
"Apples and Bananas"

The children will need several opportunities to learn the song before they are expected to engage in manipulating the sounds. For example, some classroom teachers play these songs during transitional activities (such as during clean-up time or snack time or while the children are involved in cutting, pasting, or coloring activities). This helps to promote familiarity with the songs and encourages sound play.

Once the children are fairly familiar with a given song (and can at least sing along with the recording comfortably), invite them to add their own verses. It may be necessary to provide support in constructing these additional verses, as exemplified for the song "Down by the Bay." Here is the first verse:

Down by the bay
Where the watermelons grow
Back to my home,
I will not go
For if I did,
My mother would say:
"Did you ever see a <u>bear</u>,
<u>Combing his hair</u>
Down by the bay?"

In this song, only the underlined words change in subsequent verses. The first and last underlined words always rhyme.

Once the children have sung the song several times, perhaps over a period of a few days, the teacher might model how to make up new verses (e.g., "Did you ever see a <u>car</u> parked on a <u>star</u>?"). The teacher might then encourage the children

---

[1] These songs can be found on CDs by Raffi, Nancy Cassidy, and many other children's recording artists. Dr. Jean Feldman also has a collection of CDs, including many songs that are useful for promoting phonemic analysis (see *www.drjean.org*).

to suggest verses. Initially, to make this easy for children, the teacher might ask for just the first word of the rhyming pair and generate the second word of the pair him- or herself. A sample dialogue appears below.

Sample Instructional Dialogue

TEACHER: Today we are going to make some new parts for this song. We can pick an object and make a rhyme with it. I'll do one first to show you what I mean. My object is a ball. So I have *ball,* then I need to think of a word that rhymes with *ball* . . . a word that sounds the same at the end. I know! *Ball—hall.* Those words rhyme. I am going to use those words to make a new part for my song. How about "Did you ever see a *ball* rolling down the *hall*?" Let's sing the song with that verse.

Now, let's do a verse with a fruit. What fruit would you like to use?

CHILD: Pear!

TEACHER: Oh! That's a good one. First I'll have to think of a word that rhymes with *pear.* I know—*chair*! *Pear* and *chair* rhyme—they sound the same at the end. *Pear* and *chair.* Now let's think of what the *pear* could be doing with the *chair*? How about sitting on it? Did you ever see a *pear* sitting on a *chair*! Let's sing a verse with the rhyming words *pear* and *chair.*

Once the teacher has modeled this approach several times, she should encourage the children to generate the rhyming words and to think of how the two words will be related in the song. Children can also be encouraged to think of new verses at other times and try to remember them for the next time the class sings that particular song. Silliness is an important element in the appeal of this activity.

LEARN, RECITE, AND MODIFY NURSERY RHYMES, CHANTS, AND POEMS

Well before the concept of phonemic awareness became an important focus in thinking about developmental reading, nursery rhymes and poems were commonly used to entertain children and to engage them in language play. Nursery rhymes and poems help children shift their focus from attending to the message to noticing the sounds in the words that are used to convey those messages.

Once children have learned and can recite a given nursery rhyme or poem, they are often delighted by "playing" with it and changing the verse. For example, for the nursery rhyme "Jack Be Nimble," once they have learned it, children might be invited to modify it by making a new rhyme, perhaps by assuming that Jack was slow instead of quick.

Jack be nimble,
Jack be slow,
Jack jump over
The _____ [Purple bow, or farmer's hoe, or elephant's toe].

Note

In the examples given in this section, some words are likely to be unfamiliar to many kindergarten children. This activity could be used to support vocabulary development as well as phonemic awareness—although you certainly wouldn't want to get into extensive discussions about every word that may be unfamiliar.

This activity could be made easier for children by presenting pictures (which should include objects that rhyme as well as some that do not). The children would then choose between and among the pictures. A child who finds this activity difficult might be given only two choices (e.g., a purple bow or a red car). More proficient children might be asked to choose from a larger set of pictures.

II. Sound Sorting: Sorting Pictures or Objects by Sound Similarity

---

Using the Group Snapshot

Four different sorting principles are used for sound sorting: beginning sounds, rhyme, ending sounds, and medial sounds. As the children are given the opportunity to attempt sorts based on each of these principles, the teacher should note on the snapshot whether each child can do the sorting reliably and fairly quickly.

The activities described below are included in many programs designed to promote phonemic awareness. The teaching that goes on with these activities is more explicit and more focused than the sensitivity to sound activities described in the previous section. However, the general objective is the same: to help children notice sound similarities and differences in words.

The general technique entails providing children with a group of objects or pictures of objects that can be sorted by sound similarity in a specified part of the words. For example, children might be given pictures of a *mat*, the *moon*, a bar of *soap*, and a *mouth* and be asked to put together the three that have the same sound at the beginning and/or to move the one with a different beginning sound away from the others.

Materials

Developing materials for sound-sorting exercises is relatively easy. Old (or new) phonics workbooks contain pictures that can be copied onto heavy card stock so that the pictures can be used over and over again. Alternatively, the picture set for a given day can be copied onto plain paper and each child can be given a sheet containing the pictures. The children would then cut up the sheet into individual pictures in preparation for the day's sorting activities. Things to remember when developing (or selecting) materials to use for sound sorting activities include the following:

- Choose pictures/objects that are relatively unambiguous in terms of the names that might be applied to them.
- Choose pictures/objects that have one-syllable names.
- Always apply the same name to a picture or object. If you initially labeled a picture *rug*, it will confuse children if you later use the same picture but decide to call it *mat*.

Especially for introductory purposes:

- Choose objects with names that contain a relatively simple phonemic structure in the part of the word that will be the focus of the activity. For example, for a beginning sound sort, the words *fork, fox, rope,* and *fish* would be a good group to use because the beginning sounds are comprised of single consonants. Words with consonant blends, such as *flag, frog* and *stick*, would be more challenging to analyze.
- Choose words in which the targeted phonemes can be easily stretched or emphasized without distortion (e.g., the initial sounds in these words can be stretched—*rrrrope, ffffox, mmmmmoon*) so that the children's attention can be drawn more effectively to the sounds in that part of the word.
- Use contrasts that are very distinct so that the differences in the sounds are easier to notice. For example, the sounds /f/ and /r/ are quite different from one another whereas the sounds or /f/ and /v/ are quite similar (they differ only in voicing). Thus, it would be easier for a child to notice that *rope* has a different beginning sound in the set *fork, fox, rope, fish* than to notice that *van* has a different beginning sound in the set *fork, fox, van, fish*.

Useful Resources

Pictures for use in sorting activities can be found in a book entitled *Words Their Way* by Bear et al. (2008). Alternatively, teachers might wish to order a set of prepared sorting cards, available from numerous vendors that sell early literacy teaching materials. When purchasing cards for picture sorts, it is important to know which pictures are included in the set and to attend to the guidelines provided above.

As children begin to demonstrate the ability to detect similarities and differences in the sounds in words, the restrictions on word selection can be relaxed, and word sorts can include stop consonants (i.e., *ball, top, box,* and *bike*).

Terminology

Onset—the portion of a spoken word or syllable that precedes the first vowel. The onsets in the following words are underlined: <u>s</u>ome <u>tr</u>ick <u>shr</u>ink.

Rime—the vowel and what comes after it in a spoken word or syllable. The rimes are the portions of the words that are not underlined in the examples above.

Sequence of Instruction for Sorting Activities

Research has demonstrated that there is a progression in the order in which children become sensitive to (aware of) the sound components in words. The easiest sound components for the children to attend to and learn to manipulate in single-syllable words are *onsets* and *rimes*. The next easiest component is the ending sound. In one-syllable words, the most challenging part for a child to attend to is the middle sound—usually the vowel sound and individual sounds that are parts of consonant blends (Fox & Routh, 1975; Treiman & Zukowski, 1996).

Based on the accumulated research (see Burgess, 2006, for a review), a sequence of instruction is presented in this section. Early on, children should be asked to sort words based on the sound components that are easiest for them to attend to (onsets and rimes). In our experience many children find it easier to attend to rimes initially than to onsets (beginning sounds). For other children it appears that onsets are easier. Therefore, no confident recommendations can be made about whether to start with onsets or rimes. The best advice is probably to try both and determine which sorting principle a particular group of children appears to find easier and to focus on the targeted sound component until the children can easily sort based on that principle. Then switch to working with the other sorting principle that was initially more challenging (whether onset or rime). Continue to work with that new principle until the children can sort easily based on that one as well. When children can easily sort based on both onset and rime, begin to work on sorting by ending sounds. Finally, when children are able to easily sort pictures based on similarity in ending sounds, they should begin to work on sorting pictures based on similarity in medial sounds. Table 5.1 provides a summary of the order in which the sorting principles should be pursued.

TABLE 5.1. Recommended Order for Sorting Principles

Order	Sorting principle	Sample picture set
1	Rime (rhyme)	*cat, hat, mat*; *pin, fin, tin*
	Onset (beginning sounds)	*moon, mat, mouse*; *soap, sun, sock*
2	Ending sounds	*pail, ball, seal*; *moon, fin, van*
3	Middle sounds	*coat, soap, home*; *map, rat, pack*

Odd-One-Out Sorting Activity

For an initial introduction to sorting by sound commonalities, the *odd-one-out* activity is useful because it allows children to focus on just a few words at a time. In this activity, children are presented with groups of pictures. In each group, all of the pictures except one have the same sound(s) in a specified part of the word. The children are asked to figure out which word doesn't have the same sound.

A fairly detailed description of the odd-one-out activity, using beginning sounds as the sorting principle, follows. The same format can be used to introduce and practice the other sorting principles. In general, children should work on a given sorting principle until they are both fast and accurate before moving on to a new sorting principle.

> **KEEP IN MIND**   Children are most likely to attach the intended label to a picture if the teacher labels it immediately when it is presented. Sometimes teachers hold back and wait to see if the children can label the pictures. Often the children will suggest a different label than the one intended. Once they've decided that the picture shows a *shark*, for example, it may be hard for them to remember that the teacher called it a *fish*.

BEGINNING-SOUND ODD-ONE-OUT SORT

For this activity, collect several groups of pictures. Each group should contain two or three pictures that begin with the same sound and one picture that begins with a different sound (e.g., *sun, seal, mop* see Figure 5.3). For initial demonstration and practice purposes, it is best to choose items for which the beginning sound can be easily elongated (stretched) when it is pronounced (i.e., words starting with *f, l, m, n, r, s, sh, v, z*). Using stretchable sounds makes it easier to demonstrate the sorting principle of interest. Also, keep in mind that it is important that the children assign the correct labels to the pictures (the labels you intend). This can be ensured by saying the names of the pictures frequently.

FIGURE 5.3. Pictures for phoneme sorting.

KEEP IN MIND When stretching words for children, particular emphasis should be placed on stretching the part of the word to which the children are to attend. So, for the example, in Figure 5.4, it is helpful to say *ffffan*, not *ffffaaaaannnn*. The latter rendition of *fan* would be appropriate at a later time when children are attempting to analyze all of the sounds in a word—as, for example, when they are writing.

Sample Instructional Dialogue

TEACHER: I have three pictures here. One of them doesn't belong in the group because it has a different sound at the beginning. This is a *sssseal*, this is a *sssssun*, and this is a *mmmmmop*. (*Points to each picture as she labels it.*) When I say *sssssun* and *sssseal*, do you hear that they both have /sssss/ at the beginning? *Sssssun, sssseal*?

CHILDREN: Yes.

TEACHER: Now when I say *mmmmop*, do I make that /sssss/ sound? *mmmmmop*.

CHILDREN: Yes? No?????

TEACHER: That's right, *mmmmmop* doesn't have the /sssss/ sound, so I'm going to move the *mmmmmop* away from *sssssun* and *sssseal* because it is different from *sssssun* and *sssseal*. *Mmmmmop* doesn't have /sssss/ at the beginning. We hear /sssss/ in *sssssun* and in *sssseal* (*Points to each picture as she names it.*) So I'm going to put them together because they have the same sound at the beginning. Now you try one. (*Lays out three new pictures and points to each as she names it.*) Here are *ffffan*, *rrrrrake*, and *fffffox*. Two of these sound the same at the beginning, and one of them doesn't. Let's see if we can figure out which one has a different sound at the beginning. *Ffffan, rrrrrake, fffffox.*

CHILDREN: Fan?

TEACHER: No, let's think about this one together. First we'll say each word. *Ffffan, rrrrrake, fffffox*. (*Encourages the children to join in labeling the pictures and stretching the beginning sounds.*) When we say *ffffan*, what is the first sound we make? Let's all make the first sound in *ffffffan*. /fffff/. So *ffffan* has /fffff/ at the beginning. Now let's try *rrrrake* and think about what sound we make first when we say *rrrrrake*. /rrrrr/. Do *ffffan* and *rrrrake* both have /rrrr/ at the beginning?

FIGURE 5.4. Beginning sound sort—*fan, rake, fox.*

CHILDREN: No!

TEACHER: So, *ffffan* and *rrrrake* have different sounds at the beginning—and I am going to move them apart.

Now, let's try *ffffox*. Do you hear the same beginning sound as in *fffan*? Or do you hear the same sound you hear at the beginning of *rrrrake*?

The teacher should provide the children with several examples of sorting by the beginning sound. Gradually, as the children demonstrate that they understand the task, the teacher should begin, on subsequent items, to reduce the elongation of the beginning sounds when saying the names of the pictures. Eventually, the items used can be expanded to include words that begin with stop consonants (e.g., *b, d, g, h, k*). Although adding a *schwa* sound (the /uh/ in /buh/) is unavoidable when producing stop sounds in isolation, the teacher should be careful to minimize it as much as possible because otherwise it may dominate the sound of the consonant— thereby making it harder to focus on the consonant sound.

Sorting Boards

Once children understand the general principle of separating pictures by whether or not they have the same sound in a particular part of the word, sorting boards can be used to provide additional sorting practice. The same sorting principles would be used. The sorting boards contain two or three columns, each headed by a picture that begins (ends, etc.) with a different sound. The children are then given a packet of pictures that have the same beginning (ending, etc.) sound as one of the pictures heading a column. One by one, children then place the pictures with the same sounds in the appropriate column. In using the sorting boards, children should be encouraged to say the name of each picture as they consider its placement. If they have difficulty deciding in which column to place a picture, they should be encouraged to name the pictures already in the column. Once the children have learned how to do this type of sorting they can use these sorting boards fairly independently, perhaps as a center activity.

An example of a sorting board for a beginning-sound sort is presented in Figure 5.5. The two pictures at the top are posted on the board when the child begins to work with it. The pictures at the bottom are given to the child in a packet. The child is to sort the pictures into two groups by beginning sounds. In this example, the column headers are *rain* and *sock*. The pictures for sorting include *saw, soup, rug, ring, roof, sun,* and *rope*. Clearly, it is important to make sure that the children have the correct label for each picture before asking them to do the sort.

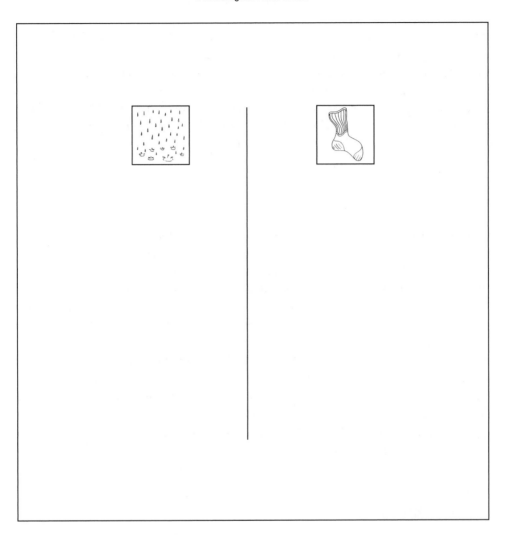

FIGURE 5.5. Beginning-sound sorting board.

Phoneme Blending and Segmentation

Phoneme Segmentation and Writing

In order to write effectively at the early stages, children must be able to segment individual words into their component sounds. For example, when children first begin to truly use the alphabet to communicate in writing, they often print the first, or the most salient, letter of each word they want to write. To do so, the child must be able to focus on the individual sound in the word and to think of it as being somewhat distinct from the remainder of the word. Then the child might articulate the sound and try to think of which letter makes that particular sound, and, finally, write the letter. The activities described in this section help the child to both attend to and isolate the individual sounds in words. When children have learned a bit about letters and their sounds, they are ready to coordinate these understandings and to begin to apply their phoneme segmentation and letter-sound knowledge in writing.

Phoneme Blending and Reading

Learning to blend phonemes is generally (but not always) easier than learning to segment the phonemes in a word. Practice with phoneme blending is helpful because, when beginning readers attempt to decode a word that they do not recognize immediately, one approach they may use is to identify the individual letters, think of the sound each letter makes (or could make), hold the individual sounds in memory while other sounds are retrieved, and finally blend all of the individual sounds together. Difficulty with the blending process (or any of the other processes involved) may interfere with retrieval of the name of the printed word and, ultimately, with comprehension of the text. Providing children with practice in blending individual (spoken) sounds into words may make it easier for them to handle the blending process while reading. In addition, having children blend individual sounds into words will help to attune them to the fact that words are comprised of separable sounds. In turn, this idea should help children develop the ability to segment words at the level of the phoneme (which then assists with sound spelling).

III. Sound Blending

> ### Using the Group Snapshot
>
> Four different types of blending activities are described below. On the checklist, these activities are listed in order of their difficulty. As with earlier portions of the checklist, a record should be made when the child reliably and quickly demonstrates the skill in question; she should then move on to the next skill.

Puppets or other character props are typically used in blending exercises. For example, children might be told that a particular character is from outer space and that he has a strange way of talking: He spreads out the sounds in his words too much. It becomes the children's job to figure out what the character is trying to say—sort of like a guessing game. Three or four pictures are then put in front of the children. The spaceman (through the teacher) then names one of the pictures using his funny (segmented) speech. The children attempt to figure out which of the pictures he named. In our research, we have typically used finger puppets that "need some help learning to talk." Children typically love these blending activities. The puppets are very popular and usually have names and personalities. These activities can have a playful tone but clearly need to stay focused on the instructional purpose: developing awareness of the phonemic nature of spoken language.

Sample Instructional Dialogue

TEACHER: We are going to play a game with this puppet and some pictures and words. This puppet has a strange way of talking. He says the sounds in his words very slowly. Because he says the sounds so slowly, we really have to think about what he is trying to say.

Here's how we start the game. I will put out [three or four] pictures [see Figure 5.6]. The puppet will tell which picture he is thinking of, and you get to figure out which picture it is. That means you'll have to put the sounds he says together to make a real word.

Let's try one. Here we have a picture of a *mouse*, a *man*, a *fox*, and a *fan*. (*Points to each picture as she names it.*) Now the puppet is going to say one of these words in his very slow way. We'll put together the sounds he says to figure out the word. Now we'll listen to the puppet. He says /ffff/ /an/. If we put /fff/ /an/ together, it says *fan*. Which picture is he saying? /fff/ /an/. (*Pauses for about one second between segments.*)

CHILDREN: *Fox!*

TEACHER: You remembered the first sound he said, /fff/. But listen to both parts of the word. /fff/ /an/. /fff/ /an/. (*Makes the pause between the segments a bit shorter so that they will be easier to blend.*)

CHILDREN: *Fan!*

TEACHER: *Fan!* Yes! When you put /fff/ /an/ together, it makes the word *fan*.

KEEP IN MIND If only one of the pictures displayed for this sample activity started with a /f/ sound, the children would not have to blend the component sounds in order to produce a correct response. All they would need to do is decide which of the pictured items started with /f/.

FIGURE 5.6. Sample pictures for onset–rime blending.

Table 5.2 illustrates the progression of difficulty for sound-blending activities.

TABLE 5.2. Progression of Difficulty for Blending Activities

Onsets and rimes with picture choices	As for the sorting activities described previously, blending activities should initially focus on onsets and rimes. When the puppet speaks, he provides the onset and the rime segments of the intended word. Thus, if he wanted to say the word *fan*, he would say /f/ /an/.
Onsets and rimes without picture choices	Once the children are able to blend onsets and rimes, as demonstrated by choosing the correct picture in the set displayed, the next level of difficulty engages them in onset–rime blending when no picture choices are available. The game-like aspect of the activity can be maintained when there are no picture choices if the teacher shows the picture of the object named *after* the children have correctly identified it.
Single phonemes with picture choices	If the children can blend onsets and rimes without picture choices, the puppet should begin to speak in individual phonemes: /m/ /ou/ /s/. Once again, picture choices are made available in order to make the task a bit easier. For example, the teacher might display pictures of a *mat*, a *leaf*, a *mouse*, and a *pig*. The puppet would name one of the pictures using his unusual speech pattern: /m/ /a/ /t/. The children must figure out which picture the puppet is attempting to name. (Note: To make the process efficient, the teacher might replace only the picture just named on each successive turn.)
Single phonemes without picture choices	If the children can identify the correct picture with the picture choices displayed, the task should be made a bit more challenging. The teacher holds all of the pictures so that the children can't see them, then the puppet peeks at one of the pictures, uses his segmented speech to name it, and the children try to guess at which picture he has looked. This activity can be made more game-like if the child who successfully blends the sounds is given the card to hold.

Hints for Individualizing Blending Challenges in a Group or Classroom Context

It is easy to make blending tasks more or less challenging to fit the child's current capabilities. For example, in a group activity, the teacher might ask one child to blend an onset–rime combination and another child, who is a bit more advanced, to blend individual phonemes. Some children might be asked to blend words with stretchable sounds, whereas others will be asked to blend words with stop consonants. A child who is struggling might be given sound segments that are only minimally separated, whereas a child who is progressing more quickly might be asked to blend segments that are presented with longer separations between them. However, teachers need to keep in mind that children who routinely demonstrate different instructional needs should probably be in different instructional groups.

IV. Phoneme Segmentation

Phoneme segmentation is, for most children, the hardest of the phonemic analysis tasks. For that reason, it comes last in the sequence of instructional procedures for promoting phonemic awareness. There are more difficult phoneme manipulation tasks, such as reversing the sequence of phonemes in a word (i.e., given the word *top*, the child would need to say *pot*), but it is not clear that developing proficiency on such tasks has any real utility for the child—aside from being a lot of fun for some children, of course.

Language Play

In a classroom setting, keep the puppet and some picture cards available as a free choice or center activity. The children may not be accurate in the way they segment and blend the words, but at least they will be thinking about the sounds in words. Over time, this language play may benefit them.

Moving from Blending to Segmenting

Some children find it quite easy to learn to segment words into phonemes, whereas others find it much more challenging. Participating in phoneme-blending activities is likely to make learning to segment easier because the blending tasks essentially provide lots of modeling around how to segment words. Practice with blending activities also makes phoneme segmentation seem like fun for many children. As the children begin to become facile at blending sounds to make words, they will usually be eager to take a turn at controlling the puppet and talking the way the puppet does. This sort of playful practice is useful and should be encouraged.

Phoneme (Sound) Counting/Segmentation

Phoneme counting involves segmenting a word into its individual phonemes and using counters to track the number of sounds.

TYPES OF WORDS

Initial instruction and practice for phoneme counting should use words with only two sounds, both of which are stretchable (e.g., *me, say*), and the child should not be required to separate the rime portion of the word into individual phonemes. For example, segmenting the word *me* into individual phonemes requires the child to separate the onset from the rime (/m/ /e/). This type of segmentation is comparatively easy for the child. Segmenting a word like *in*, on the other hand, requires breaking up the rime portion (there is no onset in the word *in*). Once children are successful with segmenting two-phoneme words with stretchable consonants,

TABLE 5.3. Progression of Difficulty for Sound-Counting/Segmenting Activities

Degree of challenge	Types of Words to Use
Easiest	Two-phoneme words with onsets and rimes and stretchable consonants (e.g., *me*)
	Two-phoneme words, stop consonants (e.g., *to*)
	Three-phoneme words, stretchable consonants (e.g., *sun*)
	Three-phoneme words, stop consonants (e.g., *bat*)
	Three- or four-phoneme words that include consonant blends (e.g., *fly*, *stop*)
Most challenging	Longer words with consonant blends

they should begin work on words with stop consonants. The general instructional sequence for introductory lessons is presented in Table 5.3. Sample lists for each type of word used in sound-counting activities are provided in the Figure 5.7.

MATERIALS

Phoneme-counting activities were originally described by Elkonin (1973). He used "sound boxes" to provide children with a graphic representation of the process of segmenting words. As children articulate each phoneme in a word, they are taught to move a counter into the box that represents that sound. Because Elkonin was the first to introduce this procedure for sound counting, many now refer to this method as *Elkonin boxes*. Since the technique has been found to be so successful in helping children learn to segment words at the level of the phoneme, and because the sound boxes provide for an easy and straightforward transition between sound counting and sound spelling, Elkonin boxes have been incorporated into many early intervention and early literacy programs.

Typically, a sound-counting activity begins with providing each child with a piece of (laminated) paper on which connected squares have been drawn. Initially, the number of squares corresponds to the number of phonemes in the words that will be used for sound counting. Often, a small symbol is drawn in or under the leftmost box to indicate that it is the "beginning box." We usually use a star to signal "start." (Although no letters are used at this point, sequencing the sounds in words from left to right will help the child to understand the left-to-right directionality of print.) The teacher provides each child with a small number of counters (poker chips, counting cubes, etc.). To start with, the teacher has the same materials as the child, perhaps in a bigger version depending on the number of children in the group. (Table 5.4 summarizes the instructional sequence for sound counting; Figure 5.8 provides and example of Elkonin boxes.)

Two Phonemes		Three Phonemes		Consonant Blends
Stretchable	Stop consonants	Stretchable	Stop consonants	
me	bow	safe	bat	fly
so	by	foam	bite	stop
new	boo	face	bike	smile
my	do	fame	cap	frog
shoe	day	man	cake	snow
say	guy	mane	dot	flag
lie	go	mice	good	plane
low	gay	moss	gate	sweep
lay	hay	mole	hike	grape
moo	high	noon	kite	prize
mow	hoe	news	keep	fry
may	who	nice	pot	float
knee	he	niece	pack	glue
no	key	name	tape	block
ray	pay	knife	tight	ski
row	pie	some	tap	bread
sew	toe	zoom	top	crib
zoo	tie	feel	take	stick

FIGURE 5.7. Words for phoneme counting.

TABLE 5.4. General Instructional Sequence Focused on Sound Counting

Teacher	Child
Models saying the sounds and moving the counters.	Watches.
Says individual sounds.	Moves counters.
Moves counters.	Says individual sounds.
Watches.	Says sounds and moves counters.

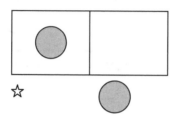

FIGURE 5.8. Illustration of Elkonin boxes.

Sample Instructional Dialogue

TEACHER: Before we were practicing listening to the sounds in words. Now we are going to figure out how many sounds there are in some words that we use all the time. If we know how many sounds there are in a word, it will help us decide how many letters we might need to use when we write that word.

Let's think about the word *me*. When I say the word *mmmmeeee*, I start with the /mmmm/ sound and then I make the /eeee/ sound. So *mmmmeeee* has two sounds: /mmmm/ and /eeee/.

I can use these boxes to help me count the sounds. The first box has a star in it to help me remember it is the box for the first sound in the word. The star will help us remember that this is where we *start*.

Let's try using these boxes to help us count the sounds in *mmmmeeee*. When I say *mmmeee*, I start by saying /mmmm/, so I put a counter in the start box. Then, when I say /eeee/, I put a counter in the next box. (*Demonstrates.*) Now, let's all say the sounds in the word *mmmeeee*. (*Encourages children to use their counters as she uses hers.*). Me /mmmm/—/eeee/. (*Puts a counter into the correct box as she articulates each sound, briefly stopping between the two sounds.*)

CHILDREN: (*Move counters into each box, with teacher guidance as necessary.*)

TEACHER: (*Provides praise and encouragement.*) Now I'll just say the sounds, and you move the counters into your boxes just as I'm saying the sounds. /mmm/ /eeee/.

CHILDREN: (*Move counters and receive feedback from teacher.*)

TEACHER: Now, who would like to say the sounds for us while the rest of us move our counters?

VOLUNTEER CHILD: /mmmm/ /eeee/.

OTHER CHILDREN: (*Move counters.*)

TEACHER: Now, let's all say the sounds in *mmmeee* and move the counters into the boxes as we say each sound.

"How Would Stretch Say It?"

One of the teachers on our staff (A. Daley) used a puppet named Stretch when she worked with her kindergarten groups. During blending activities, Stretch articulated the individual sounds and the children would identify the word that Stretch was attempting to say. Stretch's memorable way of talking was very helpful to the children when, at a later point, they were attempting to write. If they demonstrated difficulty with segmenting the sounds of the words they wanted to write, the teacher would simply ask "How would Stretch say it?" This simple prompt reminded the children of the process and engaged them in doing the sound analysis more independently (and lightheartedly) than they otherwise might have done.

As the children become more adept at this exercise, the teacher should gradually withdraw her support. The goal is for the children to be able to count the sounds in two-sound words (articulate the sounds and move the counters) independently. The teacher should continue to use words with stretchable sounds until the children can segment them easily and are, therefore, ready for more challenging words. Some children will be ready for the more challenging words sooner than others. In this case, individual children can be asked to segment and count the sounds in different words.

When the children are facile with counting the sounds in two-sound words that have stretchable consonants, they should be asked to count sounds in two-sound words with stop consonants. Later, they would work with words that have three sounds with stretchable consonants, then three-sound words with stop consonants, and so on. (Samples of appropriate words are provided in Figure 5.7.)

When it is clear that the children understand the process, it is no longer necessary (nor desirable) for there to be an exact match between the number of boxes available and the number of sounds in the words. At this point the children can have a standard set of boxes (four or five boxes) and use as many boxes as they need to represent all of the sounds in the words—realizing that there will often be boxes left over.

Transition from Sound Counting to Sound Spelling

Once children are able to use the counters to represent the sounds in words, the sound boxes can be used to assist them in figuring out spellings for unknown words.

SINGLE LETTER-SOUNDS

Initially, the teacher might use the sound boxes to teach and reinforce the sound of an individual letter. For example, if the children are learning the sound of the letter *m*, the teacher might display three sound boxes and provide a marker (or a letter tile) with the letter *m* on it. The teacher would say a series of words, each of which has the sound of *m* in either the beginning or ending position, and then model the process of stretching the word, thinking about where the /mmm/ sound was heard, and then moving the *m* marker into the box that represents the position in the word where the /mmm/ sound is heard.

After modeling the process with a few words (making sure that sometimes the /mmm/ sound occurs at the beginning and sometimes at the end), the teacher would invite the children to participate in the sound analysis and decision making concerning the location of the /mmm/ sound. By initially representing only one sound in the word, the process will be more manageable for the children. Ultimately, the goal is for the children to be able to go through the steps in the process on their own.

> **KEEP IN MIND** Sound boxes are used to represent sounds, not letters. There should be a box for each *sound* in the word. If one sound is represented in print by two letters (e.g., /sh/ or /th/), both letters would be written in the box for that sound (see Figure 5.9). Silent letters should not be placed in sound boxes. In the word *plane*, for example, the silent e should be added to the end of the word, outside the last sound box (see Figure 5.10).

FIGURE 5.9. Sound boxes representing each sound in the word *she*.

p	l	a	n	e

FIGURE 5.10. Sound boxes representing each sound in the word *plane*, with the unboxed silent *e*.

Ultimately, the children should be able to figure out how many boxes would be needed for a given word and then to figure out which letters should go into each of the boxes. If a child who has had some experience with using sound boxes wanted to write the word *plane*, he would start by thinking about how many sounds he hears. Then, he might draw a line for each sound he hears (boxes would take too long) and place the letters that represent those sounds on the lines. Depending on where he is in his knowledge of phonics, he might add the silent *e* at the end—but not on a line.

Fiddling with Phonemes, Playing with Language at Odd Times

The activities described below can be squeezed into odd moments of the day. These activities typically should not be attempted unless the skills on which they build have already been introduced explicitly and practiced. For teachers who are working with children in an intervention setting, the "talking like the puppet" activity could be used to practice phonemic analysis skills while traveling through the hallways.

Line Up by Sound

Have children line up for gym, recess, etc., in accord with whether or not a certain sound (not letter) occurs in their name. For example, the teacher might ask children whose names begin with the /sss/ sound to line up first. *Sara* and *Sam* would line up, but not *Sean*, because his name starts with the /sh/ sound.

Talking Like the Puppet

Occasionally the teacher or other children can pretend to be the robot or space person or whatever prop was used for the sound-blending activity. The teacher might use a segmented version of the child's name (e.g., "/T/ /o/ /m/, please bring me a pen") or object (e.g., "Tom, please bring me a /p/ /e/ /n/").

EVALUATING AND DOCUMENTING CHILDREN'S PROGRESS

Figure 5.11 presents the group snapshot for phonological skills. This checklist can be used to track children's development of phonological skills. Although the skills are presented in list form by necessity, it is important to remember that the various instructional techniques are mutually reinforcing. Teachers are encouraged to draw upon different techniques as needed. Within each set of instructional activities (e.g., sorting, blending) the tasks are sequenced to represent a developmental progression. In general, children should demonstrate success on the easier task within a sequence (e.g., blending onsets and rimes with pictures) before moving on to the next most challenging task (e.g., blending onsets and rimes without pictures). Children should be considered proficient when they can reliably and quickly demonstrate a particular skill.

Group Snapshot—Phonological Skills					
Student names					
I. Sensitivity in Text					
Complete rhyme in known text					
Identify rhyme in text					
Identify alliteration in text					
II. Sound Sorting					
Beginning sound					
Rhyme					
Ending sound					
Medial vowel					
III. Sound Blending					
Onset–rime w/ pictures					
Onset–rime w/o pictures					
Single phonemes w/ pictures					
Single phonemes w/o pictures					
IV. Sound Counting/Segmentation					
Two phonemes, stretchable consonants					
Two phonemes, stop consonants					
Three phonemes, stretchable consonants					
Three phonemes, stop consonants					
Words with consonant blends					

Key:

◻ *B—Beginning* indicates that instruction has addressed the objective but that the child has only a preliminary understanding or capability with regard to that particular objective.

⊠ *D—Developing* indicates that the child has some understanding of the objective but does not reliably demonstrate that understanding or capability or is not yet automatic (fluent) with the skill.

⊠ *P—Proficient* indicates that the child reliably and automatically demonstrates the understanding or capability.

FIGURE 5.11. Group snapshot for phonological skills.

CHAPTER 6

Letter Naming

ALPHABETICS GOAL 3

The child will be able to name, rapidly and accurately, all 26 letters of the alphabet, both upper- and lower-case versions.

Kindergarten and beginning first-grade children vary greatly in their letter-name and letter-sound knowledge. Those who enter kindergarten knowing the names of most of the letters of the alphabet are much more likely to experience success in the early stages of learning to read, whereas those who know few letter names are at risk of literacy learning difficulties (Scanlon & Vellutino, 1996, 1997; Snow et al., 1998). However, this does not mean that all children who enter kindergarten lacking in letter-name knowledge are destined to experience reading difficulties. Rather, their future success in reading depends, at least in part, on the experiences they have with print and the effectiveness of those experiences in attuning them, not only to the elements of print, but to the interrelationships between spoken and written language. In fact, research demonstrating that instructional experiences in kindergarten make a big difference for children who arrive with comparatively little early literacy experience provides a strong argument for initiating intervention efforts in kindergarten (O'Connor et al., 2005; Scanlon & Vellutino, 1996, 1997; Scanlon et al., 2005, 2008).

By the beginning of first grade, most children can name most, if not all, of the letters of the alphabet. At this point, the speed with which children can name the letters becomes a good predictor of progress in first-grade reading. It is hypothesized that this relationship exists because slow letter naming is an indication of some uncertainty about the names of the letters, and this uncertainly requires children to expend more of their cognitive energy on this lower-level skill. As a result, children have fewer cognitive resources to devote to word solving and to the higher-level (meaning-making) aspects of reading. Thus it is important to help children become fluent with letter names as soon as possible.

ASSESSING LETTER KNOWLEDGE

In small-group and individual intervention settings where the teacher has more opportunity to individualize instruction, it is possible to develop a more optimal instructional plan for teaching individual children about letters. To do so, it is important first to determine which letters the child can already recognize, name, and/or produce, and for which letters, if any, the child knows the corresponding sound(s). For children who know little about the alphabet, it is also important to take into consideration which letters may hold significance for them (e.g., because the letters are in their names or in the names of friends, pets, siblings). As the school year progresses it is important to determine whether the children are learning (or know) the letter-level skills that have been taught.

Such individualization is often not possible for the classroom teacher, because even the small groups are apt to include several children. However, initial assessment of letter-level skills nevertheless provides important information that contributes to grouping decisions. Periodic assessment of letter-level skills during the course of the year provides important information concerning whether children are in appropriate groups, whether they are making progress or need more intensive instructional support, and whether the class, as a whole, is making sufficient progress.

Initial Evaluation of Letter-Level Knowledge

Table 6.1 provides an overview of the type of assessment that might be done to evaluate letter-level knowledge. To make the evaluation as efficient as possible, we recommend that teachers do the following:

- Assess letter naming first.
- Assess recognition for any letters the child cannot name.
- Assess production (printing) for any letters the child can name.
- Assess letter–sound association of any letters for which the child was able to name *both* the upper- and lower-case versions.
- Assess use in decoding of any letter for which the child knows the sound.

TABLE 6.1. Assessment of Letter-Level Skills

Letter-level skill	How the skill is measured	Example
Letter recognition	The child is shown a small group of letters and is asked to point to the one named by the teacher.	The teacher displays *B S M T O* and says, "Point to the *T*." (*Note*: If a correct response seems like a lucky guess, include the letter in another set and ask the child about that letter again.)
Letter naming (identification)	The child is shown an individual letter and asked to name it. The teacher notes whether the response is correct and, if so, whether it is fast (no hesitation).	The teacher shows the letter *B* and asks, "What is this letter called?"
Letter production	The child is asked to print individual letters.	The teacher provides the child with pencil and paper and says, "Make the letter *B* for me." (*Note*: Be sure that models of the letters are not in sight.)
Letter–sound association	The child is asked to say the sound made by a letter presented in print. (*Note*: Do not name the letter when asking for its sound. The letter name often provides a good clue to the letter's sound.)	The teacher displays or points to a single letter and asks, "What sound does this letter make?"
Use in decoding	The child is asked to decode words comprising the letter being evaluated and other known elements or orthographic units that are identified for the child.	The child is shown a word family, such as *at*, and is told, "This is *at*." Then the teacher puts a *b* (or whatever letter is being evaluated) in front of the *at* and asks, "If I put this letter in front of *at*, what will the word be?"

The assumption here is that, any letter(s) a child can name, he will also be able to recognize; therefore, it is not necessary to evaluate the child for recognition of those letters. Similarly, it is assumed that the child will not be able to print letters that he cannot identify; therefore, only letters that the child can identify are evaluated for production (printing). Letter-sound knowledge is typically acquired only after the child can identify (name) the letter. Thus, letter-sound knowledge should usually be assessed only for letters that the child can already identify.

Use in decoding would be assessed only for letters for which the child knows the sounds. The child's ability to use letters sounds in decoding words can be evaluated informally by noting the child's success as he reads. Alternatively, this skill, as well as many of the letter-level skills listed above, can be evaluated using one of the many early literacy assessments that are currently on the market. The group snapshot for alphabet knowledge can be used to document children's progress with respect to letter naming, letter production, and letter sounds. This snapshot can be found at the end of this chapter (Figure 6.7, p. 125).

Note

Occasionally children are taught (and learn) letter sounds instead of letter names. If this is true for a given child, it will be evident during a letter identification assessment, since the child will provide the letter sound rather than the letter name when asked to identify individual letters.

CHOOSING LETTERS FOR INSTRUCTION

Although intervention teachers have the luxury of being able to plan instruction that is more closely tied to the knowledge and skills of the children, it is useful for both classroom and intervention teachers to give careful consideration to the order in which letters are taught. Below are recommendations for teachers who are working with *children who know very little about the alphabet.*

- *Avoid similar letters.* It is important to choose letters to teach that are as different as possible from one another in terms of their appearance and their sounds. For example, it would make sense to avoid teaching the letters *b* and *d* at the same time or in close proximity to one another because they look alike and the names of the letters rhyme. Also, teachers might want to avoid teaching *j* and *k* together because their names rhyme. When teaching letter sounds, teachers should avoid teaching sounds for letters such as *f* and *v* at the same time because of the similarity in their sounds.
- *Begin with upper-case letters.* Upper-case letters are preferable because their features are more salient, they are less visually confusable, and it is potentially very confusing for a child to have to learn the upper- and lower-case versions of letters simultaneously, particularly if the two versions are very dissimilar in appearance (approximately half of the letters have different looking upper- and lower-case versions).
- *Teach letters that are important to children.* Children are typically very interested in learning the letters in their names.
- *Teach more frequently occurring letters first.* Some letters, such as *a, s, t,* and *m,* occur more frequently than others such as *j, x,* and *z.*

SEQUENCE OF OBJECTIVES FOR LEARNING ABOUT LETTERS

In general, children demonstrate letter-related skills in the following sequence:

1. Recognition
2. Naming

3. Letter–sound association
4. Use in decoding

If a child has no knowledge of a given letter, instruction should focus initially on recognition of the letter. Once a child can reliably and quickly recognize a letter, he is ready to begin working toward reliable and quick naming of that letter. Activities that engage children in printing the letter (production) can help them learn to recognize and identify the letter. However, their ability to print the letter at the request of the teacher without referring to a visual model ("Print the letter *T* for me") will typically occur after the children can both recognize and name the letter. Once children know the name of a letter, children are ready to learn the letter's sound and ultimately to use that letter in reading and writing.

Children Do Not See Letters Backwards

Children often confuse certain pairs or groups of letters (e.g., *b/d*, *u/n*, *p/q*). Such confusions were once thought to indicate that a child somehow saw things differently or that the image was rotated or reversed as it traveled from the eye to the brain, or vice versa. Over 30 years ago, however, Vellutino and his colleagues demonstrated that such confusions arise from difficulties in remembering what visually similar letters are called. In other words, children who make errors such as substituting *b* for *d* are not having difficulty with the visual aspects of the process; it is the *verbal memory* aspect of the task that is problematic for them (Vellutino, 1979).

Rationale for the Sequence

Many teachers are initially uncomfortable with the idea of teaching about letter names and letter sounds separately and/or with the idea of teaching upper-case letters before lower-case letters. These recommendations apply primarily to children who begin with very little letter knowledge. Teaching about both upper- and lower-case letters and letter names and letter sounds simultaneously has the advantage of providing new information for all or most of the children in the class. Thus, the children who already know the names of many letters probably learn about letter sounds in this instructional context. Those who know some capital letters probably learn the lower-case version of those letters. However, those who know little, if anything, about the alphabet are faced with a huge amount of information and, potentially, little guidance concerning what they are to accomplish in these learning episodes.

For example, if a teacher were using a "letter-of-the-week" instructional format, she might introduce the upper- and lower-case printed versions of the letter *B*, tell the children that both of those letters are called *be*, and that they both make

FIGURE 6.1. *B*/ball illustration.

the /b/ sound that we hear at the beginning of *ball* (see Figure 6.1). Note that the children need to be somewhat phonemically aware in order to attend to the onset in the word *ball*. Also note that it is likely that children who know little about the alphabet will be insensitive to the importance of orientation with regard to letters. Add to these potential points of confusion the various ways in which an individual letter might be presented (in different fonts and by different hands). Clearly, the child who arrives in kindergarten knowing little about the alphabet has more to learn in a letter-of-the-week context than does a child who already knows quite a bit about the alphabet. In a classroom setting, a child with very little letter knowledge might participate with the class during the introduction of the letter, but then focus only on learning the name of the upper-case version of the letter during follow-up activities and in small-group formats.

Note

It is not necessary to work on recognition for all letters before moving on to identification of letter sounds for some of them. In general, the intention is to work forward from the child's current knowledge base. However, it is reasonable to work toward the ability to name both the upper- and lower-case versions of a given letter before beginning to work on the sound for that letter.

LETTER RECOGNITION

Whole-Alphabet Activities

There are a variety of useful ways to familiarize children with the entire alphabet and to attune them to the fact that specific forms are associated with particular names.

• *Singing the alphabet song.* While singing, the teacher and/or the children should point to the printed letters. In a small group, each child might have his own alphabet strip to use while singing the song. Such an activity requires careful teacher monitoring (or perhaps buddy work with a more knowledgeable child) to ensure that the child is, in fact, pointing to the letter that is being named in the

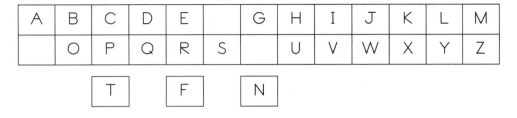

FIGURE 6.2. Missing letter illustration.

song. It is also important to slow the song down enough so that the children who most need the practice actually hear the names of the individual letters. We have all met children who believe that one of the letters in the middle of the alphabet is called "*elemeno*" (*L-M-N-O*). For children who know very little about the alphabet, most of the song initially sounds like a string of meaningless syllables (*ay-be-cee-dee-eee-ef-gee*)—which it is for them. Early on, particularly for children in intervention settings and for those with limited alphabetic knowledge, it is helpful to use letter strips that include just the upper-case letters.

• *Singing to a specific letter.* Once children have learned the alphabet song, a focus on specific letters can be accomplished by singing the song up to a specific letter and then stopping at that letter. For example, the teacher might decide to sing to the letter *K*. The group would then sing the song and point to the letters, as usual, but stop at the *K*. The teacher might also discuss the letters that come before and after *K*. The purpose of this activity is to draw attention to individual letters. The song can, of course, be sung a number of times, and children can be invited to choose which letter to sing to.

• *Singing to the missing letter(s) and filling it (them) in.* In this activity, the children are provided with alphabet strips with a few letters missing (see Figure 6.2). The group sings to the first missing letter and then fills it in by selecting from a small group of letters provided, as illustrated in the figure. Then the song is begun again and continues to the next missing letter, etc. (The teacher may need to hold up a model of the letter for which the children are looking.)

• *Reading and discussing alphabet books.* Children who have had little print exposure prior to school will enjoy listening and reacting to alphabet books almost as much as younger children do. Because such books typically devote an entire page (or more) to each letter, they are a great resource for focusing the child's attention on individual letters. They are also helpful for teaching about letter–sound correspondences.

A Note about Font

To reliably recognize a letter, a child needs to learn which features of the letter are characteristic of the letter per se and which features are irrelevant. For example, the *T*'s presented in Figure 6.3 appear in different fonts, and some contain features that are not critical to the *T*'s identity.

T T T I *I* T

FIGURE 6.3. Font illustration.

Hand-printed letters and highly embellished fonts in books add even more variations through which a child must sort to determine which features define the letter and which features are merely stylistic variations. Children who learn to identify the letters of the alphabet without explicit and focused instruction generally extract the essential elements or critical features of letters either through their supported attempts to write or through exposure to multiple exemplars. In other words, they learn what gives *T* its "*T*-ness." However, it is important to accelerate the pace of letter learning for children who begin kindergarten with limited letter-name knowledge. Thus, the letters used in the earliest phases of instruction should, ideally, consist only of the features that define the letter. For example, all but the last example among the letters in Figure 6.3 would be poor choices for introducing the letter *T* because they include unnecessary features or features that are necessary but are not sufficiently salient. The last example, comprising only the critical features of the T, is clear.

In considering instructional materials for beginning readers, teachers should look critically at the font used in the books that children are asked to read. Ideally, it should be crisp and unembellished. Teachers should also note whether the "sticks" on the letters (the ascenders and descenders) sufficiently distinguish between similar-looking letters. Below is the worst example of a primary-type font that could be found on the computer used to produce this document:

a b d p n h

Compare the font above to the example below, which is a very good primary font—also found on the same computer—called *ZB Manuscript*.

a b d p n h

Clearly, it will be easier for children to learn the letters that are presented in the second example because the height of the ascenders and descenders makes it easy to distinguish a from d, n from h, and so on.

Teaching about Specific Letters

Materials Needed

• A short text with large print (a book or a poem) that contains several instances of the letter to be taught should be selected for this teaching segment. In a Tier 2 or Tier 3 intervention setting, it would be ideal to use materials that are routinely available in the child's classroom.

• Use a letter card containing the individual letter. The letter should be large enough for all of the children in the group to see, and the font should be unembellished, containing only the critical features.

Introducing the Letter

• Present the letter to be taught on a card (the letter *M* is used in the following examples). If possible, provide all of the children in the group with a card that has the selected letter on it. Tell the children what the letter is and have them repeat the letter name.

• While leaving the letter in view, introduce the text.

• Tell the children that the words in the book contain many *M*'s and that, after the book is read, they are going to look for all of the *M*'s.

• Explain that knowing the letters helps us to read and write.

• Engage the children in a discussion of the book before beginning to read. Encourage anticipation (prediction) and personal reactions to the text.

• Read the text to the children, pointing to the words while reading. Read with natural phrasing (not word by word).

• While reading, engage the children in discussing and reacting to the text.

• After reading, briefly discuss various (meaningful) aspects of the text.

• Focus in on the letter by saying something like: "Let's look for all of the *M*'s. There were a lot of *M*'s in this book!"

• Do a letter search, encouraging the children to find the focal letter on each page. Frequently use the name of the letter during the letter search (i.e., "There's an *M*." and "You found another *M*!"). Also encourage the children to use the name of the letter. Unless the name of the letter is used frequently, some children will treat this activity as a visual matching task rather than as a letter-naming activity. (Once several instances of the focal letter have been located, ask children to find a few instances of the letters that were taught previously.)

Figure 6.4 provides an illustration of a book that would be useful for teaching about an individual letter and explaining its utility.

KEEP IN MIND The purpose of the letter hunt activity is to give children many opportunities to connect the printed letter to its letter name. Do not have children count the letters, because counting would keep them from thinking about the letter's name.

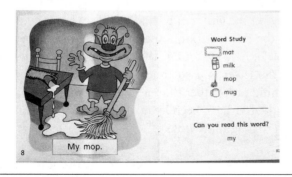

To the left is an example of a book that might be used to teach the letter M. Notice the following:

- The font is clean and unembellished

- There are enough capital M's for the children to engage in recognition activities (letter hunts for the M).

- The story is interesting despite the fact that there are only a few words per page

- There are opportunities to develop comprehension skills, including:
  - The use of picture cues.
  - Prediction ("What do you think will happen [after the spill]").
  - Text-to-self connections ("Who does the clean-up when there's a spill at your house?").

FIGURE 6.4. Example of a book that might be used while teaching the name of the letter *M*. From *Ready Readers, Monster Mop*, by Aimee Mark, illustrated by Cameron Eagle. Copyright 1997 by Pearson Education, Inc., or its affiliates. Used by permission. All rights reserved.

Practicing Letter Recognition

When the children can reliably find instances of the letter with the letter card in view, practice letter recognition without the letter card in view. If a child has difficulty recognizing a letter without the letter card present, the letter card should be provided again.

Look for opportunities to have the children find the letter(s) you are working on in other contexts (e.g., on a bulletin board or calendar, on displays while walking through the hallway). Direct children's attention to these displays and encourage them to try to find the target letter. Our purpose in having children look around the environment for letters they can recognize is to encourage them to become attuned to the fact that they are often surrounded by print and that they are beginning to acquire the skills to make some sense of it. Further, the children will, hopefully, think about the letters more frequently if they are attuned to their presence in a variety of contexts.

Games for Promoting Letter Recognition

Once several letters have been introduced for recognition, simple games can be constructed to reinforce recognition.

- *Letter bingo.* Customized bingo games can be created using only those letters on which the children are working. For each bingo card, make three or four columns, each with three or four boxes. Print one letter in each box (each letter can be used more than once, if necessary, to provide enough letters for the card). The teacher can call the letters while the children place markers on the letters as they are called. The teacher should monitor the children's performance to ensure accuracy. Also, to promote children's ability to name the letters, they should be encouraged to name each letter as they cover it. (There needn't be any winners or losers with this game—the children are generally delighted to simply cover up all of their letters.)
- *Parking lot game*—In this game, a parking lot is drawn on a piece of paper that includes two rows of parking spaces with four or five spaces in each row. One of the targeted letters is printed in each of the parking spaces in such a way that, when the paper is placed in front of the child, all of the letters will be properly oriented (right side up). Several different parking lots are made, all with the same letters but with the letters in different locations on each. To play the game, each child is provided with a different parking lot sheet and a toy car that fits in the parking spaces. Then the children are directed to park their cars in different spaces according to the letter named by the teacher (e.g., "Everyone park your car in the M space"). To encourage letter-name retrieval, a child who has "parked" his car might be asked, "What space is your car in?" Figure 6.5 provides an example of a parking lot game board.

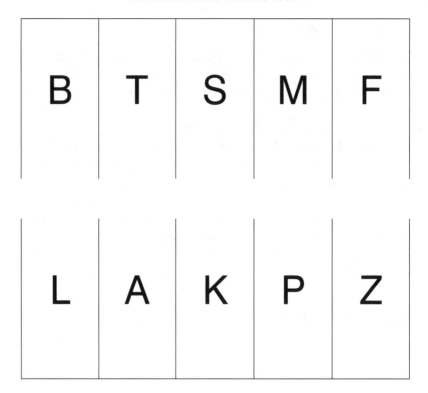

FIGURE 6.5. Parking lot game board.

LETTER NAMING

When the teacher notices that a child quickly and accurately recognizes given letters, the focus should shift to letter naming. For many children, once they can reliably recognize a letter, they are also able to identify it. However, for some children, it takes a good deal of additional practice to be able to retrieve the names of given letters. An additional goal for letter identification is that the child be able to name letters quite quickly so that, as the reading tasks become more demanding, slow letter identification skills will not limit the other processes. Thus, the goal of the letter-naming activities is not only accurate identification but fluent (fast) identification.

Introducing Letters for Identification

In preparing to teach in a small-group or intervention setting, the teacher should choose four or five letters that the children can recognize but not name reliably. During instruction, the teacher would show each letter, name it, and ask the children to repeat the name. If a child makes a mistake, the teacher would provide the correct letter name and point out the salient features of the letter. If appropriate, the teacher would point out how the misidentified letter differs visually from the letter the child named. Before moving on, the children should be asked to repeat the name of the letter. The same letters are presented a number of times, in a different order each time, to provide children with the opportunity to practice the letters' names.

Practicing Letter Identification

Children who are just beginning to learn about the letters often forget letters that were learned previously. As new letters are presented, it is important to frequently review previously learned letters. Below are some suggested activities for providing additional practice with letter identification:

- Provide each child with a collection of the letters he knows (perhaps in an envelope). Once every couple of days the children should be invited to name all of the letters they know. This activity can be used as an opportunity to evaluate letter identification skill, but the most important purpose is to promote fluency with letter identification.

- Occasionally choose a word in the text that is being read and ask the children to name all of the letters in the word. For example, while pointing to the word *cat*, the teacher might say, "Here is the word *cat*. Tell me what letters you see in the word *cat*." Or the teacher might say: "What is the first [middle, last] letter you see in *cat*?" or "Spell the word *cat* for me by telling me all of the letters in *cat* starting with the first one." (Until the children have the concept of print directionality firmly established, the teacher should always point to the letters when using words such as *first* and *last* in reference to print.)

KEEP IN MIND Classroom teachers often work with several children at once, even in a small-group setting. In such situations it is sometimes hard to ensure that all of the visual materials (in this case, letters) are oriented properly (right side up) for every child in the instructional group. Proper orientation of letters is especially important in letter study because some letters are easily confused (e.g., *b/d, u/n, p/q, b/p*).

Games for Promoting Letter Identification

Use letters on which the children are currently working for identification (and additional letters they can already identify reliably, if necessary, to make the game fun). As children begin to be able to identify a fairly large number of letters, it will sometimes be useful to include both upper- and lower-case versions of the same letter in these games. In this case *T* and *t* would be a match, as would *T* and *T*.

Use letter cards to play games of *Go Fish* or *Concentration (Memory)*. In playing such games, make sure that the letter cards are always properly oriented relative to the children. For example, if two children will be involved in a game of Concentration, make sure they are both on the same side of the table. Further, make sure that the cards are always presented right side up (a small dot at the top of each card will help—particularly if the children are frequently reminded that they need to keep the cards turned so that the dot is on the top). Also, in all games, make sure that the children name each letter as it is used. The purpose of playing the games is, after all, to help the children connect printed letters to their names.

A Common Parental Concern

Perhaps one of the most common parental concerns that primary-grade teachers are likely to encounter relative to literacy development has to do with young children's inclination to confuse visually similar symbols (e.g., *b* and *d*, *p* and *b*, *u* and *n*, and so on). Many parents believe that such confusions are a sign of a serious reading difficulty that is sometimes referred to as dyslexia.

The difficulty that some children experience with remembering what name to apply to two things that look a lot alike (e.g., *b* and *d*) is partly due to the fact that, until children encounter print, most of the objects they learn to label are called by the same name regardless of how the object is oriented in space. Thus, a pen is a pen regardless of whether its writing end is pointed to the top, bottom, left, or right of the perceiver's visual field. With letters, it is necessary to remember the symbol's orientation as well as its other critical features in order to recall the proper label.

To help children overcome their confusions with commonly confused letters, teachers can provide a model of the upper- and lower-case versions of the two confusable letters and encourage the children to refer to the model whenever they are uncertain about a letter's identity. An example of such a model is provided in Figure 6.6. Many early primary-grade teachers have found it useful to have such a model posted on all four walls of their classroom so that children can refer to it easily from wherever they are seated.

FIGURE 6.6. *B/D* example. Adapted from Scanlon and Anderson (2010). Copyright by the International Reading Association. Adapted with permission.

EVALUATING AND DOCUMENTING CHILDREN'S PROGRESS IN LETTER IDENTIFICATION

Children's accuracy in identifying letters can be evaluated through the use of a formal assessment or through observation of individual children's responses in routine instructional interactions. If informal observations are used, the teacher can note when the child can quickly and accurately name given letters over a couple of sessions. The group snapshot for alphabet knowledge, included at the end of this chapter (Figure 6.7, p. 125), can be used for capturing this information in small-group instructional situations. The first column (REC/ID [Recognition/Identification]) would be used to capture letter naming skill. Children who can recognize but not name a letter would be considered to be at a beginning point in development. Children who can name the letter but are not automatic or entirely reliable would be rated as developing.

LETTER PRODUCTION

Any writing activities attempted with children will be much more time-consuming and difficult for children who need to expend a lot of "cognitive energy" forming the letters. Therefore, it is useful to help children learn to form the letters efficiently and legibly. Concern with neatness in letter formation should be secondary (in our opinion, although many educators would take exception to this position).

Introducing the Letter

Learning to print letters can help children attend to the critical features of the letters they are learning. So, instruction designed to help children learn to write letters does not fit precisely in the sequence of alphabetic skills development. If a child in an intervention setting does not have an established method for printing a letter, it is reasonable for the teacher to teach the method employed in the child's classroom.

To help children learn to print a given letter, the teacher might:

- Provide children with a large-print version of the letter.
- Explain that they will be learning to write the letter.
- Trace the letter with her finger as the children watch, explicitly describing the process while tracing. For example, in describing how to print the letter *T*, the teacher might say, "This is how we make a *T*. For the first part of the *T*, we make a straight line down. Then a *T* needs a straight line across the top. So we make two lines when we make a *T*, a straight line down and then a line across the top of the *T*."

• Invite the children to trace the letter several times while again providing a verbal description of the process for printing the letter. As illustrated in the example above, the teacher should be sure to use the name of the letter many times as she guides the children through letter formation.

• The teacher can model the printing of the letter on a chalkboard or whiteboard while the children watch. Once again, it is essential to provide a verbal description and to say the name of the letter several times.

• Have the children print the letter on paper, a chalkboard, a whiteboard, or on whatever is available, guiding their initial printing attempts with the same verbal descriptions. The children should name the letters as they write.

• If the child has difficulty producing a recognizable letter, the teacher can assist him by guiding the child's hand (while the child holds the pencil) to form the letter.

Note

Whiteboards are especially appealing to children for these kinds of activities. They enjoy both the opportunity to write and the opportunity to erase. Teachers can capitalize on this appeal by having erasure time serve instructional purposes. For example, if several letters were printed on the whiteboard, the children could be directed to erase one letter at a time (e.g., "Erase the *T*, erase the *M*," and so on).

In letter production, in our opinion, the focus should be on general form, not on details. The goal is recognizable letters, not beautiful ones. It is also important that the child, ultimately, be able to print letters fairly quickly. If a child has already learned to form a letter fluently (as is often true of the letters in children's names), it may be difficult for him to alter the letter formation while remaining fluent. A decision about whether to attempt to change the child's approach to forming a particular letter should rest on a determination of whether this approach will reduce that child's writing fluency in the future. The purpose of handwriting instruction (especially in an age where most things are done on the computer) is to ensure that letter formation does not interfere with the process of communication. In an intervention setting, perfect handwriting should not be a focus. (This does not, however, mean that neat and legible handwriting shouldn't be encouraged.)

KEEP IN MIND Until children can form letters effortlessly and automatically, they should have ready access to an alphabet strip to use as a model.

Practicing Letter Printing

The children should be encouraged to print given letters many times until it is apparent that they do not need to refer to a model of the letter when they print. In an intervention setting, children should print letters that are being focused upon several times during each session, and they should name the letter each time it is printed. We have found that the game of *tic-tac-toe* is a particularly motivating way to engage the children in practicing the printing.

Tic-tac-toe can be used in multiple ways to reinforce the development of foundational early literacy skills. For purposes of learning the names of letters and how to print them, the game can be played in a couple of different ways.

- *One letter.* To work on just one letter, each player in the game would use a different colored marker. On their turn, they would each print and name the targeted letter. The winner of the game would be determined by having three letters of the same color in a row.
- *Two letters.* Each player would have a different letter, which each would print and name on his or her turn. The winner of the game is determined by have three of the same letters in a row (as in tic-tac-toe with *X*'s and *O*'s).
- *Multiple letters.* In this version, each player uses a different colored marker. On their turn, players each choose from a set of letter cards and name and write the letter they pick. The winner is determined by having three (different) letters of the same color in a row.

In order for tic-tac-toe to support letter-name learning, children need to name the letter as they write. Teachers have found it useful to have whiteboards dedicated to Tic Tac Toe. They make the game grid on the board using masking tape so that all that the children need to do when they play is write in the letters. Having dedicated boards allows the teacher to ensure that the boxes are large enough to easily contain the children's writing.

Print in a Variety of Media

A variety of media for printing can be used to maintain the children's interest. For example, the children might be asked to print:

- Using different colors or kinds of markers on paper
- In whipped cream or shaving cream
- Using a wet sponge brush on a chalk board
- Using markers on whiteboards
- In sand or salt on a cookie sheet
- Using drawing toys such as Magnadoodles or Ghostwriters

Remember to have children say the letter names as often as possible during these activities.

EVALUATING AND DOCUMENTING CHILDREN'S PROGRESS
IN LETTER PRODUCTION

Teachers can observe and record children's proficiency in producing a particular letter either informally by observing them as they write or by explicitly asking them to print a particular letter. To qualify as proficient, the child needs to be able to print the letter quickly and accurately and without needing to refer to a model of the letter.

Figure 6.7 presents the group snapshot for alphabet knowledge. This checklist can be used to document the progress of children within a group in letter recognition and identification, letter production, and letter sounds.

| Group Snapshot—Alphabet Knowledge | | | | | | | | | | | | | | |
Student Names	REC/ID	Print	Sound	REC/ID	Print	Sound	REC/ID	Print	Sound	REC/ID	Print	Sound	REC/ID	Print	Sound
A															
a															
B															
b															
C															
D															
d															
E															
e															
F															
f															
G															
g															
H															
h															
I															
i															
J															
j															
K															
k															
L															
l															
M															
m															
N															
n															
O															
P															
Q															
q															
R															
r															
S															
T															
t															
U															
V															
W															
X															
Y															
Z															

Note that when the upper- and lower-case versions of a letter are essentially identical in appearance, it is not necessary to evaluate the two versions separately. Therefore, the snapshot does not provide space to do so.

Key:
☐ B—*Beginning* indicates that work with this letter has begun.
☒ D—*Developing* indicates that the child can perform the task but is slow and/or sometimes inaccurate but does not reliably demonstrate that understanding or capability or is not yet automatic (fluent) with the skill.
☒ P—*Proficient* indicates that the child reliably and automatically demonstrates the skill.

FIGURE 6.7. Group snapshot for alphabet knowledge.

CHAPTER 7

Letter–Sound Association

ALPHABETICS GOAL 4

The child will be able to associate the most common sounds of individual letters with their printed representations.

To puzzle through unfamiliar words, children need to know something about the relationships between printed letters and their sounds. This chapter focuses on helping teachers (1) understand letter–sound relationships from the perspective of a novice reader and (2) teach children the conventional letter–sound relationships they need to know in order to develop their reading skills.

THE LINK BETWEEN LETTER NAMES AND LETTER SOUNDS

For many consonants, the name of the letter provides information about the letter's sound. For example, in the following letters, the initial phoneme in the letter's name is the sound represented by that letter—*b, d, j, k, p, t, v, z*, and also the soft sound of *g* (as in *gym*) and the soft sound of *c* (as in *city*). For other consonants, the final phoneme in the letter's name is the sound represented by the letter (*f, l, m, n, r, s, x*). For all of these letters, knowing the letter name provides useful information about the letter's sound. This is one of the reasons why we stress the utility of helping children learn the names of the letters before expecting them to learn the sounds. Table 7.1 illustrates the link between letter names and letter sounds by writing out the name for each letter.

When young children write, they often use letter names as a source of information about letter sounds (Bear et al., 2008; Read, 1971). Thus, if a child wants to write the word *cat* and does not already know how to spell it, she is likely to start the word with a *k* because the first sound heard in the word *cat* is also the first sound heard in the name of the letter *k*. Obviously, in order for the child to be able to do this type of complicated analysis, she needs to know the name of the letter and be somewhat phonemically aware (that is, she needs to be able to notice the similarity in the onsets in the word *cat* and in the name of the letter *k*).

It is also interesting to note (and very predictable, given what is known about the development of phonemic awareness) that children tend to learn the sounds of letters in which the letter sound is in the onset of the letter name (e.g., *b*, *k*, *t*) more readily than the sounds of letters in which the letter sound is embedded in the rime (e.g., *s*, *m*, *f*) (Treiman, Sotak, & Bowman, 2001). This is at least partially because children tend to be able to separate syllables into onsets and rimes (/b/ /e/) before they are able to segment the rime portion of a word into its separate phonemes (/e/ /s/).

For some consonants, of course, the letter sound is not contained in the letter name (*h*, *w*, and *y*). The letter–sound associations for these letters are notoriously difficult for young children to learn. However, it is often in the children's attempts to use these letters in spelling that we see the strongest evidence of their inclination to use letter names as a resource. Thus, a child might spell the word *was* as illustrated in Figure 7.1. In this example, the *y* is used to represent the /w/ sound, consistent with the first sound in its name (*why*). The *z* is used to represent the /z/ sound heard at the end of the word *was*.

Vowels are more complicated than consonants. Long vowel sounds are, of course, very transparent. The sound is the same as the name of the letter. Short

TABLE 7.1. The Link between Letter Names and Letter Sounds

Letter sound at the beginning of letter name	Letter sound at the end of letter name	Letter sound not in letter name
B (*bee*)	F (*ef*)	C (as in *cat*)
C (see as in *city*)	L (*el*)	G (as in *give*)
D (*dee*)	M (*em*)	H (*aich*)
G (*jee* as in *gym*)	N (*en*)	W (*double you*)
J (*jay*)	R (*ar*)	Y (*why*)
K (*kay*)	S (*es*)	
P (*pea*)	X (*ex*)	
T (*tea*)		
V (*vee*)		
Z (*zee*)		
Q (*kyou*)		

FIGURE 7.1. Sound spelling of *was*.

vowels, however, present children with greater challenges because, for most vowels, there is little relationship between the name of the letter and the short vowel sound associated with it. For example, for the letter *e*, the short sound is not heard in the name of the letter. Rather, the short-*e* sounds like the beginning of the name of the letter *a*.

In fact, for the vowels *e*, *i*, *o*, and *u*, the short vowel sound associated with the letter is actually heard in the name of the vowel letter that immediately precedes it in the alphabet.

Note

The discussion of vowels in this section is some of the most challenging text in this book. Try as we might, we were not able to make it clearer. Therefore, a few suggestions are in order:

- Do the exercise described below *out loud*. You really need to hear the letter sounds and the letter names in order to understand the points being made.
- If you do not engage in these exercises in a workshop or class setting, do them with a friend or colleague. Sometimes what confuses one person will be clear to someone else.
- Realize that expending the effort to understand these relationships will help you to better understand aspects of your students' literacy development. When teachers understand what children are doing and why, they have the potential to provide much more effective feedback to the children.

These letter–name/letter–sound relationships are typically very difficult for literate people (like teachers) to notice because they have been so well trained in the conventional letter–sound relationships that they seem natural. Some insight into these relationships can be gained using Table 7.2 and following the directions provided below.

Say the sound of the vowel in the middle column of the table (don't say the word—just the vowel sound it contains). As you are saying the short vowel sound, begin to say the name of the letter in the right-hand column. Do not stop—glide right from the short vowel sound into saying the name of the letter. *Do this out loud*. In doing so, most people notice that the sound of the vowel in the center column occurs at the beginning of the name of the letter in the right-hand column.

TABLE 7.2. Links between Vowel Letter Names and Short Vowel Sounds

Letter used in conventional spelling	Short vowel sound as heard in . . .	Vowel letter name containing that sound
E	Short *e*, as in <u>pet</u>	A
I	Short *i*, as in <u>pit</u>	E
O	Short *o* as in <u>pot</u>	I
U	Short *u*, as in <u>putt</u>	O

The left-hand column in Table 7.2 has the letter that is usually used to spell the short vowel sound (that is, the short-*e* sound is spelled with an *E*). If you try to glide from the sound of the vowel in the middle column into the name of the letter in the left-hand column, you'll find that you can't really glide easily into the name of the letter. That's because the *short sound of the vowel is not contained in the name of the vowel.*

What does all this mean for children? It means that a child who is beginning to include vowels in her writing and does not yet know the conventional spelling for the short-*e* sound is likely to spell it with an *A*. She would write *pat* when she wanted to talk about her *pet*. A teacher who did not understand the reason for the use of the letter *a* in this context might well provide feedback focused on helping the child to isolate the middle sound in the word *pet*. In other words, the teacher is apt to operate on the assumption that the child's difficulty in spelling this word is due to inaccurate phonemic analysis rather than to not knowing the conventional spelling of the short-*e* sound. The child is likely to be confused by this feedback because she actually did isolate the /eeee/ (short-*e* sound), which the teacher so helpfully articulates by way of feedback. The child's problem is that she just doesn't know how to spell the short-*e* sound.

SELECTING AND USING KEY WORDS (MNEMONICS)

Key words are often used to help children learn and remember letter–sound relationships—and can be especially useful for the hard-to-remember relationships discussed above. However, for key words to be helpful, they need to be "good" key words. That is, they need to provide clear and representative examples of the sounds on which we want the children to focus. An example of the key word alphabet chart used in ISA research studies appears in Figure 7.2. Our purpose in presenting this chart is not to suggest that ours is necessarily better than others that are available. It is just an example of what a planfully constructed (key word) alphabet chart might look like.[1]

---

[1]Teachers refer to such charts by various names (letter chart, alphabet chart, key words, etc.). Consistent terminology should be used across instructional settings.

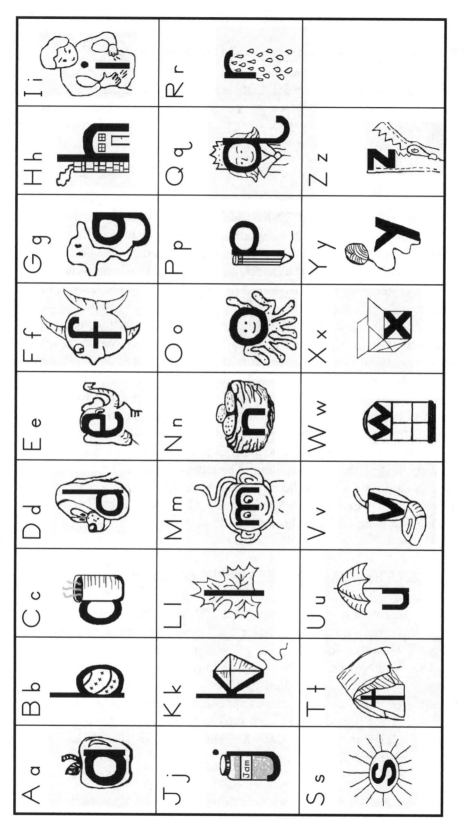

FIGURE 7.2. ISA key words.

In developing these key words, several considerations played a role. These considerations may be useful to teachers as they consider the utility and appropriateness of the key words they utilize or are considering. Thus, we share our thinking as follows:

*For the short-*a *sound*

- Avoid words in which the *a* is followed by an *n* (*ant, antlers, ankle*), an *r* (*arm*), or an *l* (*alligator*) because, as a result of coarticulation, these letters tend to change the sound of the *a* such that it is not a good example of the short-*a* sound.

*For the short-*e *sound*

- Avoid words like *elephant* and *envelope* because, for the child who is just learning, a letter name is the first sound in the words (i.e., *l* is the first sound in *elephant*; *n* is the first sound in *envelope*, and so on). To avoid this problem, we named the elephant on our key word chart *Ed the Elephant*.[2]
- Avoid the word *egg*. Many people pronounce the word *egg* such that it sounds very much like a (non)word spelled with a long-*a* sound (*aig*). (For doubters, note that *Craig* and *Greg* rhyme.) Teachers using a set of key words with *egg* for *e* have drawn a smiley face on the egg and named it *Ed* to address this problem.

*For the short-*i *sound*

- Avoid words in which the *i* sounds more like a long-*e*. For example, some people pronounce the word *igloo* such that it sounds like *ee-gloo* and *iguana* such that is sounds like *ee-guana*. Our key word for short-*i* is *itchy*.

*For the short-*o *sound*

- Avoid words in which the *o* sounds more like an *au*. For example, some people pronounce the word *ostrich* in such a way that is sounds like *austrich*.
- Do not use the word *orange* because the *r* changes the pronunciation of the vowel.

For all consonants

- Avoid words in which the focal letter is included in a consonant blend because it is harder for young children to attend to and isolate the initial sound in a word if it is part of a blend. *R* blends are especially problematic for the

---

[2]We elected to use an elephant as our key word for *E* because, although young children may think that it begins with an *L*, it does begin with a true short-*e* sound. To get past the *L* problem, we named the elephant *Ed*. So, the children learn that key word as *Ed the Elephant*.

letters *t* and *d* because when either of these letters is combined with *r* at the beginning of a word, the sound of the focal letter (*t* or *d*) cannot be isolated. (For example, the word *train* and the nonword *chrain* sound the same when pronounced. Neither of them includes a recognizable /t/ sound.)

Another characteristic of key words that may make them more useful to children is the integration of the letter and the picture representing the key word. Ehri, Deffner, and Wilce (1984) found that when letters and key words were integrated (as ours are), children seem to learn the letter–sound correspondences more readily.

An additional consideration that guided the development of our key words was familiarity. If children are familiar with the concepts that the key words represent, they will be better able to attend to the key word as it is intended to be used: to help them remember the letter–sound correspondence rather than having to learn about the concept as well. For example, *house* and *cat* are familiar but *iguana* and *leopard* are less so for most children. A related concern is that it is easier to analyze the phonemes in a known word than in an unfamiliar word.

KEEP IN MIND   If a child is receiving reading instruction in more than one setting, the key words used in the different settings should be the same. The purpose of key words is to assist memory. If children are taught several key words (because they are receiving instruction in more than one setting), then they are essentially being asked to learn more than children who are receiving instruction in only one setting. This is also a concern as children move from one grade to the next. Children who have learned the letter–sound correspondences so well that they no longer need key words will not have to recall the key words at all. Those who still need the key words often have to learn a whole new set when they move from one grade to the next!

TEACHING AND PRACTICING LETTER SOUNDS

Children are ready to learn a letter's sound as soon as they can reliably identify the letter. To begin instruction on letter sounds, teachers should demonstrate that the letter tends to make the same sound in different contexts in which it occurs. If a set of key words is to be used, the key word should be included when initially introducing the sound of the letter. A sample dialogue for teaching the sound of the letter *s*, using *sun* as the key word (see Figure 7.3) is provided.

Sample Instructional Dialogue

TEACHER: We are going to learn about the sound that the letter *s* usually tells us to make in words. When we see an *s*, it tells us to make the /ssss/ sound. (*Shows the letter s.*): /sssss/.

FIGURE 7.3. Sun key-word picture.

(*Shows the word* sun.) Here is the word *sun*. It has an *s* at the beginning. The *s* tells us to make the /ssss/ we hear at the beginning of *ssssun*.

(*Shows a picture of a sun with the letter* s *next to it* [*or in it, depending on the key words*].) Here's a picture of a sun. We are going to use this picture to help us remember the sound that the *s* makes. So when we see the letter *s*, we'll think of a sun. The word *ssssun* has an *s* at the beginning, and the *s* makes the /ssss/ sound that we hear at the beginning of *sssssun*.

(*Shows several other printed words that start with* s *and that the children know the meaning of, e.g.,* soup, sock, seat, some, said.) These words all have an *s* at the beginning: *ssssoup, ssssock, sssseat, sssssome,* and *sssssaid*. (*Points to each word as it is said.*)

The *s* makes the same sound in all of these words: *soup, sock, seat, some,* and *said*. (*Points to the* s *in each word as it is said.*) Do you hear the /s/ at the beginning of each of these words?

(*Repeats the words, stressing the* /s/ *sound.*) Sssoup, ssssock, sssseat, ssssome, and ssssaid. Often when there's an *s* in a word, it tells us to make the /ssss/ sound.

(*If some children in the classroom are at a more advanced level, the teacher would show words with an* s *sound at the end* [e.g., this, yes, bus].) Here are some words that have an *s* at the end: *thissss, yessss, bussss*. (*Points to each word as it is said.*)

When I say these words, you hear the /ssss/ sound at the end. (*Repeats the words, stressing the* /ssss/ *sound.*) So you need to remember that *s* often makes the /ssss/ sound that we hear at the beginning of *sun*. (*Points to the symbol for the key word again.*)

After this introduction, the children should be invited to think of words that have the /s/ sound. The teacher might write each word the children suggest and draw their attention to the *s* in the word. The words should be grouped by the relative position of the *s* in the words (beginning, middle, or end of the word). If a child suggests a word that has the /s/ sound but no *s* (e.g., *city, celery*), the teacher should offer praise for noticing the /ssss/ sound but explain that that word does not happen to have an *s* and that the letter at the beginning of that word will be learned at a different time. Words that start with the target sound but not with the target letter could be put on a separate list for later consideration.

Practicing Letter–Sound Associations for Consonants

Exercises designed to reinforce letter–sound associations should typically focus on the sounds of letters that occur at the beginning of words until the children are very facile with those associations. Later, the focus can be shifted to the sounds in other parts of the word. In small-group instructional settings, different skill levels among individual children may be accommodated by asking different children to focus on different parts of the word.

Below are several activities that can be used to provide practice in applying developing letter-sound knowledge.

Sorting by Beginning Letter Sound

This activity is very similar to the sound-sorting activity described in Chapter 5. In order to sort objects or pictures by the beginning letter sound, children must be able to isolate the beginning sounds in spoken words. For this activity, the teacher would do the following:

• Select several pictures of objects that either do or do not start with the sound of the letter that is the focus of instruction. Avoid objects that start with the target sound but not with the letter. Also avoid objects that start with the letter but not the sound that is being targeted (e.g., *shoe* starts with *s* but not with the /sss/ sound; *America* starts with *A* but does not have either of the commonly taught sounds of *A*).
• Name each object and have the children decide whether it starts with the sound of the target letter.
• Have the children place all pictures that start with the target letter under a printed version of the letter.
• Later, when the children know several letter sounds, have them sort groups of pictures according to the initial letter in the word. They might use a sorting board such as the one illustrated in Figure 5.5 (p. 95), with letters heading the columns rather than pictures.

"What's My Beginning Letter?"

This activity helps prepare the children to effectively apply their letter–sound knowledge in writing. Rather than thinking about multiple aspects of the writing process, they can concentrate on thinking about what letter to use to spell the first sound in a word. In this activity the teacher would do the following:

• Give children three or four letters for which they are learning the letter sounds.

• Hold up a picture, name it, and ask the children to find the beginning letter of the word. Each child should be allowed enough time to pick out her letter before the other children give their responses. (The teacher would ask the children to keep their choices private until everyone has decided which letter to select.)

• Remind children who need them to use the key words by saying something like this: "Think of the sound that you hear at the beginning of the word I say and look at the pictures of our key words (pointing to an available display) and think about which one starts with the same sound as the word I said. Then look at the letter that goes with the picture, and you'll know which letter to choose."

• As the children become more proficient with this exercise, the teacher might ask them to write the beginning letter for the word on a piece of paper or on a whiteboard instead of picking the letter from a set of alternatives (e.g., "If I wanted to write the word *tub*, what letter would I write first?"). Having the children write the letters is a more challenging task and translates more directly into writing.

KEEP IN MIND It is also important to note that, if we want children to make good use of key words, we need to show them how to use them (perhaps by thinking aloud) on several occasions. It is also important to:

• Provide them with guided practice in using the key words.
• Encourage them to use the key words during both reading and writing.
• Notice when they use the key words spontaneously and explicitly praise them for doing so (e.g., "I saw Sara look up at our key words when she wasn't sure what sound that *W* made. What good thinking, Sara!").

In order to provide every child in an instructional group with the opportunity to do her own thinking, teachers have found it useful to provide the children with "offices" in which to work. Such an office is constructed from two manila folders stapled together in such a way that, when opened and set on the table, they form a three-sided enclosure in which each child can work.

Strategic Emergent Reading

To help them understand how letters can help them identify unfamiliar words, children need instruction and guided practice in applying their letter–sound knowledge in puzzling through words encountered in text. To address this need, the teacher might do the following:

- Explain to children that they are learning about the sounds of letters because the letters will help them figure out words when they are reading.
- Engage the children in reading emergent-level texts that highlight the letter under study.
- In reading these texts, explicitly model how to use the letters in combination with other available clues for word identification. For example, if the text says *I saw a mouse* and is accompanied by a picture of a mouse-like critter, the teacher might say something like this: "Hmm, that's a puzzling word. I know it's going to start with an /mmm/ sound because I see that letter *m* at the beginning. In the picture I see a rat or a squirrel or something. But I know it must be something that starts with /mmm/. What could that word be?"

As the children engage in either shared or supported reading, encourage them to use the letter sounds they know to try to anticipate the beginning sound in an upcoming word.

Emergent Level Texts

Emergent texts are those designed to enable children to get a sense of the reading process but that do not require them to read in a conventional way. Such texts usually include repetitive language and pictures that closely parallel the print. Some emergent-level texts provide opportunities to focus on particular letters (see *Monster Mop* in Figure 6.4, p. 116).

Sound Boxes

Elkonin boxes, described in Chapter 5, can be used to reinforce letter–sound associations. The children are given a counter or a letter tile with the focal letter on it. Then the teacher dictates words, one at a time, and the children decide whether they hear the sound of the focal letter at the beginning or end of the word, and they place the marker in the appropriate box.

Writing Helper

During shared writing activities, as the teacher writes, she should invite the children to help by saying which letter should be written for the beginning of particular words. For example, if the teacher is writing a caption for a picture a child has drawn, the teacher might ask the child to say what the first letter would be for words that start with letter sounds that the child has learned. Again, it is important to remind children to use the key words they have learned for a particular letter sound if they cannot immediately recall the letter that represents the sound.

Personal Dictionaries (Appropriate for Kindergarten)

In our kindergarten intervention groups, each child developed her own personal dictionary that contained a page for each letter of the alphabet and the associated key words that were used in the classroom.

As the children learned the sound for each of the letters, they put pictures of things that start with that letter on the appropriate page in the dictionary. To save time, the children were given several pictures that had been cut from newspapers, magazines, old phonics books, etc., and told to select a few to paste into their picture dictionaries. (Note that in intervention settings, time for drawing and coloring should be strictly limited so as to fully capitalize on the intensity of the small instructional grouping.)

The child may want to label some of the pictures that she puts in the dictionary. Because the dictionary is a long-term project and because it is in book form (and, therefore, may be considered "published"), the spelling that appears in the book should be conventional. To accomplish this, in a small-group setting individual children, supported by the teacher, might work out the spelling of the word on a piece of scrap paper and then each child can copy the conventionally spelled picture label into her dictionary. Some children also enjoy copying words that start with a given letter onto the appropriate page of their dictionary by referring to a published children's dictionary. As the children's literacy skills progress, the captions for the pictures can become longer and include some of the high-frequency words that the children are learning.

The personal dictionaries should represent an ongoing project for the children. The goal should not be to fill up the entire page on the day that page is begun. Rather, the child should be encouraged to add entries over time. These dictionaries can be sent home with the children at the end of kindergarten with the invitation to continue to add pictures over the course of the summer. This may encourage the children to continue to think about the relationships between the sounds in spoken words and the letters in printed words.

Games for Reinforcing Letter Sounds

A variety of simple games for reinforcing letter–sound knowledge can be redesigned to help reinforce letter–sound associations:

- *Letter bingo.* Each playing card has letters on it, and the caller says sounds.
- *Picture bingo.* Each playing card has pictures beginning with particular sounds, and the caller says letter names.
- *Picture post office.* A "post office" is set up with three or four "mail slots," each identified with a letter. The children have cards to mail. Each card contains a picture whose name begins with one of the letters on the post office slots. The

children can check their own accuracy if the correct pictures are pasted into the box under each slot.

- *Parking lot.* The parking lot director (teacher) names objects, and the children park their cars on the letter that comes at the beginning of the word named.
- *"I spy* (with my little eye something that begins with the letter __"). The children are given the first letter in a word and perhaps some meaning-based clue. They are encouraged to guess the word. When they offer guesses that are wide of the mark, there should be discussion about why their guesses don't fit the clues.

Useful Resource

Words Their Way, by Bear et al. (2008) contains an abundance of appealing games and activities that provide practice with letter sounds.

EVALUATING AND DOCUMENTING CHILDREN'S PROGRESS IN LETTER–SOUND KNOWLEDGE

Periodically, teachers might opt to use a formal early literacy assessment to document children's skills with respect to letter sounds. For ongoing documentation, teachers can observe and record children's proficiency with letter sounds, as well as other aspects of alphabet knowledge, informally through instructional interactions. To qualify as proficient, a child needs to be able to quickly and reliably provide the sound for a particular letter and/or identify the letter that represents a particular sound.

The group snapshot for alphabet knowledge (Figure 6.7, p. 125, in Chapter 6) can be used to document the progress of children within a group in letter recognition and identification, letter formation, and letter sounds.

CHAPTER 8

The Alphabetic Principle and the Alphabetic Code

In order to progress as readers and writers, children need to understand how to use the alphabetic code to decipher printed words. In the previous chapter we discussed teaching letter–sound relationships. In this chapter we focus on ways to help children learn how to apply that knowledge. Children develop proficiency with alphabetic coding at different rates, and depending on the materials they read and the instruction they receive, they learn about different aspects of the alphabetic code in different sequences. The ISA is not tied to a particular curriculum. Therefore, although in what follows we suggest a sequence for teaching about aspects of the code and provide a rationale for that sequence, we recognize that the curricula in place will play a large role in determining how instruction proceeds. In this and the next chapter, we offer approaches to helping children to develop various decoding and spelling skills but stress that the order in which particular skills are taught and practiced will, to a great extent, be determined by what the children already know and by the materials that they will be reading. In other words, *the sequence in which we present the skills is not necessarily the sequence in which the skills should be taught.*

In this chapter we describe instructional activities that help children develop a conceptual understanding that the letters in printed words represent the sounds in spoken words and to understand how to apply this insight in emergent reading and writing. We then discuss ways to further the development of skill with decoding (reading) and encoding (writing) by teaching children about consonant digraphs, consonant blends, short and long vowels, and vowel digraphs. In Chapter 9 we discuss teaching children how to use larger units of print in reading and spelling words.

EARLY DEVELOPMENT OF SKILL IN USING THE ALPHABETIC CODE

Grouping and Pacing

The instruction described in this section is appropriate for children who know at least a few letter sounds and who are able to attend to the beginning sounds in spoken words. These skills generally develop in kindergarten. Older children who do not yet demonstrate these skills will benefit from instruction designed to promote phonemic awareness (Chapter 5) and knowledge of letters and their sounds (Chapters 6 and 7).

Sequence of Development

Generally, understanding of the alphabetic principle and skill with the alphabetic code develop gradually and in a predictable sequence. The sequence tends to parallel the sequence described for phonemic awareness:

1. Beginning letters and sounds
2. Ending letters and sounds
3. Middle letters and larger orthographic units (chunks)

Therefore, in teaching children about the alphabetic principle, we begin by engaging them in making (building), reading, and writing words that involve changes only in the beginning letter (e.g., *bat, mat, fat,* cat). These activities are useful both for introducing the alphabetic principle and for giving children practice with the letter sounds they are learning. Once the children appear to be proficient with beginning letters, we work on the ending sounds in written words, once again using word building, word reading, and written spelling activities. When children are proficient with reading and spelling words that require changes just at the beginning or end, they are prepared to attend to the middle of words. Ultimately, they need to process larger orthographic units, as is discussed in Chapter 9.

TEACHING THE CONCEPT OF THE ALPHABETIC PRINCIPLE: BEGINNING LETTERS

Materials needed: Three or four letters for which the children know the sounds and a phonogram that, when combined with the individual letters, will produce several words.

Sample Instructional Dialogue

TEACHER: When we read, the letters tell us what sounds to make. They help us figure out what each word is.

(*Displays the word* it.) This little word is *it*. I can put a letter in front of the word *it*, and I will have a new word.

(*Puts an* s *in front of* it.) When I put an *s* here, *it* becomes *sssssit*. The *s* makes the /sssss/ sound, and when I put /sssss/ and /it/ together, it makes the word *sssit*.

(*Displays the letters* f, b, *and* l.) I can change *sssit* to *ffffit* by changing just one letter. *Ssssit* and *fffffit* have different sounds at the beginning of the word, so I need to change the beginning letter. So, I'll take the *s* away. Now the word is *it* again. I need to put another letter in front of *it* to make the word *ffffit*.

What letter makes the sound that you hear at the beginning of *fffffit*?

(*Reinforces.*) Yes, the letter *effff* makes the /fffff/ sound.

OR

(*Scaffolds.*) If you are not sure what sound each of these letters make, you can look at your key words. Which letter has a key word that starts like *ffffit*?

(*Models, if necessary.*) If I am not sure what letter to use to make *ffffit*, I can look at my key words to find one that starts like *ffffit*. I've only got three letters here, so that makes it easy. I'll start with the letter *b*. I look up at the key-word chart and I find the *b*. The key word for *b* is *ball*. /b/b/b/ is the sound at the beginning of ball. That is not the same as the beginning sound in *ffffit*. So *b* is not the letter that I need. Next, I'll try *f*. I go to my key words and find the *f* and I see that the key word for *f* is *fan*. *Fffffan* and *ffffffit* have the same sound at the beginning. So *f* is the letter I need.

Guided Practice: Changing Beginning Letters to Build, Read, and Spell Words

Once the concept of the alphabetic principle has been introduced, children should be provided with guided practice in applying it. Three practice activities are used: word building, word reading, and written spelling. The teacher should explicitly demonstrate the task before asking the children to do it.

Word Building

This is the easiest of the practice activities and so should be used first. The children are given a phonogram (e.g., *it, an, op*) that can be used to form several different words. The teacher names the phonogram and then asks the children to make words by changing just the beginning letter. For example, the teacher might use letter tiles to show the word *make* (see Figure 8.1) and say "This is the word *make.* If I take the *m* away, all I have left is *ake.* If I add one of these other letters, I can make a new word. If I put a *b* in front of *ake,* I have the word *bake.*"

Once the process has been demonstrated, the children can be asked to form the words that the teacher dictates. As needed, they should be encouraged to refer to the key words that have been taught to help them recall the sounds for the letters. Word building is relatively easy for the children because the number of letters that might be used to form the new word is limited and the key words are readily available for reference.

Word Reading

In this activity the teacher changes the beginning letter in the word and asks the children to read the new word. This task is somewhat more challenging than the word-building activity because the children need to recall both the sound of the beginning letter and the sound of the phonogram, and then blend the sounds together.

Written Spelling

In this activity children are asked to spell the words they have been building and reading. For children at this point in development, the phonogram would be left in view and they would be expected to refer to it in order to properly spell the word dictated by the teacher. Their major task is to analyze the word spoken by the teacher and then to decide which letter to use to represent the beginning sound in the word.

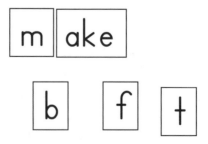

FIGURE 8.1. Word building with *ake.*

The Role of Phonograms and Word Families in Early Decoding and Encoding Activities

In the activities described above, we use phonograms to form multiple words in a word family by changing just the beginning letter. In these early activities it is unlikely that the children will actually learn the phonogram that is the central component of the word family because most of their attention is drawn to the beginning of the word, which is the only part that changes. The goal in the activities that focus on beginning letters is for the children to become facile with using the beginning letters to read and spell words.

Ultimately, however, it is important that children learn that words containing the same sound pattern often share the same phonogram. Once a child learns a number of frequently occurring phonograms and understands how they can be generalized, he will be better able to efficiently analyze and identify unfamiliar words. A more thorough discussion of teaching to promote the effective use of phonograms for reading and writing words in a family is provided in the next chapter.

Independent Practice: Real or Nonsense?

Once children have learned to build and read words by changing the beginning letter, additional independent practice can be provided by giving children a phonogram and several individual letters and asking them to make two lists of words using that phonogram: real words and nonsense words. Teachers sometimes use a letter slide for this activity to encourage the children to be a bit more systematic (see Figure 8.2).

Strategic Emergent Reading and Writing

It is easy to assume that children understand the connections between phonics activities and literacy—because they are so obvious to us! However, such assumptions should not be made. It is important to explicitly help children understand the relationship between decoding and constructing the meaning of printed language. Some suggestions for helping children to make these connections while reading to and with them are provided below.

To promote word solving during shared reading, the teacher might:

• Periodically point to individual words in the text and draw the children's attention to the beginning letter. Ask them to think about with what sound the word will start.

• Identify a character or object in the picture and ask the children to try to find the printed word for it. ("Can you find the word *bear* on this page? What letter do you think it will start with?") In order to find the word, the children must first

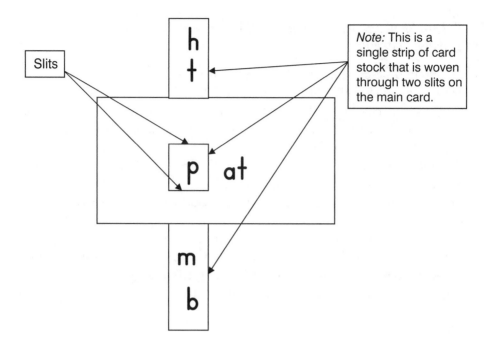

FIGURE 8.2. Example of a letter slide.

attend to the initial sound in the word, think of what letter represents that sound, and finally, examine the printed words to find one that starts with that letter.

To promote effective sound spelling during shared writing, the teacher might:

• Encourage the children to participate in isolating the beginning sound in the word that is about to be written and then deciding what letter should be used to represent that sound.

• Write the first letter of the upcoming word and ask the children to figure out what the word will probably be, based on information provided by the context and by the first letter.

TEACHING THE CONCEPT OF THE ALPHABETIC PRINCIPLE: ENDING LETTERS

Grouping and Pacing

In the ISA, teachers continue working on single-consonant sounds using initial consonant substitution with phonograms until children are quite facile with the sounds for most of the consonant letters. When children know these sounds well, and when they are able to attend to the ending sounds in spoken words (i.e., sort

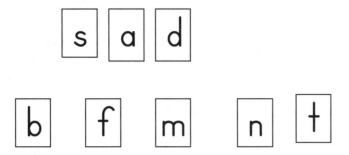

FIGURE 8.3. Word building beginning and ending sounds.

by ending sound), they are ready to learn to build, read, and spell words by making changes to both the beginnings and ends of words.

Materials needed: Six or seven consonants for which the children know the sounds and a single vowel (see Figure 8.3).

Sample Instructional Dialogue

TEACHER: When we read, the letters tell us what sounds to make. We have already practiced reading words with different beginning sounds. Now we are going to learn to pay attention to the letters at the ends of words too. This will help us figure out even more words when we read. (*Displays the word* sad.) This is the word *sad*. I can change one letter and make the word *mad*. Watch, I take the *s* away and put an *m* at the beginning, and that makes the word *mad*. Now I will change *mad* to *man*. I need to think about the sounds in *mmmmaaaannnn* and decide which letter I need to change. *Mmmmaaannnnn* has an /mmmm/ sound at the beginning, so the *m* needs to stay. So, I'm going to think about the end of the word *mmmmaaannnn*. I hear the /nnnn/ sound at the end of the word *mannnnnn*—so I'll need to change that ending letter to the letter that makes the /nnnn/ sound—that's the letter *n*. [The teacher might elongate the pronunciation of the name of the letter *n* to emphasize the /nnnn/.]

Guided Practice: Changing Beginning and Ending Letters to Build and Read Words

Following this initial introduction, the teacher would engage the children in collaboratively making (building) several additional words by changing just one letter at a time. Thus, the teacher might ask the children to change *man* to *mad*, *mad* to *bad, bad* to *bat, bat* to *fat, fat* to *fan*, and so on.

In subsequent lessons the children would be engaged in word building, word reading, and written spelling of words in which changes are made at either the beginning or end of each word to form the new word.

Independent Practice: Making Words

Once children have learned to build and read words by changing the beginning and ending letters, additional independent practice can be provided by giving children a single vowel, for which the sound has been taught, and several individual letters. The children would be asked to make a list of as many real words as they can make, keeping the vowel in the middle.

Strategic Emergent Reading and Writing

Children who are able to build words by making requested changes to both the beginning and ending sounds/letters are ready to apply that knowledge while reading and writing. Thus, in addition to drawing the children's attention to the beginning letters as they puzzle over unfamiliar words, they should be encouraged to attend to the ending letters as well to confirm their attempt at identifying the word.

Strategic Reading: An Example

We once observed a kindergartner reading an emergent-level text with a picture of a log laying on the ground. The text read "Look at the log." The child read it as "Look at the land." Because the teacher had just begun to draw the children's attention to the ending sounds in words, she was able to reinforce what the child had done right ("Good thinking, we do see land in that picture and the word does begin with *l*") and to extend the child's thinking about how to use print ("Remember, we've been talking about how we need to look all the way through to the end of the word to make sure that we think about the sounds that the ending letters make").

Similarly, children who are beginning to attend to ending sounds in isolated word-study activities should be encouraged to participate in analyzing and spelling the final sounds in words both during shared writing and in their own independent writing. Teacher modeling of this more complete analysis of the printed word is, of course, important.

KEEP IN MIND When a child hesitates over reading or spelling a word, it is appropriate to scaffold his attempts by referring to the key words that are being used to support letter-sound learning. For example, the teacher might say:

- "If you can't remember what sound that letter makes, check your key words."
- "If you are not sure what letter will make the sound that you hear at the end of that word, check your key words."

The purpose of this type of scaffolding is to build independence in reading and spelling unfamiliar words.

LATER DEVELOPMENT OF SKILL IN USING THE ALPHABETIC CODE

Grouping and Pacing

The activities described in this section are intended for children who

- Know the names of most of the letters and the sounds of most of the consonants.
- Can build and read words using initial and final consonant substitution.
- Are at least beginning to be able to segment single-syllable words into their individual phonemes.
- When writing, can represent the prominent consonants with an acceptable letter and are beginning to include vowel markers (i.e., they frequently represent long vowels with the vowel letter; e.g., CAK for *cake*), and they occasionally represent short vowel sounds with a letter that is unconventional (e.g., PAT or PNT for *pet*) or they don't represent short vowel sounds at all.

Some children may reach this point in kindergarten or even before. Others will be in first grade before they are ready to focus on the aspects of the alphabetic code discussed in this section. Further, some children will move very quickly through the content of this section, whereas others will move more slowly and will need many more repetitions and reinforcements. *It is important to remember that education is about teaching children, not about teaching the curriculum regardless of what the children are learning.*

Assessment for Grouping

One of the most efficient ways of evaluating children's skills with the alphabetic code is through an evaluation of their written spelling. Bear et al. (2008) provide developmental spelling inventories that can help teachers identify groups of children who have similar understandings about the workings of the alphabetic code. Once such groups are identified, instruction can be more explicitly targeted to what the children in the groups are ready to learn.

Consonant Combinations

Consonant Digraphs

When two letters together represent a single sound, the letter combination is called a digraph. Consonant digraphs include *th, sh, ch, wh, ck, ph, gh*, etc. For most of the digraphs, the letters do not make their most common sound (e.g., in *th* the /t/ and /h/ sounds are not heard). The digraphs *th, sh, ch, ck*, and *wh* occur more frequently and therefore should have a higher priority for instruction than *ph* and *gh*. Generally, only one digraph would be introduced on any given day.

Two Sounds for th

The *th* digraph makes two sounds. For one, the vocal chords vibrate a bit as the sound is pronounced (e.g., the /th/ sound in the word *the*), whereas for the other pronunciation the vocal chords do not vibrate (e.g., the /th/ sound in the word *thing*).

In teaching a digraph, the teacher might show the children several words that include the digraph, read the words to them, and draw their attention to the fact that the two letters go together to make just one sound. For digraphs such as *th* and *ch*, it is important to point out that the sound made is different from the sound that either of the letters makes alone. The children should be encouraged to listen to each of the words and to isolate and say the beginning sound.

For use in word-building and word-reading activities, the digraph should be treated as a single decoding element (see Figure 8.4). Some teachers do this by printing the digraph on a card, others tape two letter tiles together. Using the letter cards in Figure 8.4, the children might be asked to change *tap* to *chap*, *chap* to *chat*, *chat* to *mat*, *mat* to *pat*, *pat* to *pack*, and so on.

Consonant Blends

In a consonant blend the sounds of two or three consonants are blended together, but the individual sounds of each of the consonants are still fairly discernable (*cl*, *cr*, *bl*, *br*, *fr*, *scr*, *sm*, etc.). In the ISA, we teach blending as a process rather than teaching every possible consonant blend as a unit because there are far too many blends.

WHEN ARE CHILDREN READY TO LEARN ABOUT CONSONANT BLENDS?

The concept of blending consonants can be introduced when children know the sounds of most, if not all, of the single consonants and can use those consonant sounds in decoding and spelling single-syllable words. At the very least, children

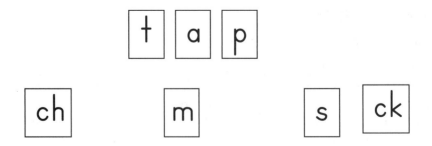

FIGURE 8.4. Word building with digraphs.

need to know the sounds of the individual consonants in the blends on which they are working.

ORDER OF DIFFICULTY FOR CONSONANT BLENDS

Some blends appear to be easier for children to analyze and read than others. As with all instruction, it is helpful to begin with the clearest, easiest examples and to move to more challenging items once the children are facile with the easier ones.

- *Easiest blends.* Because it is easier to draw children's attention to consonant sounds that can be elongated (stretched) without distortion (e.g., *s, m, n, f, r, l*) than to stop consonants (e.g., *p, b, d,* hard *c* [as in cat], and hard *g* [as in *goat*]), it makes sense to start teaching the blending process with a blend in which both consonants are stretchable (*sm, fr, sl, fl, sn,* etc.). The specific blends selected for instruction should be determined by the reading the children will do in the near future (the same day or the next day). Work with a variety of blends composed of stretchable consonants should continue until the children are fairly proficient with them.
- *More difficult blends.* Consonant blends that have a combination of stretchable and stop consonants (*pr, br, bl, cl, sc, st,* etc.) are somewhat more challenging because it is difficult to draw children's attention to the stop consonant portion of the blend.
- *Most difficult blends.* Some of the most challenging consonant blends in the initial position are *dr* and *tr.* These are challenging because the stop consonants *d* and *t* are not easily detected in these blends due to coarticulation. That is, because of the way that the mouth naturally positions itself to make the /r/ sound as it is articulating the /d/ or /t/ sound, the sounds of the *d* and *t* are distorted. (This is the reason why a child might spell the word *drip* with the letters *jrip* or *jip* or spell *truck* with the letters *chrk*.

Confusing Writing System

We once observed a kindergarten child reading an emergent-level book about a toy bear. The story unfolded something like this. "My bear can sit. My bear can swing. My bear can swim. My bear can dry." The child read the book quite comfortably until the very last page, which showed the bear hanging on a clothesline. The child puzzled over the last word for a bit and then said, "It's not *dry* because it doesn't start with a *j*."

Some of the most challenging consonant blends in the final position are those in which a nasal consonant (i.e., *m* or *n*) precedes a stop consonant (e.g., *t, p*). These are difficult because children use changes in mouth position as clues to the sounds in words. The subtle changes in mouth position when the nasal consonant is present or absent are hard to detect. This can be experienced by saying the words *wet* and *went* or *rap* and *ramp* and carefully attending to the various parts of the mouth that are involved in the pronunciation. Most would agree that the mouth movements for each pair of words are very similar.

Note

In pronouncing a "nasal consonant," air flows through the nose (nasal passage) instead of through the mouth. *M* and *n* are the only nasal consonants.

TEACHING CHILDREN TO READ AND WRITE WORDS WITH CONSONANT BLENDS

Word building, word reading, and written spelling can be used to teach and practice the use of consonant blends. Starting with word building, the teacher might begin by modeling the formation of words with blends in the initial position.

Step 1: Phoneme Blending		
Teacher	What the teacher says	Comments on the activity
Says:	"Many of the words that we read have two consonant letters together, and each letter makes its own sound. When we see these words, we need to think of the sound made by each letter and then blend them together. We'll start by practicing blending with Stretch [or whatever character is used in phoneme analysis activities]. Stretch is going to say some words one sound at a time, and you need to figure out what Stretch is saying. We are going to work with words that have two consonant letters together."	After this introduction, the teacher articulates the sounds in several words that contain (stretchable) consonant blends. After the sounds for each word are articulated, the children attempt to blend them to form a whole word. Ideally, the children should be able to do this type of blending before they are asked to do the more challenging task of looking at the letters, thinking about the sounds they make, and then blending them to form words. By the time children are learning about consonant blends, they shouldn't need the picture choices to successfully complete the phoneme blending. However, if they struggle, continued work on phoneme blending with words containing consonant blends is warranted, perhaps with picture choices if necessary to support the development of this skill.
Words with two stretchable consonants for phoneme blending: *flake, snow, smile, frog, fly, slide, smoke, sleep, flat, free, etc.*		

Step 2: Decoding of Consonant Blends (Using the *ip* Phonogram)

Teacher	What the teacher says	Comments on the activity
Displays and says:	"Some of the words we are going to make today have consonant blends in them. That's when there are two consonants, like *s* and *l*, next to each other. When you read words like that, you make the sound of each letter and then blend them together."	The letters to be used in word-building activities are displayed. All of the consonants to be used in the initial consonant blends are stretchable.
Displays phonogram and says:	"All of the words we are going to make now have these two letters: *i* and *p*. When they are together in a word, they sound like this— /ip/. There are a lot of words in the /ip/ word family. Let's make some words with /ip/."	The *ip* phonogram can be printed on a single card rather than on two separate letter cards.
Says:	"If I put an *l* in front of /ip/, what word would it make?"	The teacher places an *l* in front of *ip* for all children in the group to see.
Provides feedback:	"Right, the word would be *lip*."	If the children cannot respond accurately at this step, they are not ready to work on consonant blends. They need continued work with single consonants.
Demonstrates blending consonants:	"Watch, now I am going to put an *s* in front of *lip*. So I have the /sss/ sound and then *lip*. /ssss/ /llllliiipppp/—when I put them together, it will sound like . . . *slip*."	The teacher should move through these steps slowly so that the children can see what she is doing.
Removes one consonant from the blend and says:	"Now, if I take the *s* away, I would have . . . *lip* again."	The teacher should pause to give the children the opportunity to predict what the word will be when the *s* is removed.
Adds the *s* again and says:	"If I put the *s* back on, it would be . . . *slip*."	Again, the teacher should pause briefly before saying the word *slip* so that the children have the opportunity to think of it on their own.
Removes the *l* and says:	"Now, what will happen to the word *slip* if I take the *l* away?"	The teacher should, again, give the children enough "think time" before answering the question.

Teacher	What the teacher says	Comments on the activity
Adds the *l* back and asks:	"Now, what word do I have if I put the *l* back again?"	
Explains:	"So, when we see a word with two consonants together, usually we will need to make the sound of each consonant and then blend them together to try to figure out what the word is."	
Reminds children of exceptions:	"There are some times when this doesn't work. You already know, for example, that when *t* and *h* are together, you usually don't hear the sound of either the *t* or the *h*; instead, you hear the special sound that *t* and *h* make together."	The teacher might remind the children of any other consonant digraphs that have already been taught.

Step 3: Word Building

Teacher	What the teacher says	Comments on the activity
Presents letter and phonogram cards and says:	"We are going to make some words in the /ip/ word family. You need to listen carefully to the words I say and put letters at the beginning of the word so that you make the word I say. Sometimes you'll need one letter at the beginning and sometimes you'll need two letters."	The teacher should provide the children with the phonogram and the letters needed to make all of the words in the family.
Dictates words in the set:	"Make the word sip." "Change sip to lip." (Refer to the sample word set in Figure 8.5, p. 154.)	The teacher watches as children attempt to build the words and provides needed scaffolding, which may include elongating sounds, reminding the children to use the key words, etc.
Provides feedback and reinforcement:	Sample comments: • "I like the way you stretched that word when you were trying to figure out what letter[s] you needed." • "I noticed you looking at the key words when you weren't sure what letter to use."	The teacher would continue to work with the children on sets of words that include consonant blends comprising stretchable consonants until the children appear to be fairly proficient. With slight modifications, the sample comments provided to the left could be used as scaffolds (e.g., "Stretch that word to figure out what letter you need").

Step 4: Word Reading
The teacher forms words with one or both elements of the consonant blends and asks the children to read them. Assistance is provided, as needed.

Step 5: Written Spelling
The teacher presents the phonogram to be used for word formation, tells the children that all words will be in that word family, and then dictates words with one or both elements of the consonant blend that is the focus of the activity. The children write the words on a piece of paper or on a white board.

For initial instruction with consonant blends, we have found it helpful to use groups of words that can be formed with one or the other of the single consonants in the blend as well as a combination of the two (or three) consonants. Often during initial instruction, we use a family of words in which the phonogram remains constant, and the children focus on changing and modifying the elements of the blend. Once the children can do this easily, changes in other parts of the word are made. Some examples of families of words that might be used for instruction on consonant blends are provided in Figure 8.5.

Vowels

Learning to decode and encode vowel sounds is significantly more complicated than learning to decode and encode consonant sounds. This is true for several reasons, including the following:

- Within a word or syllable, the sound of the vowel tends to be influenced by (coarticulated with) the surrounding consonants.
- Most of the "rules" for representing vowel sounds in print are quite unreliable. For example, the "silent-*e* rule" only works about 50% of the time (Clymer, 1963).
- The printed representations of many vowel sounds, other than the short vowels, are complex. It generally takes more than one letter to represent the vowel sound. Sometimes the two letters are separated by one or more consonants, as in *cake* and *time*. Sometimes the two letters represent more than one vowel sound. For example, the *ea* combination is used to represent the long-*e* in *bead*, the short-*e* in *bread*, and the long-*a* in *great*. Moreover, sometimes the same vowel sound is spelled in many different ways. For example, all of these words have the long-*a* sound: *cake, great, weigh, play, rain, prey.*

Because of this complexity and unreliability, in the ISA we teach the children to be *flexible* in decoding vowels. We teach that when they encounter a vowel, they should be prepared to try different pronunciations if their first attempt does not

	Initial word	**Change to**	**Change to**	**Change to**	**Change to**	**Change to**
Easiest blends (both initial consonants are stretchable)	sip	lip	slip	sip	lip	slip
	lake	fake	flake	fake	lake	flake
	mock	sock	smock	mock	sock	smock
	sag	nag	snag	nag	sag	snag
More difficult blends (one stretchable and one stop consonant)	boom	loom	bloom	loom	boom	bloom
	camp	ramp	cramp	ramp	camp	cramp
	gain	rain	grain	rain	gain	grain
	pay	lay	play	lay	pay	play
	pill	sill	spill	sill	pill	spill
	sack	tack	stack	tack	sack	stack
	tick	sick	stick	sick	tick	stick
DR and TR blends	dip	rip	drip	rip	dip	drip
	dug	rug	drug	rug	dug	drug
	tack	rack	track	rack	tack	track
	tail	rail	trail	rail	tail	trail
	tap	rap	trap	rap	tap	trap
	tip	rip	trip	rip	tip	trip
Three-letter blends	sip	tip	rip	trip	strip	trip
	lit	sit	pit	spit	split	lit
	sand	stand	strand	stand	sand	stand
	seam	team	steam	stream	steam	seam

FIGURE 8.5. Word sets for practicing consonant blends.

result in a real word or a word that makes sense in the context of what they are reading.

Instruction for Short Vowels and Long Vowels with the Vowel–Consonant–e Spelling Pattern

To help children develop flexibility with vowels, we teach the most common spellings for the two most common sounds when we begin to teach about a given vowel. That is, we teach the long and the short sounds for the vowel on the first day that we begin to work on sounds for that letter. This is not as challenging for the children as it may initially seem because, by the time we teach the sounds for a particular vowel, they already know the name of the letter and may have already been using the vowel letter in their writing. It would not be unusual, for example, for a kindergartner to use the letters *A* and *T* to spell the word *ate*, or the letters *B* and *I* to spell the word *buy*. Thus, children generally have a sense that the letter *A* can be used to represent the long-*a* sound before we begin to teach the vowel sounds. From our perspective, it makes sense to build from this knowledge and teach one additional association for each vowel (i.e., the short vowel sound). Moreover, over the many years that we have recommended this approach to teaching vowel sounds, teachers have consistently reported success.

A suggested order for introduction of the vowel sounds is provided below. This order is based on the similarities between and among the vowel sounds (the vowel sounds that are most different from one another are taught first) and on the usage frequency of the vowels. Teachers who are using a basal or phonics series obviously should follow the progression recommended by that series for teaching short vowel sounds. However, since many published programs teach all of the short vowels before the long vowels, it will be necessary to deviate somewhat from the program guidelines in order to teach for flexibility.

The suggested order is as follows:

• Long and short sounds for *a*, using long-*a* words spelled with the silent-*e* pattern (as in *make* and *late*). This pattern is sometimes referred to as the vowel–consonant–*e* pattern and is abbreviated as VCe. (The spelling pattern that characterizes many one-syllable, short-vowel words is the consonant–vowel–consonant [CVC] pattern.)

• Long and short sounds for *i*, using long-*i* words spelled with the VCe pattern.

• Review of long and short sounds for both *a* and *i*.

• Long and short sounds for *o*, using long-*o* words spelled with the VCe pattern.

• Review of long- and short-*a*, -*i*, and -*o* sounds.

• Long and short sounds for *e*, using long-*e* words spelled with the double-*e* pattern (because there are very few long-*e* words spelled with the VCe pattern).

- Review long and short vowel sounds and spellings for *a, i, o,* and *e.*
- Long- and short-*u* sounds, with the long-*u* spelled with the VCe pattern. Note that it is important to initially introduce long-*u* words that have a true long-*u* (*mute* and *cube*) rather than words with an /oo/ sound, as in *toot* (and *tube, rude, dude, blue,* etc). Of course, the later type of long-*u* words are quite common and should ultimately be included in practice activities.
- Review vowel sounds and spellings taught thus far.

Ideally, as each vowel is taught, the children would be provided with enough practice to allow them to really learn the sounds for the vowel and how the sounds are often represented in print. The children should not be rushed on to the next vowels in the sequence before they are fairly secure with those that have already been taught.

Lists of words that can be used for teaching and practicing each of the vowel sounds are provided in Figure 8.6. Below we describe procedures for teaching about the vowels.

Note

We try to avoid referring to the silent-*e* rule because the silent *e* is far from entirely reliable and therefore does not really constitute a "rule." Many one-syllable words that end in *e* do not have the long vowel sound (e.g., *have, come, give, one, some, live*). Some teachers refer to the *e* at the end as a clue that the other vowel might say its name.

Teaching Children to Decode and Encode Long and Short Vowel Sounds

Below we illustrate the process we use for teaching about the long and the short sounds of a vowel simultaneously. We begin with a brief overview of the process and then provide a more detailed explanation in the form of a sample script for each step. The instructional routine is abbreviated once the first couple of vowels have been taught.

- *Locating vowel sounds.* This involves having the children listen for the vowel sounds to be taught and deciding whether the sound occurs at the beginning, in the middle, or at the end of given words. The purpose here is to ensure that the children are able to notice and isolate the vowel sounds.
- *Comparing and contrasting vowel sounds.* This is a sound-sorting activity in which the children listen to spoken words and sort them into long and short vowel groups. Some teachers use pictures as an initial step in the sorting process. The comparing and contrasting step is, again, intended to attune children to the sounds of the vowels before they begin to attend to the written representations of those sounds.

Long and short *a* (*m, a, t, e, f, d,* *s, p, c, n, k, g,* *h, r*)	Long and short *i* (*b, i, t, k, h, m,* *d, e, r, w, n, p,* *f, s, l*)	Long and short *o* (*m, o, m, p, e,* *d, r, b, s, t, n, c,* *h, p, l*)	Long and short *e* (*s, e, e, d, f,* *w, k, n, t, m, b,* *r, p*)	Long and short *u* (*c, u, b, e, t, j,* *m, s, f, b, g, h*)
mat	bit	mom	seed	cube
mate	bite	mop	feed	cub
fate	kite	mope	fed	cut
fat	kit	mode	wed	cute
fad	hit	mod	weed	jute
fade	him	rod	week	jut
made	dim	rode	seek	but
mad	dime	robe	seen	cut
sad	time	rob	teen	cute
Sam	tide	sob	ten	mute
same	hide	sop	men	muse
tame	hid	top	met	fuse
tape	rid	tone	meet	use
tap	ride	cone	beet	us
cap	wide	con	bet	bug
cape	wine	cop	bed	hug
came	win	cope	fed	hub
cane	pin	hope	feed	cub
can	pine	hop	feet	cube
man	dine	pop	meet	tube*
mane	line	pope	met	tub
make	fine	rope	net	
take	fin	rode	need	
tame	sin	rod	seed	
game	sit	cod	weed	
gate	site	code	wed	
hate	side	cob	red	
hat	ride	lob	reel	
rat	ripe	lobe	peel	
rate	rip	lone	pen	

*Tube does not have a true long-*u* sound. Rather it is pronounced with the double-*o* sound as in *toot.* However, since the children ultimately need to learn to decode words with this spelling–sound relationship, it is fine to include it once the children are fairly secure with the more rule-based spelling–sound correspondence for long *u*.

FIGURE 8.6. Word lists for working on long and short vowel sounds. *(page 1 of 2)*

Review of *a* and *i* (*b, i, t, a, f, m, e, d, n, c, p, s, k, h*)	Review of *a, i,* and *o* (*c, o, t, a, f, i, e, n, p, d, r, b, g, w, l, k*)	Review of *a, i, o,* and *e* (*f, e, ee, i, d, a, m, b, r, o, n, w, t, g, l, h, p, k*)	Review of *a, e, i, o,* and *u* (*c, u, t, e, ee, a, p, o, i, d, k, b, t, s, n, m, f*)
bit			
bat	cot		
fat	cat	feed	cute
fate	fat	fed	cut
fame	fit	fad	cat
tame	fin	fade	cap
time	fine	made	cop
dime	pine	mad	cope
dim	pane	bad	cape
Tim	pan	bid	cap
tin	pad	bide	tap
tan	pod	ride	tip
fan	cod	rode	dip
fin	code	rod	did
fine	rode	nod	deed
mine	rod	need	did
mane	rid	weed	dip
man	ride	wed	deep
can	ripe	wet	keep
cane	rope	get	beep
cape	robe	got	bop
cap	rob	lot	top
tap	rib	let	tap
tip	rig	net	tab
sip	rag	not	cab
sap	tag	rot	cub
sat	bag	rob	cube
sit	big	robe	tube
site	bin	rope	tub
kite	win	hope	sub
kit	wine	hop	sun
hit	line	top	sin
hat	like	tap	tin
hate	lake	tape	tan
	rake	take	teen
		tame	ten
		time	men
		Tim	met
		Tom	meet
			mat
			mate
			fate
			fit

FIGURE 8.6. *(page 2 of 2)*

158

• *Explaining the silent-*e *generalization*. This involves providing an explicit explanation of how the silent *e* works. Since the silent *e* is one of the most common ways of representing the long vowel sound, it is important that children understand the generalization well.

• *Introducing the short vowel key word*. The short vowel sounds are among the hardest letter sounds for children to remember. Therefore, encouraging children to actively use the key words is important. Early on, children benefit from explicit guidance in how the key words can support their reading and writing efforts.

• *Word building*. This involves making words that the teacher dictates, using moveable letters.

• *Word reading*. This involves reading words that the teacher either writes or makes using moveable letters.

• *Written spelling*. This involves writing words dictated by the teacher.

Each of these instructional steps is elaborated more completely below:

Step 1: Sample Instructional Dialogue for Locating Vowel Sounds		
Rationale:	It is important that the children can notice the targeted vowel sounds in words. By asking them to decide whether the targeted sound comes at the beginning, middle, or end of the word, we are able to determine whether they are ready for the more challenging task of using letters to represent those sounds.	
Materials needed:	A large-print letter *A* and the key word to be used for the short sound of *A*.	
Teacher	What the teacher says	Comments on the activity
Says:	"We are going to start learning about vowel sounds. Vowels are special letters. One of the things that makes them special is that every word has to have a vowel in it. Another thing that makes vowels special is that every vowel can make more than one sound. The vowel letter that we are going to start with is the letter *a*."	
Displays letter *a* and says:	"Sometimes when there is an *a* in a word, the sound it makes is the same as its name, /ā ā ā/. Listen for the /ā ā ā/ sound at the beginning of these words: *aaaage, aaaache, aaaate, aaaape*."	The teacher elongates the long-*a* sound in each word as she says it. (*Note*: An *a* [or any vowel] with a straight line over it—*ā*—denotes the long-*a* sound. The line is called a macron.)

Says:	"Now listen for the /ā ā ā/ sound at the end of these words: *maaaay, plaaaay, saaaay.*"	The teacher elongates the long-*a* sound as she says each word.
Asks:	"Listen to this word and tell me where the /ā ā ā/ sound is—at the beginning, in the middle, or at the end: *aaaape?*"	The teacher might use Elkonin boxes as a support/scaffold to ensure that every child has an opportunity to respond.
Provides feedback:	"Yes, the /ā ā ā/ sound is at the beginning." Or: "Listen again—*aaaape*—we hear the /ā ā ā/ sound at the beginning of *aaape*. The /ā ā ā/ sound is the first sound I make when I say *aaape*."	
Continues with activity, adding new words:	*make, play, aid, tape, ace, say, shake, fame, ape, safe, tray*, etc.	The teacher says each word and provides feedback. Practice continues with various one-syllable long-*a* words until the children are fairly quick at locating the sound in words with two or three sounds.
Says:	"So far we've learned that a lot of times when there is an *A* in a word, it means we are supposed to say its name. But sometimes we are supposed to make a different sound /ă ă ă/—like the sound we hear at the beginning of the word *aaaapple* [or whatever key word is to be used]."	The word used to introduce the short vowel sound should be the key word that will be used to remind the children of the vowel's sound. The teacher should show the picture of the key word when she mentions its first sound. (*Note:* An *a* with a curved line over it—ă) denotes the short-*a* sound. The curved line is called a *breve*.)
Directs:	"Everyone say the sound of *a* that comes at the beginning of the word *aaaapple*."	
Asks:	"Now listen to the word *aaaat*. Do you hear the /ă ă ă/ sound at the beginning or at the end of the word *aaaat?*"	The teacher elongates the short-*a* sound when presenting the first couple of items.
Provides feedback:	"Yes, the /ă ă ă/ is at the beginning of the word *aaaat*." Or: "Listen again to the word *aaaaaat*. The /ă ă ă/ sound is at the beginning."	If the response is incorrect, the teacher should say the word again, elongating the vowel sound even further.

Continues:	"How about the word *maaat*? Is the /ă ă ă/ sound at the beginning, in the middle, or at the end of the word *maaat*?"	The teacher should provide practice with locating the short-*a* sound in different words until the children are facile at locating the sound in words.
Reduces support and continues:	"Where is the /ă ă ă/ sound in the word *add*?"	Ideally, the children should be able to identify the location of the vowel sound without the teacher elongating it for them. The teacher should reduce the amount of elongation as quickly as possible while still ensuring the children's success. The teacher may need to do different amounts of stretching for different children.

Additional practice words for short *a*: *cap, as, back, add, sat, mad, axe, tap, bat, sad, at, pack, act, had*, etc.

Additional practice and feedback at Step 1 should be provided until the children can easily locate the short-*a* and long-*a* sounds in spoken words.

Short-*a* with coarticulation problem: If the children can easily locate the short-*a* sound in the words listed above, have them try some short-*a* words where the vowel sound is altered somewhat by the nasal consonant. Examples of these words include *am, ran, an, and*. Although these are not good examples for introductory purposes, ultimately the children need to categorize these words as containing the short-*a* vowel sound.

Step 2: Sample Instructional Dialogue for Comparing and Contrasting Vowel Sounds	
Rationale:	In order to ultimately use letters to represent vowel sounds, the children need to be able to distinguish between the two sounds associated with the vowel.
Preparation:	Steps 2 and 3 should occur in the same instructional episode, so be sure to allow enough time for both.
Materials needed:	A chart with two columns, one headed by a familiar word with the long-*a* sound in the middle and one headed by a word that has a short-*a* sound in the middle. We'll use *tap* and *tape* as column headings in this example. A highlighter is also used in this activity. (*Note:* Do not use words with an *n* or an *m* following the vowel for the headings of the columns because these letters distort the sound of the vowel a bit, and this may confuse the children. All of the words used for the long-*a* column should be spelled using the silent-*e* pattern. Lists of words for these activities are provided in the Figure 8.6 (pp. 157–158).

Teacher	What the teacher says	Comments on the activity
Says:	"We are going to make a chart with words that have the /ā ā ā/ (long-*a*) sound and words that have the /ă ă ă/ (short-*a*) sound. In the first column on the chart, I have written the word *tap* and in the second column I've written the word *tape*."	If this activity occurs on a different day than Step 1, it may be helpful to have the children locate the sound of the short and long *a* in the words at the top of each column.
Points to each word as it is said:	"Now I'm going to say another word, and I want you to decide if the middle sound in the word I say sounds like the middle sound in *taaap* or if it sounds like the middle sound in *taaape*."	
Presents words:	"The first word is *maaaake*. Does the middle sound in *maaaake* sound like the middle sound in *taaaaap* or the middle sound in *taaape*?"	At least on the first couple of items, the teacher should emphasize the middle sounds in the words by elongating them. However, the goal should be to reduce or remove this scaffold as soon as the children are ready. (*Note*: If children struggle with determining in which column a word belongs, it may be necessary to revert to more focused phonemic analysis instruction before proceeding with the decoding instruction.)
Writes the word in the appropriate column as the children look on, engaging the children in the process of spelling the word as much as possible:	"What's the first sound we hear in *make*? And what letter do we need for that /mmm/ sound? And we know the middle sound is . . .? And the last sound in *make*?"	The words on the list should be conventionally spelled. So, for long vowel words, the teacher would add the *e* and say something like "In the dictionary [book] spelling for *make*, there's an *e* at the end—so we'll put that on."
Asks:	"Our next word is *cat*. Which column does *cat* go in? Does the middle sound in *cat* sound like the middle sound in *tap*? Or like the middle sound in *tape*?"	Again, if need be, the teacher should elongate the vowel sounds in the words to help children make their decisions.

Continues:	*face, cat, bake, gate, nap, dad*	The teacher says additional words, asking children to decide in which column to place each word, and engaging the children in interactive writing of the words until four or five words have been added to each column.
Says:	"Now let's read our lists and see what we notice about the letters in these words."	The teacher should read down the first column, pointing to each word as she reads.
Asks:	"What do you notice that's the same in all of these words?"	Generally children quickly notice that all of the words have an *a*. If they don't, the teacher should direct their attention ("What letter do you see in every word?").
Confirms:	"Yes, all of the words under *tap* have an *a*."	
Says:	"Now let's read the words in this next column. See if you can figure out what's the same in all of these words."	The teacher reads down the column, pointing to each word as she reads.
Asks:	"What did you notice that's the same in all the words in this column?"	Sometimes a child will notice just the *e*'s or just the *a*'s. If the teacher is working with an individual, it may help to have the child highlight all of the vowels in the word to make the pattern more apparent. In a group, with group effort, usually both the *e*'s and the *a*'s are noticed—but it may help, nevertheless, for the teacher to highlight all of the vowels to emphasize the pattern.

Step 3: Sample Instructional Dialogue for the Explanation of Silent e

Rationale:	English orthography (the writing system) is quite complicated. It is helpful to provide children with clear explanations about some of the conventions of the orthography.
Preparation:	Step 2 should immediately precede this step the first time the explanation is given. It may well be necessary to repeat this explanation, perhaps in abbreviated form, on several occasions.
Materials needed:	The chart that was created during Step 2.

Teacher	What the teacher says	Comments on the activity
Explains:	"For all of the words on this list that have that /ā ā ā/ sound, there's an *a* in the middle and an *e* at the end. All of the words on this other list have an a in the middle but no *e* at the end. They all have the /ă ă ă/ sound because they don't have an *e* at the end."	The teacher points to the words in each list as she explains the similarities and differences, not necessarily providing labels for the different sounds (i.e., short and long).
Continues:	"The *e* is a clue we can use when we are sounding out words. When the *e* comes at the end of words like these, it tells us we should probably say the name of the vowel that's in the middle of the word."	The teacher points to the words in the column under *tape*.
Continues:	"When there's no *e* at the end, and there's only one vowel in the word, that usually means that we are supposed to say the vowel's other sound. For the letter *a*, that's the /ă ă ă/ sound."	The teacher points to the words in the column under *tap*.

Step 4: Sample Instructional Dialogue for the Introduction of the Key Word		
Rationale:	The short vowel sounds are among the hardest letter–sound correspondences to remember. Key words, when used effectively, allow children to independently remind themselves of the vowel sounds.	
Materials needed:	The picture for the key word for the letter *A*.	

Teacher	What the teacher says	Comments on the activity
Shows vowel key word and says:	"We are learning that, when we are looking at the letters in a word and trying to figure out what the word will sound like, we need to think carefully, especially about the vowel letters. The *a* may be telling us to make the /ā ā ā/ sound, or it may be telling us to make the /ă ă ă/ sound. If there's an *e* at the end of the word, we try the /ā ā ā/ sound first. If there's no *e* at the end, we'll try the /ă ă ă/ sound. "It's easy to remember that /ā ā ā/ sound because it is just the same as the letter's name. But the /ă ă ă/ sound is harder to remember. To help us remember	

the /ă ă ă/ sound, we have this picture of an apple [or of whatever key word is used].

"The word *aaapple* starts with that /ă ă ă/ sound. So, if you are looking at the letter *a* and you can't remember it's other sound, then you could find the letter *a* on the key word chart and look at the picture that goes with it. The /ă ă ă/ at the beginning of *aaaaaapple* will remind you of the other sound of *a*."

Step 5: Sample Instructional Dialogue for Word Building		
Rationale:	In word building, the children are given a fairly small set of letters with which to work. This simplifies the task of building the words. We are, in essence, providing the children with a scaffold by limiting the letter set from which they are to choose.	
Preparation:	Word building can be done with a single large set of letter cards that all of the children can see, or each child might be given a set of letters with which to work. Often teachers use both large cards and letters for individual children. That way each child can work on a given word independently, and then the children can check their attempts against what is displayed with the large letters.	
Materials needed:	Word list for long-*a* and short-*a* words (provided in Figure 8.6) and the moveable letters needed to make all of the words on the list.	
Teacher	What the teacher says	Comments on the activity
Says:	"Now we are going to use these letters to make some words. Today, all of the words we are going to make will have an *a* in them. Sometimes the words will need that silent *e* to show that the sound of the *a* is just like the sound of its name. Sometimes, we won't need an *e* at the end because the sound of the *a* will be /ă ă ă/, like in *aaapple*."	The children are provided with all of the letters they will need to make the words that will be dictated.
Makes the word with the letter tiles and says:	"Let's have everyone use three letters to make the word *mat. Mmmaaat.* "Change *mat* to *mate.* "Change *mate* to *fate.* "Change *fate* to *fat.* "Change *fat* to *fad.* "Change *fad* to *fade,*" etc.	Early on the teacher should provide as much support as the children need—stretching the sounds, isolating and articulating sounds individually, reminding them to use the key words, etc. The teacher should also monitor children's attempts at each word and provide corrective feedback as needed (commenting on what they did right and what needs

		further thought). However, the goal is for the children to be able to independently analyze and represent the sounds as soon as possible. Therefore, the teacher should always be thinking carefully about with which aspects of the task the children need help and which aspects they might be able to handle alone.

Step 6: Sample Instructional Dialogue for Word Reading

Rationale:	After building the words during Step 5, the children are familiar with the words that they will be asked to read. They have been "primed," so to speak. As a result, it will be easier for them to identify these words than it would have been without the word-building step.	
Preparation:	In this activity, the teacher uses moveable letters to form the same words that the children were making during the word-building activity.	
Materials needed:	Letters large enough for all of the children in the instructional group to see; the word list for long-*a* and short-*a* words (in Figure 8.6).	
Teacher	**What the teacher says**	**Comments on the activity**
Says:	"Now I am going to make some words, and I want you to figure out what each word is. Remember to check for that silent *e*. Also remember, if you are not sure about the sound of one of the letters, you can use your key words to figure it out."	Drawing from the words on the long-*a* and short-*a* word list (and other words the children may see in texts they will be reading soon), the teacher uses the moveable letters to form words that the children attempt to read. The teacher again provides scaffolding on an as-needed basis by reminding the children to attend to the presence or absence of the silent *e* and by guiding them to use the key words.

Step 7: Written Spelling

Rationale:	Spelling out an entire word can be very challenging, as it requires being able to do both the sound analysis and the alphabetic coding component. Having children spell words that they have been working on in other ways helps to build their confidence and competence and to increase their proficiency with the types of analysis required for spelling.

Materials Needed:	Word list for long-*a* and short-*a* (in Figure 8.6) and writing materials (paper and pencil, white boards and markers, chalkboards, etc.).	
Teacher	**What the teacher says**	**Comments on the activity**
Says:	"Now we are going to write some words. All of the words we write will have the letter *a* in them. You need to listen to the words carefully and decide whether the word has an /ā ā ā/ sound. If it does, you need to be sure that the word you write ends with a silent *e*. If the word has a short-*a* sound, /ă ă ă/, then you don't need to put an *e* at the end."	The teacher should monitor the children's spelling of each word and provide any needed scaffolding. The children should discuss their decisions (e.g., about whether or not to include a silent *e*).

Similar procedures might be followed as each new vowel is introduced and practiced. However, as children demonstrate that they understand the processes involved, it may not be necessary to spend as much time or do as much explanation as the example above indicates.

Organizational Tip

Some teachers make a sheet with the letters needed for each of the word lists used for practice activities. Each child is given a sheet, which he cuts apart in preparation for the word-building activities. After the letters are used, they can be stored in an envelope or snack bag to be used by the child on subsequent days. When they are fairly proficient with spelling and reading the words on the list, the children can take the list and the associated letters home for additional practice.

Instruction for Vowel Combinations

When two vowels occur next to each other in a word, they usually represent one sound. Teachers sometimes teach students, "When two vowels go walking, the first one does the talking." Unfortunately, this "rule" does not work for many words, including some of the highest-frequency words (e.g., *been, great*). Perhaps a better "rule" would be "*When two vowels are together in a word, usually only one vowel sound is heard.*" Or, "*When two vowels go walking, somebody says something.*"

Vowel Flexing in Word Solving

We have encouraged teachers to teach children to be flexible with the vowel sounds for many years. Many teachers are initially skeptical about children's ability to use this strategy. However, every teacher who has reported back after teaching this strategy has indicated that the strategy is very useful. In fact, one experienced teacher who was working with fourth-grade children identified as learning disabled reported that she thought it was the most powerful decoding strategy she had ever taught her students.

Usually when two vowels are together in a word the sound of one of them is heard. Most often it is the long sound of the first vowel (e.g., *bean, rain, boat*). Sometimes it is the short sound of the first vowel (e.g., *head, been*). Occasionally, it is the long sound of the second vowel (e.g., *great, break*).

Sometimes, of course, two vowels together signal a sound that is different from the sound made by either letter individually (e.g., *oy, au, ei*). Still other vowels are influenced by the letter that immediately follows—this is especially true of *r*-controlled vowels (*ar, er, ir, or,* and *ur*) in which neither the long nor the short sound of the vowels can be distinctly heard.

For purposes of instruction, the various kinds of vowels are handled differently in the ISA.

VOWEL COMBINATIONS THAT CAN BE DECODED WITH VOWEL FLEXING

Figure 8.7 presents a listing of the vowel combinations that can usually be decoded by trying the long and short sounds for each of the vowels, including the /oo/ sound for *u* as in *blue*. These combinations do not require explicit instruction beyond teaching the two sounds of the vowel and the vowel flexing strategy. *Practice with vowel flexing must occur in context, as only context will allow the reader to determine if the decoding attempt is accurate.*

ai	ea	ie	oa	ue
ay	ee		oe	ui
	eu*			

*As in *pseudo*.

FIGURE 8.7. Vowel combinations that can be decoded with vowel flexing.

VOWEL DIGRAPHS THAT MAY NEED TO BE EXPLICITLY TAUGHT

Several digraphs represent vowel sounds that cannot be identified via vowel flexing. Some of the digraphs include two vowels (e.g., *au* and *oi*) and some include a vowel and a consonant (e.g., *oy* and *ow*). The vowel digraphs that may need to be explicitly taught include:

- Digraphs with only one common pronunciation:

au aw ew oi oy

- Digraphs with two common pronunciations:

oo	ou	ow
(as in *look* and *boot*)	(as in *out* and *soup*)	(as in *now* and *snow*)

- *r*-controlled vowels: When a single vowel is followed by the letter *r*, the sound of the vowel is altered (coarticulated) such that is it hard to distinguish the sound of the vowel from the sound of the *r*. Therefore, *r*-controlled vowels are generally taught as decoding units.

ar er ir or ur

INSTRUCTION FOR VOWEL COMBINATIONS THAT CANNOT BE DECODED USING VOWEL FLEXING

Children's knowledge of these various vowel combinations and the ease with which they acquire new knowledge about the alphabetic code should determine the amount of emphasis that is placed on teaching these decoding details. It may be, for example, that simply showing and discussing a word or two that includes the vowel combination will suffice to allow the child to successfully puzzle through words with that combination, especially when they are encountered in a meaningful context. However, some children may need the type of practice that is provided in the word-building and word-reading activities described above.

Note that it may be difficult to use some of the vowel combinations in word building exercises because there are several different ways a given sound might be spelled (e.g., the sound at the end of the word *drew* could be spelled with an *ew*, a *ue* [as in *blue*], or an *oo* [as in *too*]). These letter combinations can, however, be included in word-reading exercises.

For vowel combinations that have two common pronunciations, students need to learn both pronunciations and need to be encouraged to be flexible in decoding the combination—alternating the sound until a word is identified that fits the context in which the word is encountered.

THE SCHWA SOUND

In words with more than one syllable, one or more of the vowels may not make any of the traditionally taught sounds, but instead may represent the *schwa* sound (e.g., the first vowel sound in the words *about* and *oven*). Every vowel letter is pronounced as a *schwa* sound in some words. If a child has tried both sounds for a particular vowel and is still puzzling over a word, it may help to suggest that she try the *"uh"* sound.

Vowel Flexing and Word Learning

In Chapter 10, we discuss the use of vowel flexing as an important tool for word solving. Children are taught that, when they encounter an unfamiliar word in a text, one of the things they can do to solve the word is to "Try different pronunciations for some of the letters, especially the vowels." For example, if they are puzzling over the word *great*, they would be encouraged to try the long sound of the *e*, the short sound of the *e*, and then to move on to the long and the short sounds of the *a* until they identify a real word that makes sense in the context of what they are reading. In order to be able to approach vowel teams in this way, children need to be very familiar with the two sounds of each of the vowels and they need to view vowels as "decision points" which often require them to do some thoughtful problem solving.

Diphthongs

Some may wonder where diphthongs fit in our approach to teaching about vowel sounds. A diphthong (pronounced di*f*-thong) is a vowel sound that changes quality, due to changes in mouth position, during pronunciation. For example, in pronouncing the diphthong /oy/, the mouth position is initially similar to the one used in pronouncing a long *o* sound, but then changes to the position similar to that used in pronouncing the long *e* sound. The sound that is emitted changes accordingly. The English language has several diphthongs including the /ou/ sound as in *shout* and the long *a* and long *i* sounds. In teaching about vowels sounds, we do not make distinctions between diphthongs and monophthongs (vowels that don't change quality during pronunciation).

EVALUATING AND DOCUMENTING CHILDREN'S PROGRESS

Figures 8.8 and 8.9 present group snapshots for the alphabetic principle and code. Early and later development forms are presented separately, as the level of detail varies between them. Teachers should use one or both forms depending on their students' stage in development.

Group Snapshot—Alphabetic Code, Early Development					
Student names					
Reading isolated words					
Initial consonant substitution					
Final consonant substitution					
Writing isolated words					
Initial consonant substitution					
Final consonant substitution					
Reading words in text					
Uses initial consonant sound					
Uses final consonant sound					
Writing words in text					
Represents beginning sound in word					
Represents ending sound in word					
Represents middle sound with a vowel					

Key:

☐ *B—Beginning* indicates that instruction has addressed the objective but that the child has only a preliminary understanding or capability with regard to that particular objective.

☒ *D—Developing* indicates that the child has some understanding of the objective but does not reliably demonstrate that understanding or capability or is not yet automatic (fluent) with the skill.

☒ *P—Proficient* indicates that the child reliably and automatically demonstrates the understanding or capability.

FIGURE 8.8. Group snapshot for early development of skill with the alphabetic code.

Group Snapshot—Alphabetic Code, Later Development						
Student names						
Short vowel sounds in CVC words	Decoding					
	Encoding					
Long vowel silent-e pattern (VCe)	Decoding					
	Encoding					
Consonant digraphs (*sh, ch, th* . . .)	Decoding					
	Encoding					
Consonant blends (*fl, st, br,* . . .)	Decoding					
	Encoding					
Other vowel patterns via vowel flexing	Decoding					
	Encoding					
Other vowel patterns (*aw, ow, or, ar* . . . etc.)	Decoding					
	Encoding					

Key:

◻ *B—Beginning* indicates that instruction has addressed the objective but that the child has only a preliminary understanding or capability with regard to that particular objective.

▨ *D—Developing* indicates that the child has some understanding of the objective but does not reliably demonstrate that understanding or capability or is not yet automatic (fluent) with the skill.

▧ *P—Proficient* indicates that the child reliably and automatically demonstrates the understanding or capability.

FIGURE 8.9. Group snapshot for later development of skill with the alphabetic code.

When children are initially working toward an understanding of the alphabetic principle, it is important to attend to the developmental progression, introducing and building proficiency first with consonants at the beginnings of words, then at the ends of words, for both reading and writing activities. Eventually, the goal is for children to be able to represent beginning, middle, and ending sounds in their attempts to write words, even if those representations are not conventional. In order to be considered proficient, children should be spontaneous and consistent (but not necessarily accurate) in their attempts to use letter sounds for reading and spelling words.

Once a rudimentary understanding of how the letters in printed words are used to represent the sounds in spoken words has been established, that understanding can be further developed through instructional activities that focus on consonant digraphs and blends, short and long vowel sounds, and vowel digraphs. The order in which these elements are introduced varies somewhat, depending upon the instructional materials in use and the knowledge of the children in the group. Typically, these elements are introduced through working with words in isolation. However, children should be able to apply the skills when reading and writing connected text in order to be considered proficient.

CHAPTER 9

Larger Orthographic Units and Multisyllabic Words

ALPHABETICS GOAL 6

The child will develop the ability to use a variety of larger orthographic units (word families/phonograms, prefixes, suffixes, etc.) to read and spell words.

Orthography refers to letters and spellings and the representation of speech in writing (Venezky, 1998). Many languages, including English, have alphabetic orthographies in which letters or letter combinations represent the phonemes of the spoken language. In alphabetic orthographies, certain spelling–sound patterns, involving multiple letters and sounds, tend to occur with some regularity. For example, the letter string *ight* occurs in several different words, such as *light, slight, might,* and *night,* as do patterns such as *tion, ness,* and so on. Proficient readers process these spelling patterns as units rather than processing all of the letters individually. Processing these larger orthographic units allows the reader to read more efficiently and fluently. In this chapter we discuss several different types of orthographic units and suggest approaches to instruction that can help children learn to notice and use these units effectively as they read and spell single-syllable and multisyllable words.

PHONOGRAMS AND WORD FAMILIES

Phonograms as Decoding and Encoding Units

As children learn more and more words, they begin to become attuned to (and are often taught) recurring spelling patterns (e.g., *ing, ook*). Over time, they come to use these patterns in attempting to read and spell words. For example, children who can easily read the words *look* and *took* are likely to find it easier to identify the word *cook* than children who only know the sounds for each of the letters that make up the word *cook*. The children might have learned *-ook* as a *phonogram* or *word family*, or they might have learned to use an analogy strategy that allows them to apply what they know about the pronunciation of *look* and *took* in their attempts to read the word *cook*. Either way, they are learning to use these larger orthographic units in attempting to figure out words, and this makes their attempts more efficient. As students engage in more and more reading and writing, these units become consolidated in their memory, and they become able to use these units when attempting to identify words with more than one syllable. Thus, for example, children who can readily read the words *thing, ring*, and *sing*, and who can read *look* and *took*, might be able to effectively puzzle out the word *cooking*.

In this section we discuss teaching children to use phonograms to decode and spell words. As we use the term, *phonogram* refers to frequently occurring spelling patterns that represent the rime portion of a syllable (the vowel and what comes after it). Teachers often use the term *word family* to refer to both the spelling patterns and the group of words that can be formed using the phonogram. As it is unclear whether children will benefit from understanding the distinction between a phonogram and the family of words that can be generated from the phonogram, we think that the general term *word family* is appropriate to use for instructional purposes. Other terms, such as *chunk* or *decoding key*, are also used for these elements. For instructional purposes, it is important that, at least for beginning readers, one term be used rather than a variety of terms. Further, the same term should be used in all settings for children who receive reading instruction in more than one setting.

Research done by Ehri (1998) suggests that children need to be fairly familiar with individual letter–sound correspondences and how they are used in encoding and decoding before they can learn to effectively use larger orthographic units such as phonograms. Therefore, the expectation for children to use these larger orthographic units is probably best delayed until after they are fairly competent with using individual letter sounds, especially the consonants, in their reading and writing attempts. Ultimately, it is important for children to learn that words containing the same sound pattern often share the same spelling pattern, and vice versa. When children learn a number of common spelling patterns and have learned how spelling patterns can be generalized, they will be better prepared to efficiently analyze and identify words that they do not immediately recognize, and they will also be more strategic in their attempts to spell words.

Phonograms are more efficient decoding and spelling units both because they allow the reader to avoid potentially tedious letter-by-letter processing and because the pronunciation of the vowels in words that contain phonograms is often more reliable than the pronunciation of individual vowels as determined by letter-by-letter decoding and spelling "rules."

Figure 9.1 provides a list of phonograms from which over 500 primary-grade words can be derived. The list includes 37 phonograms identified by Durrell (1963), plus a few others that teachers have felt should be added.

Note that some of the phonograms listed here (e.g., the *r*-controlled vowels and *aw*) were also discussed as vowel digraphs in the previous chapter. If a vowel digraph can be used to generate multiple words, it can be treated as a word family. Thus, *aw* is treated as a phonogram because it comes at the end of several common words—for example, *saw, raw, claw, paw,* and *jaw.* However, *au* is not treated as a phonogram because additional letters would need to be added to the end to form words.

Selecting Phonograms for Instruction

The phonograms selected for instruction should be drawn from books the children will read in the near future. Ideally, the phonogram would occur several times in the book in order to provide sufficient practice. In our intervention studies we have recommended that the earliest phonograms taught should be as distinct from one another as possible so that the children are more apt to treat the phonogram as a unit rather than to analyze it letter by letter. For example, if the first few phonograms taught were *an, ap,* and *at,* the child would need to attend very carefully to the final letter in order to distinguish them from one another. On the other hand,

ack	eat	ice	ock	uck
ail	ell	ick	oke	ug
ain	er	ide	op	ump
ale	est	ight	ore	unk
ame		ill	or	ur
an		in		
ank		ine		
ap		ing		
ar		ink		
ash		ip		
at		ir		
ate		it		
aw				
ay				

FIGURE 9.1. Phonograms that can be used to form over 500 primary-grade words.

if the first few phonograms taught were *an, op*, and *it*, the child could process them more holistically because they look so different from one another.

Teaching Children to Read and Write Words Using Phonograms

Step 1: Introducing a New Phonogram

Provide children with a card containing the phonogram and tell them what the phonogram is. Explain that the phonogram is contained in many words that they will see in books and that it will be helpful to know the phonogram so that words containing this combination of letters will be easier to figure out. Give them several individual letter cards as well. Dictate words for them to build using the individual letter cards and the phonogram. Words containing consonant blends and digraphs can be used if instruction on blends and digraphs has already occurred.

Step 2: Word Building

Provide cards containing one or two previously taught phonograms as well as the new phonogram. Have the children build words using the various phonograms and individual letter cards. For example, the children might be presented with the phonograms *it* and *an* and asked to build the words *fit, fan, pan, pit, bit, ban*, and so on.

Step 3: Word Reading

Using individual letter cards and cards containing the phonograms, the teacher forms words and asks the children to identify them.

Step 4: Written Spelling

The children write words dictated by the teacher. It is often helpful to start a spelling activity by creating a column for each of the phonograms that will be used. Then the teacher dictates words and the children decide in which column each word belongs and then write the dictated word in the correct column. Teachers sometimes use a graphic of a house and talk about these charts as two- or three-family houses—the children need to decide in which family each dictated word belongs (see Figure 9.2)

Further Phonogram Practice

Once a phonogram has been introduced and practiced, the children can be asked to generate as many real words as they can think of using the phonogram and make a list of them. Alternatively, they could be asked to systematically use a set

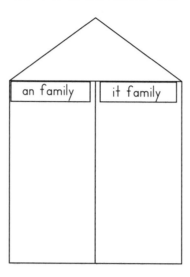

FIGURE 9.2. A two-family house used for word family practice.

of consonants, blends, and/or digraphs to try to form words with the phonogram and to read each resulting combination and make a list of all of the real words and nonwords that are formed.

Note

Making decisions about which combinations yield real words and which result in nonwords is, potentially, a helpful activity in promoting self-monitoring when the children read continuous text. If a decoding attempt results in a nonword, they are more likely to notice it.

Maintaining a Focus on Phonograms

After each phonogram has been introduced and practiced, the goal is for children to use it in decoding words they do not immediately recognize and in spelling words for which they have not memorized the conventional spellings. The activities described below are designed to promote the use of phonograms for these purposes.

The Phonogram Display

The phonograms that have been introduced and practiced should be prominently displayed for the children to refer to during reading and writing. For this display, the phonograms should be organized by the vowel they contain. Long- and short-vowel phonograms should be grouped separately. Phonograms that have neither a long nor a short vowel (e.g., the *a* in *all*) would also be grouped separately. An example of a phonogram display is provided in Figure 9.3.

Note that by grouping the phonograms by vowel sound, the phonogram chart provides the children with an additional clue about how the phonogram will be pronounced. In addition, for phonograms with which children have particular difficulty, it is helpful to provide a familiar high-frequency word to facilitate their recall of the sound of the phonogram (see Figure 9.3). This is especially helpful for phonograms that are contained in high-frequency words that the children can readily identify.

Reading Connected Text

When children are reading a text and encounter a word they do not immediately recognize, and the context is not sufficiently helpful to allow for word identification, they should be encouraged to see if there are any familiar phonograms contained in the word. The vowel or vowels in the word should serve as the starting point for looking for known phonograms. Ideally the children would remember the phonograms that they have learned. However, if they don't, the phonogram display will facilitate their attempts to make use of the phonograms. The children must find the first vowel in the word they are attempting to identify and then check the phonograms in the column for that vowel. If the word in question contains more than one syllable, more than one phonogram that has been taught may help the children to identify the word. For example, if the phonograms displayed in Figure 9.3 had been taught, and the children encountered the word *entertain*, they could make progress toward identifying the word by recognizing the three phonograms contained in the word (*en*, *er*, and *ain*). Children should always, of course, be encouraged to determine whether their decoding attempts make sense in the context of the text they are reading.

Spelling

Children should be encouraged to use phonograms in attempting to spell words when they do not know the conventional spelling. In order to do so, the children must first determine the number of syllables that are contained in the word they wish to spell (by counting the number of "beats" in the word). Often, it is helpful to have the children draw a line for each syllable in the word. Next, for each syllable, the children should determine what the initial sound(s) is and how it (they) should be represented in print. Next, the children should think about whether they know any phonograms that sound like the remainder of the syllable. If so, that phonogram should be used to complete the spelling for that syllable. Subsequent syllables in the word would be analyzed in a similar fashion.

Children will become more efficient in using phonograms in their spelling if they periodically have "spelling tests" in which they use a phonogram-based spell-

Word Families We Know

A	E	I	O	U
at	en	it	ot	up
an	ess		op	ug
ain	eet	ite	oat	ute
ame	ean	ight (night)	ope	
ay (play)			old	
all	er	ir	or	ur
ar		ing	oy	
			ook (look)	

FIGURE 9.3. Phonogram/word family display for children.

ing strategy. For example, by referring to the Word Families We Know display illustrated in Figure 9.3, the children might be asked to spell *mess, feet, shop, smell, raining,* and *daylight*. While the use of phonograms as one spelling strategy will certainly, on occasion, lead to incorrect spellings (e.g., some children will provide *daylite* as the spelling for *daylight*), the use of phonograms will considerably improve the initial spelling attempts of many children.

Games for Promoting Fluent Use of Phonograms

The games described below can be used in centers and/or for practice at home.

• *Phonogram guessing game.* The clue giver thinks of a word containing one or more of the phonograms on the chart and provides a clue concerning the meaning of that word (e.g., "I'm thinking of something kids usually don't like to have to clean up"). The children try to think of a word that fits the clue and contains one of the phonograms. If they cannot think of the word with only the meaning clue, the clue giver would provide another clue that focuses attention on a smaller group of phonograms (e.g., "The word I'm thinking of has one of the short-*e* phonograms in it"). If the children are still unable to think of the word, the clue giver might point to the phonogram contained in the word, tell the children that the word contains that phonogram, and then remind the children of the meaning clue initially provided.

- *Go Fish.* Go Fish games can be created using words derived from phonograms that have been taught. In this game the children ask for words containing a specific phonogram. Thus, a child might ask for a word that has *ake* in it (pronouncing the phonogram rather than naming the letters). A match is created by having two words with the same phonogram.

- *Tic-tac-toe.* For this game the children are provided with two or more phonograms that have been taught. On each turn, the player has to think of a word using one of the phonograms and write it in the square of choice. Repetitions of words are not allowed. All words need to be real when pronounced (although if the children are playing without an adult, there may be unconventional spellings of real words). Children use different colored markers to write the words, and the winner is determined by the colored entries on the game board.

- *Phonogram hunt.* Children are given a text in which they are to go on a "phonogram hunt." That is, they are invited to see how many phonograms they can find in the text. The text may be covered with a transparency or plastic sheet protector, and children can underline or circle all of the phonograms they find. This game helps to increase children's awareness of phonograms.

- *Great big words.* The children are encouraged to find words that contain a large number of phonograms. A cumulative list of words containing several phonograms might be maintained with an eye toward finding a really big word by the end of the school year. The children can be on the lookout for such words in their classroom as well as at home.

DECODING WORDS WITH MULTIPLE SYLLABLES

Because words with more than one syllable come up early in children's reading experience, it is important to provide guidance on how to handle such words.

Vowels and Syllables

A syllable is a unit of pronunciation. Every syllable contains one and only one *vowel phoneme*—although that vowel phoneme may be represented by more than one letter. As discussed previously, usually when two vowels are together in a word, they represent just one vowel phoneme. In attempting an unfamiliar word, it may help the child to look for the vowels in the word—recognizing, of course that the silent *e*'s will sometimes cause problems with syllables. The reader may find it useful to group sounds around the vowels, thereby forming syllables. For example, with the word *recognizing*, looking for vowels allows the reader to accurately note that there are four syllables in the word. However, such an approach will not always work. For example, looking for vowels in the word *therefore* might lead one to expect three or four syllables (i.e., *the, re,* and *fore* or *the, re, for,* and *e*).

Meaningful Word Parts: Root Words, Prefixes, and Suffixes

Words often consist of more than one meaningful part (*morpheme*). There is always a *root word*, which is a unit of meaning that can stand alone. *Cat, want, run,* and *green* are all examples of root words. Some words have prefixes or suffixes that change the meaning of the root word in some way. A prefix comes before the root word and a suffix comes after the root word. For purposes of decoding an unfamiliar word, it is helpful for children to learn to recognize common prefixes and suffixes and to temporarily ignore them while attempting to identify the root word (Lovett et al., 2000).

Inflectional Endings

The first suffixes that children are likely to encounter in their reading are inflectional endings such as *-ing, -s* (or *-es*), and *-ed.* The teacher might begin by helping children to notice these endings and temporarily cover them with their fingers while thinking about the root of the word. The various endings present different levels of challenge.

• The *-ing* ending is pronounced the same way in all contexts and so is a fairly easy ending for the children to grasp.
• The *-s* (or *-es*), used to mark plurals and third-person present tense, can be pronounced as /s/ as in *cats* or *wants,* as /z/ as in *balls* and *wades,* or as /ez/ as in *cages* or *watches.* Teaching children that *s* and *es* are units of meaning that can be temporarily ignored and then added back on once the root word is identified usually allows them to assign the proper pronunciation to the marker because they know implicitly what the plural or third-person present tense form of the root word sounds like in spoken language.
• The *-ed* used to mark past tense is also pronounced in different ways depending on the final sound in the root word. It is pronounced as /d/ in *played,* as /ed/ in *wanted,* and as /t/ in *missed.* Here again, if children are taught to temporarily ignore the ending while they puzzle through the root word and then add it back on once the root word is identified, they are likely to assign the correct pronunciation (or the pronunciation they would use in their typical spoken language).

Common Prefixes

The prefixes *un-* (meaning, *not*) and *re-* (meaning, *do again*) are the two most common prefixes and so are useful to teach. Other prefixes that might be considered as children progress include *in-, im-, dis-, en-,* and *non-.*

Common Derivational Suffixes

Derivational suffixes change a word's part of speech. For example, adding *-ly* changes an adjective to an adverb (*nice–nicely*) and adding *-ness* changes an adjective to a noun (*happy–happiness*). While is it not critical that children understand how these suffixes function, it does help them to recognize these "chunks" so that they can, again, temporarily ignore them while attempting to decode the root word. Among the most common derivational suffixes are *-ly*, *-ment*, *-ness*, *-less*, and *-ful*.

Teaching Children to Use Meaningful Word Parts in Decoding

The teacher explains that a single word sometimes has more than one meaningful part, using, as an example, a word with a prefix or a suffix that the children will soon encounter in their reading. The teacher would present the root word on a card and the prefix and/or suffix on separate cards and demonstrate how adding or removing the prefix or suffix changes the meaning. The same prefix and/or suffix can be used to modify additional root words to further illustrate the process. The teacher should explain that noticing the parts will help readers to puzzle out words by letting them focus on one part at a time. Children should be encouraged to notice the prefix/suffix, think of how it will sound, and then temporarily cover it up while thinking about what the rest of the word will sound like (and what would make sense in context).

As new word parts are taught, previously taught word parts can be integrated into instruction to help children become automatic in noticing and interpreting them and in using them to assist in their decoding of words with multiple syllables. Word-building activities using root words and the prefixes and suffixes that have been taught can be periodically revisited until the children are quite facile in using them. So, for example, if the prefixes *re-* and *un-* and the suffixes *-ly*, *-ful*, *-ness*, *-ed*, *-er*, and *-ing* have been taught, children might use several different root words to build and read multisyllabic words. For example:

- *Build—rebuild, building, rebuilding, builder*
- *Watch—watches, watchful, unwatchful, watchfulness*
- *Event—eventful, uneventful*
- *Swim—swimming, swimmer*
- *Bright—brighter, brightly, brightness*

When children read, they should be periodically reminded of the utility of thinking about, and temporarily ignoring, prefixes and suffixes while they puzzle through root words (see the "break the word into smaller parts" strategy in Chapter 10).

Breaking Words into Parts That Aren't Meaningful

Many multisyllabic words are made up of syllables that do not have individual meanings. Readers can often find these syllables and decode the word if they attempt one or more of the following:

- For words with double consonants, break the word between the two consonants and decode each part (syllable).
- For words with the *consonant + -le* syllable structure (e.g., *ap-ple*, *lit-tle*, *scram-ble*) go back one letter from the *-le* and treat that consonant plus the *-le* as a syllable. Decode the first syllable and then decode the *consonant + -le* syllable by making the sound of the consonant and adding /ul/.
- For words with two different consonants together in the middle of the word, try breaking the word between the consonants (e.g., *basket*, *chimney*, *servant*).
- Try different pronunciations for the vowels—trying the long and short sound of the vowels alternately until a word that fits the context emerges. It may be helpful to tell/remind children that all of the vowels sometimes represent the /uh/ (*schwa*) sound, as in *about*, *effect*, *other* (as these words are pronounced in everyday conversation).
- For words that include spelling units that are difficult to decode (e.g., *tion*, *ture*), provide the pronunciation (e.g., "That part says *shun*") and explain that it will be seen in lots of words and is therefore useful to try to remember.

To initially make these approaches explicit, challenging words that are encountered while reading text can be written out and then analyzed briefly in isolation. It is useful to illustrate that multiple approaches can be applied together in attempting to decode a multi-syllable word. It is also important to stress the need to think of words that would make sense in the context and to always confirm that the decoded word fits the context.

Decoding by Analogy to Known Words

When proficient readers encounter an unfamiliar word, they typically do not consciously engage in the types of analysis discussed above. Rather, they are likely to identify the word by analogy to known words (e.g., the word *prattle* would be read effortlessly by analogy to words such as *battle* and *cattle*). Teachers should be alert for opportunities to move children toward this type of word-solving approach. For example, when a child encounters a word that is unfamiliar but very similar to one or more words that the child knows well, the teacher might comment, "You can figure out that word easily if you notice how similar it looks to. . . . " Initially the teacher would name the similar word. Over time, the teacher would reduce the support by asking, rather than telling, "Can you think of another word you know that looks like that one?"

> **KEEP IN MIND** While multisyllabic words may present a word identification challenge, for some readers they can also present a vocabulary challenge. It is difficult for readers to ascertain that a word has been accurately identified if there is no word in their lexicon that corresponds to it. For that reason, a critical element of instruction is anticipating unfamiliar vocabulary and using it in prereading discussions. Since children differ widely in their vocabulary knowledge, it is important that teachers be alert to terms that may be challenging for some children and be prepared to individualize the vocabulary terms addressed. As the texts that children read become more challenging, a significant part of planning should involve teacher's prereading of the text selection and choosing multisyllabic words that are appropriate to focus on both for the purpose of decoding and for the purpose of building children's vocabularies.

EVALUATING AND DOCUMENTING CHILDREN'S PROGRESS IN USING LARGER ORTHOGRAPHIC UNITS

Figure 9.4 presents the group snapshot for larger orthographic units and multisyllabic words. Although presented in a list format, it is important to point out, once again, that instruction does not always proceed from the top to the bottom of the list. Some phonograms (e.g., *at, ake*) might be introduced much earlier than others (e.g., *ean, ight*). Likewise, the inflected ending *-ing* (as in *going, playing*) might be encountered in earlier-leveled texts than *-ed* or *-es*. The point is, instruction around larger orthographic units and multisyllabic words is not likely to move in a linear fashion, but will be highly dependent on the instructional materials in use. Thus, children should *not* be expected to demonstrate proficiency with all of the phonograms, then all inflected endings, then prefixes and suffixes, etc. Rather, children should demonstrate an understanding of how these various word parts can be used to read and spell words. For example, a child who is considered proficient with respect to phonograms will be able to read and spell the phonograms that have been taught, will be able to use those phonograms to read and spell new words, and will find it easy to learn to use new phonograms as they are introduced. In other words, a child who is "proficient" knows quite a few of the larger orthographic units, appears to make effective use of them in reading and writing, and is expanding her repertoire of orthographic units easily. Recall that one major purpose for the group snapshot is to help teachers identify areas where additional instructional emphasis appears to be needed.

Group Snapshot—Larger Orthographic Units and Multisyllabic Words							
Student names							
Phonograms (*at, ain, ope . . .*)	Decoding						
	Encoding						
Inflected endings (*ed, ing, es*)	Decoding						
	Encoding						
Prefixes (*re-, un-* . . .) and suffixes (*ness, ly,* . . .)	Decoding						
	Encoding						
Syllables	Decoding						
	Encoding						

Key:

◻ *B—Beginning* indicates that instruction has addressed the objective but that the child has only a preliminary understanding or capability with regard to that particular objective.

⊠ *D—Developing* indicates that the child has some understanding of the objective but does not reliably demonstrate that understanding or capability or is not yet automatic (fluent) with the skill.

⊠ *P—Proficient* indicates that the child reliably and automatically demonstrates the understanding or capability.

FIGURE 9.4. Group snapshot for larger orthographic units and multisyllabic words.

PART III

WORD LEARNING

INTRODUCTION

A written word that a reader can identify quickly and accurately and in all contexts is said to be in the reader's *sight vocabulary*. Fast and accurate word identification is critically important to comprehension for both beginning and more proficient readers, because readers who know most of the words in a text can devote most of their thinking to understanding the text rather than to figuring out the words. In this part we focus on ways to help beginning and struggling readers learn words so well that they become part of their sight vocabularies.

Share (1995) estimates that a competent seventh- or eighth-grade reader can quickly and accurately identify 50,000 words or more. How does such phenomenal skill develop? Surely all of these 50,000 words are not taught to children; there is no way a teacher could possibly teach the thousands of words that would be needed to help a child reach this level by eighth grade. Rather, it appears that children learn the vast majority of the words that ultimately become part of their sight vocabularies by effectively puzzling through and figuring out unfamiliar words that they encounter while reading. Share (1995) suggests that the ability to figure out unfamiliar words serves as a *self-teaching mechanism* that allows children to gradually increase the size of their sight vocabulary through reading. This is not to suggest, of course, that correctly identifying a word just once will necessarily allow it to become part of a reader's sight vocabulary. Rather, for most words, it is through multiple encounters with, and correct identifications of, the words that students come to learn them to the point of automaticity. Thus, the first time readers encounter an unfamiliar word, they may need to devote quite a bit of effort to thinking about what that word might be. On the next encounter, a bit less thinking may be needed for correct identification. On each subsequent encounter, readers are likely to be able to identify the word more and more easily and fluently until ultimately it becomes part of their sight vocabulary.

Exactly how a child comes to "know" a previously unfamiliar word has been the source of much debate over the years (Adams, 1990; Chall, 1967; Goodman, 1967; Pressley, 2006). And, although some experts assert that a consensus has been reached (Pressley, 2006), we are far from having reached scientific certainty as to how children accomplish this remarkable word-learning feat. However, there are a few points on which near unanimity exists:

- Children need to do extensive amounts of reading to build their sight vocabularies.
- Children need guidance and feedback while they are reading to become effective word learners (word solvers). However, the amount of guidance needed varies substantially among children.
- The texts that children read need to be somewhat, but not too, challenging if they are going to be useful in helping to build children's sight vocabulary.

These points of agreement, however, still leave unanswered the question of what readers actually do when they encounter an unfamiliar word in context. One of the reasons this question is so difficult to answer is that what readers do depends on:

- Readers' knowledge and skills
- The text that they are reading and the types of supports that the text provides
- The instruction that they have received about how to approach unfamiliar words in text.

Difficulties with Word Learning

Children in the early primary grades who are identified as being at risk of experiencing literacy learning difficulties, and especially those who do not accelerate with Tier 1 instruction alone, are particularly likely to demonstrate difficulties with word learning. Many children experience difficulty due to limitations in their ability to make effective use of the alphabetic code. However, as is discussed in some detail below, learning to read words encountered in context requires much more than alphabetic decoding skills. Rather, alphabetic skills and strategies need to be coordinated and orchestrated with other word-learning strategies as well as with language skills and other knowledge sources. And children need to do a great deal of reading in order to encounter the many words they need to learn.

Characteristics of the Reader

Word solving is dependent on what readers know about the alphabetic writing system and on what they know about the language and concepts presented in a particular text. While beginning readers are often taught the most common correspondences between letters and their sounds (as discussed in Part II, "Learning the Alphabetic Code"), it is important to keep in mind that written English is characterized by many, many irregularities in spelling–sound correspondence. Therefore, it is simply not possible for readers to rely exclusively on alphabetic information for the purpose of identifying unfamiliar words. Such an approach would lead to far too many inaccuracies in word identification—even for some of the most commonly occurring words such as *have, of, was,* and *to.* Nevertheless, virtually all words consist of letters that at least partially signal their pronunciation. Therefore, knowing the most common correspondences between letters and their sounds and knowing how to apply that knowledge are critically important for building sight vocabulary.

Knowledge of the workings of the alphabetic writing system develops gradually and, at least for some children, requires explicit instructional guidance and practice.

- Readers who are just beginning to learn about letters and their sounds will make limited use of the alphabetic information in attempting to identify an unfamiliar printed word encountered in context because their alphabetic knowledge is limited and tenuous. Even if children know most or all of the common letter–sound correspondences, it is quite taxing to think about all of the letters in the word, the sounds those letters may represent, hold those sounds in memory, and then blend them together and say the resulting word. Moreover, the kinds of texts that beginning readers encounter provide many other sources of information that assist them in identifying unfamiliar words. For example, students at this point in reading development are often given texts that are repetitive (or predictable) and that have pictures that provide so much contextual support that they are able to "read" the text successfully by relying primarily on the pictures and the repetitive language (see Figure III.1). Children reading such texts do not necessarily need to attend carefully to the letter- and word-level information provided in the text.
- Readers who are more familiar with the workings of an alphabetic writing system and more fluent at recalling the most common sounds associated with printed letters will find it less taxing to look through the word for more alphabetic clues about the word's possible identity. Such readers do not need texts that make heavy use of repetitive language patterns and pictures.
- Readers who have done quite a bit of reading and who have learned to read many words automatically will begin to recognize larger units of print, such as *bl, ink, er,* etc. These larger orthographic units will allow readers to be more efficient in puzzling through unfamiliar words. Instead of having to think about each

FIGURE III.1. An example of an emergent-level text.

separate sound in the consonant blend *bl*, these readers will process it as a unit or "chunk." Thus, identification of the word *blinker* might require readers at this point in development to think about only three orthographic units rather than the seven letters that comprise the word.

With regard to readers' familiarity with the language and concepts presented in the text:

• Readers must know the meaning of unfamiliar words encountered in text in order to know whether the word has been accurately identified. For instance, in reading a book, about a farm, that relies on repetitive language and pictures to make reading the text easier, children might read sentences such as

"Look at the cow. Look at the horse."

quite easily because the pictures and the repetitive pattern are so helpful. However, if the text included the sentence

"Look at the hen."

the children might experience difficulty because the word *hen* is less likely to be in their spoken vocabulary than the word *chicken*. Even though the word *hen* is relatively easy to decode (if one knows the most common letter–sound correspondences), children will not be able to conclude that their decoding efforts are accurate if they do not know the meaning of the word.

• Readers' sensitivity to the syntactic or grammatical aspects of a text also influence their ability to successfully puzzle through unfamiliar words. For example, the sentence "I have a . . . " leads grammatically sensitive readers to expect either an adjective (e.g., *big*) or a noun (e.g., *cow*). This sensitivity will limit the number of options readers might consider and/or may signal them that an initial attempt at a word was inaccurate because it didn't fit the syntactic/grammatical constraints of the sentence.

• Readers' general knowledge (or schemas) for the circumstances or events portrayed in the text can also influence their ability to accurately identify unfamiliar words. For example, children who know a fair amount about farms are likely to more readily identify the last word in the sentence

> "Look at the goat."

because they know that goats are apt to be found on farms.

Characteristics of the Text

There are multiple kinds of texts that might be used to promote the development of reading skill. The variety and types of texts that children encounter may play a substantial role in their approach to word solving. Below we describe some of the types of texts that are often used in early reading instruction.

Predictable Texts

In the earliest phases of reading development, highly predictable texts are often used. Predictable texts generally have one line of print per page, which may be only a phrase (e.g., "The cow") or a complete sentence (e.g., "Look at the cow"). Generally, only one word changes from one page to the next, and that word is frequently something that can be illustrated pictorially. The picture on each successive page highlights the thing that changed. With this type of book, once children know the pattern (e.g., "Look at the . . . "), they can rely primarily on the pictures to "read" the entire text. One advantage of these texts for emergent readers is that they help to build motivation for reading, because children can generally experience the positive feeling of success when they correctly "read." Another advantage is that these texts can be used to teach about print concepts, such as the concepts of *letter* and *word*. A significant potential disadvantage is that exclusive reliance on these kinds of texts can serve to confuse children about what it means to read, because many of these texts can be "read" primarily by looking at the pictures. They do not require that children devote much attention to the print. Extended use of such texts may ultimately serve to slow the reader's progress (Tunmer & Chapman, 1998).

Decodable Texts

Texts in which most of the words can be identified by applying knowledge of common letter–sound correspondences are often referred to as *decodable texts*—because most of the words can be sounded out. A decodable text might include a sentence like:

"Ben and Jen can pet the cat."

In this sentence, all of the words except *the* can be decoded (if one knows the commonly taught letter-sound correspondences). The text might continue:

"The cat can sit. Ben sits. Jen sits. Jen pets the cat. Ben pets the cat."

The advantage of this kind of text is that it provides practice with using the alphabetic code to decipher words. A potential disadvantage is that the structure of the sentences tends to be quite different from typical spoken and written language (e.g., "Ben sits. Jen sits.") and thus may lead the child away from using syntax as a source of information in identifying words.

Early Sight Word Readers

Many high-frequency words are not entirely decodable, and they often occupy roles in sentences that make them hard to identify using contextual cues. Therefore, these words are often given special instructional attention. Several publishers have developed "sight word readers" to help to build automaticity with these words. These materials are intended to help make these frequently occurring words part of children's sight vocabulary. However, sight word readers are not all of a kind. Indeed, several series consist of books that look quite like the predictable texts described earlier. Thus, the book *The Farm,* described in that section, contains text that repeatedly uses the phrase "Look at the. . . . " *Look, at,* and *the* are all high-frequency words. As noted above, in reading this text, beginning readers may attend very little to the printed words once they know the pattern, and therefore reading this text may not help them learn these high-frequency words. Although many series devoted to the teaching of high-frequency words feature predictable patterns, we are aware of at least one series, published by The Short Books (1999; *www.myshortbooks.com*), that varies the language structure in a way that encourages more careful attention to the print. These texts use a few high-frequency words over and over in the context of a single book, but the words are used in slightly different syntactic structures. As a result, readers need to attend more carefully to the words in order to read the text; such books seem more likely to help children build high-frequency sight vocabulary. For example, the book *The Farm* could be rewritten as:

"Look at the cow. Look at the horse. Look! The pig. The cat. Look, look, look!"

Clearly, this version of the text would require readers to attend more carefully to the print. As a further illustration, Figure III.2 presents two versions of the book *See My Pets,* only one of which is likely to help children learn the high-frequency words that are utilized.

FIGURE III.2. Two renditions of a book called *See My Pets*. The version on the left is much more likely to help children learn the words *I*, *see*, and *my* than is the version on the right. From Scanlon and Anderson (2010). Copyright by the International Reading Association. Reprinted by permission.

More Advanced Sight Word Readers

For children who are a bit more advanced in their reading skills but who are having difficulty learning high-frequency sight words, we have found that books that include many repetitions of very high-frequency words help to facilitate the development of skill with these words. Books by Margaret Hillert and by Babs Bell Hajdusiewicz (both published by Modern Curriculum Press), for example, are particularly helpful in this regard. Several of the books by Margaret Hillert involve retellings of fairy tales such as Cinderella and Hanzel and Gretel. Because these books emphasize the use of high-frequency words, the language patterns are far from natural. For example, the book entitled *The Three Little Pigs* (Hillert, 1963, p. 12) reads

"See my house. It is a little house. It is yellow."

However, because these books tell a story that is apt to be familiar to many children (or that may be made familiar through read-alouds of the originals), and because they look like small chapter books, the books are more appealing and engaging for children than might be expected. We have observed that many children who are initially slow to develop high-frequency sight vocabulary have shown rapid gains in this regard when provided with the opportunity to read some of these books.

Strategy-Promoting Texts

Strategy-promoting texts is a term we have coined to describe texts that present readers with problem-solving opportunities that promote the interactive use of a variety of informational sources for purposes of identifying unfamiliar words. Thus, readers may need to consider information provided by the picture, the general context of the text, and the print in order to puzzle through an unfamiliar word. Below are two examples taken from a series called Ready Readers (Modern Curriculum Press).

The first example in Figure III.3 is taken from a book titled *My Room* (Spevack, 1997), in which the labels for several of the pictures are somewhat ambiguous and readers are required to attend to the print in order to determine the exact word. For example, to confidently read the words "my rabbit" (as opposed to "my bunny"), the emergent reader needs to think about at least three different sources of information: the repetitive pattern in the book, the picture, and the printed word *rabbit*. The second example presents a similar task within a somewhat more challenging text. In this example, taken from the book *Eggs!* (Robinson, 1997), readers who are relying primarily on the repetitive pattern of the text and picture cues are likely to read "Look at the *fire*." Careful attention to the print, in conjunction with the other sources of information, is needed to accurately read the word *smoke*. Note that, although the word *smoke* adheres to commonly taught decoding generalizations, children reading this level of text have probably not attained that level of decoding skill and will therefore require multiple sources of informa-

my rabbit,

7

Look at the smoke.

6

FIGURE III.3. Examples from strategy-promoting books. Left: From *Ready Readers, My Room* by Judy Spevack, illustrated by Joan Holub. Right: From *Eggs!*, by F. R. Robinson, illustrated by Randy Verougstraete. Both copyright 1997 by Pearson Education, Inc., or its affiliates. Used by permission. All rights reserved.

tion to solve the word. We have found that books such as these are particularly conducive to promoting the interactive use of a variety of informational sources for word solving. Indeed, the use of strategy-promoting books, which can be found in a number of different series intended for beginning readers, is quite central to promoting the interactive use of a variety of word identification strategies.

In our work with beginning readers, we have found use for all of the kinds of texts described above. The highly predictable and patterned books are particularly useful for children who know little about how the alphabetic writing system works. Occasional use of decodable books can be helpful for children who find it difficult to stabilize their knowledge of the alphabetic code. However, we do not use these texts exclusively for any extended period of time for fear that children will adopt an attitude toward reading that is exclusively code-focused. Because there are so many words in English that are not entirely decodable, it is important for children to learn to use other sources of information to check and confirm their initial decoding attempts. We have found that some children are slow to develop automaticity with high-frequency words. For these children, some series of sight word readers seems to be especially useful. However, in our early intervention programs we turn to strategy-promoting texts most frequently, and many kindergarten and first-grade classroom teachers have also found them helpful for the broad spectrum of children whom they teach. From our perspective, these texts capitalize on the advantages provided by many of the other kinds of texts described above, but do not suffer from their potential disadvantages.

Characteristics of Instruction

In addition to the characteristics of the child and the characteristics of the texts, the other major factor that influences children's ability to build their sight vocabulary is the instruction that guides their thinking about word solving. Whereas some children seem to learn to word-solve easily, without much instructional guidance, others need explicit guidance and extended opportunities for guided practice in order to become proficient word solvers. As Gerald Duffy (2003) puts it in his book *Explaining Reading*:

> Some students struggle with reading because they lack information about what they are trying to do and how to do it. They look around at their fellow students who are learning to read easily and say to themselves, "How are they doing that?" In short, they are mystified about how to do what other students seem to do with ease. (p. 9)

Because many children who struggle with learning to read have particular difficulty with learning to use the alphabetic code, schools and teachers often respond to these difficulties by emphasizing decoding strategies to the near exclusion of the other sources of word-solving information that texts provide. As a result, when these children encounter a word that is not fully decodable—a word such as *have*, for example, which, when decoded, would rhyme with *gave*—they have no other problem-solving strategies at their disposal. They are stuck. They have made no progress toward adding the word *have* to their sight vocabulary, and their ability to negotiate the remaining text is impaired.

On the other hand, some instructional approaches encourage children to rely primarily on the meaningful context in which a word occurs when attempting to solve unfamiliar words. Children are directed to attend to the alphabetic information provided in the word primarily to confirm their prediction of what the word will be. In fact, many children have been taught to think of a word that would make sense in the context in which the unfamiliar word is encountered, and then check the letters to see if they are consistent with their guess. Often a match on the first letter is considered a satisfactory match. Thus, for example, in reading the book *The Farm,* suppose a child reads the page that says "Look at the cow" as "Look at the calf" because she knows a lot about cows, and the particular cow pictured looks young to her. By some instructional philosophies, this error would be considered acceptable and would provide evidence that the reader was accessing the important sources of information for word identification. Further, because such an error did not substantially change the meaning of the text, teachers aligned with this instructional approach might decide that there was no value in redirecting the child's thinking on this particular word. This may be the appropriate reaction depending on the child's understanding of the alphabetic writing system. However, it is important to realize that a child who makes such an error has made little progress toward adding the word *cow* to the set of words that she can identify easily. Thus, the next time she encounters the word *cow*, it will be no more familiar than the first time she encountered it.

A child who is reliably able to use the beginning letter in a word to guide her identification attempts is ready to learn how to use more of the available alphabetic information to word solve. Directing such a child to consider both the beginning and ending letters in the word *cow*, as well as the general context and picture cues, would help to disconfirm *calf* and encourage her to think about other possible identities for the word. Most likely, this guidance would lead to the accurate identification of the word in this particular example.

In the ISA we explicitly teach word-solving strategies that are intended to help children negotiate such trouble spots by encouraging the use of as much of the alphabetic information as they are ready to handle, in combination with the contextual and pictorial cues that are available. Although there is little research that explicitly evaluates the specific effects of the ISA to teaching word-solving strategies, because it has always been only one component of the larger instructional approach, testimonials from both classroom and intervention teachers suggest that it is an extremely important and powerful component and may be *the* most important contribution that the ISA makes to teachers' effectiveness with children who struggle with literacy acquisition. In fact, in a small study recently completed by Anderson (2009), which compared the effects of teaching teachers about just the content of the material covered in Part II or just the content covered in Chapter 10 (strategic word learning), it was found that first-grade struggling readers whose intervention teachers learned about the strategic word-learning component out-performed students whose teachers learned the alphabetics content on measures of word identification and oral reading accuracy.

Although most of the words that children ultimately learn to identify will be learned through the use of strategic word solving, we do encourage teachers to explicitly teach some of the most frequently occurring words (e.g., *have, the,* and *was*) because these words are often difficult to identify strategically and because they occur so frequently that being able to identify them allows children to be more strategic. We discuss ways to promote the development of strategic word solving in Chapter 10; we discuss approaches to teaching high-frequency words in Chapter 11.

CHAPTER 10

Strategic Word Learning

WORD LEARNING GOAL 1

The child will develop flexibility and independence in applying code-based and meaning-based strategies to identify and learn unfamiliar words encountered in text.

Proficient readers are able to effortlessly identify virtually every printed word they encounter. Most of those words are learned through effective word solving. This chapter focuses on the development of effective word-solving skills that will enable readers to accurately identify unfamiliar words encountered while reading. Accurate identification of words in context, over time, helps readers learn the words so well that they become part of their sight vocabulary. Thus, effective word-solving skills allow readers to "teach" themselves to read the vast number of words they must ultimately be able to identify without effort. Share (1995) refers to effective word solving as a *self-teaching mechanism*. According to Share, "the ability to translate printed words *independently* into their spoken equivalents assumes a central role in reading acquisition" (p. 155). He credits the use of letter–sound relationships to identify unfamiliar words as the primary path toward the attainment of reading proficiency. However, he argues that beginning readers need to develop a variety of word identification strategies that can be used to build their sight vocabularies. While he places primary importance on decoding, Share acknowledges the significance of context in the word identification process. Indeed, he asserts that it is the individual's sensitivity to the constraints of the text, used in combination with a "willingness to test multiple alternative pronunciations for 'goodness of fit.'" (Share, 1995, p. 166), that allows for even the partial decoding of unfamiliar words to take on a self-teaching value. Moreover, experiences with successful decoding help children become familiar with new letter–sound correspondences and patterns, thus expanding the power of the self-teaching mechanism (Share, 1995). According to the self-teaching hypothesis, automatic word recognition depends on both the number of times the child has been exposed to a particular word and the nature and success of the child's previous attempts to read the word. When children independently apply skills and strategies to read unfamiliar words encountered in text, they learn more words, and more about words, each time they read.

To facilitate the development of effective self-teaching in the ISA, word identification strategies are explicitly taught to beginning and struggling readers. Two general types of strategies are taught: code-based strategies, which focus on the use of letters and larger orthographic units to arrive at an approximation of the pronunciation of a word, and meaning-based strategies, which encourage children to focus on whether the attempted pronunciation produces a word that fits the context. When children have difficulty settling on what a word is, they are encouraged to utilize additional strategies. For example, readers might try alternative pronunciations for some of the letters, or they might read beyond the as-yet unidentified word for additional contextual information that might inform their word-solving efforts. The goal is for children to learn to use both types of strategies in interactive and confirmatory ways.

APPROACHES TO WORD IDENTIFICATION

In the ISA, we discuss three general approaches that children might use in identifying a word: a selective cue approach, a strategic approach, and an automatic approach. The strategic approach is the focus of this chapter. However, because many beginning and struggling readers initially rely heavily on a selective cue approach, we discuss that one first. The automatic approach is, of course, the approach that is taken when a word is part of the reader's sight vocabulary.

The Selective Cue Approach

As children begin to learn a basic sight vocabulary, they are often inclined to attend to prominent cues to help them remember individual words. Sometimes the cues they choose have little or nothing to do with the printed letters in the words. They may, for example, attend to the overall shape of the word, to a picture (or even a smudge) that appears on the same page as the word, to the color of the paper on which the word appears, etc. Using these prominent cues, in many instances, will allow children to rapidly and accurately identify the word but only if it appears in the same context and/or if the children have encountered no other words with similar visual characteristics. For example, many years ago, we had a child in our clinic who was able to reliably identify the word *not* when it appeared in isolation on a word card that his tutor was using for sight word practice, but he was consistently unable to identify the word when it appeared in the context of a book. After much debate about what the problem might be, we finally thought to ask the child. He told us that the way he identified *not* on the word card was by the presence of a small pencil dot that appeared on that card and no other. In other words, he wasn't even looking at the word; the errant pencil mark was sufficient for him to do what he understood was expected of him—speak the word *not* when that particular card was displayed. Gough, Juel, and Griffith (1992) found that attention to such selective cues was common among 4- and 5-year-olds.

Most primary-grade teachers have encountered children who can identify a word in one context but not another and have found it rather mysterious. Understanding children's inclinations to use selective cues helps to demystify the behavior and has implications for how words are displayed on word walls and in other instructional resources. For example, early primary teachers often post word wall words on cards that highlight the shape of the word or on different colored cards or using different color markers for different words. Although these shape and color cues may help children find a particular word on the display, these cues may also lead them to attend less thoroughly to the alphabetic information and thus impede their learning of the word.

The selective cue use approach is quite natural because children who are just beginning to learn to read do not yet know what features of words are most relevant for reliable identification. And, in fact, the use of selective cues can be an effective way of identifying words early on if the words that are being learned are fairly distinct from one another. Further, in some cases, selective cues may completely suffice—particularly for words that are very distinctive (e.g., a McDonald's sign that includes the golden arches) and that occur in limited contexts (e.g., the names of characters in Russian novels). However, as the number of written words that children encounter grows, reliance on nonalphabetic cues such as the shape of the word or on very limited alphabetic cues such as the first letter and the general context will lead to confusion. Children who do not analyze the words they are learning fairly thoroughly are likely to confuse similar-looking words such as *was* and *saw*; *on* and *no*; *of, from,* and *for*; etc. Reliance on a selective cue approach is likely to result in stagnation in the growth of sight vocabulary and confusion about the reading process more generally.

The Strategic Approach

Word identification strategies are deliberate (conscious) actions that readers employ in an effort to identify an unfamiliar word. To move children beyond the selective cue approach to word identification, the ISA focuses on helping children learn to use code-based and meaning-based word identification strategies flexibly and interactively while reading texts. The ultimate goal is for unfamiliar words to be learned so well that they can be identified effortlessly in all contexts (i.e., they can be identified automatically). In order for this automaticity to occur, readers need to carefully analyze the word both in terms of its phonological and orthographic characteristics and in terms of the way it is used in context. The instruction that children receive can play a critical role in the development of such a strategic approach (Brown, 2003). We encourage teachers in the early primary grades to explicitly teach and model strategic word solving and to help children internalize the strategies that are taught such that they, ultimately, become skilled word solvers. To fully account for the complexity of the English writing system, two major types of strategies are taught: code-based strategies and meaning-based strategies.

What Is a Strategy?

Word identification strategies are a particular type of cognitive strategy. According to Dole, Nokes, and Drits (2009), "a cognitive strategy is a mental routine or procedure for accomplishing a cognitive goal" (p. 348). The goal of using word identification strategies is to accurately identify an unfamiliar word encountered in context.

Code-Based Strategies

Code-based strategies are taught because one major aspect of reading, for novice literacy learners, involves translating printed language into spoken language and translating speech into print. Ehri (1998, 2005) theorizes that, for the printed version of a word to be thoroughly stored in memory so that it ultimately becomes part of the reader's sight vocabulary, the reader needs to have mapped the sounds in the spoken word onto the letters in the printed word. That is, the reader needs to attempt to connect each of the sounds in the spoken word to one or more letters in the written word. In order to effectively use code-based strategies a reader must:

- Understand that spoken words are composed of smaller units of sounds (called *phonemes*) and have the ability to attend to and manipulate those phonemes.
- Be familiar with how the English alphabetic writing system works; readers need to understand that the phonemes in spoken words are represented by the letters in printed words.
- Over time, readers need to recognize that the alphabetic code for English is not entirely reliable and that there are alternative ways of pronouncing the same letter or letter combination, just as there are alternative ways to represent the same sound in writing (e.g., the long-*e* sound can be represented in multiple ways including: *ee, ea, ei, ey*, and *y*).

Meaning-Based Strategies

Meaning-based strategies serve to direct and check decoding attempts by allowing readers to anticipate what an unknown word might be and/or to test whether an initial decoding attempt fits the context. The use of meaning-based strategies also allows readers to evaluate, on an ongoing basis, whether the text is making sense and, if not, such strategies lead readers to institute some sort of "fix-up" strategy to recover meaning. In order to effectively use meaning-based strategies, readers must:

- Construe reading as a communicative process.
- Have sufficient background knowledge, vocabulary, and general language skill to notice when communication has broken down.
- Read materials that present some but not too much challenge; when a text is too challenging, readers are unable to build the context needed to enhance their word-solving efforts.

Interactive Strategy Use

In order to effectively puzzle through unfamiliar words, students generally need to use both code-based and meaning-based strategies in an interactive and confirmatory way. Because the English language includes many words that are not spelled in entirely predictable ways, decoding attempts often result in only an approximate pronunciation of the printed word. To settle on the actual pronunciation, the reader needs to think of a word that sounds like the result of the decoding attempt *and* that makes sense in the given context.

Children Tend to Learn What We Teach Them

Sometimes children who struggle with literacy acquisition come to believe that reading is about saying the words quickly and accurately and that writing is about accurately spelling and neatly writing the words. These beliefs may result from an emphasis placed on accuracy by the children's teachers. While we fully support and encourage teachers' efforts to address the needs of their students with respect to foundational skills, we also caution that this focus should not supersede a focus on understanding and enjoyment. Teachers need to emphasize that reading is about *meaning making* if we want children to focus on meaning.

In the ISA we build the foundation for establishing an active use of meaning-based strategies through the interactions we have with children during read-alouds and in other reading contexts in which we seek to develop general world knowledge, vocabulary and language skills, and active engagement with the meaning of the texts that are read or heard.

The Automatic Approach

The goal of teaching children to be strategic in their attempts to identify unfamiliar words is to help them learn words so well that they become part of their sight vocabulary. Thus, although a strategic approach to word solving may result in accurate word identification, a word would not be considered to have been learned until the child could identify it effortlessly and in all contexts. That is the level of learning that is needed to free up the cognitive resources needed for meaning construction.

Reading Skill and Approaches to Word Identification

As children progress as readers, the proportion of words they identify using each of the three approaches shifts. Early on, most children use a selective cue approach to identify a small number of words. As children begin to understand how the alphabetic writing system works and how printed words are used to convey complex ideas, they develop (with appropriate guidance) the ability to be strategic in their word identification. At this point, most of the words they can identify while reading may be the result of using a strategic approach, although those that have been identified successfully on several occasions may be so familiar that they are automatically identified. Proficient readers identify the vast majority of words automatically, although they will continue to encounter words that require a strategic approach and perhaps even a few words (e.g., characters in Russian novels) that they will identify via a selective cue approach.

STRATEGIC WORD LEARNING

There has been remarkably little research on word identification strategy instruction in terms of systematically testing which strategies are most effectively taught and when and how to effectively teach strategy use (Brown, 2003). However, summaries of the scientific research on literacy acquisition have generally concluded that it is critical for children to learn to use all of the graphic (letter) information in printed words as soon as possible (see Pressley, 2006, for a review) because *children who do not use all of the graphic information when attempting to read an unfamiliar word do not effectively store that word in memory* (Ehri, 2005; Share, 1995). As a result, upon future encounters with the word, it is no more familiar than it was the first time. Children who attend to all of the graphic information in printed words store more complete word information in memory and are more likely to successfully identify the word on subsequent encounters.

Because accurate word solving is critical to word learning, and because written English is not entirely decodable, it is also important that children learn to use the context in which the word occurs to direct and verify their decoding attempts. Thus, children who rely too heavily on decoding strategies will produce many,

many word identification errors when attempting to read unfamiliar words and will fail to make sense of the materials they read.

One of the biggest differences between children who experience difficulty with learning to read and those who learn to read with relative ease is in their abilities to use the phonological code. Strong readers learn to use the code more quickly than do children who struggle and who depend more on meaning-based strategies, presumably because their phonological skills are weaker and therefore are not as useful to them (Nicholson, 1991; Tunmer & Chapman, 2004). However, because they do not make adequate use of the alphabetic code, they do not effectively store words in memory, and, as a result, their sight vocabulary develops more slowly, thus impeding their ability to read grade-level texts.

Such a finding might lead some to conclude that code-based strategies should be the primary focus of early reading instruction, at least for children who struggle with literacy acquisition. However, acting on such a conclusion has the potential to move the children away from focusing on the meaning of the things they read and may move them away from the expectation that what they read should make sense.

Based on the logic articulated above and on research on strategy instruction in the comprehension domain (Pearson & Gallagher, 1983; Roehler & Duffy, 1984), we have developed an approach to word identification strategy instruction that teachers report is very effective for beginning[1] and struggling readers.[2] The strategies are taught explicitly, and the children are provided with extensive guided practice in applying the strategies. The ultimate goal is for the children to internalize the strategies so that they can effectively word-solve without teacher guidance. In order to help children internalize the problem-solving approach, we teach a small set of strategies of each type: four code-based strategies and four meaning-based strategies. Thus, we do not teach an exhaustive list of all of the things an active reader might do in attempting to solve an unfamiliar word. However, the strategies that we do teach are representative of the kinds of things that readers might do. Our goal in keeping the strategy list fairly short is to make it more likely that readers will be able to learn the list well enough that they will be able to prompt their own word-solving attempts by recalling the strategies on the list.

Code-Based Strategies

Code-based strategies include using individual letters and larger orthographic units (digraphs, blends, phonograms, inflectional endings, etc.) to figure out unfa-

---

[1] The vast majority of the research on the ISA has involved the implementation of the entire approach. Therefore, we cannot attribute the effects of the ISA to the approach to teaching word-learning strategies.

[2] The potential utility of a variant of the ISA for accelerating reading development among older students identified as learning disabled is currently being researched. Initial results are encouraging (Gelzheiser, Scanlon, Vellutino, & Hallgren-Flynn, under review).

miliar words. The aspects of the code to which children are expected to attend in utilizing the code-based strategies change as children's skill with the alphabetic code develops. Teachers are cautioned to be sure that children demonstrate the needed code-based skills in isolation before they are expected to apply them in the context of reading connected text (see Part II). We teach the following code-based strategies:

- *Think about the sounds in the word.* At the earliest points in development, children are taught to attend to just the beginning letter/sound in the unfamiliar word and to use that information in conjunction with pictorial or other contextual supports to identify the word. As children progress, the teacher focuses on encouraging them to use both beginning and ending sounds. Ultimately, children are expected to look all the way through the word, thinking about the sounds and blending them to make a word that fits the context.

- *Look for word families or other parts you know.* In using this strategy, readers look for word parts that have been explicitly taught (e.g., phonograms) or for word parts that are familiar (e.g., consonant and vowel digraphs, spelling patterns such as *tion*).

- *Try out different pronunciations for some of the letters, especially the vowel(s).* In using this strategy, students retrieve from memory alternate sounds for letters to determine which sound produces a meaningful word that fits the context. This strategy is particularly useful for vowels that have been taught and practiced. For example, in puzzling through the word *break*, the child might try the long sound for the *e*, the short sound of the *e*, and finally the long sound of the *a* before deciding that a real word that fits the context has been identified. The strategy of trying different pronunciations is also useful for the hard and soft sounds of *c* and *g* and for vowel digraphs that have more than one common pronunciation (e.g., *oo* and *ow*). This strategy can also be used to deal with silent letters in some letter combinations (e.g, *kn, gh, wh, pn*).

- *Break the word into smaller parts.* This strategy is useful in identifying words with inflectional endings (*ed, ing, s*), words with prefixes and suffixes, and multisyllabic words. By breaking a word into smaller parts, the decoding of an unfamiliar word can be somewhat simplified. As with other word identification strategies, this strategy would generally be used in combination with other code- and meaning-based strategies in efforts to accurately identify an unfamiliar word encountered in context. In initially teaching this strategy, the teacher would encourage students to cover known parts of unfamiliar words, attempt to decode the part of the word that isn't covered, rely on the context of the sentence and larger text to get a better idea of what the word might be, and, having formed a hypothesis about what the word is, read it with the covered part added back in and check to see if the resulting word fits both the meaning and the syntax of the sentence. Because using the "break-the-word-into-smaller-parts" strategy requires facility with several other strategies, this tends to be one of the last strategies taught.

Meaning-Based Strategies

Meaning-based strategies include the use of picture clues and the context of the sentence and the larger text. We teach the following meaning-based strategies:

- *Check the pictures.* In using this strategy, students check the picture to see if there is information that is useful in identifying a puzzling word. This strategy is particularly useful for students who are just beginning to learn about the reading process and who do not yet have the ability to use code-based strategies to puzzle through unfamiliar words.
- *Think of words that might make sense.* In applying this strategy, readers use the meaning and syntax[3] of what has been read to generate a hypothesis about what a puzzling word is or to confirm the identity of an unknown word that has been identified using other strategies. While it is sometimes possible to accurately identify an unfamiliar word encountered in context by relying solely on this strategy, this practice should not be encouraged because such an approach would not draw students' attention to the printed form of the word and would therefore not help the word to become part of their sight vocabulary.
- *Read past the puzzling word and then come back to it.* In using this strategy, students read on, often to the end of the sentence, to gain more insight into what the puzzling word might be. The strategy can be especially helpful when used early in a sentence or paragraph, when readers have not yet acquired much sense of what the sentence or paragraph is about. However, this strategy is also useful if the puzzling word occurs later in the sentence; sometimes reading the next sentence will help to clarify the identity of an unfamiliar printed word.
- *Go back to the beginning of the sentence and start again.* Sometimes when readers encounter an unfamiliar word, taking the time to puzzle over it causes them to forget what has already been read. In using this strategy, readers go back to the beginning of the sentence and start again to regain the context that the earlier part of the sentence provides. This additional context sometimes provides the needed information to confirm a hypothesis about the word's identity.

TEACHING TO PROMOTE THE USE OF WORD IDENTIFICATION STRATEGIES

Although the ultimate goal is for children to learn to use the code-based and meaning-based strategies in a confirmatory way, we generally teach the strategies one at a time, since learning to use a new strategy takes effort. We explain what the strategy is, how it works, when to use it, and so on. Children are provided with a good deal of guided and independent practice with a strategy in order to ensure

---

[3]In the ISA, we do not try to get children to make a clear distinction between semantic (meaning) and syntactic (grammatical) sources of information for word solving as two sources are often intricately connected.

that it becomes part of their repertoire. However, we do not wait until children are proficient in the use of one strategy before introducing another. Rather, we provide focused practice with each new strategy as it is introduced and offer guidance in the interactive use of all of the strategies that have been taught.

> **KEEP IN MIND** The way we talk about the process of identifying unfamiliar words may influence children's willingness to engage in the process. Referring to words as *hard* may lead some children to feel defeated before they even begin. Referring to unfamiliar words as *puzzling* or as *detective words*, however, may be a bit more motivating.

Resources That Support Strategy Use

Reading is a complicated process for beginning readers. Often they are asked to access a great deal of information as they read. For example, they may need to remember the word identification strategies they have learned, the sounds associated with each of the letters and letter combinations (including digraphs and phonograms) that have been covered, and the high-frequency words that have been taught. Meanwhile, they need to make sense of the text they are reading by drawing upon their prior knowledge and integrating it with the information in the text.

Early in reading development several of these knowledge sources are not automatically available. Therefore, it makes sense to provide resources to support children's processing. For the strategy component, as children develop a repertoire of strategies they can use, we provide a listing of the strategies and encourage them to refer to this list, if necessary, when trying to figure out a word. The list of strategies used in the ISA is provided in Figure 10.1. In the left-hand column is a symbol that is intended to serve as a mnemonic for the strategy listed in the right-hand column. Obviously, the mnemonics require a bit of explanation if they are to serve their intended function. For example, the children might be told that the little picture is a reminder that the pictures in a book might help them to figure out what a word is. The word *fun,* which serves as the mnemonic for the "think-about-the-sounds-in-the-word" strategy is used, we might say, because you can figure out the word *fun* just by thinking of the sounds of the letters—and it is *fun* to figure out words by yourself.

> **KEEP IN MIND** Strategies should generally be introduced one at a time. A strategy list containing only those strategies that have been introduced should be posted and made available to the children as they read. As new strategies are taught, they should be added to the list.

In addition to the strategy list, it makes sense to have other supports available, including the *key words* that are used to remind the children of the sounds

To figure out a word:

 Check the pictures.

 Think about the sounds in the word.

 Think of words that might make sense.

 Look for word families or other parts you know.

 Read past the puzzling word.

 Go back to the beginning of the sentence and start again.

aeiou Try different pronunciations for some of the letters, especially the vowel(s).

 Break the word into smaller parts.

FIGURE 10.1. Word identification strategy list. From Scanlon and Anderson (2010). Copyright by the International Reading Association. Reprinted by permission.

that letters make, the list of *word families* or *phonograms* that have been taught, and a *word wall* (perhaps personalized for individuals or groups) with the high-frequency words that have been taught. We have observed that children who are provided with such resources and who are explicitly taught to use them when they encounter difficulty ultimately become more active and effective word solvers.

The Components of Strategy Instruction

Research on strategy instruction in reading has, for the most part, focused on comprehension strategy instruction and has yielded a general consensus with regard to the critical components of strategy instruction (Duffy, 2003; Paris, Lipson, & Wixson, 1983; Pearson & Gallagher, 1983). In the ISA we have used the same general approach in the context of teaching about word identification strategies. In general, the components of strategy instruction involve (1) clear explanations of the strategies, (2) teacher think-alouds to model and illustrate the strategy, (3) guided practice in the use of the strategy, and (4) gradual release of responsibility for strategy use to the student for the purpose of promoting independent application. Each of these components of strategy instruction is described below.

Clear Explanations: Using Explicit Language to Communicate What the Strategy Is and When and How to Use It

Beginning readers and especially children who are struggling with the beginning stages of learning to read are often confused about how the process works. In explaining a strategy, it is important to try to take into account what each child understands about the process. Word identification strategies need to be explained from a child's perspective. This may be more difficult than it initially seems. It is often hard to explain how to do something that one does without conscious thought. Therefore, in preparing to teach a word identification strategy, teachers should think about how to explain the strategy before beginning instruction.

The *check-the-picture* strategy is typically taught first because, when highly predictable and patterned texts are used, it makes the least demands on children's literacy skills. In explaining this strategy, the teacher might say: "When you are reading and you come to a word you don't know, sometimes it helps to look at the picture. The picture might give you some ideas about what the word is." Explaining the strategy this way, rather than simply saying "Check the pictures," will help to make it clear that it is the *word* that needs to be identified and that the picture may provide an assist.

In first teaching the *think-about-the-sounds* strategy the teacher might say:

> "When we read, the letters in the words help us figure out what the word is. We
> have been learning the sounds of some of the letters, and now you are ready
> to use those letter sounds to figure out words in books. To start with, we are

going to think about the first letter in our words because that will give us some ideas about what the word might be. Thinking about the sounds that the letters make is a strategy that we will use a lot as we learn to read. So, now we know about two things we can do to figure out words when we read: We can check the picture, and we can think about the first sound in the word."

The teacher would then demonstrate how the strategies would be applied in reading an emergent-level book (see Think-Alouds, below). As children progress as readers, the *think-about-the-sounds* strategy would be extended to include thinking about both the beginning and ending sounds and, ultimately, to thinking about the sounds all the way through the word.

Eventually, the strategy prompts should evolve into a shorthand way of reminding children of how they might figure out an unfamiliar word. The children should be taught to use the mnemonics to trigger their memory for the strategies. However, when a strategy is first introduced, it is important to try to ensure that the children really understand what the strategy entails.

Think-Alouds: Modeling the Use of the Strategy

Teachers can use think-aloud techniques to help students understand the kind of thinking that a strategy involves. Research on the use of think-alouds in the context of comprehension strategy instruction indicates that they are most effective when they are explicit, leave students little to infer about how the strategy should be applied, and when they are flexibly adjusted to reflect the demands of the text (Duke & Pearson, 2002). In a think-aloud, teachers talk about their thinking as they demonstrate their approach to solving a cognitive problem. During a shared reading activity, for example, teachers might occasionally puzzle through a word that they pretend not to recognize, or they might, in advance, cover up all or part of a word in the text. For example, in a think-aloud for the picture cue strategy, teachers might use a simple patterned/predictable book and put stickies over some of the words that change from one page to the next.

The teacher might say: "I have covered up some of the words in this book so I can show you how checking the pictures can help you figure out a word that you don't already know." Then the teacher reads through the book, pointing as she proceeds, until coming to the first covered word. At that point the teacher might say: "Hmmm. I don't know what that word is, so I am going to look at the picture to see if it gives me any ideas about what the covered word is. I see a . . . . in the picture, so I think that the word may be. . . . " The teacher would then uncover the word to confirm, saying, "I was right. For this word, checking the picture helped me figure out what the word is!" Once the think-about-the-sounds strategy has been introduced, the teacher might engage in the same type of think-aloud, except that she would generate a short list of possibilities for the covered word and then uncover just the first letter to confirm what the word actually is.

When children have learned multiple strategies and are proficient in the use of several of them, the teacher might use multiple strategies during a think-aloud:

> "Hmmm, I don't know this word. I'll have to figure it out. I know lots of things I can try. I can look at the letters in the word and think about their sounds. Maybe I'll notice a word family or some other part I know. I can think about words that would make sense in the story. Maybe the picture will give me some ideas."

Guided Practice and Gradual Release of Responsibility

Upon first attempting to use a given strategy, children need to work collaboratively to develop the thinking processes involved. The first few opportunities for children to use the strategy may be contrived to ensure that the utility of the strategy is very clear. For example, for the strategy of *trying different pronunciations for some of the letters, especially the vowels,* the first time the teacher asks the children to use this strategy, she might show a sentence containing the word *child*.

Jason is a child.

For children who know a fair amount about the alphabetic code, the most reasonable first attempt at the word *child* would be to pronounce it with a short vowel sound. After discussing that this decoding attempt did not result in a word that made sense in the sentence, the teacher would prompt the students to use the new strategy that had been taught (and perhaps reiterate the strategy). Once the word is successfully identified, the students and teacher would briefly reflect on the utility of the strategy.

Across many different reading episodes, teachers should provide the children with practice in using newly taught strategies in contexts in which the particular strategy will work effectively (e.g., when children encounter a word they do not immediately recognize, and the new strategy is likely to facilitate word identification, the teacher would suggest that they try the new strategy). Once children have experienced some success in applying the strategy, they need experience with attempting to use the strategy when it doesn't work. This will help them to understand the need to be flexible in applying the various strategies and to use multiple sources of information.

Thus, during guided practice the teacher should act as a coach, initially advising children to try the strategy only when she is fairly sure that it will work and later encouraging them to try the strategy both when it will work and when it is not clear that it will work. Early on, when a strategy does not work, the teacher and children should reflect on the fact that the strategy did not work in that particular situation. For example, the teacher might say: "Hmm, sometimes checking the pictures does not help us to figure out the word. Later on, we will learn some other strategies that might have worked for this word." Or, "What other strategies do we know that we could try?"

Our goal is for the children to internalize the problem-solving strategies and to become independent in their use. One way to encourage internalization is to have them periodically rehearse the strategies they have learned initially by referring to the strategy list, but later by relying on memory. For example, before reading a book, children might be asked: "What are some of the things we can do when we come to a word we don't know in this book?" In addition, when a child gets stuck on a word while reading, the teacher might say: "That word is puzzling you—what could you do to try to figure it out?" Engaging children in thinking aloud about the problem-solving strategies serves to enhance their awareness of the process (Prawat, 1989). When a teacher responds to difficulties in this way on a consistent basis, the children are likely to ask themselves the same questions when they encounter an unfamiliar word. They might say to themselves: "I don't know what that word is. What can I do to figure it out?"

KEEP IN MIND "Guided practice is something we too often skip. We teach, assume the teaching has paid off in learning, and then go straight to independent practice, the next step in the learning process" (Saunders-Smith, 2003, p. 50).

Independent Practice

The ultimate goal of strategy teaching is for children to be able to independently apply word-solving strategies. To ensure that the children do, in fact, use the strategies when not engaged with the teacher, it is helpful to reflect on and discuss their strategy use when they are reading independently. Some teachers encourage children who are learning word identification strategies to use sticky notes to mark places in text where they have relied on strategies for word solving during independent reading.

Encouraging Interactive Strategy Use

While teaching the individual strategies is certainly important, it is critical that children learn to use strategies in combination and in mutually supportive and confirming ways. Thus, for example, a child who has learned to effectively use the strategy of trying different pronunciations for some of the letters, especially the vowels might reasonably decode the word *read* such that it rhymes with *seed*. However, before settling on this pronunciation, he would evaluate whether that word fit the context in which it occurred and, if not, would try a different pronunciation (such as pronouncing it with the short-*e* vowel sound) and then check to see whether that word fits with the context. Thus, interactive strategy use often involves an iterative process in which different pronunciations of individual words are checked against the reader's evolving understanding of the text. To illustrate this interactive and confirmatory use of strategies, teachers often find it useful to use a *cloze* task.

A description of how this procedure might be used with children who often make oral reading errors that do not fit the context of the passage is illustrated in Figure 10.2, using a page from the book *Six Fine Fish* (Dobeck, 1996). For this example, it would be useful to stress how just thinking about the meaning of the sentence gave the children some pretty good ideas about what the covered word might be. If the read-past-the-puzzling-word strategy had been taught, it would be appropriate to discuss this as well as other strategies that were utilized.

Assessing, Reinforcing, and Planning from Strategy Use

As children progress, it is important to carefully evaluate the strategies they do and do not use effectively while reading. Some teachers find it useful to take running records for this purpose. However, because the use of running records can limit the teacher's ability to respond to the student's word-solving attempts, we do not encourage frequent use of them. Rather, we encourage teachers to make note of the strategies they observe the children using, or neglecting to use, and to offer assistance and guidance as opportunities arise. For children who are first learning to be strategic word solvers, teachers should note which strategies are used spontaneously and which are used only with prompting. Such notations allow teachers to plan instruction more effectively. Thus, for example, if children are routinely and reliably using a particular strategy, that strategy probably does not need to be discussed at length or modeled in future lessons. If, on the other hand, children are using a particular strategy effectively but only when prompted to do so, the teacher needs to plan ways to promote independence in the use of that strategy. For strategies that children do not utilize effectively, even when prompted, additional explanation and modeling would be needed.

Evaluating and Documenting the Use of Word Identification Strategies

Figure 10.3 presents a group snapshot for strategic word learning that might be used to track the development of word identification strategies among children in a small-group instructional situation. To document strategy use in any given lesson, the teacher might listen to an individual child read and make notes, using two-letter codes to represent each strategy, to record which strategies the child uses spontaneously or with prompting. Although it is certainly not always possible to determine which strategies children are using, especially for children who do a lot of their word solving in their heads, careful attention to the types of errors they make and to where their eyes go as they puzzle over a word can provide insights. By reviewing observational notations made over a week or so, the teacher would be able to update the snapshot for the children in each of her groups. Looking across

(text continues on p. 217)

This big fish is puffed up like a ball.
It has sharp _____ all over it.
The sharp spikes tell other fish to
stay away!

Prior to meeting with students, the teacher selects a page in a book and identifies a word on the page that is fairly, but not entirely, predictable based on context. Covering the word with a sticky note (in this example, the word *spikes* is covered), the teacher reminds the students that often they can make some pretty good guesses about what a word will be if they read up to the word, think about what they know about the book so far, and look at what the pictures show. The teacher would then:

- Have the children read the text to the end of the sentence that contains the covered word.
- Ask the children to generate guesses about what the missing word might be. (In the current example, they might guess *points, things, spots, spikes, needles*, etc.).
- Make a list of the possibilities the children provide (trying to ensure that the list contains the covered word).
- Engage the children in a conversation about the other information they would need in order to figure out the covered word (perhaps by encouraging them to think of the strategies list).
- Reveal some of the print information to the children (in this example, uncovering the beginning consonant blend would be most appropriate; however, in other examples, it might be appropriate to uncover just the initial letter or possibly a word family). Encourage children to use the print information to narrow down the list of possibilities they generated.
- Ask them to think about what else they would need to ultimately confirm whether the hidden word is *spots* or *spikes*.
- Uncover the word and talk about the need to use lots of different kinds of information to figure out a word.

FIGURE 10.2. Illustration of a cloze activity to promote interactive strategy use. From *Ready Readers, Six Fine Fish,* by Maryann Dobeck, illustrated by Tom Leonard. Copyright 1996 by Pearson Education, Inc., or its affiliates. Used by permission. All rights reserved.

Group Snapshot—Strategic Word Learning, Use of Word Identification Strategies							
Student names							
CP—**C**heck the **P**ictures							
TS—**T**hink about the **S**ounds in the word	First						
	Last						
	Medial						
MS—Think of words that might **M**ake **S**ense							
WP—Look for **W**ord families or other **P**arts you know							
RP—**R**ead **P**ast the puzzling word							
SA—Go back to the beginning of the sentence and **S**tart **A**gain							
DP—Try **D**ifferent **P**ronunciations for some of the letters, especially the vowel(s)							
BW—**B**reak the **W**ord into smaller parts							
IC – Use multiple strategies in an **I**nteractive and **C**onfirmatory way							

Key:

◻ *B—Beginning* indicates that instruction has addressed the strategy but that the child has only a preliminary understanding or capability with regard to its use.

◻ *D—Developing* indicates that the child has some understanding of the strategy but does not reliably and/or spontaneously use the strategy.

◻ *P—Proficient* indicates that the child reliably and spontaneously demonstrates use of the strategy.

FIGURE 10.3. Group snapshot for strategic word learning: Use of word identification strategies.

the children's application of strategies, she might notice patterns of use and nonuse that would inform planning for upcoming lessons.

WORD IDENTIFICATION STRATEGY-FOCUSED INSTRUCTION

We describe how word identification strategy instruction, and the teacher thinking that goes along with that instruction, might unfold before, during, and after children engage in reading a book.

Strategy Instruction Before Reading

Preparing to Read a New Book

Until children are routinely and effectively strategic, it is important to provide them with guidance and instruction in the use of word identification strategies prior to reading each new book. The characteristics of the books used for the purpose of promoting strategic reading are important to consider both because the level of challenge that the children encounter in each book will influence their ability to be strategic and because some books facilitate strategy instruction and practice more than others (see "Characteristics of the Texts" section in the introduction to Part III, p. 191).

Selection of Texts That Will Be Somewhat Challenging

Generally, texts that children can read with 90–95% accuracy are considered to be appropriate for instructional purposes. A determination of which texts will fall in this range for particular children can be accomplished by taking running records (Clay, 1985; Johnston, 1997) on leveled texts and determining the highest text level (Fountas & Pinnell, 1996) at which the child is able to maintain this level of accuracy. Alternatively, following the sequence in a structured series of texts, such as a basal series or the Ready Readers (Pearson Publishing Company), may help to keep students in the appropriate range of challenge; many such series attempt to systematically develop the decoding skills and high-frequency sight vocabulary that students need to negotiate upcoming texts.

Attention needs to be given to the level of challenge a text presents because, when there are many unknown words and/or when the content is too unfamiliar, it is extremely difficult, if not impossible, for children to be effectively strategic in working through it. A wide range of factors contributes to the level of challenge that a text provides for a particular child (see Mesmer, 2008). Teachers who work closely and thoughtfully with small groups of children will, ideally, come to know their students well enough that they are able to select books that provide sufficient challenge and thereby opportunity to observe and guide strategic processing but not so much challenge as to frustrate or overwhelm the child.

KEEP IN MIND Children learn to read by reading. Some reading series engage children in reading and rereading the same passage for an entire week. If this is the only reading that children do, their rate of progress *and* their motivation are likely to be more limited than if a greater variety of texts were read and they, therefore, had more opportunities to be strategic in their word-solving efforts.

Preparing Children to Read a Specific Book

The supportiveness of the introduction of a new book should be based on the characteristics of the text and the skills and strategies of the children. If we provide more support than the children need to read a book, their opportunities to grow as readers will be limited because they will not have the opportunity to use their developing word identification strategies. If we provide too little support, they may become frustrated. Further, they will not be able to effectively apply their developing word identification strategies because, when a text is too difficult, children are unable to attend to whether or not what they are reading makes sense. Thus, it may be difficult for children to determine if word identification errors have occurred.

Several different approaches to the provision of support prior to reading a new book are presented below. The procedures are listed in order of their supportiveness, with the most supportive approaches listed first.

More Support

↑

• *Read the text to the child(ren).* Children at the earliest stages of reading development often benefit from having a book read to them before they attempt to read it. This approach allows them to focus more of their attention on the printed words when they ultimately read, since they had the opportunity to enjoy and comprehend the text when it was read to them. However, it is important to keep in mind that, for children to become independent readers, they need to have the opportunity to engage in the strategic thinking and problem solving that reading a new book entails. If every text is read to them before they attempt it, which is the practice in some basal series, it will limit their opportunities to become strategic thinkers.

• *Introduce the book.* Previewing a book by looking at and discussing the pictures (sometimes called a *picture walk*) can help children develop schemas for the book and provide the teacher with the opportunity to introduce some of the language structures and concepts that will allow children to read the text more easily. Book introductions typically include several of the following components:

- Introducing the title and author of the book.
- Relating the book to something the children know about, care about, have read or heard previously, etc.

- Collaborative wondering about what the book might be about; this often includes making predictions about what will happen in the text.
- Flipping through the pages of the book and discussing what is happening and possibly refining predictions.
- For books that include challenging language or language patterns, incorporating the language from the text into the discussion.

• *Teach important unfamiliar words and/or decoding elements before children read the text.* For a given text, it is generally possible to anticipate which words and/or decoding elements (e.g., word families) will cause difficulty for children. The important words or elements to teach ahead of time are those that both occur frequently in the text and would be difficult for children to figure out, given the contextual supports in the book and the children's current level of decoding skill. Teaching these words and/or decoding elements prior to having the children read the text will allow them to read more fluently on their first attempt.

• *Provide a brief book introduction and allow the children to independently preview the text before reading.* Children who have had extensive experience with book introductions can often gather a good deal of information about a text by flipping through the book independently before reading. The teacher might provide an overall schema for the text by briefly telling the children the topic of the text. For example: "Today we are going to read this book about snakes; before you read, look through the book a bit to see what you'll be learning about snakes." The children are then given time to preview the text on their own before reading.

Less
Support

KEEP IN MIND It is possible to do too much in preparing children to read a new book. For example, we have observed teachers who teach far too many words from the book before asking the children to read. Only words that are important for understanding the text and that the children are unlikely to be able to figure out, given the contextual/pictorial support and their current word-solving strategies, should be taught prior to reading. We have also observed teachers routinely having children locate the most challenging language in the text prior to having them read the book. As a result, when the children come to this portion of the text while reading, their opportunities for problem solving will be reduced because they have already looked at and read the language. As an alternative, the teacher might use the challenging language during the book introduction but not directly draw the children's attention to the print. That way, the children will be primed for the unusual language but will have the opportunity to puzzle through it when they encounter it in print.

Strategy Talk

The nature of strategy discussions that are provided before a new text is read will depend on the children's point in development with word identification strategies. If new strategies have been taughty recently, these might be reviewed fairly thoroughly, whereas strategies that the children understand and use well might only be briefly mentioned or not mentioned at all. Alternatively, if all of the strategies have been taught but the children need more support in effectively using some more than others, a brief lesson concerning the use of one or two strategies might be offered. Sometimes strategy talk before reading might involve having the children list the strategies they know, in an effort to help them internalize the strategies so that they can call upon them when neither the teacher nor the list is available.

Strategy Instruction During Reading

Teachers should attempt to listen to individual children read as often as possible—particularly children who are identified as at risk for reading difficulties—because observing children's approaches to word solving provides opportunities for the teacher to coach and guide students' strategic behaviors and will inform the teacher's planning of future strategy instruction. In small-group contexts, teachers should listen to one child read during each reading opportunity. As a child reads, it is important for the teacher to attend to each of the components described below.

Allowing the Child Enough (Relaxed) Time to Puzzle through Difficult Sections of Text

It takes a good deal of time for a young child to orchestrate the various strategies. If the child is given assistance with puzzling through an unfamiliar word before he has had time to think things through, he may not develop the independence that is critical to becoming an effective word learner. Teachers need to think carefully about how to respond to children's difficulties when they read. As we've noted previously, children's development can be limited by providing either too little or too much assistance. The assistance given needs to take different forms for different students at different points in time (and in different contexts). Thus, the recommendation to "allow the child enough time" does not come with an explicit recommendation concerning how long one should wait.

In some contexts it may be appropriate to provide assistance almost immediately—as when a child encounters a word that the teacher knows he cannot decode, and the context is not helpful. In other situations, it may be appropriate to wait as much as 10 seconds or more if the child appears to be problem-solving productively.

When they are involved in partner reading, children who need more time to puzzle through words may feel anxious about taking the time they need, and/or their partners may provide the word before they have had time to think it through. When children routinely have the words that they are puzzling over solved for them, their sense of efficacy with regard to reading may be undermined, and they may come to view themselves as unable to word-solve.

Rather than allowing partners to provide the word that other children are puzzling over, it is helpful to encourage children to view taking the time to figure out a word as something positive ("It's fun to be able to figure out the word yourself—it's like being a detective"). If a child is really stuck on a word, the partner might be encouraged to make suggestions concerning different word-solving strategies to try, but it should be done only when the child who is reading indicates that he needs some ideas. For example, the teacher might say, "Take the time you need to figure out the word and let your partner know if you would like him to suggest a strategy that might work." This approach not only provides the reader with a bit more time to think, but engages the other students in thinking about the strategies and can lead to productive conversations about how multiple strategies can be used to figure out the same word.

Noticing and Acknowledging Children's Strategic Word Solving

One of the values of listening to children read and noting their strategic word solving is that it focuses teachers' attention on what the children are doing to solve words—both when they are successful and when they are not. We have long known that guiding children's thinking and problem solving (and behavior) is more effective when we attend more to what they have done right than to what they have not done right. This principle applies to word solving as well. Teachers should look for occasions when children use one or more of the strategies spontaneously and praise their efforts even if they are not entirely successful in identifying unfamiliar words. Indicators that a child is being strategic include the following:

- The child spontaneously corrects a word identification error.
- The child hesitates briefly over an unfamiliar word before identifying it accurately.
- The child refers to resources such as a strategy list, key-word chart, or word wall for assistance in identifying a puzzling word.

When a child begins to demonstrate the inclination to be strategic, it is important to provide explicit praise. Examples of explicit praise include the following:

- "I noticed that you looked at the key-word chart when you puzzled through that word—that helped you remember the sounds of some of those letters and figure out what word would fit there."
- "I noticed you looking at your strategy list when you came to that puzzling word—that is a very good way to help you remember some of the things you could try when you need to puzzle through a word."
- "Wow! Good thinking! When you got to the end of that sentence you realized that something didn't make sense and you went back and reread the sentence and tried a different pronunciation for that word, and it worked."

Gradual Release of Responsibility

In order for strategy instruction to have the desired effect, children ultimately need to become independent in strategy use. For some children, teachers will need to hand over responsibility for strategic word solving in a very planned and gradual way. Teachers should provide enough support for word solving to allow the child to be successful but not so much support that the child doesn't need to do much thinking. Thus, for example, in some cases it might be appropriate to suggest a specific strategy for a child to use; in other cases, patient waiting will be the most helpful thing to do. Below is an ordering of prompts that a teacher might provide or actions that a teacher might take that range from more to less supportive. In general, we want to provide the child with the least support possible while still ensuring success.

More Support

- Tell the child the puzzling word if there is little likelihood that, given his current skills, he could figure it out.

- Suggest a specific strategy or combination of strategies that is likely to work well for the child in the given context and help him apply the strategy if need be (e.g., "Look at the first letter in that word and then look at the picture to see if it gives you some ideas").

- Remind the child to look at the strategy list for ideas on how he might solve the word (e.g., "That word is puzzling you; look at your strategy list for some ideas on how to figure it out"). The purpose here is to teach the child to use available resources.

- Ask the child to think of the strategies that he could use without explicitly referring him to the list (e.g., "That word is puzzling you; what are some of the things you could try?"). Here, the purpose is to encourage the child to begin to internalize the strategies. He may refer to the list if he wishes, but if the teacher believes that he is beginning to internalize the strategies, the teacher may not want to direct him to the list.

- Wait patiently while the child puzzles through the word and try to notice what the child does to figure it out and explicitly praise him (e.g., "You had to do some thinking on that word; I noticed that you covered up the ending while you were trying to figure it out—that worked, didn't it!").

- Wait patiently while the child puzzles through the word and then ask how he figured it out (e.g., "I noticed that you had to think about that word a bit; what did you do to figure it out?"). This reflection helps the child internalize the strategies by engaging him in talking about how he used them.

- Wait patiently while the child puzzles through the word and then briefly compliment him and move on (e.g., "Good! I see you are really thinking like a reader!"). This is partly just a pat on the back, but it also helps to reinforce the notion that reading involves (*is*) thinking.

Less Support

Promoting Self-Regulation, Not Dependence

In the context of reading, *self-regulation* refers to the ability to independently notice and solve problems that arise with either word identification or comprehension. Teachers have a fair amount of control over whether children become self-regulated learners. In our experience, particularly in intervention settings, teachers are often inclined to do too much of the thinking for the students; as a result, the students come to depend on the teacher in ways that are counterproductive for their reading growth. When a child routinely looks at the teacher upon encountering difficulty with a word, it is usually a pretty good sign that the teacher has been too helpful to the child. It is important for teachers to reflect on what they do (or do not do) to promote self-regulation with regard to word learning. Many times fairly small changes in how the teacher reacts to a student's difficulties will lead to big advances in the student's ability to problem-solve independently. Table 10.1 provides a listing of some common student reading behaviors along with the teacher behaviors and responses that either promote dependence on the teacher or promote independence of the teacher.

Encouraging Self-Correction among Children Who Are Capable But Disinclined

Some children who clearly demonstrate the ability to use word identification strategies when prompted by the teacher do not readily develop independence in using those strategies. They make many word identification errors and do not correct their errors unless prompted. These children can often be coaxed into independence by the institution of a brief period of competition between the student and the teacher. The competition involves tallying who notices an error first—the teacher or the student. The teacher, of course, waits until the child has read far enough into the text for the error to become evident—at least to the end of the sentence. Whoever notices the error first gets a star. (The stars are drawn quickly in one of two columns on a piece of scrap paper—the record keeping should be a minor focus.) After a word identification error has been noted, the child is expected to make use of his strategies to repair it.

Generally, the teacher gets most of the stars the first time this competition is instituted. Within a few days, however, the child is usually getting most or all of the stars. At that point, the teacher should begin to fade the reinforcement system, dropping it altogether as quickly as possible. If the child asks to have it reinstated, the teacher can simply explain that it is just a little game played to help students remember to check themselves when they read. Since the child is already checking himself, there is no need to play the game anymore.

The use of this "gimmick" for promoting self-monitoring should be reserved for those few children who truly understand the strategies and would be capable of noticing their errors if they had the mind-set to do so. This approach would not be appropriate for students whose word identification errors are caused by difficulties with comprehension of the text or for students for whom misidentified words are not part of their spoken vocabulary.

TABLE 10.1. Teacher Behaviors That Promote Dependence or Independence in Word Learning

Student reading behavior	Teacher response that promotes dependence	Teacher response that promotes self-regulation and independence
Child looks at the teacher upon encountering an unfamiliar word.	Teacher tells child word. Or Teacher gives a partial response (e.g., articulates the first sound in the unfamiliar word).	Teacher continues to look at word rather than making eye contact with the child. Or Teacher asks, "What could you try there?" Or Teacher prompts with a word identification strategy that has recently been taught.
Child reads many unfamiliar words with a rising (questioning) intonation.	Teacher confirms or disconfirms for the child ("Uh-huh" or "Nooo . . . ")	Teacher waits for the child to do the confirmation, saying nothing and keeping her eyes on the text. Or, if need be, Teacher prompts the child to confirm/disconfirm (e.g., "Keep reading [or reread] to see if that makes sense").
Child produces words that don't fit the context.	Teacher asks "Does that make sense?" before the child has read far enough along to realize that meaning has been lost. Or Teacher asks "Does that make sense?" *only* when it doesn't make sense.	Teacher does not comment on word identification errors until the child has read far enough along to notice that something doesn't make sense. Or Teacher asks, "Does that make sense?" both when it does make sense and when it doesn't; thereby making the question a genuine one rather than a signal that a word identification error has occurred.
Child seldom if ever self-corrects.	Teacher does all the monitoring for the child and prompts the specific strategies the child needs to use in order to solve word identification problems.	Teacher notices and praises the child when the child self-corrects without being prompted to do so. And/or, teacher encourages the child to be independent in strategy use by briefly making error monitoring a bit of a competition between the teacher and the child (see *Encouraging Self-Correction* box).

Strategy Instruction After Reading

When children have finished reading a text, it is helpful to focus on the strategies they used effectively. For example, teachers might prompt them in one or more of the following ways:

- "What strategies do you think you used well today?"
- "What strategies do you think you need more practice with?"
- "Are there any strategies that you forget to use? If so, what can you do to remember to use that strategy?"
- "I like the way you puzzled through this word. Tell me what you did."

It is also a good idea to compliment the children on what they did well.

- "I like the way you used the word family chart to help you figure out some words."
- "I heard a lot of people thinking like readers today. I like the way you are helping each other remember to use your strategies."
- "You guys are really getting good at being flexible with those vowel sounds!"

EVALUATING AND DOCUMENTING CHILDREN'S PROGRESS

In addition to using the snapshot in Figure 10.3 to document strategy use, Figure 10.4 can be used to document the ease with which children build their sight vocabulary through strategic word solving. As with several of the snapshots, the primary purpose of this form is to prompt teachers' thinking as to which of the children in their groups might benefit from extra, more focused, instructional attention. To use this form, the teacher would record observations of the ease with which sight words are acquired (*readily, slowly,* or *very slowly*). Such observations should be made at several points in time. This snapshot allows for this. Thus, in the first column the teacher would record the data on which her ratings are entered for the group of children. She would then record her rating for each child in the column under that child's name. Ratings can be recorded up to 10 different times. Children who appear to be building their sight vocabulary slowly or very slowly relative to peers may be in need of more explicit instruction and/or more guided practice in the use of word identification strategies. Further, they clearly need more opportunities to read texts that are not too challenging.

KEEP IN MIND All of the discussion in this chapter has been focused on word identification strategy instruction. This is one major goal that is pursued in the context of engaging the children in reading text. The other major goal is for the children to become active, engaged comprehenders. For children who are at the early stages of learning to read and for those who are struggling with reading, it is easy for teachers to become so focused on facilitating the development of skill in word identification that the focus on meaning is lost—at least to the child. So, while in this chapter we discussed instruction that is intended to promote the development of skill in word identification that should occur before, during, and after children read a text, this instruction should not replace instruction intended to develop meaning-focused reading.

Group Snapshot—Observations of Strategic Sight Word Learning						
Student names:						
Builds sight vocabulary through strategic word identification while reading Code as: **R**eadily **S**lowly **V**ery slowly	Date:					
	Date:					
	Date:					
	Date:					
	Date:					
	Date:					
	Date:					
	Date:					
	Date:					
	Date:					

FIGURE 10.4. Group Snapshot for sight word learning.

CHAPTER 11

High-Frequency Word Learning

WORD LEARNING GOAL 2

The child will be able to read the most frequently occurring words accurately and quickly.

High-frequency words are those that occur very often in print (and in spoken language). Most high-frequency words refer to abstractions (i.e., they do not refer to things that can be seen or envisioned). As a result, they are relatively difficult to learn and often difficult to identify through the use of contextual cues. Further, many high-frequency words are not entirely decodable. For all of these reasons, it is useful to explicity teach the most frequently occurring words and to provide sufficient practice so that children can identify them automatically.

EARLY INSTRUCTION OF HIGH-FREQUENCY WORDS

The first words that children learn to read need special instructional consideration because the children have little or no conceptual framework for understanding the reading process and the role of printed words. Therefore, in this section we focus on ways to help children learn to read and write a small set of very-high-frequency words. When we talk to kindergarten and first-grade teachers about teaching high-frequency words, we almost always get questions about how many words should be in this "small set." Since, to our knowledge, there is no research to guide a response to this question, we generally turn the question back to the teachers and ask about the expectations in their schools. Their answers have ranged from a low of six high-frequency words to a high of 100 words by the end of kindergarten. In our kindergarten intervention work, where we provided small-group instruction for half an hour twice a week to children identified as being at risk for literacy learning problems, it was not unusual for these children to know 50 or more high-frequency words at the end of kindergarten. So, clearly even children who begin kindergarten with limited early literacy skills can learn quite a few high-frequency words by the end of the year. Because knowledge of high-frequency words provides children with so much access to reading materials, and allows them to be strategic in learning new words, setting higher expectations for sight word knowledge is probably in the children's best interest. That said, it is important to note that, in our approach, teaching high-frequency words entails much more than the drill-type activities that are often associated with teaching high-frequency sight words.

Note

Although the term *sight words* is often used when discussing high-frequency words, the two terms are not synonymous. As defined in Chapter 10, sight words are any words that can be identified automatically—without cognitive effort. While a proficient reader's sight vocabulary will contain many high-frequency words, it will also contain many words that occur with less frequency. Since the goal of instruction around high-frequency words is for these words to become part of the individual's sight vocabulary, both terms are used in this chapter.

Selecting Words for Instruction

A child who can identify few written words will generally be most interested in learning words that are important to her (e.g., her name, the names of family members or friends, words for feelings [e.g., *love, like, happy*], words for favorite toys, animals). Therefore, some of these words should be included in early sight word instruction. The most frequently occurring words, on the other hand, are neither important nor particularly interesting to children. They are, nevertheless, important for children to be able to identify. Figure 11.1 presents a list of some of the most frequently occurring English words. These words are taken from a list compiled by Eeds (1985) based on a sampling of children's trade books. They represent the 52 most frequent words in the texts.

the	and	a	I
to	said	you	he
it	in	was	she
for	that	is	his
but	they	my	of
all	on	me	be
go	can	with	one
her	what	we	him
no	so	up	are
will	look	some	day
at	have	your	come
not	like	than	get
when	thing	do	out

FIGURE 11.1. High-frequency words.

Some of the earliest words taught should be drawn from this list of very-high-frequency words. Other considerations in selecting words for early instruction include:

- The instructional materials in use in the classroom.
- The words the children are expected to know at the next grade level.
- The texts which are available for the children to read in the near future.

An additional consideration in selecting words for instruction is that a high-frequency word should *not* be introduced until the children can identify all of the letters in that word. Otherwise, the children are more apt to attempt to learn the word through the use of selective cues. Further, the first several high-frequency words that are introduced should be as different as possible from one another in terms of the way they look. Thus, for example, one would not want to introduce both *they* and *the* among the first several high-frequency words.

Teaching High-Frequency Words

For children who know few, if any, sight words, we would introduce only one new word at a time. In preparing to teach a new high-frequency word, it is important to have a text available that contains opportunities for children to read the words in context. It is often possible for the teacher to construct a text (such as the morning message) that uses the target high-frequency word repeatedly and also carries a lot of meaning for the children. Many book publishers also have developed series of little books that, in a single book, use specific high-frequency words frequently enough that the children have the opportunity to become very familiar with them. As noted in the introduction to Part III, in our studies we have used the Ready Readers series (available through Pearson Learning) and felt that it was particularly useful. The Short Books, Inc., also publishes a very useful set of books for helping students to develop high-frequency-sight vocabulary.

Introducing Words

The first several high-frequency words should be introduced very explicitly, presented in context and in isolation, and the children should be given a rationale for learning the word as well as practice to support that learning. Thus, the teacher might do the following:

• Choose a text in which the word appears several times. Read the text to the children, discussing the material, allowing the children to respond to it as usual.

• Point to the targeted word in the text that was read and say something like this: "Here's a word that the author used a lot in this book. The word is _____. This word is used in a lot of things we will be reading, so we are going to learn this word. That way, when we see it in other books and stories, we'll already know it."

• Write the word in large print on a card or chart paper, naming each letter as it is written. Invite individual children to name the word and to spell it while everyone in the instructional group is looking at the word.

• While leaving the word in view, invite individual children to find the word in several different locations in the book (or other text) that was originally read. As the children find the word, either they or the teacher should label the word (e.g., "There's the word *he*" or simply "*he, he, he*" each time the word is encountered).

If a child chooses an incorrect match for the word, the teacher should discuss how the selected word is similar to, and differs from, the target word and talk about the letters in the word. For example, "The word you picked starts with *h*, just like the word *he*. I'm glad you noticed the *h*'s in those two words. Now let's look at the end of those two words. *He* ends with an *e*. Do you see an *e* at the end of this word [*her*] (*pointing to the end of the word*)? This is the word *her*; it has an *r* at the end. So the word you picked looks a lot like the word *he* that we are searching for. To make sure we have the right match, though, we need to look at the beginning and the end of the word and sometimes in the middle, too."

As illustrated in this example, when providing feedback following an incorrect response, we should always make note of what the child did correctly as well as what aspect of the response needs more attention. If feedback conveys only inaccuracy, some children will lose their motivation to engage in the challenging activities that are being pursued.

When a child finds a correct match, the teacher might read aloud the sentence in which the matching word occurs, emphasizing the target word when it is read with both voice and pointing. Once children can find the word reliably with the model available, the word card might be removed from view while they continue to look for the target word in the text, as before.

Group or Classroom Alternative

With a larger group of children, it is often useful to give each child a card with the target word on it. The cards for individual children do not need to be particularly big. However, the teacher should still use a large-print version as a model.

If children each have their own copy of the word, they can be given the choice of whether they want to refer to the model in the context of word search and word-spelling activities. Children can also be encouraged to use the word card to find other instances of the word in print displayed around the classroom or school.

Making a Collection of the High-Frequency Words That Children Can Identify

When children are first learning some high-frequency words, they often enjoy having a collection of the words they have learned. Giving each child a special way to store her words is very motivating. Allowing children to decorate their collection device (whatever it may be) may encourage them to keep the words together and to practice them periodically. A variety of games can be played with word cards, so these collections can come in very handy.

Parents should also be kept informed of the words the children are learning and be given suggestions for how they can help their children learn those words. For example, if a weekly newsletter is sent home with students, one section might be devoted to providing the parents with a list of the newest high-frequency words that have been taught and practiced.

Communication between classroom and intervention teachers is important concerning the words that children are expected to learn in the classroom, especially for children in a Tier 2 or Tier 3 intervention. Intervention teachers should consider initially teaching and practicing the most frequent words that their children do not yet know. Over the course of intervention, the ultimate goal is, of course, to ensure that each child knows what the average child in the classroom knows. Therefore, intervention teachers should be helping children to add to their collections of known words.

Practicing Early High-Frequency Words

Reading and Writing

READING LITTLE BOOKS

Provide the children with the opportunity to read little books that include the high-frequency words they are learning. (Sometimes it may be possible to create an appropriate book by building on a classroom theme and/or modifying a book that has been read to the children.) Read these books several times with the children. Consider utilizing the types of sight word readers that were described in the introduction to Part III (see example on the left side of Figure III.2, p. 193). Books of the sort described can be made easily using clip art.

REPEATED READING

The more children read, the faster they grow as readers. Children should frequently have the opportunity to read and reread books that are at an appropriate level of challenge for them. Little books that have been read with the teacher should be made available for the children to read independently or with a partner. Ideally, children would be able to take these books home to read to family members as well. In addition, many publishers provide reproducible *Take Home* books that incorporate the same phonics skills and high-frequency words that the instructional series addresses. Children and families can be encouraged to accumulate such *Take Home* books in a folder at home so that children always have a ready source of appropriately challenging reading material. It is important to help parents understand the value of children reading the emergent-level books that they (appear to) have memorized. Otherwise, with the best interest of their child at heart, parents sometimes engage the child in interactions with books that are potentially counterproductive (e.g., some parents have reported that they cover the pictures or have children begin reading on the last page of the book and read the pages in reverse order!). Therefore, we suggest that teachers provide parents with insights into the purposes of having children read and reread these books and specific guidance on what parents can do while interacting with their children in this context (see Figure 11.2 for suggestions to parents of beginning readers).

WRITING

Be alert for opportunities to include the high-frequency words that have been taught in writing activities. The words that are in the children's sight vocabulary should be made available to them in list form and they should be "given permission" to spell these words conventionally in their writing by referring to the list. (Think for a moment about the message that is conveyed by a statement such as "If

Dear Parent,

Your child is beginning to learn to read. At this early point in development, children "read" books that provide them with the opportunity to develop familiarity with important skills but that do not require them to be able to read the words on the page in a conventional way. In fact, to a great extent, children "memorize" the repetitive refrain in these books and "read" them by using the pictures to remind them of what changes from one page to the next.

Parents are encouraged to spend some time listening to their children read these beginning-level books on a daily basis. When your child reads, encourage him/her to point to the words because this will help your child to:

- Become familiar with the directionality of print (that it goes from left to right).
- Begin to learn some of the words that occur frequently in the book by focusing his/her eyes on each word as it is said.
- Begin to use the letters at the beginnings of words to trigger his/ her memory of what the text says.
- Understand that the pictures help to tell the story and may help him/her to remember what a particular word says.

It is also important to discuss the information presented in the book with your child so that he/she develops the understanding that we read for the purpose of understanding what we read. By discussing books with your child, even these beginning-level books, you can help to build your child's comprehension skills. Below are some examples of the kinds of conversation starters that you might use both when your child reads to you and when you read to your child.

Before reading,

If your child has read or heard the book before, you might ask questions such as these:

- "What was this story about?"
- "Is it like any other stories we've read?"

If your child has not read or heard the book before, then you might ask:

- "What do you think this book will be about?"

During reading, you might ask questions directly related to events in the story. Ideally, the questions would be rather open-ended:

- "Why do you think . . . ?"
- "What do you think would have happened if . . . ?"

During and after reading, you might share your reactions to the book and encourage your child to do so as well:

- "I liked the part where. . . . "
- "I thought it was funny when. . . . "

An important goal for parents is to support their children's interest in reading by making these early reading experiences enjoyable.

Sincerely,

FIGURE 11.2. Helping parents to support early reading development: An example.

the word is on our list, you must spell it the right way whenever you use it in your writing" versus "Since the word is on our list, you will be able to spell it the right way whenever you use it in your writing." The subtle difference in wording in these two statements could make a substantial difference in how a child approaches a writing activity.)

When using word lists to facilitate conventional spelling, try to ensure that the list is readily accessible to all of the children. We are all more likely to use resources if they are handy. Some teachers post the list prominently at the front of the room (in letters big enough for all of the children to see, regardless of where they are sitting). Other teachers post copies of the list at each table, often on all sides of the supply box that is kept there.

SENTENCE BUILDING

Once children can readily identify several words, use the words to create simple sentences. Some additional, more meaningful words would need to be added to the set in order to allow for the creation of these sentences. These additional words should be of interest to children and be very distinct from the other words in use for a particular sentence-building episode. These words might include the children's names or those of friends or family members, favorite animals, toys, etc.

The first example of sentence building is appropriate for children who know very few words. The sentence used is *My doll is nice*. The major goal for this particular example is that children will have the opportunity to learn the words *my* and *is*, as these words occur more frequently than do *doll* and *nice*. While *doll* and *nice* receive as much attention in this activity as do *my* and *is*, *my* and *is* will be used more in other practice activities and so are more likely to be learned to the point where the children can identify them automatically.

For this activity, a sentence is written on a sentence strip (which could be just a strip of paper):

$$\boxed{\text{My doll is nice.}}$$

The teacher would:

- Display one strip and read it with the children several times, while pointing to the words.
- Have individual children read the sentence a few times, while pointing.
- As the children watch, cut the sentence strip into words and display the words in a mixed up order.

The teacher might then *think aloud* about how to reconstruct the sentence, as illustrated below:

Teacher	Think-aloud
Says:	"Hmm. I know the sentence said, 'My doll is nice.' So the first word I need is the word *my*. My. MMMyyy. It sounds like the first letter is *m*, so I'll need to look for a word that starts with *m*."
Finds the word *my* and observes:	"This word starts with an upper-case *m*. My is the first word in my sentence, so it needs to have an upper-case letter—so this must be the word *my*. So I am going to put it first. "OK. The sentence said, 'My doll is nice.' My doll. The next word I need is *doll*. /d/d/d/doll. What letter makes that /d/d/d/ sound? Maybe my key words will help. I need to check to see if I know a key word that starts like /d/d/d/doll. I see the key word *dog*—dog starts with a *d*—/d/d/d/dog, /d/d/d/doll—those words sound the same at the beginning, so they probably start with the same letter. Let's see which of the words that I have left here starts with the letter *d*?"
Finds the word *doll* and says:	"I think this word probably says *doll* because it starts with a *d*. So now I've got My doll. (*Points to each word as it is said.*) "My doll is nice. My doll is. . . . I need to find the word *is*. Hmm. I am not sure which one of these words says *is*. My doll is . . . nice. . . . Nice is the last word in my sentence so it should have a period. This word has a period at the end and it starts with an *n*. NNNNNice probably starts with an *n*, so this word must be *nice*. So that word goes at the end of the sentence. This word that is left over must be *is*. Wait a minute! Is is one of our sight words. I wonder if this word is on our sight word list."
Finds the word on the list and says:	"There it is, this is the word *is*!"
Reads the entire sentence:	"Let's see if this all works. The sentence says: *My doll is nice.*"

Afterward, the teacher would mix up the words in the sentence again and invite the children to collaborate in reconstructing the sentence by arranging the words in the proper order. The teacher would provide prompts on an as needed basis with some of the strategies that she modeled earlier. Below are some examples of what the teacher might say:

- "What kind of letter will we need at the beginning of the sentence?"
- "What is the first sound you hear in *nice*?"
- "How could you figure out what letter will be at the beginning of the word *nice*?

Note

The first several times that the children are engaged in these kinds of sentence-building activities, it may be helpful to leave an intact model of the sentence in view as the children do the reconstruction.

The teacher would gradually withdraw these supportive prompts as she notices the children being able to handle things on their own. As children collaborate with each other, the teacher should be sure to openly notice and encourage the problem-solving skills they demonstrate (e.g., "I like the way that Jared stretched the sounds in that word when he was trying to figure out what it was").

• *Variations for children with larger sight vocabularies.* As children progress, the sentences can be longer; eventually the initial sentence strip can be eliminated and children can be challenged to form a meaningful sentence from a set of words. One teacher with whom we worked used sentence building as a center activity toward the end of the kindergarten year. She provided the words to build four or five different sentences. The words for each sentence were on different colored cards so that it was easy to keep all of the words for a given sentence together. During their time at the sentence-building center, children were to take all of the cards of the same color and assemble a meaningful sentence. Different children could work on different sentences, or two children could collaborate. Once a meaningful sentence was assembled, the children wrote the sentence on their paper. When they finished with one sentence, they moved on to the next group of cards.

Below are the word cards for one of the sentences that the children might be asked to build. Clearly children would need to read all of the words multiple times before managing to build the meaningful sentence: *The cat likes to play with the hat.*

As should be evident from the preceding description, sentence-building activities provide practice with high-frequency words but also help to reinforce several print concepts (e.g., the first word in a sentence starts with a capital letter, the last word has a period or some other punctuation mark after it). They also provide children with opportunities to practice sound segmentation and letter–sound correspondences in a somewhat more meaningful way. Moreover, the process of reconstructing the sentence requires that children attend to the meaning of the sentence to ensure that it is properly ordered. Thus, sentence building gives children the opportunity to exercise many important literacy skills. The teacher should be alert for opportunities to reinforce these concepts and the problem-solving strategies associated with them.

Lists and Games

The words that the children are learning can be used in a variety of games and activities that will help to build their fluency in identifying them. We describe several such activities below, for which there are many possible variations.

PRACTICE READING THE LIST

Keep a list of high-frequency words (or a set of word cards) that have been taught and ask the children to read them a few times in isolation. Words that the children readily identify in isolation over several occasions need not be practiced as often, but they should be reviewed periodically. Children who continue to be uncertain about some of the words should be provided with additional practice with the most frequent of these words. Having children form the words using letter tiles or by writing them several times will help them to focus on the letters and the order of the letters that form a given word. Children should name the letters in the word and then name the word each time they build it or write it.

TIC-TAC-TOE

For this version of tic-tac-toe, each player uses a different colored marker to write high-frequency words in the squares of the board. For children who know very few words, each child might write the same word on his/her turn. As they write it, children name the letters and then say the word. For children who know more words, the game would involve selecting a word card from a deck of cards containing words that have been taught. They would then read the word, write it in their selected square (naming the letters as they do so), and then name the word again. In both versions of the game, the winner is determined by having three words of the same color in a row.

PARKING LOT

The parking lot game described on page 117 can be used to reinforce sight word knowledge if the sight words are written into the parking spaces. The parking director then tells the players in which parking space to park. It is important that words be arranged differently on each player's parking lot so that children actually need to find the correct word rather than simply parking in the same relative position as their neighbor (see Figure 11.3)

CONCENTRATION (MEMORY)

Using a deck of cards that includes two copies of each of the high-frequency words under study, a traditional game of Concentration can be played. It is important

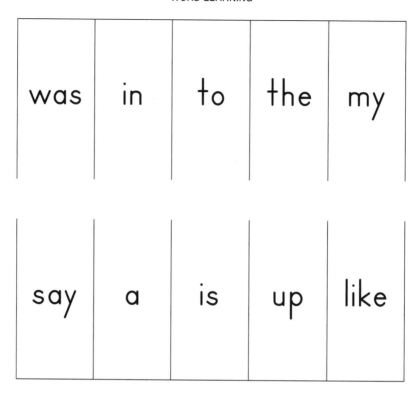

FIGURE 11.3. A parking lot game for high-frequency sight words.

that all players be on the same side of the playing surface so that all of the words are viewed in the proper orientation. It is also important that each player, on her turn, says each word as it is turned over, otherwise some of the children will treat the game as a visual matching activity and come no closer to being able to identify the words automatically.

STICKY NOTE BINGO

Bingo boards with 12–16 squares are set up. Each square contains a high-frequency word. The caller says the word, and players cover the word with a sticky note and try to write the covered word from memory (on the sticky note). In preparation for the game, each child can prepare her own playing board by writing in the words that the teacher dictates in the square of her choice. It may be important to display the words that are dictated to ensure proper spelling.

READING THE ROOM

Using a pointer or a flashlight, children are encouraged to search the print posted around the room for the high-frequency words they can read. (This assumes, of course, that the classroom has lots of poems, posters, language experience charts, and/or morning messages displayed.)

LATER INSTRUCTION OF HIGH-FREQUENCY WORDS AND BUILDING AUTOMATICITY

The development of accuracy and automaticity in identifying and spelling high-frequency words should be a particular emphasis for all children until they have mastered the most frequently occurring words. More than 50% of the words that one encounters in any given text consist of a fairly small number of high-frequency words (about 100 of them). Therefore, the 100 or so most frequently occurring words are of particular priority because when children are able to identify and/or spell these high-frequency words effortlessly, they are able to devote more attention to the message of the text and, if necessary, to figuring out the less frequent (and often more meaning-bearing) words. Once children have begun to understand how the reading process works, they begin to learn new words through reading (as discussed in Chapter 10) instead of needing to have the words taught directly. Therefore, as children grow as readers, the high-frequency words that need the most explicit instructional attention are those that children are unlikely to be able to figure out, given their current word-learning strategies.

Lists of High-Frequency Words

Over the years, several different researchers and reading educators have compiled lists of high-frequency words to provide educators with insight into which words occur most frequently and might, therefore, be of high priority for children to learn (e.g., Dolch, 1936; Eeds, 1985; Fry, Kress, & Fountoukidis, 1993). Because each list represents a ranking of words in terms of their frequency of occurrence in written text, these lists are pretty similar to one another. We have reproduced Eeds's version in Figure 11.4. This list contains approximately 230 of the most frequently occurring words, based on a count of words appearing in a sampling of children's literature. For convenience, we have broken the longer list down into 9 lists of approximately equal length. The first list contains the most frequent words, the second list the next most frequent words, and so on.

Grouping and Pacing

The instructional procedures described in this section are appropriate for children who already know a small set of high-frequency words (10–20). In general, the more words a child knows, the more quickly she will learn additional words. This is true for a variety of reasons but primarily because, as for virtually all learning situations, the more you know about something, the easier it is to learn more about

(text continues on p. 242)

Student name _____

List 1	List 2	List 3	List 4	List 5
the	with	too	walk	any
and	one	want	came	right
a	her	did	were	nice
I	what	could	ask	well
to	we	good	back	old
said	him	this	now	night
you	no	don't	friend	may
he	so	little	cry	about
it	out	if	oh	think
in	up	just	Mr.	new
was	are	baby	bed	know
she	will	way	where	help
for	look	there	very	grand
that	some	every	play	boy
is	day	went	let	take
his	at	father	long	eat
but	have	had	here	body
they	your	see	how	school
my	mother	dog	make	house
of	come	home	big	morning
on	not	down	from	yes
me	like	got	put	after
all	than	would	read	never
be	get	time	them	or
go	when	love	as	sleep
can	thing		Miss	made
	do			first
Total ____/26	____/27	____/25	____/26	____/24

FIGURE 11.4. Eeds's (1985) list of high-frequency words. *(page 1 of 2)*

List 6	List 7	List 8	List 9
self	say	hurry	mama
try	took	hand	use
has	dad	hard	turn
always	found	push	thought
over	lady	our	papa
again	soon	their	lot
side	ran	watch	blue
thank	dear	because	bath
why	man	door	mean
who	better	us	sit
saw	through	should	together
mom	stop	room	best
kid	still	pull	brother
give	fast	great	feel
around	next	gave	floor
by	only	does	wait
Mrs.	am	car	tomorrow
off	began	ball	surprise
sister	head	sat	shop
find	keep	stay	run
fun	teacher	each	own
more	sure	ever	
while	says	until	
tell	ride	shout	
pet			
Total ____/27	____/25	____/24	____/21

FIGURE 11.4. *(page 2 of 2)*

that same thing. That said, it should be clear that while we might start teaching high-frequency words by introducing only one new word at time, as children progress, they can generally handle increasingly larger groups of new words.

Assessment for Instructional Grouping

In the early primary grades, children who are at similar points in their knowledge of high-frequency words often have similar instructional needs related to reading. Thus, assessing children's ability to read the words on a high-frequency list can provide useful information to guide grouping decisions. The word lists in Figure 11.4 can be used to make a rough determination of a child's high-frequency word knowledge. For administration, each list should be typed in primary font on a separate card or sheet of paper. On the first administration, the assessment would begin with List 1 and continue until the child is unable to read more than half of the words on a given list (continuing past this point would be too frustrating for the child). Words identified both accurately and automatically should be marked with a checkmark (✓). Those identified accurately but more slowly should be identified with an X. When a child misidentifies a word, it is helpful to record what she says, as this will provide insights into the child's approach to word identification. On subsequent administrations, it is not necessary to readminister lists on which the child read all or nearly all of the words accurately and automatically.

Teaching High-Frequency Words

Selecting Words for Instruction

As discussed above, the earliest words taught should be highly distinct from one another because children's primary approach to word learning at the early stages is apt to be through selective cue use (i.e., using salient visual features, but often not the word's letters and sounds). By working with these words in a variety of ways, children begin to attend to their letters and sounds in addition to their overall visual configuration. The potential confusability of words will remain an issue for a while as children's sight vocabularies grow. This as well as other factors to consider in selecting high-frequency words for instruction are discussed in Table 11.1.

Teaching High-Frequency Words in Preparation for Reading a New Text

In the ISA, the first time a high-frequency word is taught and practiced is in the context of preparing children to read a new book (see Chapter 10, p. 219). Teachers periodically remind children that learning these words is helpful because they are used a lot in reading and writing. When introducing a new word, it is presented on a card or sticky note. The teacher names the word and then the children read it a few times before reading the text.

TABLE 11.1. Considerations on Selecting High-Frequency Words

Things to consider	Advice
Is the word likely to be easily confused with another word(s) that has recently been taught?	Avoid teaching visually confusable words in close succession. Children at the earlier stages tend to use the overall configuration of the word as a prominent cue for word identification.
How frequently is the word used?	Words that appear very frequently in print should be among the earliest words taught.
Do children have the decoding skills to identify the word on their own?	Words that follow regular spelling–sound correspondences that the children have already learned probably do not need to be taught explicitly. We want children to have opportunities to apply their decoding skills and to be strategic in their reading.
Will children encounter the word in continuous text in the near future?	Explicitly teaching high-frequency words prior to having children read a text containing those words helps them to be more fluent on the first reading. The high-frequency words will serve as anchors that allow children to be more strategic in analyzing other unfamiliar words in the text and in constructing an understanding of the text.

Logistical Tip

Our intervention teachers found it helpful to write the new words that would be taught for a given book on sticky notes and to place the notes inside the front cover prior to the lesson. In preparing the children to read the book, the sticky notes are taken out and placed on the table. The words remain on the table during the reading. Children often find it useful to refer to these words while reading. After the book has been read, the words are reviewed and then placed back in the book, ready for the next group of children.

Practicing High-Frequency Words

Once a high-frequency word has been taught, it is incorporated into a set of words that will be practiced until children are fairly automatic in identifying them. Many of the practice activities described for children at the early stages of learning high-frequency sight words are appropriate for students who are a bit further along (see the section on "Practicing Early High-Frequency Words," page 232). However, as children progress, the number of words with which they work in practice activities will be larger. Practice activities include reading and rereading books, using a resource to spell high-frequency words conventionally while writing, and using various game-like word-reading drills.

For children who receive intensive intervention in very small groups or in one-to-one settings, we have found a word game we call Your Pile/My Pile to be helpful for practicing high-frequency words to the point of automaticity. This game is described below.

YOUR PILE/MY PILE: A GAME FOR PRACTICING HIGH-FREQUENCY WORDS

This game is designed to promote accuracy and automaticity in identifying high-frequency words that have already been taught. The game can be used as part of a small-group or one-to-one lesson but should only constitute a small part of the lesson. The game can also be suggested as a playful way to practice high-frequency words at home.

Selecting Words for the Game. High priority should be placed on the highest-frequency words in helping children build their sight vocabulary. Thus, the most frequent words on high-frequency word lists should be among those learned first. It is also reasonable to provide practice on words that are of high priority for a particular child either because of her interests or because of the text(s) that the child will be reading in the near future. Depending on children's current competence, the number of words in a drill may vary from a small number (i.e., 3–5 words with several copies of each word included) to 20 or more words. Words for any given game should generally consist of the following:

- Some that the child routinely identifies accurately and relatively quickly.
- Some that the child can usually identify accurately but slowly.
- A few that have only recently been introduced to the child.

This combination of words serves to make the game manageable yet challenging enough to hold children's interest.

Preparing the Words for the Game. The words to be used should be written on cards. The cards should all be the same color and the words should all be printed in the same color so that children do not try to rely on color cues, as noted above, as a means of trying to remember the word on a given card.

Preparing Children for the Game. It is important to explain to children why learning to recognize the words quickly will help them when reading. Explain that the more words they can recognize right away, the easier it will be to read stories and other kinds of books. It is also helpful to explain that the words that are being practiced are in a lot of different books and that learning those words will help them read and write many different things.

Explain How to Play the Game. Tell the child that you will present the words one at a time and that she is to tell what the word is as quickly as possible without making mistakes. Explain that, if she does make a mistake, you will tell her what the word is called and that the word will go back in the deck for more practice. Further, explain that if the child gets stuck on a word, you might give her a hint, but that if you give a hint, the word needs to go back in the deck for more practice. Finally, if the child recognizes the word accurately, but it takes a long time, the word will also go into the pile for more practice. Words that the child recognizes quickly and accurately go into the "finished" pile for any given drill. The goal is for the child to quickly get all of the words into the finished pile. Often in playing the game, teachers refer to the two different piles of words as *your pile* (the child's pile of finished words) and *my pile* (the teacher's pile of words that needs more practice).

Playing the Game. Show the words one at a time, placing words in the finished pile if the child is accurate and relatively fast (for that child) in identifying the word. Words that the child identifies either inaccurately or slowly (taking longer than about 2 seconds) go into the teacher's pile for more practice. The game continues until all of the words are in the child's pile. That is, when all of the words in the original pile have been played, the teacher goes on to draw the words from her pile and continues to do so until the child quickly names it and, therefore, gets it placed in her pile.

> **KEEP IN MIND** The major purpose of these drills is to help children get to the point where they are both *fast* and *accurate* in identifying high-frequency words. Being automatic in their identification of the most frequently occurring words will allow children to devote more of their cognitive resources to constructing the meaning of the text and to puzzling through unfamiliar, less frequent, words.

Eliminating Words from the Deck. For subsequent games of Your Pile/My Pile, words that the child routinely identifies accurately and quickly (within 1 or 2 seconds) can be removed from the deck and replaced with others. One way of easily tracking a child's knowledge of particular words is to mark word cards with a small checkmark if the child identifies it quickly and accurately *the first time it is shown* on a given day. Generally, when words have three or four checkmarks, they can be removed from the deck. When words are removed from the deck, they can be added to the child's "Words I Know" chart (see p. 247).

Using "Words I Know" Charts and Word Walls to Encourage Automaticity with High-Frequency Words

Charts listing the high-frequency words that children have learned serve as important resources for them as they continue to practice accurate and rapid identification of these words and as they work toward internalizing the conventional spellings. At a classroom level, teachers often maintain word walls on which are listed all of the high-frequency words that the majority of the class is expected to know. In small-group and one-to-one intervention settings, teachers can develop similar "Words We Know" or "Words I Know" charts that include only the words that the children in the group or the individual child knows. These charts are useful in supporting the needs of children who might find the classroom word wall to be overwhelming.

Children should be given permission to spell words on the word wall and/or from their Words I/We Know charts conventionally (using "book spelling") by referring to the wall or the charts. Children are expected to spell the "Words I Know" words correctly in their writing because allowing invented spelling of these high-frequency words is likely to slow down the process of getting these words to the point where they can be identified automatically. For example, the child who often spells the word *was* as *yz* is likely to have difficulty recognizing the word *was* accurately and quickly when she encounters it in text. Although sound spelling is an important contributor to the development of phonemic awareness and phonics knowledge, allowing children to use invented spellings for known high-frequency words is not recommended.

The use of the "Words I Know" chart to promote conventional spelling of these high-frequency words will highlight for children the fact that sound (invented) spelling is only a temporary means of facilitating communication.

CHARACTERISTICS OF USEFUL CLASSROOM WORD WALLS

In order for classroom word walls to be effective for the children in the classroom, the words should be listed alphabetically by first letter, so that it is reasonably easy for children to find the word for which they are looking. Further, the words should be printed in a font that is large enough that the children can read them no matter where they are in the classroom—that is, so that children do not need to leave their seats to find a word on the word wall. Finally, it is important that most of the words on the word wall be printed on a standard background color with a standard color of ink so that children are not tempted to rely on something other than alphabetic features when they attempt to find a word.

CHARACTERISTICS OF USEFUL WORDS I/WE KNOW CHARTS

A "Words I Know" chart is an important resource for children who are slow to develop skill with high-frequency words. The words that are placed on these charts are high-frequency words that have been taught explicitly and that the teacher believes the children can identify accurately. In our intervention work, decisions about which words to add to a chart were often based on a student's performance in the *Your Pile/My Pile* game (see above). Early on, the "Words I Know" charts could be ordered in accord with the order in which children learn the words. Thus, words that a child learned to read first would appear at the beginning of the list whereas words learned more recently would be at the end. This ordering of the words gives the child who has yet to learn anything about alphabetization a positional cue for finding the words she wants to write.

An alphabetized "Words I Know" chart should be used starting when children know 15–20 high-frequency words. This chart would look much like a classroom word wall except that the chart is much smaller, since the words need be visible only to the children in a small group or to the individual. Moreover, they would typically include fewer words than the classroom word wall. An example of a Words I Know chart appears in Figure 11.5.

The use of this chart should be clearly explained to children when there are only a few words on it. The children should be told that all of the letters of the alphabet are on the chart and that, when they learn a word that starts with a particular letter, it will be put on the chart under that letter. When they want to find a word to use in their writing, they need to think of the sound at the beginning of the word and then think about what letter(s) might make that sound. Next, they need to find the word's first letter on the chart and read the words under the letter to see if the word they are looking for is there. This, of course, implicitly requires that children review some of the sight words they have learned as they read through the list and either accept or reject each word listed under a given letter.

For children who seem to have difficulty with reading and spelling the words on their "Words I/We Know" charts, it is helpful to make their personal charts of high-frequency words readily available. Some teachers tape a page protector to

Words I Know

Aa and	Bb big	Cc can come	Dd down did does	Ee	Ff for	Gg good	Hh has him her	Ii is	Jj
Kk keep	Ll love	Mm make	Nn nice	Oo of on	Pp put	Qq	Rr run	Ss said says	Tt the to
Uu us	Vv very	Ww was want	Xx	Yy you yes your	Zz				

FIGURE 11.5. "Words I Know" chart. A chart of this type might be stapled on the facing pages of a manila folder. That is, the columns headed by A–E would be on the left-hand side, and the columns headed by F–J would be on the right-hand side. Such an arrangement would allow substantial space for adding words under each letter.

children's desks for their "Words I Know" charts. That way, a chart can be easily removed for updating. For children who have a larger sight vocabulary and for whom spelling is a major concern, teachers have found it useful to provide the words in a personal dictionary format, which is either kept in their desks (often in the writing folder) or attached to their desks with a string that allows it to hang off the desk out of the way but be readily available when a child needs it.

"Spelling Tests" to Encourage Usage of "Words I Know" Charts or Word Walls. Periodic administration of spelling tests, for which children are encouraged to refer to their charts, can help them learn to use a chart effectively. During the spelling "test," the teacher can walk the children through the process of finding the needed word on their chart as often as necessary. On these tests, every child has the opportunity to score 100% if she understands how to use the chart.

Guessing Games. There are a variety of ways to encourage children to make efficient use of word walls and "Words I Know" charts. For example, it is helpful to periodically play guessing games using the displays. Guessing games might take the form of the teacher providing verbal clues and the children using displayed words to assist them in guessing the correct response. For example, if the word *in* were on the word wall, the teacher might say something like "I'm thinking of a word that begins with *i* and is the opposite of *out*." Such activities can also contribute to vocabulary development.

KEEP IN MIND   Procedures to ensure that every student has the opportunity to respond are easily incorporated into word wall activities. For example, in the guessing game described above, rather than having individual students make guesses, every child could be asked to write her guess on a whiteboard before anyone is asked to share a guess.

EVALUATING AND DOCUMENTING CHILDREN'S PROGRESS

Figure 11.6 provides a vehicle for teachers to record their observations of children's acquisition of high-frequency sight words. The form allows space for teachers to record their observations of individual children multiple times over the course of a school year. For children in intervention settings, teachers will probably want to closely document their progress in learning high-frequency sight words. This can be done most easily by counting the number of words that appear on a child's individual "Words I Know" chart. Alternatively, for students who are not receiving intensive intervention, the high-frequency word assessment (p. 240) can be periodically readministered and the number of the Eeds's list which the child reads with 90% or better accuracy can be recorded.

Group Snapshot—Observations of High-Frequency Word Learning						
Student names:						
Number of known high-frequency words (can be identified automatically at sight). (Record the number of words on the child's "Words I Know" chart *or* the number of the highest Eeds's list the child reads with 90% accuracy.)	Date:					
	Date:					
	Date:					
	Date:					
	Date:					
	Date:					
	Date:					
	Date:					
	Date:					
	Date:					
	Date:					
	Date:					

FIGURE 11.6. Group snapshot for high-frequency word learning.

PART IV

MEANING CONSTRUCTION

INTRODUCTION

Meaning construction is the goal of reading and reading instruction. As was high-lighted in Chapter 1, reading is a complicated process that requires readers to draw on a wide array of knowledge sources and strategic processes. In order to understand a printed text, readers must be able to do much more than simply read the printed words. They must know what the words mean and understand the con-cepts to which they refer. Readers must be able to assemble the individual words into idea units, which become the building blocks for a more comprehensive under-standing of the text. Ultimately, in order to fully understand a text, readers need to draw on and use their existing knowledge to interpret and construct the meaning of the text being read. Readers who have limited language skills and background knowledge will have limited ability to understand the things they read. Further, readers who do not actively think about the meaning of a text as they are reading are likely to have little recollection of what they have read.

In the previous chapters we have focused largely on the word-reading com-ponent of the reading process. Because this component is often a major stumbling block for children at the early stages of learning to read and for older struggling readers, it clearly needs to be addressed. However, the other processes need to be addressed as well, since, once skill with the alphabetic code is established, lan-guage, knowledge, and comprehension skills and strategies are the major determi-nants of reading comprehension. Further, unlike decoding skills, which represent a rather finite set of abilities, knowledge and language skills are rather infinite.

Therefore, whereas children who begin school with limited early literacy skills may be readily helped to catch up to their peers with regard to their knowledge of the alphabetic code (because their abler peers stop growing), it is much more difficult to close the knowledge gaps that tend to be especially evident between more and less economically advantaged groups (Hirsch, 2006; Neuman, 2006). In fact, Neuman argues that "although the 'have-nots' gain knowledge, the 'haves' gain it faster. And by gaining it faster, they are able to gain more" (2006, p. 33).

There is also substantial concern that language and knowledge gaps develop as a result of reading difficulty because limited engagement in reading results in limited opportunities to acquire new vocabulary and language structures and to encounter and develop new knowledge. Stanovich (1986) described this phenomenon as the *Matthew effect*, which is a biblical reference to the notion that the "rich get richer and the poor get poorer." While the research to date has yielded mixed results with regard to whether Matthew effects actually do arise for struggling readers (see Scarborough & Parker, 2003, for a review), it is hard to argue with the logic that such an effect could accrue.

In the chapters in this section, we focus on the knowledge, strategies, and dispositions that need to be developed and integrated in order for children to be able to make sense of the things they read (or listen to), and we discuss approaches to instruction that will help them do so. Two major goals are addressed in this section: (1) the development of vocabulary and more general language skills, and (2) the development of comprehension skills and strategies as well as the general background knowledge that will enable children to construct the meaning of the texts they read. The division between the two chapters is somewhat arbitrary. Language and knowledge are, obviously, intricately interconnected, and comprehension is heavily dependent on both.

Meaning Construction and Early Intervention

The existing research on RTI has generally not attended to the role that limitations in language skills and background knowledge may play in the evolution of reading difficulties. We think this is unfortunate because we suspect that both persistent and "late-emerging" reading difficulties are often attributable to limitations in these areas. Further, we fear that because of the common emphasis on oral reading skills, children who need support in developing language skills and world knowledge may be largely ignored until they begin to encounter texts that make heavier demands on these skills (in the middle elementary grades and beyond). Therefore, we encourage attention to the development of language and general knowledge of young learners in hopes of preventing later reading comprehension difficulties.

As is discussed in some detail in the next two chapters, language and knowledge develop incrementally over extended periods of time. The goal of increasing vocabulary and knowledge development needs to be at the forefront of teachers' thinking as they plan and deliver instruction for children with limitations in these aspects of development. Teachers should be constantly asking themselves whether their students understand the language (both vocabulary and syntax) and the concepts that they encounter in instructional interactions, and teachers need to be prepared to take steps to intervene for children who do not have the requisite knowledge. Knowledge and vocabulary development can be promoted by engaging children in reading and listening to informational books, watching information-rich videos, providing experiential learning opportunities, and the like. All such instructional opportunities are more productive for children when they have extensive opportunities to discuss what they are reading and learning.

Of course, even children with well-developed knowledge and language skills sometimes have difficulty comprehending the texts that they "read" with relative ease. For at least some of these children the comprehension difficulties may be attributable to failure to attend to the meaning of the text as it is being read. Virtually every reader has had the experience of reading something and then having no clue what was just read. When this happens on occasion, it is due to the fact that the reader had his mind on something else while reading. When this happens routinely, it can be a signal that the reader does not fully understand that the purpose of reading is to make sense of the text and to integrate the knowledge gained with already existing knowledge. This lack of understanding can arise for a variety of reasons; for struggling readers, it is apt to be due to the type of guidance and feedback they receive while reading. Thus, for example, if the feedback primarily focuses on word-reading accuracy, the child is likely to focus on such accuracy and attend little to the meaning of the text. Over time, such an approach may become habitual and, once established, will require explicit intervention to help the child overcome this inclination and to actively attend to the meaning of the text. In the ISA, we strive to prevent children from ever adopting such an attitude toward reading by engaging them in active meaning construction in all interactions around texts.

CHAPTER 12

Vocabulary and
Oral Language Development

MEANING CONSTRUCTION GOAL 1

The child will learn the meanings of new words encountered in instructional interactions and will be able to use the words conversationally. Further, the child's ability to understand and use more complex grammatical structures will improve.

Reading is a language skill. Thus, to a great extent, this entire book is about language development. However, in this chapter we focus on the development of two aspects of language: knowledge of word meanings (vocabulary) and familiarity with sentence structure (syntax). We discuss both how these aspects of language develop during the primary grades and how they are related to reading development in the primary grades and beyond. Our major focus in this chapter is to help teachers become attuned to the language challenges that children encounter while reading or listening to text and to become knowledgeable about methods of instruction that may help strengthen these critical language skills, particularly among children who struggle with literacy acquisition.

LANGUAGE AND READING

There is a strong predictive relationship between language skills, especially vocabulary, measured in the preprimary and early primary grades and reading comprehension performance all the way through high school (Dickinson & Tabors, 2001; Cunningham & Stanovich, 1997; Gallagher, Frith, & Snowling, 2000; Senechal, Ouellette, & Rodney, 2006; for reviews, see Dickinson, McCabe, & Clark-Chiarelli, 2004, and Scarborough, 2001). That is, children who have relatively limited language skills when they are young are likely to have difficulty understanding the things that they read when they are older—even when they can identify all of the words effortlessly. The association between language skills and later reading comprehension is generally considered to be causal in nature and has led to calls for instituting efforts to improve early language skills in order to improve reading comprehension and academic performance more generally (e.g., Biemiller, 2006; Dickinson, McCabe, & Essex, 2006).

Vocabulary knowledge and general language skills are strongly linked to children's home lives. Children arrive in kindergarten with very disparate experiences which, at least partially, account for their differing levels of vocabulary and language development. Children from low-income homes often have had more limited language experiences than children from more economically advantaged homes. In fact, Hart and Risley (1995) found that, on average, preschoolers from professional families experienced approximately 16 times more utterances per year than children from economically impoverished backgrounds. Further, Graves and Slater (1987) found that first graders from higher-income backgrounds knew the meanings of about twice as many words as those from lower-income backgrounds. Moreover, there is evidence that these early differences do not disappear. Low vocabulary knowledge relative to peers at the end of kindergarten typically means low vocabulary knowledge throughout schooling. This may, in part, be due to the fact that there tends to be little emphasis on explicit vocabulary instruction in schools (Scott, Jamieson-Noel, & Asselin, 2003; Watts, 1995) and that being in school does not seem to substantially impact vocabulary size. For example, one study found that January-born kindergartners (the oldest in their class) had about the same size vocabulary as December-born first graders who were only a month older than the kindergartners but had been in school a year longer (Christian, Morrison, Frazier, & Massetti, 2000).

Vocabulary

Most of the words for which children know the meanings are learned in the context of conversations and/or through being read to and reading. The words are not learned through direct instruction provided by someone who has the specific intention of teaching their meanings. Although words certainly can be learned through purposeful instruction, children need to learn so many words that it

Vocabulary and Sight Vocabulary

In Part III, word learning, the focus was on the development of *sight vocabulary*—words that readers can identify automatically and in all contexts when they are seen in print. In this chapter, the focus is on *knowledge of word meanings*. When one knows the *meaning* of a word, it is considered to be in one's *vocabulary*. At early points in literacy development, the number of words in a child's vocabulary is much larger than the number of words in his *sight vocabulary*. That is, the child knows the meanings of many more words than he can read. For proficient readers, on the other hand, sight vocabulary and vocabulary are about the same size; these readers can read all of the words for which they know the meaning.

People sometimes confuse vocabulary and sight vocabulary when talking about developing readers. The distinction between the two is important because it impacts instructional decision making. Children's knowledge of word meanings (their vocabulary), particularly if it is very limited, has the potential to influence the development of their sight vocabulary. As discussed in Part III, most items in children's sight vocabulary are learned through successful word-solving efforts. An important step in word solving involves confirming that the hypothesized pronunciation of a word constitutes a real word that fits the context in which it is encountered. If the hypothesized pronunciation is a real word that is not in a child's vocabulary, that child, if he has learned to be strategic in word solving, is apt to reject the hypothesized pronunciation. For example, in reading the sentence *He wore a plaid shirt,* the word-solving efforts of a child who does not know the meaning of the word *plaid* are likely to yield a pronunciation with a long-*a* sound. Realizing that *played* does not fit the context, the child would reject that pronunciation and perhaps try the short-a sound (being flexible with the vowels). This would yield the correct pronunciation but the child would be unable to confirm it because the word is not in his vocabulary. The child might try a few more pronunciations, perhaps trying both the long and short sounds of the *i*, still to no avail. At this point it would be reasonable for the child to settle on one of the pronunciations and move on. However, this encounter with the unknown word will have served to disrupt the child's reading of the text and to undermine his confidence in his word-solving skills. Further, the child will have made no progress in adding the word to his sight vocabulary. This is just one of the many ways in which vocabulary development and reading development are reciprocally related—development in one influences development in the other.

would be virtually impossible for teachers (or anyone else) to specifically teach all of them. Therefore, teachers need to provide supportive contexts and strategies that will enable children to learn word meanings and that will generate enthusiasm for doing so. In addition, teachers can, and should, selectively teach and provide ongoing engagement with some words. Indeed, numerous studies demonstrate that direct and explicit teaching of word meanings has a positive impact on young children's vocabulary (e.g., Beck & McKeown, 2007; Coyne, McCoach, Loftus,

Zipoli, & Kapp, 2009; Silverman, 2007). The basic premises of these instructional approaches are described later in this chapter.

Of course, knowing a word's meaning is not an "all-or-nothing" phenomenon. Gradations exist in knowledge of word meanings, with knowledge ranging from knowing nothing about a word to having elaborated knowledge of the word's meaning, how it relates to other words, being able to use it fluently and appropriately in conversation and in writing, etc. Ouellette (2006) suggests that deep knowledge of word meanings is the type of vocabulary knowledge that is most strongly related to reading comprehension. For most words, deep knowledge of meaning develops gradually through multiple encounters with the words in different contexts. In fact, Bloom (2000) suggests that children do not learn 10 words a day, as some estimates suggest (Nagy & Herman, 1987), but rather that they learn "one-hundredth of each of one thousand different words" (p. 25) each day. If Bloom's characterization is accurate, which we suspect it is, it becomes clear that vocabulary development is largely incidental and occurs through children's efforts to infer and refine the meanings of words as they participate in various language contexts. Teachers can assist in this incremental learning process by providing supportive language contexts for vocabulary acquisition and by being alert for occasions when children encounter words that are unfamiliar to them and providing explanations of those words.

Syntax

Syntax is a component of grammar that involves knowledge of sentences and their structures (Fromkin, Rodman, & Hyams, 2003). For most people, syntactic knowledge is largely implicit. For example, people can generally identify when a sentence sounds right (e.g., *The boy found the dog*) and when a sentence does not sound right (e.g., *The boy found quickly*). However, explaining what's wrong with a sentence is often difficult. By the time children enter kindergarten, they generally have a fairly well-developed implicit grasp of the syntax of the language spoken in their homes. For example, the order of the words in their sentences and the types of words that follow one upon the other are likely to be quite like the sentence structures used by family members.

As children read, they rely heavily on their implicit syntactic knowledge to help them assemble the words they have read into the meaningful ideas that become the building blocks for their overall understanding of the text (see Chapter 1). Syntax also plays a role in the development of sight vocabulary. Thus, when children are "testing the fit" of a word's hypothesized pronunciation, one factor that would signal a poor fit is whether or not the sentence sounds right. If it does, the word's identity would be confirmed and the word would be a step closer to being part of the student's sight vocabulary.

As with vocabulary, children vary in their syntactic competence, and that variation is at least partially related to their language experiences. The syntax in books is often quite different from, and more complex than, the syntax of everyday spoken language. Therefore, if children have had limited experience with being read to, they are likely to find book syntax challenging. Teachers and proficient readers are so familiar with book syntax that they may not recognize the challenge it poses for some children. Consider this excerpt from *The Turkey Girl* (Pollock, 1996) below:

> "Hear me, hear me, children of the Sun Father and Earth Mother, in four days time, before the harvest moon, the dance of the Sacred Bird will be held. It is fitting that you all attend."
> Murmurs of plans for the festival rippled throughout the crowd. (no page)

This book is a Zuni folktale that bears resemblance to the European folktale known as Cinderella, and young children are the intended audience. Children who have been read to widely and frequently and who have discussed such books with their reading partners will have encountered the types of syntactic structures (e.g., multiple embedded clauses and phrases) and gained experience in interpreting those structures. For children without such experience, the syntactic challenges provided by this portion of the text will be difficult or impossible to negotiate without assistance.

Even books written to be read by emergent and developing readers sometimes include challenging syntax that could interfere with word-solving attempts. For example, a book entitled *Where Is the Queen?* (Minkoff, 1996) includes the following as part of the description of a queen's preparation for giving a ball: "First, she set the table for eating in the green room" (p. 4). The phrase *set the table for* **eating** is at odds with the more typical phrase *set the table for* **dinner** and may well confuse children and lead them to reject even an accurate decoding of the word. The more unfamiliar children are with the types of syntax encountered in books the more likely they are to experience difficulty with such structures.

Much more is known about the role of vocabulary development in reading than is known about the role of syntactic knowledge. Therefore, this chapter focuses more on vocabulary than on syntax. However, this imbalance should not be taken as an indication that syntax is somehow less important than vocabulary. Further, because language skills are tightly interrelated, it is likely that whatever teachers do in the name of enabling children to expand their vocabularies is likely to promote children's syntactic development as well.

INSTRUCTION TO SUPPORT VOCABULARY DEVELOPMENT

In working with teachers involved in implementing the ISA, we have addressed vocabulary development in three basic ways. Firstly, we encourage teachers to be generally attentive to the need to support vocabulary development among their students and to "think vocabulary" across the school day. Secondly, we encourage them to explicitly teach and provide practice with a few "generally useful" words from each book they read during interactive read-alouds and to rely on instructional recommendations provided by Beck et al. (2002) in doing so. Thirdly, we encourage teachers to develop content-area concepts and vocabulary by immersing students in thematically organized units of study for the purpose of building the knowledge base upon which reading comprehension depends. The need to develop content-area knowledge and vocabulary is addressed in the next chapter. In the remainder of this chapter we discuss instruction to develop knowledge of words that have broader utility and other more general language skills.

Attention to Vocabulary All Day Everyday

The goal of reducing the vocabulary gap that exists between more and less economically advantaged children is unlikely to be accomplished if vocabulary instruction is relegated to a few minutes in the day during which it is explicitly delivered. Therefore, we encourage teachers to be mindful throughout the school day of the vocabulary challenges that children encounter (especially those with the weakest language skills) and to be alert for opportunities to enhance children's development. This mindful approach entails engaging children in conversation as much as possible, providing multiple opportunities for children to engage in conversations with their peers, recognizing (and anticipating) when limitations in vocabulary might interfere with word solving, using vocabulary that has been explicitly taught while engaging in genuine conversations, and so on.

Explicit Vocabulary Instruction

Which Words Should Be Taught?

Unfortunately for teachers, vocabulary researchers are not in agreement about how to go about selecting words for vocabulary instruction. Biemiller (2006) argues that words tend to be acquired in a rough sequence and that instruction should respect this sequence. Thus, for children with limited vocabularies, from Biemiller's perspective, the words that are taught should be words that most children at that age already know. Beck and her colleagues (2002), on the other hand, suggest selecting words for instruction based on such characteristics as their utility and interest value. Research on vocabulary instruction is ongoing and will hopefully provide clearer guidance in the near future on how to select words for specific instruction. Below we share the guidance we provided to teachers in the most recent ISA study (Scanlon et al., 2008).

In this study, we encouraged teachers to follow the guidance provided by Beck and her colleagues (2002) who divide words into three large groups which they refer to as Tiers.[1]

---

[1]Use of the word *tier* in this context has nothing to do with the use of the word *tier* in discussions of RTI.

- *Tier 1* consists of the most basic words (e.g., *house, boy, hand*) that rarely require instruction in school, at least for children who are native speakers of English.
- *Tier 2* consists of words that are relatively high in their frequency of usage by mature language users and are useful in a variety of contexts (e.g., *remarkable, extraordinary, hesitant, pursue*). Beck et al. recommend explicitly teaching Tier 2 words.
- *Tier 3* consists of words that are low in frequency of usage and their application is typically limited to a specific domain (e.g., *stamen, voltage*). Instruction of these words, Beck et al. (2002) argue, is best left to occur in the content area when they are needed.

According to Beck et al. (2002), instructional emphasis should be placed on Tier 2 words, because they are most likely to be useful to children in a variety of contexts, and children are likely to encounter them often enough that their meanings can be learned well.

A further consideration in choosing words to teach is the importance of understanding the meanings of particular words relative to the text or texts that the children will read in the near future. If understanding a particular word is crucial to understanding the text, obviously that word should be taught either before the text is read or at the point where it is encountered in the text. In fact, Pressley (2006) concluded that highly effective teachers teach vocabulary opportunistically; that is, they are aware of when children may not know the meanings of words, and they teach the meanings of the words as they come up.

Finally, Beck and her colleagues (2002) argue that children will learn new words more readily if they already have ways of expressing the concepts to which the new words refer. Thus, in learning these words they are not learning entirely new concepts but more precise ways to refer to concepts that they already understand. Below is a list of Tier 2 words and the expressions that children would be likely to use to refer to the concepts.

Tier 2 words	Students' likely expressions
merchant	salesperson or clerk (or guy in the store)
required	have to
tend	take care of

(Beck et al., 2002, p. 17)

Beck et al.'s Criteria for Tier 2 Words

Teachers are encouraged to review reading materials prior to reading the texts with their students and to select a few words that will be used for focused instruction. The words should meet all three of the criteria listed below:

1. *Importance and utility:* Words that are characteristic of mature language users and appear frequently across a variety of domains.
2. *Instructional potential:* Words that can be worked with in a variety of ways so that students can build rich representations of them and of their connections to other words and concepts.
3. *Conceptual understanding:* Words for which students understand the general concept but which provide precision and specificity in describing the concept. (Beck et al., 2002, p. 19)

General Principles for Helping Children Learn Word Meanings

Both Beck et al. (2002) and Graves (2006) suggest a variety of ways that teachers can help children build their vocabulary skills. A listing of their combined recommendations is provided below along with our commentary.

- *Provide a language-rich environment.* Children should have many opportunities throughout the course of the school day to talk and listen for both social and academic reasons. Further, they should be read to on a daily basis and provided with the opportunity to discuss things that are read.

- *Develop a fascination with learning and using more sophisticated words.* Young children tend to value what their teachers value (at least, if they like their teachers). If teachers express an interest in and a love of words, the children are likely to catch the excitement. In classrooms that focus on vocabulary development, we often hear teachers exclaiming "Isn't that a great word!" or "Oh! I love that word—let's put it in our Great Word Box!" or "Did you hear that word that Sara just used? It's one of our sparkle words!" In these same classrooms we also notice children asking about the meanings of words and being motivated to use more sophisticated words when speaking and writing.

- *Teach words by providing both definitional and contextual information.* Dictionary definitions are generally weak sources of information for children, particularly those with limited word knowledge and limited reading skill. Such definitions are often vague, circular, and cryptic (Beck et al., 2002). For example, the definition of the word *coax* is "to persuade or try to persuade by gentle urging or flattery" (*American Heritage*, 2003). Children who do not know the meaning of *coax* may also not know the meaning of the words *persuade, gentle, urging*, and/or *flattery*. Using a context in which the word occurs, such as the sentence in the book where the word was first encountered, as the initial point of departure for teaching the word's meaning will help children to more readily understand the meaning. For example, if the word *coax* occurred in a book about a poorly behaved dog, in a sentence such as "Mom tried to *coax* the dog into the house," by the time the children encounter this word they are likely to already have a sense of the what the mother and the dog are like and so will have both the broader context of the passage and the more immediate context of the sentence to help them learn the meaning of the word.

Promoting an Interest in Words

In my (JMS) reading groups when we encounter a Tier 2 word in our reading, we put the word on a sticky note (each group has its own section around the small room and a different colored sticky note). This simple act encourages students to become more word conscious, and it helps me be more mindful when planning my lessons to revisit specific vocabulary. Occasionally, if there are a few minutes left at the end of a lesson, we'll play a game where a student selects a word from the wall and, by using pantomime, tries to get the other students to identify the word. These activities have generated enthusiasm around learning new vocabulary.

- *Explain the new words using words and concepts that the children already understand.* Children definitely know about *coaxing*, although they are unlikely to know the word.
- *Use "child-friendly" language.* For example, "To *coax* means to get somebody to do something that he or she doesn't really want to do and to do it in a nice way."
- *Provide multiple examples of how the new word might be used and use the word in a variety of contexts.* For example, after children encounter the word *coax* in a book, the teacher might say "This week I am going to try to *coax* you into keeping the cubby area neat" or "If we get all of the scraps of paper cleaned up quickly, you may be able to *coax* me into reading an extra book before lunch."
- *Teach groups of words that are related in meaningful ways.* In order to have a deep understanding of the meaning of a word, students need to know how the word relates and compares to other words. So, teaching multiple words relating to the same general meaning can provide opportunities to analyze word meanings more fully. Thus, for example, synonyms (words that mean the same or similar thing) and antonyms (words with opposite meanings) might be taught together. Synonyms for *coax* include *cajole, persuade,* and *entice.* Antonyms for *coax* include *command, demand,* and *force.* Children will learn the meanings of these words well if they use them in describing how they interact with their parents and friends and how characters in books interact.
- *Keep using new words so that they become a stable part of children's vocabularies.* Words whose meanings have been specifically taught will be retained better if they are revisited periodically. Teachers and students should use the words in their everyday interactions and in their writing. Many teachers who have instituted vocabulary instruction of this type have developed some method for reminding themselves of the words that have been taught. For example, some teachers keep a list of the words so that they can quickly refer to it. Others keep a word box or a word can with the individual words written on strips of paper, and they periodically draw out a few of the words and discuss their meanings with the students. In one school with which we have worked, a schoolwide effort to enhance vocabulary

development has been instituted. There is a schoolwide word of the week, each week, which the principal announces on Monday and then uses in his morning announcements for the rest of the week. Teachers have lists of the words of the week and the words have been stenciled on the walls in the hallways. Everyone in the school is encouraged to incorporate these more sophisticated words in their interactions both during the week when they are introduced and thereafter.

"Isn't That Dreadful?"

One of the kindergarten intervention teachers (P. Connors) who was responsible for instigating the greater focus on vocabulary in the school mentioned above, which is a school that serves a high-needs population, tells the following story. One of her students reported to her on an incident that he had heard about on the television news. An elderly woman had been attacked and beaten for her pocketbook. Having conveyed the story to his teacher, the child concluded with "Isn't that dreadful?" *Dreadful* was a Tier 2 word in his classroom. Clearly, the child owned it!

INTERACTIVE READ-ALOUDS AND CONVERSATIONS TO PROMOTE THE DEVELOPMENT OF VOCABULARY AND ORAL LANGUAGE

There are two basic techniques that have been cited widely and consistently recommended by child language researchers (e.g., Biemiller & Boote, 2006; Dickinson et al., 2006; Dickinson & Smith, 1994; Whitehurst et al., 1994) as powerful ways to promote vocabulary knowledge and syntactic skills:

- Reading to children and engaging them in conversations about what is read.
- Engaging children in lots of conversations throughout the day.

A Great Read-Aloud Website

www.storylineonline.net

This is an online streaming video program featuring actors reading children's books aloud. Accompanying activities and lesson ideas are included.

Interactive Read-Alouds

Reading aloud to children and engaging them in conversations about what is read is a powerful tool for promoting vocabulary and literacy development more generally (e.g., McGee & Schickendanz, 2007; Morrow & Gambrell, 2001). In fact, virtually all of the studies on ways to enhance vocabulary development in the primary grades have utilized read-alouds as a central component of the intervention (Biemiller & Boote, 2006), and Graves (2006) reports that the most successful attempts at bolstering vocabulary come from interactive read-alouds. In this section we focus on the role of interactive read-alouds in enhancing vocabulary and oral language development. Read-alouds are, of course, useful in many other ways, including for the purpose of modeling and engaging children in the active construction of the meaning of text, for developing the background knowledge upon which comprehension depends (discussed in Chapter 13), and for providing a context in which children can—and often do—become captivated by books and thus develop and sustain their motivation to learn to read.

The major difference between an *interactive* read-aloud and a read-aloud is the expectation that, while reading the book, there will be extensive interaction between and among the teacher and the students and that the interaction will not all be directed and controlled by the teacher. Both the children and the teacher should have opportunities to ask and answer questions, to share their reactions and expectations, to revisit parts of the book, and so on.

Overactive Interactive Read-Alouds

In order to avoid total chaos during read-alouds, teachers need to have well-established routines and signals that let the children know when they need to quiet down so that individuals can be heard or that they need to stay on topics directly related to the book they are reading. To quiet down the class, one teacher we know simply sits up a little straighter and folds her hands in her lap (i.e., she models silence). To ensure that an individual child is heard, she simply says, "Let's listen to what Alex is saying"—which is a much more collaborative and inviting statement than something like "Shh! Alex is talking!" When a child's comments venture too far from the topic at hand, she might say something like, "I see that this reminded you of your visit to the dentist, but right now that's not what we're talking about. Can you tell me (or a friend) more about going to the dentist during snack time?"

Selecting Books for Read-Alouds

A number of factors need to be considered in selecting books to read aloud to children in a classroom or small-group context. While sometimes a book might be read just for the pure enjoyment of it, virtually every book lends itself to helping teachers address some of the many curricular goals that they have for their children. In order to most effectively address those goals, some planning is required. At the very least, the teacher needs to be thoroughly familiar with a book before she reads it to students. Previewing a book for the purpose of determining how it might be used to enhance students' language development, the teacher needs to think about the following considerations:

- *The students*
  - What do they already know?
  - What are they ready to learn?
  - What are their interests?

- *The classroom curriculum*
  - How does the book fit with the topics and themes that have been and will be covered in language arts, science, social studies, and/or math?
  - How does the vocabulary in the book fit with other vocabulary words that have already been taught?

- *The book*
  - What kinds of language challenges does the book present?
    - What words and/or syntactic structures will need explanation or clarification?
    - How will those words and structures be explained?
    - Is the language so advanced relative to students' current language skills that they will feel overwhelmed?
  - Will the text be interesting and engaging for the children in the instructional group?

Conducting Interactive Read-Alouds

Once a book has been selected for use, the teacher needs to plan for how to use it. As part of this planning, the teacher needs to think about engaging the students in discussions of the book before, during, and after reading in order to take full advantage of all instructional opportunities that a read-aloud provides. Much of the discussion will revolve around the events and the information presented in the book (see the section on interactive read-alouds in Chapter 13). During these discussions, however, teachers have the opportunity to address vocabulary encountered in the book and some of the more complex syntactic structures. They also have the opportunity to encourage children to use more complete and ultimately more complex sentence structures and more sophisticated vocabulary in their conversations.

Instruction to Enhance Syntactic and Grammatical Skills

Clarification of potentially confusing syntactic structures generally takes the form of reading the segment of text, as stated by the author, and then restating that segment using a more familiar syntactic structure. For example, in the book *The Turkey Girl* one of the pages starts with the following sentence: "The Turkey Girl caught the excitement, imagining herself dancing with the others" (Pollock, 1996, no page). Both phrases in this sentence use syntax that is different from the syntax that is likely to be used in everyday conversation, wherein we might say "The Turkey Girl got excited too and started to think about dancing with the others." The teacher might choose to simply restate the sentence, or she might read to the end of the page and then engage the children in a conversation about how the Turkey Girl was thinking and feeling and, at this point, explain the meaning of "caught the excitement." On a second or subsequent reading of this book, it probably would not be necessary to explain this particular syntactic structure again, but when the children hear it again, their syntactic competence will be slightly extended. When they hear other, similar structures such as "caught the spirit," they are more likely to understand them too.

Instruction to Enhance Knowledge of Word Meanings during Interactive Read-Alouds

In any given book, there are likely to be a number of words for which the children do not know the meanings. They cannot all be taught thoroughly. Rather, several might be explained incidentally while reading, with a few selected for more thorough instruction and discussion. Before meeting with students, the teacher should identify the words that will need explanation and plan child-friendly explanations for them. Words that will be the focus of more detailed discussion should be selected and instructional activities planned before the book is read to the group.

Ambiguous Words

Many words in the English language carry more than one meaning. Examples include *can* (the container and the ability to do something) and *bank* (the side of a river or the place where money is stored). Further, if spelling is disregarded, as it must be in the context of read-alouds (since children cannot see the words), there are many more ambiguous word pairs. Examples include *herd/heard*, *higher/hire*, *flower/flour*, and so on. It is important to be mindful that ambiguous words may be responsible for creating confusion in young learners. Proficient readers generally access context-appropriate word meanings effortlessly. However, young children often don't, and confusion may be the result. If such a word occurs in a context that doesn't provide clarity regarding the intended meaning of the word, the teacher should be prepared to clarify things.

BEFORE READING

- Discuss critical vocabulary before beginning to read the text (e.g., "This book is about volcanoes. Does anyone have any idea what a volcano is?").
- Ensure that children can pronounce the new word acceptably (e.g., "Let's all say that word, *volcano*"). This will help them store the word in memory.

DURING READING

- Stop and briefly explain or discuss the meanings of words that are novel for children but that they are likely to encounter in other contexts.
- On occasion, reread the portion of the text that includes the novel vocabulary item, but substitute a word that the children already know.
- When a child comments on or asks a question about an aspect of the text to which the new word could reasonably be applied or incorporated, encourage him to use the newly introduced word (or the teacher can use it in responding to the inquiry).
- Notice when children use the new words and compliment them.

AFTER READING

- Review the meanings of new words that were discussed either before or during the reading of the text. Children need multiple exposures to a word in order for it to become part of their useable vocabulary.
- After the words have been introduced, the teacher should look for multiple opportunities to both use them in her own speech and to encourage children to use them in speaking and writing.
- Some texts introduce enough new words that it is reasonable to compare and contrast the new words after reading the text.
- Have children think of other words they may know that mean the same thing, or almost the same thing, as the new words encountered in the text.
- Let children know how impressed you are when they begin using the new and interesting words right away.

Beck et al. (2002) provide specific recommendations for helping children establish new vocabulary after a text has been read. These recommendations are presented below:

- Present the word in the context in which it occurs in the story.
- Ask the children to repeat the word to help them establish a phonological representation of it.
- Explain the meaning of the word.
- Provide examples of the word's usage other than the one used in the story.
- Have the children interact with the examples or provide their own examples.
- Have the children say the word again to reinforce its phonological representation.

Next is a sample instructional dialogue taken from video of D. Rutnik, one of the teachers who participated in the Scanlon et al. (2008) study. She was implementing the text talk procedure described by Beck et al. (2002) following a read-aloud of the book *Swimmy* (Lionni, 1963). The focus of this vignette is on the word *fierce*, which occurred in the context of the book.

Sample Instructional Dialogue

TEACHER: In the story it said, "One bad day, a tuna fish, swift, *fierce*, and very hungry, came darting through the waves." The word I want to talk about is *fierce*. Say the word with me—*fierce*.

STUDENTS: (*Say the word.*)

TEACHER: When something is *fierce*, it is very powerful and strong. We have had some really bad weather lately, with lots of very hard rain and very *fierce* winds. The winds were very, very strong. Show me how they were blowing.

TEACHER AND STUDENTS: (*Move arms to demonstrate strong, powerful, indeed . . . fierce winds.*)

TEACHER: Tell me something you know that might be *fierce*. Try to use the word *fierce* when you tell about it.

STUDENT: A fierce shark!!!

TEACHER: Yes, a fierce shark. *Fierce* means strong and powerful, in a mean kind of a way. (*Several children were given the opportunity to use the word, and the teacher commented on and clarified usage for each one.*) You might want to use the word *fierce* today when you are talking or writing.

TEACHER: Lets say the word *fierce* again.

STUDENTS: (*Say the word.*)

Helping Children to Effectively Learn Words from Context

Clearly children will not always have a supportive adult available to help them learn the meanings of new words. As noted above, most words are learned from context. For this reason it can be helpful to provide children with guidance on how to try to figure out the meanings of words encountered in context. Graves (2006) offers some suggestions with regard to helping students at least get an approximate idea of a word's meaning. He suggests that teachers start by helping students understand that context *may* provide hints or clues about a word's meaning. If the reader does some thinking, he may be able to generate a hypothesis about what the word means. A better understanding of the word's meaning may come if the reader is persistent and continues to look for clues about the word in other contexts. Graves (2006, p. 99) suggests that it is useful for readers to do the following:

- Monitor whether what they are reading makes sense.
- Slow down when they don't know the meaning of a word.

- Reread the sentence that is causing confusion and the previous sentence, looking for clues to word meaning.
- Make their best guess at the meaning of the unknown word, substitute the hypothesized word meaning, and then read the sentence to see if it makes sense.

Teachers can model the process of using context to infer word meanings during the course of interactive read-alouds. For example, we once observed a teacher reading the Beatrix Potter book entitled *The Tale of Peter Rabbit* (Potter, 2002) to her class. One line of text read "Now run along, and don't get into any mischief." One of the children piped up and asked "What does *mischief* mean?" (a sure sign that this teacher had successfully developed an interest in words among her students). Rather than explaining the word to the children, the teacher said, "Let's see if we can figure it out." She then went back to the beginning of the paragraph and reread. After reviewing what had happened up to that point, children hypothesized that the word *mischief* might mean *trouble*. The teacher then reread the sentence, substituting the word *trouble* so that the children could decide whether *trouble* made sense in the sentence. They concluded that it did and therefore decided that *mischief* probably meant something like *trouble*.

In the example above, it was possible to effectively infer the meaning of the word. However, there are many instances where context is not helpful or may be downright misleading. It is important to be clear with children that context is not always helpful. Beck et al. (2002) describe a continuum of contexts from directive to misdirective. They offer the following as an example of a context that might actually serve to move children toward an incorrect meaning of the word *grudgingly*:

> Sandra had won the dance contest, and the audience's cheers brought her to the stage for an encore. "Every step she takes is so perfect and graceful," Ginny said *grudgingly* as she watched Sandra dance. (p. 4)

If students make hypotheses about word meanings in contexts that are not supportive, the result may be an inaccurate or confused understanding of the words. Future encounters with the same words may, however, serve to correct and refine their meaning. This again supports the notion that students need to encounter words in a wide variety of contexts in order to develop rich and accurate understandings of their meanings.

Additional Suggestions for Learning Word Meanings

WORD PARTS

As described in Chapter 9, many words consist of a root word and one or more affixes (prefixes and suffixes). If a child knows the meaning of the root word, he may be able to figure out the meaning of the word with affixes by thinking of the meaning of the root word and the meaning of each affix.

DICTIONARIES

As children gain proficiency in reading, dictionaries can sometimes be useful to them in learning about the meanings of words they encounter while reading. Children should be encouraged to look up words and then consider the definitions they find in light of the contexts in which the words were first encountered. Children's dictionaries should be made available for this purpose. Teachers might also consider making a Franklin Talking Dictionary (Franklin Electronic Publishers, Inc.) available. This is a small electronic device with a standard QWERTY keyboard. Unknown words can be typed in and, with the click of a button, the device pronounces the word and provides a spoken definition. (Because these devices have considerable play value, the conditions for their use need to be clearly delineated.)

GLOSSARIES AND OTHER TEXT CONVENTIONS

Nonfiction books often provide explicit definitions of important words introduced in their texts. The important words are often signaled by bold-face font in the text. Children need to be alert to this convention for signaling importance and to look for the definitions that may be provided either in the same section of text where the word is first encountered, in a text box or illustration on the same page, or in a glossary at the end of a text.

Conversations

Discussions between teachers and students and among students provide important opportunities for language development. Some children have had few experiences with conversing and so may need some explicit modeling and coaching relating to how to engage in conversations. In the primary grades, snack time can provide a good opportunity to model and engage children in conversations because the teacher can focus on a small number of children and engage them in more extended conversations than would be possible or appropriate if the entire class were expected to participate.

The accumulated research on classroom supports for language development (see Dickinson et al., 2004, for a review) suggests that conversations across instructional contexts are especially helpful when:

- *The children are given the opportunity to do a lot of the talking.*
- *There are several conversational turns between the child and his conversation partner.* Some researchers have observed that it is rare for children in classroom settings to engage in true conversations in which the participants have more

than one or two turns each (see Snow et al., 1998). In classrooms where more extended conversations occur, children's language develops at a faster rate.

- *The child's responses are more than single-word utterances.* Teachers encourage the use of longer and more complex sentences by asking open-ended questions. These are questions that call for more than a one-word response. Thus, instead of asking "Did you like the movie?" which calls for a yes or no response, the teacher might say "Tell me about the movie" or "Tell me what you liked about the movie."

- *Teachers restate answers or comments made by children that do not represent well-formed sentences,* especially when well-formed sentences are called for. Restatements should be made in the form of elaborations and comments on what students say and should *not* come across as corrections of students' language. For example, if the student says "He a big one!" the teacher might say "Yes, he *is* a big one!", with the emphasis on the word *is* suggesting agreement rather that correction. The hope is that providing students with opportunities to hear their thoughts expressed using standard syntax will help them develop that syntax.

- *Teachers elaborate on a student's statement* by using a somewhat more complex syntactic structure than the structure used by the student. For example, if the student says "The dog is sad," the teacher might agree by saying "Yes, the dog does seem to be sad" and extend the conversation by asking "Why do you think that he's feeling sad?"

- *Teachers occasionally notice and compliment children on using well-formed sentences* (e.g., "What a nice sentence that was!").

- *Teachers do not talk down to children.* When adults use mature vocabulary and more sophisticated syntax (within reason), children have more opportunities to advance their language skills. For example, in noting what a child is eating at snack time, the teacher might say "My! That looks absolutely scrumptious!" rather than "That looks good!"

- *Conversations often focus on nonpresent topics and pretend play* (e.g., what the child did yesterday, what the child saw on a field trip, who is going to play what role in the housekeeping area). Such conversations call for more explicit language because the child cannot rely on shared knowledge in the same way as is possible when talking about an immediate experience in which both conversation partners are involved. Experience and support with such decontextualized language helps to prepare children for the world of print, which requires them to think beyond the here and now.

There are, of course, many ways to encourage conversations among students. A few are described below.

"Describe and Guess"

"Describe and guess" is a group-sharing activity in which one child describes an item that is kept out of sight. The other students ask questions about the item and try to guess what it is, based on the description. When children (and adults) are describing things that are not visible, they have to use more sophisticated language. They cannot just point, and they cannot assume that others know what they are talking about. As compared with the more traditional show and tell, describe and guess promotes more complex language on the part of the child doing the describing, and on the part of the children doing the guessing as they refine their questions in attempts to solicit the information needed to make an accurate guess.

Sociodramatic Play

Research summarized by Snow et al. (1998) indicates that participation in sociodramatic play increases oral language use (p. 183), because such play typically requires a good deal of negotiation among the children as they determine who will play what role, how the storyline will unfold, whether events are unfolding as planned, and so on. Research has also found that, for the purpose of promoting the development of reading and writing skills, play settings are more attractive and engaging to children when they represent authentic literacy contexts in the children's real-world environment. In other words, children seem to play best at what they know. Their play will be more complex and involved in, for example, a housekeeping or grocery store setting than in a bank or post office setting because, for most children, the latter two are comparatively unfamiliar contexts. (See Morrow and Schickedanz [2006] for a review of the relationship between sociodramatic play and literacy development in early childhood.)

There is also evidence that, in settings in which there are more literacy artifacts, children engage in more literacy acts, and the acts tend to become more complex over time (Neuman & Roskos, 1993). Thus, pretend play settings should be well supplied with literacy props such as notepads, phone books, pencils, markers, cookbooks, recipe cards, magazines, newspapers, labeled food packages, message boards, envelopes, stamps, tape, and, if possible, a computer—or even a nonfunctioning computer keyboard.

Many children who enter school with limited language skills will have had limited verbal interactions and/or limited experiences with these kinds of props and/or with sociodramatic play prior to entering school. Therefore, for them, it will be important for the teacher to model and provide guidance and feedback across these contexts.

Cooperative Projects

When children work together to accomplish a common goal, they generally need to do a good deal of conversing in order to clarify aspects of what needs to be done, to negotiate roles and responsibilities, to evaluate progress toward the intended goal, and so on. Cooperative projects might include conducting and documenting the results of science experiments, gathering information about the local community and preparing and sharing what was learned, writing a book on a topic of mutual interest, etc. Cooperative projects are especially useful for encouraging conversations among children who are beyond the point of engaging in sociodramatic play in the classroom.

Share Your Thinking

This is a form of "every student response." During whole-class and small-group instruction only one child gets to talk at a time if the teacher leads every discussion. If teachers frequently ask children to turn to their neighbors or to partners at their tables and talk about whatever the topic is, all of the children will have more opportunity to engage in conversation. This approach is becoming more and more common in the context of interactive read-alouds and is often referred to as "think, pair, share" (Lyman, 1981). However, virtually any context that might lend itself to a classroom conversation can incorporate opportunities for children to share their thinking with one another.

EVALUATING AND DOCUMENTING CHILDREN'S PROGRESS

Figure 12.1 provides a record form for documenting teachers' observations of children's acquisition of new vocabulary and their sense of children's general status in vocabulary and general language skills relative to grade-level peers. The form allows space for teachers to document their observations of individual children multiple times over the course of a school year. Children who appear to be slow or very slow in adding new words to their vocabulary or who appear to have language skills that are less well developed than those of their peers will likely benefit from having increased opportunities to work in small-group and one-on-one situations wherein they are exposed to extended opportunities to engage in conversations focused on books read or heard.

Group Snapshot—Observation of Vocabulary (Word Meaning) and Language Development						
Student Names:						
Vocabulary Development—Learns and uses newly introduced vocabulary words: **E**asily **S**lowly **V**ery slowly	Date:					
	Date:					
	Date:					
	Date:					
	Date:					
	Date:					
	Date:					
	Date:					
	Date:					
	Date:					
Vocabulary and language skills relative to grade-level peers: **W**ell developed **A**ppropriately developed **N**eeds development	Date:					
	Date:					
	Date:					
	Date:					
	Date:					
	Date:					
	Date:					
	Date:					
	Date:					
	Date:					

FIGURE 12.1. Group snapshot for vocabulary and language development.

CHAPTER 13

Comprehension and General Knowledge

MEANING CONSTRUCTION GOAL 2

The child will develop the foundational knowledge and comprehension skills and strategies that will enhance her ability to construct the meaning of, and learn from, texts heard or read.

THE PROCESS OF COMPREHENSION

Comprehension occurs as the reader builds a mental representation of the text (Perfetti et al., 2005). Comprehension is an active, constructive process in which the ultimate understanding of the text is determined by a combination of what is stated directly in the text and the reader's preexisting knowledge related to the topic of the text. That understanding is reflected in the wording of the meaning construction goal above. The instructional goal is to help children to both develop the knowledge upon which comprehension depends and to become self-regulated learners who are motivated to understand the texts they read and hear and who, therefore, notice when things are not making sense to them and take action to resolve the confusion that arises. Thus, instruction to foster comprehension goes beyond helping children comprehend a particular text at a particular point in time to helping them develop productive ways of thinking about texts that will enhance their comprehension of texts they encounter in the future.

ACTIVE MEANING CONSTRUCTION

In the example below, we provide the reader with the opportunity to become conscious of the type of active meaning construction in which proficient readers engage. The example is three sentences long. After reading the first sentence, the reader should stop and think about the main character a bit.

Sentence 1: Sam walked slowly on the way to school.
(Stop and think.)

Sentence 2: She was worried about today's math text.
(Stop and think.)

Sentence 3: While walking, she wondered how she could be more effective in helping her students understand place value.

Most readers who participate in this exercise find that their thinking changes quite radically from one sentence to the next. Many think *Sam* is a young boy in the first sentence and make attributions about the reasons for his slow pace—some think he doesn't like school, others suggest that he does most things slowly. Often people have an image of Sam and the setting in which he is walking. Upon reading the second sentence, many readers immediately alter their interpretation of the first sentence: Sam is now an older girl. The gender change is due to the pronoun *she*, and the age change is due to the fact that young children are unlikely to be worried about math tests. Readers now attribute the slow pace to anxiety about the test or the desire to avoid it. After reading the third sentence, readers' perceptions of Sam again change radically—Sam is now a teacher rather than a student, and she takes on an entirely different set of characteristics in readers' minds.

This illustration demonstrates that active and engaged readers integrate information directly stated in the text with their existing knowledge to "fill in the gaps" left by the author and then to go well beyond the information directly stated in the text. Further, they shift their thinking about a text as they encounter new information that doesn't fit with their unfolding interpretation of it. Essentially, proficient readers expect the texts they encounter to be coherent, and they interact with those texts in efforts to make them so. Thus, when things don't make sense, proficient readers change their thinking or reread the text to seek clarification—or, more commonly, do both in an iterative fashion until the confusion is resolved. Often, proficient readers take all of these steps without being conscious of them. Mostly they are just thinking about the text—not their approach to comprehending it, unless, of course, the process has been purposefully slowed (as we have done in the example above).

> ### *Constructing and Reconstructing Meaning*
>
> The active, fluent, construction and revision of the meaning of the text that pro-
> ficient readers experience when reading the example of Sam represent the kind
> of comprehension processing that we would ultimately like to see all readers
> achieve. Such an achievement requires that they (1) know something about the
> topic of the passage they are reading, (2) access that information, (3) recognize
> when things don't make sense, and (4) be willing to exert the cognitive effort it
> takes to revise their thinking about the text.

LEVELS OF COMPREHENSION

In constructing the meaning of a text, readers may engage in different types or
levels of thinking. Three levels of comprehension are typically identified: literal,
inferential, and critical.

- *Literal comprehension* involves the understanding of information stated
directly in the text. Examples of literal comprehension from the Sam example
include knowing that:

  - Sam walks slowly.
  - Sam is worried.
  - There is a math test today.

- *Inferential comprehension* involves making inferences that bridge the information directly stated in the text with information that the reader already pos-
sesses. Effective readers draw on their knowledge to make inferences that fill in the
gaps left by the author; ineffective readers fail to do so (Yuill & Oakhill, 1991).
Early in the Sam example, the reader is left to make inferences about:

  - Sam's age.
  - Sam's gender.
  - Sam's reasons for walking slowly and for worrying.

- *Critical comprehension* involves evaluating the information in the text relative to what it means to the reader and relative to the intentions, expertise, and/or
perspective of the author. In the Sam text, the reader is likely to conclude that the
author developed the text with the intention of misleading the reader and might
read additional text by the same author with this in mind.

Research suggests that children who struggle with comprehension, but not
with decoding, differ from their abler peers primarily in their ability to engage in
inferential thinking (see Perfetti et al., 2005, for a review). The reasons for this

difficulty are still being researched. However, Yuill and Oakhill (1991) suggest several possibilities, including that (1) less skilled comprehenders do not have the knowledge needed to make the necessary inferences, (2) they do not know when it is appropriate to make inferences, and/or (3) they have processing limitations that interfere with their ability to integrate text information with prior knowledge. Cain and Oakhill (1999) also suggest that failure to make inferences may be attributable to a focus on reading the words in the text rather than on deriving a coherent understanding of the text. Clearly all of these possibilities could play a role in limiting comprehension, and most of them are at least partially amenable to instructional interventions. In what follows, we describe the types of knowledge sources that need to be developed and describe how interactions around texts, particularly in the context of interactive read-alouds, can help to promote the type of active thinking about text that needs to be established in order to enable the inferential thinking that is so critical to comprehension.

KNOWLEDGE AND COMPREHENSION

"World knowledge is an essential component of reading comprehension, because every text takes for granted the readers' familiarity with a whole range of unspoken and unwritten facts about the cultural and natural world" (Hirsch, 2003, p. 28).

When an individual listens to or reads a text, a complex interaction takes place between what the individual already knows and what is presented in the text. Thus, differences between individuals in the amount of text-relevant knowledge they bring to a reading task will have a substantial influence on their ability to make the required inferences and to comprehend the text (e.g., Gaultney, 1995). For example, someone who has taken a college chemistry class will learn more from reading an article about some aspect of biochemical engineering than will someone who has no background in chemistry. In fact, if someone with no background knowledge persists with the reading at all, she is likely to read the text quite passively and with little expectation of understanding. If, on the other hand, a biochemical engineer were to read the article, she is likely to learn much more than the individual with only college chemistry because she is more thoroughly versed in the terminology and concepts and in how various biochemical processes work. Before even beginning to read the article though, the biochemical engineer is likely to consider the quality of the journal in which it was published and the credentials of the author(s) in order to determine whether the article is likely to provide trustworthy information and therefore warrant the time to read it. If she does decide to read it, she is likely to read very actively and to begin forming hypotheses and questions about what she will learn even before she has finished reading the title (Anderson & Pearson, 1984). As she reads, she is likely to think actively about the content and to compare it to what she already knows about the topic. If there are discrepancies between her knowledge and the information presented in the text, the engineer may change her thinking on the topic, reject the new information, and/or decide that she needs to seek out further information so that she can be more confident in her understanding of the topic.

Types of Knowledge That Influence Comprehension

As illustrated above, how one interprets a text and what one learns from a text depends, to a great extent, on what one already knows. Several types of knowledge play a part in comprehension, including general world knowledge, topic-specific knowledge, schematic knowledge, and genre knowledge. Although the various types of knowledge clearly overlap, it is useful to consider them individually because they carry somewhat different instructional implications. Each of the knowledge types is discussed below.

General Knowledge

General knowledge is sometimes referred to as world knowledge, background knowledge, or prior knowledge. This is an overarching term that encompasses the other types of knowledge described below. General knowledge incorporates the facts and concepts that an individual "knows" and includes the interrelations among more isolated bits of knowledge. General knowledge accumulates over time, often in small increments. This type of knowledge would include the knowledge that readers draw on when they infer, in the Sam example, that Sam is a boy because most people named *Sam* are male—this type of knowledge is not explicitly taught. General knowledge would also include the knowledge that the engineer drew upon when she evaluated the credentials of the author and the quality of the journal in which the article appears. This kind of knowledge might or might not be taught explicitly.

In working with young children, teachers should try to be alert for general knowledge gaps that may interfere with children's ability to understand instructional interactions. Knowledge of word meanings is one general area where this will be an issue. However, there are a myriad of other points of confusion that can arise because children lack specific bits of information that the teacher assumes they have.

Topic-Specific Knowledge

Topic-specific knowledge refers to knowledge that relates directly to topics covered in a text. Thus, for example, the engineer had a good deal of topic-specific knowledge that would give her an advantage in reading a research article that addresses a problem in biochemical engineering. The individual who had never even taken a chemistry course, on the other hand, would probably have very little topic-specific knowledge to assist her in reading the article. The individual with just one course in chemistry is somewhere in between. As this example illustrates, having topic specific knowledge is generally not an all-or-nothing matter. For any given topic, individuals vary along a continuum ranging from little or no knowledge to a level of expertise that requires a substantial investment of time and energy to acquire.

During the course of the elementary years and beyond, children are expected to become knowledgeable about many social studies and science topics. In the early primary grades, engaging children in read-alouds of informational books on topics that will be revisited in later grades will help to prepare them for content they will be expected to master.

Schematic Knowledge

Schematic knowledge refers to knowledge that is structured and organized. Because individuals encounter so many, many bits of information in a typical day, it would be impossible to store and retrieve much of the information unless it were organized in some way. An individual's *schemas* affect how she perceives, notices, and interprets information (Anderson, Osborne, & Tierney, 1984). For example, most of us have a school schema that was probably activated in reading the Sam example. While each individual's school schema is likely to be somewhat unique, there are likely to be some commonalities for those who have experienced typical American educational settings, such as a school having multiple classrooms, with each classroom having children of similar ages, a teacher, work surfaces and chairs, books, etc. Incorporated in the school schema are likely to be schemas for student and teacher, which were also activated in the Sam example. Having a schema related to the topic plays a big role in facilitating one's understanding of a text. For example, understanding the text below is challenging for most people.

> The procedure is actually quite simple. First, you arrange things into different groups. Of course, one pile may be sufficient depending on how much there is to do. If you have to go somewhere else due to lack of facilities, that is the next step; otherwise, you are pretty well set. It is important not to overdo things. That is, it is better to do too few things at once than too many. In the short run this may not seem important but complications can easily arise. A mistake can be expensive as well. At first, the whole procedure will seem complicated. Soon, however, it will become just another fact of life. It is difficult to foresee any end to the necessity for this task in the immediate future, but then one can never tell. After the procedure is completed one arranges the materials into different groups again. Then they can be put into their appropriate places. Eventually they will be used once more and the whole cycle will then have to be repeated. However, that is a part of life. (Bransford & Johnson, 1972, p. 722)

The authors of the passage intended it to be ambiguous and challenging to understand in order to evaluate the extent to which schemas influence comprehension. And, indeed, most proficient readers find it difficult to retell or summarize the passage after reading it. However, readers who were given the title of the text, Washing Clothes, activated the proper schema and found it much easier to comprehend. Thus, without any changes in the text, the reader who knew the title would know that the *things* and *materials* were items of clothing, and that *facilities* referred to washers and dryers. The expensive mistake is also perfectly comprehensible. Clearly, having an appropriate schema relevant to the text and activating that schema are both important to the comprehension process. Book introductions can help children to activate relevant schemas and thus facilitate richer comprehension of a text. In fact, as noted in the example above, even just providing a descriptive title for a book can make a big difference in the reader's ability to integrate the information in the text and make the necessary inferences.

Genre Knowledge

Genre knowledge is a specific type of schematic knowledge that involves understanding the characteristics of different categories of text. *Fiction and nonfiction* represent major subdivisions relative to text structures, and each type carries different expectations for the reader. For example, fiction is meant to entertain and not to be factual, whereas nonfiction is meant to be believed and may or may not have entertainment as a purpose. Within each of these major subdivisions are several genres that have characteristic features, which, if understood, may help the reader more readily comprehend a text. For example, narrative stories tend to follow the structure of a story grammar in which the author provides information about the setting, the characters, one or more problems, attempts to solve the problems, and the resolutions. Children who are familiar with this genre and its characteristics are likely to read/listen to the text with an expectation that these story elements will be provided by the author, and they are therefore apt to read the text in a more active way. Knowing the characteristics of informational text, on the other hand, would lead to a different set of expectations.

INSTRUCTION AND KNOWLEDGE DEVELOPMENT

Because knowledge is so critical to comprehension and because the vehicles for knowledge development are so unevenly distributed in American society, teachers need to consider whether or not children have the various types of knowledge that a particular text takes for granted. Taking this area into consideration may mean that, in planning to read a book in which the setting is a farm, one teacher may need to explicitly tell children who are urban dwellers about farms and what they are for, whereas a teacher using the same book in a rural farming community can reasonably assume that the children have a schema that allows them to analyze/

interpret the text. Similarly, teachers of children who have recently moved to a country may need to carefully support the children's understanding and knowledge of cultural traditions and expectations relating to holidays, national heroes, and the like, and, if possible, help the children draw parallels between and among traditions in their former country and in their adopted country.

Knowledge discrepancies also characterize children who come from homes of differing socioeconomic status. There is a widely recognized "knowledge gap" between economically advantaged and less advantaged children, at least when it comes to the knowledge that children are expected to have to facilitate school learning. Further, there is growing concern that too little attention is devoted to knowledge development in school, at least in the primary grades (Hirsch, 2006; Neuman, 2006). As a result, children who begin school knowing the least are at a particular disadvantage and are, essentially, being asked to learn much more than their more advantaged peers (because they have to learn what their peers already know *plus* what their peers are learning). Without additional instructional attention and support for this level of knowledge development, it seems likely that many economically disadvantaged children would be unable to accomplish this daunting task.

Although we certainly do not have a ready solution for addressing this knowledge gap, we encourage teachers to think carefully about the extent to which it affects their students and to consider how they might begin to address it. For example, technological advancements have made many vehicles for knowledge development much more readily available than in the past. Most children have access to television and cable or satellite programming options. A wealth of educational programming can be accessed and thus used to help expand children's knowledge. Teachers might consider compiling a list of appropriate educational programs and encouraging children to view them at home. Many children also have access to the Internet, which is a wonderful resource for knowledge building. Here again, teachers are encouraged to investigate appropriate websites for students to explore and to communicate their recommendations to the children's families.

Sample Websites for Knowledge Enhancement

Listed below are several websites that teachers might find useful in the classroom or recommend to families for exploration and online learning at home. Please note that while all of these websites are sponsored by nonprofit organizations (.org) or the federal government (.gov), in many cases commercial websites are only a click of the mouse away. For this reason, and because the content on Internet sites can change so quickly, adult supervision of Internet use is always recommended.

www.ala.org/greatsites
www.Kidsclick.org
www.ipl.org/div/kidspace
www.smithsonianeducation.org/students
www.kids.gov

Teachers also, of course, need to take responsibility for addressing the knowledge gap in their classrooms. Neuman (2006) is a staunch advocate of the need to address the knowledge gap and has provided five research-based principles for improving the knowledge base of young children (pp. 35–36). These principles are very consistent with the advice we provided to teachers in an earlier iteration of the ISA professional development handbook. Below we list Neuman's principles (in *italic*) and elaborate a bit on each.

- *Children's learning benefits through integrated instruction* (p. 35). By this Neuman means that instruction should be organized around themes or projects that have coherence and depth and therefore provide children with the opportunity to develop concepts and apply them in new learning situations. Reading and discussing several books on the same or related topics will help children develop a depth of understanding that is not likely to occur when reading selections are not organized topically or thematically.
- *Learning requires children's minds (not just their bodies) to be active* (p. 35). This principle harkens back to a principle discussed in Chapter 1: Engagement leads to learning. We need to try to ensure that children's minds are engaged in the thinking that is intended. Instruction should be goal oriented, not activity oriented.
- *High levels of teacher interaction optimize children's learning* (p. 35). One of a teacher's major roles is to guide children's thinking by modeling ways of thinking about and analyzing situations and then supporting children as they begin to grow as strategic learners. Effective teachers interact with their students almost constantly—at times in whole-class contexts, at other times in small groups or one to one.
- *Play supports children's learning* (p. 35). As long as the adults around them don't make it seem like work, much of what children are asked to do in the primary grades can be fun even if it is not play per se. Thus, for example, children can be given props related to a book they just read and be allowed to "play" at reenacting the story. Or, they can "play" teacher and read a book to a couple of their friends, lead a book discussion, or respond to their writing.
- *Developing competence enhances motivation and self-esteem* (p. 36). Successful learning experiences breed more successful learning experiences and the good feelings that go along with them. Unfortunately, for children who suffer from a knowledge gap, success in school learning endeavors is less certain. Repeated failures have the potential to reduce a student's willingness to engage in learning activities, thereby increasing the likelihood of repeated failure.

COMPREHENSION INSTRUCTION

In the last several years, a great deal of research has focused on what "good" comprehenders do. We put the word *good* in quotation marks to signal our discomfort with it in this context: *Good* often serves as the opposite of *bad*, and certainly we don't want anyone who is not yet a *good* comprehender to be considered *bad*. Therefore, in what follows, we substitute the word *proficient*. In 2003 Duke and Bennett-Armistead summarized research on proficient readers in which competent adult readers were asked to *think aloud* as they read; that is, people were asked to describe their thinking as they read. There was a good deal of commonality in the reports that the participants made. They tended to be very active as they read, used a large number of strategies, and were routinely monitoring their understanding. Figure 13.1 reproduces a summary of proficient reader strategies provided by Duke and Bennett-Armistead (2003).

Comprehension Strategies

As the strategies used by proficient readers came to be understood, researchers began exploring whether it was possible to teach these strategies to people, including children, who were not using them and, if so, whether such strategy instruction would help to improve comprehension. The results of these studies indicated that a variety of approaches to comprehension strategy instruction are effective in helping

---

When Proficient Readers Read, They . . .

- Have clear purposes for their reading and constantly evaluate whether they are achieving those purposes.
- Often read selectively, continually making decisions about their reading—what to read carefully, what to read quickly, what not to read, what to reread, and so on—based on their goals.
- Use their prior knowledge to construct meaning from/with the text.
- Think ahead to what might come next in the text.
- Monitor their understanding of the text, making adjustments in their reading or thinking as needed.
- Try to fill in gaps or inconsistencies in a text so that the text makes sense. If they encounter unfamiliar words or concepts, they try to figure them out.
- Ask themselves questions as they read.
- Think about the authors of the text—their perspective, agenda, qualifications, and so on.
- Respond to the text in many different ways, both intellectually and emotionally.
- Read different kinds of text differently.
- Think about the text not only before and during reading, but also after reading. Often, good readers apply what they learned from the text in appropriate situations later on.
- Draw inferences.

When Reading Informational Text, Good Readers Also . . .

- Construct summaries of what they are reading.
- Pay attention to the organization or structure of the text, both overall and for particular sections.

FIGURE 13.1. Characteristics of proficient readers. Adapted from Duke and Bennett-Armistead (2003, p. 60). Copyright 2003 by Nell K. Duke and C. Susan Bennett-Armistead. Adapted by permission.

children to learn and use the strategies and thereby improve their reading comprehension (e.g., Brown, Pressley, Van Meter, & Schuder, 1996; Fuchs, Fuchs, & Burish, 2000; Guthrie et al., 2004; Klingner, Vaughn, & Schumm, 1998). However, most research on comprehension strategies instruction has focused on children beyond the early primary grades, and, as pointed out by Paris and Paris (2007), when children in the early primary grades are included, the effects of comprehension strategy instruction can be confounded by differences in decoding skills.

In developing the ISA, we were mindful of the studies of comprehension strategy instruction but leery of emulating their procedures with the young children who were our primary focus because we place considerable emphasis on strategic word solving (see Chapter 10), which, like using comprehension strategies, is a cognitively demanding enterprise. We did not want to overwhelm beginning and struggling readers by asking them to be consciously strategic about both word solving and meaning construction. However, certainly we did want them to be involved in the process of meaning construction and to have meaning making as their primary purpose for reading.

Therefore, rather than specifically teach and practice comprehension strategies, we opted to engage children in meaning construction by engaging them in conversations about the texts they read or heard, and, in the context of these conversations, teachers modeled some of the most commonly taught comprehension strategies. Because some comprehension strategies are widely accepted as being useful to share with elementary-age children, we identified those strategies and encouraged teachers to become familiar with them and to use them to prompt and structure their conversations with students during read-alouds and shared and supported reading. The strategies we encouraged teachers to consider are listed and briefly described in Table 13.1. We have provided a brief commentary on what each strategy entails and why it is thought to be useful.

Too Much of a Good Thing?

Having spent a good deal of time observing in kindergarten and first-grade classrooms, we have, on occasion, been concerned that comprehension strategy instruction is sometimes overdone or even misguided. Teachers need to be mindful of the fact that the primary purpose of strategy instruction is to ensure that children are active thinkers as they read (and listen). When too much emphasis is placed on the strategies, and too little on the material being read, children may come to believe that it is the application of the strategies that is valued and important rather than comprehension of the text. Indeed, we have noticed that, for some students, the explanation of the strategy they have used becomes their end goal when strategies are emphasized heavily. The challenge for teachers is to model active engagement in meaning construction in a way that allows students to generalize this mind-set when reading new texts. (Hirsch, 2006, has articulated this same concern in *The Knowledge Deficit*.)

TABLE 13.1. Comprehension Strategies Discussed in the ISA

Strategy	What it involves	Why it is useful
Activating prior knowledge	Thinking about what one already knows about a topic or concept	New information from the text will be easier to interpret if readers think about what they already know about a topic. That way, when something is read that doesn't fit with the existing schema or knowledge base, readers will be alert to that fact and will be more likely to take steps to clear up the discrepancies (e.g., by rereading, reading on for more information, altering the existing schema). Connecting information encountered in a text with existing knowledge is the essence of meaning construction. Harvey and Goudvis's (2007) approach to enhancing comprehension focuses heavily on making connections.
Prediction	Anticipating what will occur in the text and then checking to see whether the prediction matches the events in the text	Readers need to integrate prior knowledge and information from the text in order to make predictions. Generally, when readers have made a prediction, they become invested in determining whether their prediction is validated. This serves to sustain their interest in, and engagement with, the text.
Visualization	Imagining what events in the text would look like if illustrated or made into a movie	In order to construct a visual image, readers must attend to the text in an active way, modifying their images as the text unfolds.
Summarization	Retelling the events from the text, typically using some sort of organizational structure, such as sequencing (*first, then, finally*) or story grammar (setting, characters, problem, resolution)	When, after reading a text, readers reflect on it in such a way as to be able to summarize it, it is likely that they will retain more of the information. Perhaps more importantly, over time, it is assumed that the practice of summarization will lead to more active engagement during the reading of the text because readers will use the summarization structures to guide their thinking as they read. In fact, in support of this, Almasi (2003) encourages teachers to have children complete graphic organizers such as story maps *while* they are reading rather than after reading.
Questioning	A very broad strategy that entails asking questions related to the content of the text and/or directed to the author of the text (e.g., "I wonder why . . . , " "Why didn't he . . ., ?" "How come . . . ?")	When readers frequently generate questions they would like to ask the characters or author, they are likely to read upcoming text with an eye toward answering those questions. Further, the questions that they generate often lead them back into previously read text to look for clarification. Pressley et al. (1992) report that teaching children to ask "why" questions is especially effective, because children often have the necessary knowledge to understand a text but they do not apply it.
Comprehension monitoring	Throughout the reading of a text, noticing whether it makes sense and, if not, taking steps to clarify the areas of confusion	To an extent, this strategy involves all of the others discussed above and can be considered a *metacognitive* strategy, in that it involves individuals in thinking about their own thinking (Weinstein & Mayer, 1986). This strategy is particularly important to develop because it emphasizes the need for readers to take responsibility for determining whether the text makes sense to them and to take steps to clarify when comprehension breaks down.

Conversations about Text

While our decision not to encourage explicit comprehension strategy instruction in the early primary grades was partly driven by the concern that teaching both word identification strategies and comprehension strategies would overextend the cognitive capacities of young children, it was also driven by the conviction that there are multiple less formalized ways of engaging children in meaning construction while reading or listening to books. And, we suspected that these less formal forms of engagement could be more enjoyable and motivating for the children. Enjoyment and motivation struck us as particularly important elements for children who begin school with limited early literacy skills and limited literacy experiences more generally. The type of conversation-focused approach that we endorsed has been dubbed a "content" approach by McKeown, Beck, and Blake (2009) because it entails focusing most of the interaction around a text on constructing its meaning rather than on strategies that might be used to enable that construction. Although there has not been a great deal of research on the role of discussion in promoting comprehension, the research that exists indicates that discussion around text can promote problem solving, comprehension, and learning (Anderson, Chinn, Waggoner, & Nguyen, 1998; Nystrand, 1997; Wegerif, Mercer, & Dawes, 1999). Furthermore, McKeown et al. (2009), in a recent comparison of a comprehension strategy-focused approach with a content-focused approach as used in fifth-grade classrooms, found that students in classrooms using a content-focused approach were found to recall more from the texts that were read, produce higher-quality retellings, and talk more during the course of book discussions. While, to our knowledge, this is the only study of its kind, the results do support our general sense that conversations focused on the content of texts being read may be at least as useful in promoting comprehension as a comprehension-strategy-focused approach. We await further research on this important issue.

Using Interactive Read-Alouds to Enhance Knowledge and Promote Engagement

Because many of the books that primary-grade children are able to read provide limited comprehension challenges and few opportunities to build knowledge about the world, a good deal of the comprehension-focused instruction in the ISA occurs in the context of interactive read-alouds in the classroom. In addition, classroom teachers are encouraged to use classroom volunteers and other available personnel to address knowledge and comprehension needs of the children about whom they have concerns.

Research evaluating the effects of reading frequently to children has demonstrated its value (McKeown & Beck, 2006). In fact, Marriott (1995) argued that "it is almost impossible to overemphasize the value of this activity for children of any age or reading level" (p. 65). Morrow and Gambrell (2000) and Snow et al. (1998)

summarized the results of several studies that compared children from classrooms where there were daily read-alouds with children from classrooms where read-alouds occurred only occasionally. In general, these studies found that children who were read to often demonstrated greater motivation to read, greater gains in vocabulary, better comprehension of new stories they heard, greater familiarity with literary language, and better decoding skills.

KEEP IN MIND While this section focuses on read-alouds, many of the same types of interactions around the meanings of texts can occur in the context of a shared reading experience. In a shared reading activity, however, the teacher generally addresses several additional goals, including talking about the purposes and conventions of print and how the writing system is related to spoken language.

Similarly, as children begin to engage in reading texts themselves, both in supported reading groups and independently, the teacher needs to establish a specific focus on the meaning of the text. The events and/or information in the text should be discussed before, during, and after the reading of the text.

Implementing Interactive Read-Alouds

The effectiveness of read-alouds in supporting the development of active thinking during reading depends on the qualities of the interactions between the teacher and the children (see McKeown & Beck, 2006). As discussed briefly in Chapter 3, the teacher's level of enthusiasm for the books read and the reading activity in general are important. So too is the level of freedom children feel they have to initiate conversations about the book. If reactions and questions have to wait until the end of the book or until the teacher initiates a discussion, then the children might well react less and comprehend less altogether.

Virtually everyone has had the experience of missing a point midway through a passage while reading and then having difficulty understanding everything that comes later. When children encounter a confusing part of a text, it would be ideal if they could clear up their confusion almost immediately by asking questions of the teacher or perhaps the other children in the group. We certainly expect older students to attempt some sort of "fix-up" when they realize that they are not comprehending what they are reading. Such active monitoring of one's understanding has been found to be vitally important to comprehension (Cain, Oakhill, & Bryant, 2004; see Baker & Beall, 2009, for a review). In the context of a read-aloud, the only option children have for addressing a breakdown of comprehension is to rely on someone else—they cannot go back and reread. So, teachers are strongly encouraged to make read-alouds as interactive as possible.

In addition to answering questions as they arise, teachers can also be proactive, anticipating potential points of confusion and addressing them before a comprehension problem arises. In a study of exemplary literacy teachers at the kindergarten level, Block and Mangieri (2003) found that, when a portion of a book was likely to be unfamiliar to their students, exemplary teachers were likely to stop and rephrase the confusing aspect of the text or to create an example from students' life experiences.

Studies of the influences of reading aloud to children suggest that the greatest benefits accrue when the children are actively engaged during the course of the read-aloud (Beck & McKeown, 2001; Fisher, Flood, Lapp, & Frey, 2004; Hickman, Pollard-Durodola, & Vaughn, 2004; Santaro, Chard, Howard, & Baker, 2008). Participation can occur before, during, and after reading.

- Participating *before reading* might include:

  - Previewing the text through discussions of the title and the cover illustration.
  - Discussions of the author and/or illustrator, particularly if the group is familiar with other texts by the author and/or illustrator.
  - Making predictions about the text's content.
  - Encouraging the children to think about the elements of story grammar (setting, characters, problem, resolution, etc.) in anticipating the book's content.
  - Setting a purpose for listening, perhaps by relating it to a classroom theme or area of inquiry that the group is exploring.

- Participation *during reading* should include spontaneous discussions of the text. Ideally, the discussions would be initiated by both the students and the teacher. Further, when the teacher initiates discussion, she needs to encourage thinking beyond the literal level and model and prompt inferential and critical analysis of the text. This kind of guidance might include:

  - Encouraging children to ask questions and make comments as the book unfolds. Welcoming questions and comments in a conversational way will send the clear message that spontaneous reactions to the book are appropriate.

    o "Ah, good question! Does anyone have any ideas about that?"
    o "Interesting question! I'm not sure. Let's read to find out."
    o "Don't forget, if you are confused about something, listen a little longer to see if you can figure out what's going on. If not, you may want to ask a question."
    o "I agree, . . . "

  - Noticing and discussing elements of story grammar.

    o "So, it looks like this story is set in the winter. Look at how they are all bundled up."
    o "What's the problem between our characters?"

o "That is a solution I never would have guessed!"

o "So, now we know what the problem is. Any ideas on how it will be resolved [solved]?"

- Comparing predictions to the events in the texts. Note that it is important to avoid talking about predictions as being either right or wrong, as some children really don't like to be wrong—and a prediction cannot really be wrong if it follows logically from what was known at the time it was made.

  o "That's just what Jared thought would happen."

  o "What did the author do that was different from what we expected [predicted]?"

- Making further predictions based on what has already happened in the text.

  o "Before I thought that. . . . But now I think. . . . "

- Generating questions or comments relating to the text and/or the characters.

  o "I wonder why he didn't. . . . "

  o "Did you notice the look on his face? I bet he's. . . . "

  o "I wonder why the author. . . . "

  o "How do you think . . . is feeling right now?"

  o "Why do you think . . . ?"

  o What do you notice . . . ?

  o "If you could talk to the author right now, what would you ask?"

  o "Why . . . ?"

  o "Why . . . ?"

  o "Why . . . ?" (Research suggests that teaching children to ask *why* questions is particularly helpful in getting them to apply their knowledge in interpreting text; Pressley et al., 1992.)

- Asking open-ended questions.

  o "Who has something they would like to say about this page?"

- Offering personal reactions and connections.

  o "I just love the way he keeps. . . . "

  o "I really don't like the way. . . . "

  o "How would you feel if . . . ?"

  o "How would you handle this situation?"

  o "Does this book remind you of . . . ?"

  o "Did you ever . . . ?"

- Visualizing

  o "Just listen to this page as I read it to you and make a picture of it in your head."
  o "The illustrator didn't make a picture for that part. What do you think it would look like?"

- Comparing information in the current text with other texts with which the children are familiar.

  o "This is sort of like the . . . [book] we read."
  o "This is the second book we've read where the. . . . "

- Restating (perhaps using simpler vocabulary) any confusing portions of the text when it is encountered.

- Participation *after reading* might include:

  - Discussions of how predictions compared to the events in the text.
  - Discussions of whether the purposes that were set were accomplished.
  - Discussions of parts that may have been a bit confusing and then returning to those parts to reread for the purpose of clarification.
  - Discussing or writing alternative endings (e.g., "What would have happened if . . . ?").
  - Rereading the entire text either with the specific purpose of clearing up points of confusion or simply for the sake of enjoying it.
  - Encouraging children to draw a scene from the text as they envisioned it.
  - Reflecting on what was learned and talking or writing about it.
  - Reflecting on why the author might have written the book.
  - Reenacting the story with the aid of story-related props.
  - Retelling the stories for authentic purposes (e.g., retelling into an audio recorder for the benefit of a child who was absent).
  - Reconstructing stories using pictures (for very beginning readers).

The comments and questions that teachers use to foster conversations serve to help children develop ways of thinking about and reacting to texts. The hope is that the ways of thinking encouraged through these conversations will ultimately be internalized by children and thus be useful to them when they are reading independently. In conducting these conversations, however, the teacher also needs to be mindful of the fact that too much talk can disrupt the flow of the story. As in all aspects of instruction, striking the right balance is important.

Using Informational (Nonfiction) Texts to Promote the Development of General World Knowledge

While there is much that can be learned from interactive read-alouds of storybooks, the wealth of knowledge that prepares children for later academic pursuits is most readily addressed via nonfiction books and other types of information-rich books, such as historical fiction and fantastical science books such as the *Magic School Bus* series (published by Scholastic). Children generally encounter greater amounts of new information with these types of text than with storybooks. As a result, children will likely need more teacher support to integrate the new information. This extra support might include:

- Reading simpler texts on a given topic before reading more challenging ones.
- Careful planning by the teacher, with the goal of anticipating the portions of the text that might confuse children and preparation of explanations that will help to clarify points or prevent the confusion altogether.
- Lengthier discussions before, during, and after reading the text.
- Frequent think-alouds in which the teacher models her thinking while reading.
- Extended discussions focused on specific concepts or causal relationships encountered in the text—often connecting new concepts to ideas that are familiar to children.
- Periodic encouragement to summarize what has already been learned in the text; children will typically need assistance with such summaries.
- Rereading the entire book, perhaps more than once; each time a child listens to a book, she is likely to understand the content at a deeper level and is therefore more likely to integrate the knowledge more effectively.

Useful Resource

Duke, N. K., & Bennet-Armistead, V. S. (2003). *Reading and writing informational text in the primary grades: Research-based practices*. New York: Scholastic.

This book is a very useful resource for teachers wishing to use more informational texts in their classrooms. It provides both teaching strategies and an extensive list of interesting nonfiction texts.

Comprehension Instruction/Focus during Shared and Supported Reading

This discussion of the development of active comprehenders has largely focused on read-aloud interactions because there are richer opportunities to focus on content in the types of books that are read aloud to early primary-grade children than there are in the types of texts that most children are able to read. However, this focus on read-alouds should certainly not be taken to suggest that comprehension should be ignored during shared and supported reading. To the contrary, a major reason for encouraging active thinking during a read-aloud is so that the children will be more inclined to be active thinkers when they, themselves, read.

Virtually all of the suggestions made relative to read-aloud situations can be applied to shared and supported reading situations. Texts should be discussed *before, during*, and *after* reading. The discussion should involve open-ended questions and reactions that prompt inferential and critical thinking. Discussions should give children the opportunity to think through what they are reading and integrate it with what they already know. (See the discussion of supported reading in Chapter 14.)

Writing to Enhance Comprehension and Knowledge Development

As the children's literacy skills evolve, their comprehension can be supported through writing. For example, during independent reading, the children might:

- Use sticky notes to record their questions and thoughts and apply them to the appropriate pages. Later, when it is time to discuss the text, the children will have these reminders to help them participate in the discussion.
- Keep a reading journal wherein they record their reactions to, and learning from, the texts that they read. For example, they might draw a picture of how they envision a scene, write one or two of their predictions and whether the text matched them, or write questions they wish they could ask the author or main character.
- Write book reviews to post as a way to encourage others to read particular books.
- Describe texts using structural formats such as story grammar (setting, characters, problem, and resolution of the story) or sequencing (*first, then, next, finally*).
- Keep a learning log in which they record information gleaned from non-fiction readings—perhaps using a *know–w*ant to know–*l*earned (KWL) format (Ogle, 1986).
- Write their own texts (e.g., non-fiction books, short stories) modeled after the book they've read and/or drawing on what they have learned through their writing.

EVALUATING AND DOCUMENTING CHILDREN'S PROGRESS

Figures 13.2 and 13.3 provide vehicles for teachers to systematically record their observations of children's level of, and strategic approach to, comprehension in the context of read-alouds (Figure 13.2) and reading (Figure 13.3). Figure 13.4 provides a vehicle for teachers to record their observations of children's relative standing in the area of knowledge acquisition. The purpose of these forms is, primarily, to help teachers notice aspects of children's development that may need extra instructional attention in order to prevent future academic difficulties.

Group Snapshot—Listening Comprehension						
Student names:						
Ability to understand texts: **W**ell developed **A**ppropriately developed **N**eeds development	Date:					
	Date:					
	Date:					
	Date:					
	Date:					
	Date:					
	Date:					
	Date:					
	Date:					
	Date:					
Actively engages in discussion of texts (e.g., makes predictions, offers reactions, asks questions): **W**ell developed **A**ppropriately developed **N**eeds development	Date:					
	Date:					
	Date:					
	Date:					
	Date:					
	Date:					
	Date:					
	Date:					
	Date:					
	Date:					
Ability to retell/summarize text in authentic situations (i.e., for the purpose of communicating with someone unfamiliar with the text): **W**ell developed **A**ppropriately developed **N**eeds development	Date:					
	Date:					
	Date:					
	Date:					
	Date:					
	Date:					
	Date:					
	Date:					
	Date:					
	Date:					
Connects information in text to own life, other texts, broader contexts: **W**ell developed **A**ppropriately developed **N**eeds development	Date:					
	Date:					
	Date:					
	Date:					
	Date:					
	Date:					
	Date:					
	Date:					
	Date:					
	Date:					

FIGURE 13.2. Group snapshot for listening comprehension.

Group Snapshot—Reading Comprehension						
Student names:						
Ability to understand texts: **W**ell developed **A**ppropriately developed **N**eeds development	Date:					
	Date:					
	Date:					
	Date:					
	Date:					
	Date:					
	Date:					
	Date:					
	Date:					
	Date:					
Actively engages in discussion of texts (e.g., makes predictions, offers reactions, asks questions): **W**ell developed **A**ppropriately developed **N**eeds development	Date:					
	Date:					
	Date:					
	Date:					
	Date:					
	Date:					
	Date:					
	Date:					
	Date:					
Ability to retell/summarize text in authentic situations (i.e., for the purpose of communicating with someone unfamiliar with the text): **W**ell developed **A**ppropriately developed **N**eeds development	Date:					
	Date:					
	Date:					
	Date:					
	Date:					
	Date:					
	Date:					
	Date:					
	Date:					
	Date:					
Connects information in text to own life, other texts, broader contexts: **W**ell developed **A**ppropriately developed **N**eeds development	Date:					
	Date:					
	Date:					
	Date:					
	Date:					
	Date:					
	Date:					
	Date:					
	Date:					
	Date:					

FIGURE 13.3. Group snapshot for reading comprehension.

Group Snapshot—Knowledge Acquisition and Background Knowledge						
Student names:						
Knowledge acquisition—Learns and uses new information: **E**asily **S**lowly **V**ery slowly	Date:					
	Date:					
	Date:					
	Date:					
	Date:					
	Date:					
	Date:					
	Date:					
	Date:					
	Date:					
Background knowledge relative to grade-level peers: **W**ell developed **A**ppropriately developed **N**eeds development	Date:					
	Date:					
	Date:					
	Date:					
	Date:					
	Date:					
	Date:					
	Date:					
	Date:					

FIGURE 13.4. Group snapshot for knowledge acquisition and background knowledge.

PART V

IMPLEMENTING INTENSIFIED INSTRUCTION

INTRODUCTION

Children who struggle at the early stages of learning to read are at high risk of experiencing long-term reading difficulties unless efforts are made to help them overcome their early difficulties. In the foregoing chapters, we discussed the complexity of the reading process and how difficulties with any of the components could lead to long-term reading difficulties. The major emphasis in this book is on the provision of effective instruction to help alleviate early difficulties and limitations in foundational literacy skills and to support the accelerated growth in literacy skills that must occur if children who are at risk are to close the gap with their higher-achieving peers.

For children who struggle at the early stages of literacy acquisition, we believe that instruction is the most important determiner of their ultimate success. Therefore, it is important that teachers have the knowledge and skills needed to identify and respond to the instructional needs of early literacy learners, especially those who experience difficulty with the literacy acquisition process. The development of teacher knowledge related to each of the instructional goals discussed in the previous chapters has been a major focus of the book. In the two remaining chapters, we attempt to integrate the various goals into a cohesive plan for small-group and one-to-one instruction for early literacy learners, particularly those who have been identified as being at risk for experiencing literacy learning difficulties, and to provide some guidance concerning the distribution of instructional resources (e.g., teacher time) so as to maximize the outcomes for the array of children who must be served.

As discussed, in order to close the gap with their more knowledgeable peers, children who begin school with limited early literacy skills need to learn more in a given period of time than do their peers. That is, they need to learn faster or at an accelerated rate. In order to accomplish this accelerated learning, the children need intensified, high-quality instructional interventions. In Chapter 14 we discuss small-group and one–to-one instruction that is designed to be both responsive to the children's needs and comprehensive. That is, instruction needs to emphasize the aspects of the process that children find particularly challenging and to be comprehensive enough that the children fully understand the reading process. To illustrate this dual goal, we describe lesson planning in some detail as well as the type of thinking in which teachers might engage as they plan, deliver, and reflect upon instruction for children who are at various points along the continuum of early literacy development. In doing so, we hope to demonstrate how the various instructional goals discussed in the preceding chapters are integrated into coherent and comprehensive small-group and one-to-one lessons. Themes that were addressed earlier in the text reemerge in this chapter, including (1) the need for instruction to be targeted just beyond students' current capabilities (i.e., the zone of proximal development; Vygotsky, 1978); (2) the need for children to be actively engaged in the thinking that enables learning; (3) the need to help children develop a *self-teaching mechanism* (Share, 1995) so that they become more effective readers with each encounter with text; (4) the need for children to learn the alphabetic code well enough that they can be both flexible and efficient in applying their knowledge in the context of both word solving and writing; (5) the need for instruction to keep the construction of meaning at the forefront so that the children understand, from early on, that the purpose of reading and writing (and reading and writing instruction) is to enable communication; and (6) the need to enhance the development of world knowledge and language skills because such knowledge sources are central to the meaning-construction process.

In the final chapter we discuss the implementation of RTI using the ISA. While acknowledging that there is still much to be learned about the optimal implementations of RTI processes, we offer suggestions for how they might be implemented at the kindergarten and first-grade level. The model we propose involves four levels (or tiers) of intervention and is depicted graphically in Figure V.1. We present this depiction in this introductory section because it allows us to contextualize the small-group and one-to-one intervention discussed in Chapter 14.

At its core, RTI entails identifying children who are at risk for experiencing reading difficulties, monitoring the progress they make over time, and making adjustments to the instruction provided based on their progress. The first step in the process involves making decisions about the criteria (or criterion) to be used in determining whether a student should be considered at risk. Multiple measures

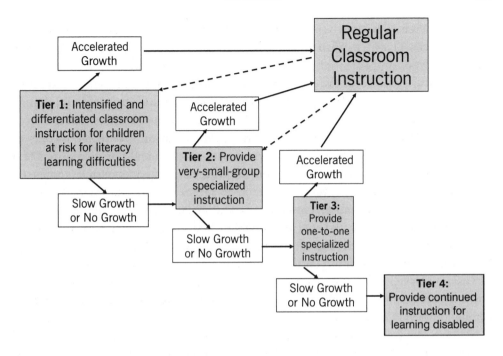

FIGURE V.1. A graphic depiction of a possible RTI approach. Adapted from Scanlon and Sweeney (2008). Copyright 2008 by the International Reading Association. Adapted by permission.

of early literacy skill are available for this purpose, some of which provide specific guidelines for identifying children as being at risk of experiencing literacy learning difficulties. Generally, such assessments identify children scoring below the 20th to 30th percentile as being at risk. In schools that serve high-needs populations, using such a criterion will result in a higher percentage of children qualifying as "at risk" for literacy learning difficulties than in schools that serve more economically advantaged communities. Ideally, all children who qualify as being at risk should be provided with intensified instructional interventions. Thus, in some schools this approach may involve providing intervention for a high percentage of the entering kindergartners, whereas in other schools the number identified will be substantially smaller.

Once children who may be at risk are identified, instructional interventions are initiated. Figure V.1 provides a graphic representation of an RTI process. The first step in the intervention process involves providing intensified and differentiated small-group intervention in the classroom context (Tier 1). Intensification can involve providing more time in small-group instruction, smaller instructional groupings, or both. When provided with intensified, classroom-based instruction, some children will demonstrate accelerated growth in early literacy skill and can be appropriately served with classroom instruction alone. Eventually, these children may not need intensified instruction at the classroom level. However, some children who are provided with Tier 1 instruction will show limited or no growth and will therefore be best served by receiving an additional intervention beyond the classroom (Tier 2). With this added instruction, some children will experience rapid gains and eventually may no longer need instructional intensification in order to meet grade-level expectations. Other children, however, will make more limited gains and should be provided yet greater intensification of intervention (Tier 3), which would, ideally, be more individualized than the instruction offered at Tiers 1 and 2. In Figure V.1 the third tier of intervention is depicted as one-to-one specialized instruction, which we think is not only ideal but also critical for the small number of children who do not show accelerated gains with less intensive forms of intervention. Intervention offered at Tier 3 should be provided in addition to, rather than instead of, classroom-based instruction (Tier 1). Further, as for the other tiers, it is expected that some of the children will experience accelerated gains when provided with Tier 3 intervention and will ultimately be able to progress without additional intervention. Children who continue to struggle in spite of intensive intervention would be considered for classification as learning disabled, and instruction in the special education setting would serve as an additional tier of intervention (Tier 4).

There are some important general trends that should be observed when an effective RTI model is implemented. First, there should be substantial coordination between and among the tiers of intervention so that children are not faced with attempting to integrate fragmented and contradictory information related to literacy. In fact, the intervention lessons offered at each of the tiers should look quite similar to one another, with the major differences involving group size (the higher the tier number, the lower the number of children in the group) and individualization (more intensive forms of intervention allow instruction to be planned for the specific needs of the children in the group) and, perhaps, the expertise of the teacher who delivers the lessons. A second general trend that should be evident is that, at each tier of intervention, some children should follow the accelerated growth path (see Figure V.1) and no longer need intensified intervention. As a result of this general trend, the number of children who are served at each successive tier should be smaller and smaller, with only a very small number eventually being considered for classification as learning disabled. If the RTI process instituted in a given school does not follow this second general pattern, the quality and characteristics of the instruction offered at each of the tiers need to be reconsidered.

Finally, it is important to note that the model depicted in Figure V.1 provides for the possibility that children who experience accelerated progress when participating in an intensive (Tier 3) intervention may benefit from some less intensive ongoing support once Tier 3 intervention is ended. The dashed arrows pointing from regular classroom instruction to Tiers 1 and 2 represent this possibility. The need for such ongoing support will depend in part on the strength of each child's knowledge, skills, and strategies at the point when Tier 3 intervention ends and in part on the nature and quality of the instruction that is provided in the classroom.

CHAPTER 14

Small-Group and
One-to-One Intervention

This chapter focuses primarily on the small-group and one-to-one instruction that might be offered to children who are considered to be at risk for experiencing reading difficulties. The small-group instruction offered in the classroom as part of Tier 1 intervention and the small-group instruction provided at Tiers 2 and 3 should look very much alike, with the major differences being that, at Tiers 2 and 3, the instruction would typically involve:

- Smaller groups (three or four children at Tier 2 and one or two children at Tier 3),
- More focused teacher attention, which can occur because the teacher is not simultaneously overseeing the rest of the class. This intensity of instruction, in turn, allows for:

  - More careful and thorough documentation of children's skills and abilities, and, as a result,
  - Instruction planned to more specifically address the needs of the individual children.
  - More opportunities for the children to respond and receive guidance and feedback.

Given the instructional needs of children at Tier 3, *daily* intervention, in addition to Tier 1 instruction in the classroom, is strongly recommended.

The implementation of additional instructional opportunities for children with limited skills should begin as early in their schooling as possible. For children in the early primary grades, the additional support might be offered only at the classroom level (Tier 1) for a period of time, as initial limitations may be due primarily to inadequacies in their literacy experiences either at home or in preschool settings. Children whose difficulties are primarily attributable to limitations in experience are apt to show a strong response (e.g., rapid growth) to comprehensive classroom language arts instruction that includes intensified small-group (Tier 1) experience, if the instruction is appropriately differentiated and targeted and competently delivered. These children may not need support beyond Tier 1. However, other early primary-grade children may need additional tiers of intervention in order to meet grade-level expectations. Decisions about instituting these additional tiers of intervention should be made as soon as possible and certainly not later than 6–8 weeks into the school year.

Small-group and one-to-one instruction for all young children, but particularly for children who struggle at the early stages of learning to read, should take account of what the children already know and are able to do and should reflect continua of skills development as described in the previous chapters. Moreover, instruction should focus on helping children to develop a *self-teaching mechanism* (see Chapter 10) and on keeping them involved in the meaning-construction process that is central to reading development.

COORDINATION ACROSS INSTRUCTIONAL SETTINGS

Given that one important goal of intervention is to increase children's ability to profit from classroom instruction, it is essential that intervention teachers be knowledgeable regarding instruction occurring in the classroom. This does not mean that intervention teachers simply reteach or preteach classroom content. Rather, it means that intervention teachers should adjust their instruction to ensure that what the children are learning in Tier 2 or Tier 3 intervention is as congruent and as coordinated as possible with what the children are doing in the classroom.

To this end, ideally, teachers within a given school will share a common philosophy and approach to early literacy instruction, use common instructional language, provide common resources for their students, and have common expectations as to what should be accomplished by the end of the school year. However, even if teachers are using a highly scripted, rigidly paced program (which, from our perspective, is not ideal), instruction is likely to vary between classrooms. Intervention teachers should, therefore, begin by meeting with each child's classroom teacher in order to learn about the classroom language arts program and how differentiation for the at risk students is being accomplished. Figure 14.1 lists aspects of literacy instruction that should be coordinated across instructional settings in the primary grades. Figure 14.2 lists aspects of classroom language arts

- Expectations for literacy competencies at the end of each grade level.
- Approaches to teaching about the alphabet and decoding skills more generally.
- Strategies to be taught to promote word solving.
- Terminology teachers use for important concepts such as:
  - Upper case (*capital, big*)
  - Lower case (*small, little*)
  - Word families (*chunks, phonograms, keys*)
  - Silent *e* (*magic* e, *bossy* e)
- Comprehension strategies taught.
- Approaches to assessing and documenting progress.

FIGURE 14.1. Target areas for consistency and consequences across instructional settings.

- The books and other instructional materials that are available in the classroom.
- The themes or instructional units that are to be covered.
- The foundational skills that are currently being worked on in the classroom and have been covered in the past. For example:
  - High-frequency words
  - Spelling words
  - Decoding skills
  - Strategies
- The extent to which the classroom and intervention teachers have a shared vision of what individual children are able to do.
- The group snapshots.

FIGURE 14.2. Important areas of ongoing communication between classroom and intervention teachers.

instruction that intervention teachers should keep abreast of as they work with children from particular classrooms. To facilitate communication, it is useful for classroom teachers to keep file folders in which they put both notes for the intervention teacher and communications that are sent home with the children. Intervention teachers can pick up their folders when they pick up the children.

GOALS OF INSTRUCTION

Table 14.1 lists the goals for intervention and the components of intervention lessons during which the goals might be addressed. All of the goals can be addressed in more than one of the intervention components, with several being addressed across most of the components. Our purpose in including this chart is to make the point that small-group and one-to-one interventions, like classroom instruction

TABLE 14.1. The Intersection of the Goals of Instruction and the Components of Language Arts Instruction

Language arts components	Motivation	Alphabetics			Word learning		Meaning construction	
		Print concepts	Phonological analysis	Alphabetic coding skills (letter names, sounds, alphabetic principle, etc.)	Strategic word identification	High-Frequency sight words	Language and vocabulary development	Knowledge and comprehension
Read-aloud/shared reading/rereading	✓	✓	✓	✓	✓	✓	✓	✓
Phonological awareness	✓		✓	✓	✓		✓	
Letters and sounds	✓	✓	✓	✓	✓	✓		
Reading new book(s)	✓	✓	✓	✓	✓	✓	✓	✓
Writing	✓	✓	✓	✓	✓	✓	✓	✓
High-frequency words	✓	✓	✓	✓		✓	✓	

Adapted from Scanlon and Anderson (2010). Copyright 2010 by the International Reading Association. Adapted by permission.

more generally, should be goal oriented. Teachers are encouraged to think about their instructional goals as they plan, deliver, and reflect upon each component of a lesson.

In the ISA, intervention lessons at Tiers 2 and 3 are typically 30 minutes long. In the classroom small-group lessons may need to be a bit shorter, given scheduling constraints. The time devoted to different components of a lesson is not fixed but rather varies based on students' instructional needs. In general, however, we would expect children to be engaged in reading and writing as part of every lesson and that, as children progress as readers, the allocation of time would shift from more time spent on the development of foundational skills to more time spent on authentic reading and writing.

INTERVENTION LESSONS: GENERAL OVERVIEW

Ideally, small-group instruction in classroom and intervention settings and in one-to-one intervention lessons should look quite similar, as teachers in all three contexts are working toward the same instructional goals. Of course, classroom teachers may be working with larger groups than intervention teachers and will also be responsible for simultaneously overseeing the rest of the class. Therefore, the level of individualized planning, instruction, and record keeping that a classroom teacher can manage will be different from what an intervention teacher can do.

In Chapter 2 we identified the major components of an ISA lesson and illustrated how a lesson might differ as the children progress as readers and writers

(Table 2.3, p. 47). In this chapter we describe each component of the lesson (read-aloud/shared reading/rereading, phoneme awareness, letters and sounds, reading new books, writing, and high-frequency words) in greater detail and attempt to provide glimpses of a teacher's thoughts and reflections before, during, and after she teaches a small-group lesson. Figure 14.3 provides a modified version of the lesson sheet that was used in small-group intervention lessons in our most recent study (Scanlon et al., 2008). We refer to this tool as a lesson *sheet* rather than as a lesson *plan* because teachers used it in planning the lesson, during the lesson to make note of what the children were able to do and what the teacher wanted to do in upcoming lessons, and after the lesson to aid in planning future lessons and to provide information for updating the group snapshots. Although teachers working with larger groups might find this form cumbersome to use during lessons, they may find it helpful to use as a guide for thinking about both the general structure and the specific plan for their small group lessons. For teachers working one-to-one with children, we provide, at a later point, a lesson sheet that allows for more detailed documentation of individual lessons.

When first encountering the lesson sheet, teachers often comment that they feel a bit overwhelmed by the level of detail. However, after using the sheet for a while, teachers generally acknowledge that the detail serves to remind them of the multiple aspects of literacy teaching/learning that might be addressed in any given lesson and that should be addressed, at various points, during the course of instruction. In fact, one teacher indicated that, for her, the lesson sheet served as a quick review of the ISA professional development program.

As a general overview to the lesson sheet, note that it is set up to be used with groups of three children. Children's names are listed at the top of each column, and room is provided for teachers to make notes pertaining to individual children in the appropriate section of the lesson sheet either in preparation for the lesson or as the lesson unfolds. This will be explained more fully below as we discuss each segment of a small-group lesson. Such a lesson generally follows the order depicted on the lesson sheet. However, some lessons include some elements but not others. For example, early in kindergarten, the high-frequency word segment would not be included for children identified as at risk because they would not yet be prepared to profitably focus on high-frequency words in small-group lesson.

Below we provide a general description of each of the lesson segments and, for each segment, one or two more detailed examples of how a teacher might plan, deliver, and reflect on that lesson for a particular group of children. We have tried to avoid becoming mired in the details while still providing enough information about what the lesson components might look like and how they fit together. For some lesson components we discuss "Using the Lesson Sheet" and "After the Lesson." To limit redundancy, we do not discuss these for all segments. However, teachers are encouraged to use the lesson sheet in similar ways for all segments and to routinely reflect across the group snapshots and the lesson sheets to identify instructional priorities.

(text continues on p. 312)

Lesson Sheet

Date _____   Session # _____

Child 1 _____   Child 2 _____   Child 3 _____

1. Read-Aloud/Shared Reading or Rereading		
Title (and Level):		
Text Comprehension: GU, AE, RET, PC, CON		
Word Identification Strategy: Code (TS [F, L, M], WP, DP, BW), Meaning (PIC, MS, RP, SA), Interactive and Confirmatory (IC)		
Letter/Sound: REC, NAM, ID		
Print Concepts: LR, TB, CW, CL, COM, PUN, 1-1		
High-Frequency Words: REC, ID		
Phonological Awareness: CR, IR, IA		
Vocabulary		
Comments/Notes for Next Session:		

FIGURE 14.3. Lesson sheet for small-group instruction. *(page 1 of 4)*

Child 1 ____________ Child 2 ____________ Child 3 ____________

2. Phonological Awareness		
Sound Sorting RH, BEG, END, MID		STRETCH??
Sound Blending Onset–Rime, Single Phonemes w/Pics, w/o Pics		STRETCH??
Sound Counting/Segmentation 2 Phonemes, 3 Phonemes		STRETCH??
Comments/Notes for Next Session:		

3. Letters and Sounds, Alphabetic Mapping, Word Families, Decoding		
Letter Names: RE, NAM, PR Letter Sounds: LS, CS-B, CS-E Other Decoding Elements: SV, VCe, D, Bl		
Word Building		
Word Reading		
Written Spelling		
Comments/Notes for Next Session:		

FIGURE 14.3. *(page 2 of 4)*

4. Reading
Title (and Level):

Text Comprehension: GU, AE, RET, PC, CON

Word Identification Strategy: Code (TS [F, L, M], WP, DP, BW), Meaning (PIC, MS, RP, SA), Interactive and Confirmatory (IC)

Letter/Sound: REC, ID

Print Concepts: LR, TB, CW, CL, COM, PUN, 1-1

High-Frequency Words: REC, ID

Phonological Awareness: CR, IR, IA

Vocabulary

Comments/Notes for Next Session:

FIGURE 14.3. *(page 3 of 4)*

5. Writing		
Writing Prompt or Dictated Sentence:		
Letters/Sounds: PR, LS, BS, ES Other Elements: SV, VCe, DI, BI		
Print Concepts: LR, TB, CW, CL, COM, PUN		
High-Frequency Words: CP, CS		
Comments/Notes for Next Session:		

6. High-Frequency Words		
Practice Plan:		

FIGURE 14.3. *(page 4 of 4)*

In what follows, we draw examples from children who are at a variety of developmental points to provide a sense of how teachers would think about, and plan for, different children. Following this overview, we describe a complete lesson for one group of children who are receiving Tier 2 intervention. We do this to provide a sense of the flow of a lesson and to illustrate that the components are interrelated and mutually supportive. Finally, we illustrate the shift in intensity that occurs when intervention is provided in a one-to-one context.

Segment 1: Read-Aloud/Shared Reading or Rereading

Depending on the children's point in development, the first segment might involve the teacher in reading to or with the children or it might involve the children rereading one or more books that were read in previous lessons. For children with very limited literacy experience and/or for children with little or no understanding of the writing system, read-alouds and shared reading are commonly used in this first segment. For children who are further along, rereading of emergent-level (and eventually more challenging) texts is routine for this segment. Below we describe what the teacher might do before, during, and after a lesson in which she uses one or the other of these activities during the first segment of a lesson.

Small-Group Read-Aloud: Before the Lesson

CONSIDER THE CHILDREN

For children who have very limited early literacy skills (e.g., those who are identified as at risk at kindergarten entry), small-group read-alouds provide important opportunities to help children learn about the pleasure that books can bring and to begin to familiarize them with foundational literacy skills. In planning, the teacher might review the snapshots for purposes and conventions of print, phonological skills, and alphabetic knowledge for the group. For these children (we'll call them Alex, Michael, and Sara), the teacher notes that they are just beginning to learn about the left-to-right directionality of print, are learning to attend to the sounds in words, and that each knows a couple of the letters in his or her name. The need to move the children forward with these skills influences the teacher's choice of the book for the read-aloud. Of course, motivation, comprehension, and knowledge building are goals addressed in every read-aloud.

SELECTING THE BOOK

The teacher chooses *Dr. Seuss's ABCs* (Seuss, 1963) because it is a playful introduction of the entire alphabet and because the alliteration in the book will help to draw the children's attention to the sounds in spoken words. While she realizes that the font used for the focal letters on each page is fairly fancy and is not ideal for teaching about the alphabet, the teacher also realizes that if she were to limit her choices to alphabet books that utilized a clean font, she wouldn't have many alphabet books to read! Given the phonemic analysis and motivational opportunities that the book offers, she decides to go ahead and use the book.

PREPARING THE LESSON SHEET

The teacher prepares for the lesson by listing the names of the children at the top of the Lesson Sheet, the name of the book to be read in the title line, and by making brief notations regarding which instructional goals and objectives she will address during the course of the read aloud. In examining the listing of goals and objectives that might be addressed during the read aloud, the teacher might plan as follows:

• *Text comprehension.* Draw the children's attention to some of the pictures and discuss how the pictures help to clarify the text. This might be noted on the lesson sheet by simply circling/highlighting the *PC*, which stands for *picture clues*, on the text comprehension line. (The codes for the small-group lesson sheet are presented in Figure 14.4.)

• *Word identification strategy.* This book does not lend itself to supporting this goal for children at this early stage of development. Therefore, no notations would be made here.

• *Letter/sound.* For children who know little about the alphabet, becoming familiar with the names of the letters is a preliminary step, even if the children are not yet connecting those names with the printed letters. Reading this book and pointing to the individual letters will help children begin to recognize the letters and become familiar with their names. The teacher would indicate that objective by circling/highlighting the *REC* (for *recognize*) in the Letter/Sound section.

• *Print concepts.* The teacher plans to point to the words and perhaps draw the children's attention to print concepts by occasionally talking about where on the page she starts reading, where she goes once she gets to the last word on a line, and so on. This will help the children begin to understand some of the most basic conventions of print. The teacher would note this plan by circling/highlighting *LR* (for *left-to-right*) and *TB* (for *top-to-bottom*) directions of print.

• *High-frequency words.* The book does not lend itself to supporting this goal. Further, for the children in the group under discussion, this is not an appropriate goal at this point.

• *Phonological awareness.* Although the alliteration in this book will help to heighten children's sensitivity to the beginning sounds in words, the teacher chooses not to explicitly address this area because the book's primary utility is its usefulness in helping children learn the names of the letters of the alphabet. There would be no notation in the Phoneme Awareness row or in the corresponding columns for the children.

• *Vocabulary.* The teacher does not plan to teach the meanings of any particular words. There would be no notation in this row.

READ-ALOUD/READ (Segments 1 and 4)

Text Comprehension
GU—general understanding
AE—active engagement
RET—retell
PC—picture cues
CON—connect to existing knowledge

Word Identification Strategy
TS-F—Think sounds—first
TS-L—Think sounds—last
TS-M—Think sounds—middle
BW—break word
DP—different pronunciation
WP—word part
PIC—picture cues
MS—make sense
RP—read past
SA—start again
IC—Interactive and confirmatory

Letter/Sound
REC—recognize
NAM—name

Print Concepts
LR—left-to-right directionality
TB—top-to-bottom directionality
CW—concept of a word
CL—concept of a letter
COM—print as communication
PUN—punctuation
1-1—voice–print match

High-Frequency Words
REC—recognize
ID—identify

Phonological Awareness
CR—completes rhyme
IR—identifies rhyming words
IA—identifies alliterative words

PHONOLOGICAL AWARENESS (Segment 2)

Sort by Sound
RH—rhyme
BEG—beginning
END—ending
MID—middle vowel

Sound Blending
w/Pics—with pictures
w/o Pics—without pictures

LETTERS and DECODING (Segment 3)
REC—recognize
NAM—name
PR—print or produce
LS—letter–sound association
CS-B—consonant substitution, *begin*
CS-E—consonant substitution, *end*
SV—short vowel
VCe–vowel consonant e
DI—digraph
BL—blend

WRITING (Segment 5)

Letters and Sounds
PR—print or produce
LS—letter–sound association
BS—beginning sound
ES—ending sound
SV—short vowel
VCe—long vowel
DI—digraph
BL—blend

Print Concepts
LR—left-to-right directionality
TB—top-to-bottom directionality
CW—concept of word
CL—concept of letter
COM—print as communication
PUN—punctuation

High-Frequency Sight Words
CP—copy from resource
CS—correct spelling without model

HIGH-FREQUENCY WORDS (Segment 6)
(no codes needed)

FIGURE 14.4. Codes for lesson objectives. From Anderson (2010). Copyright 2010 by the International Reading Association. Reprinted with permission.

This illustration of the planning phase is intended to underscore the points that multiple goals should be addressed with a given book and that not all goals need to be addressed with each book.

Small-Group Read-Aloud: During the Lesson

READING THE BOOK

As the teacher reads the book, she holds it so that the children can see the words and pictures, and she points to the letters as they are named. Once every couple of pages, she points to each word on the page as she reads it. At least once, she explicitly explains how reading proceeds—for example, "When we read, we usually start at the top of the page and over on this side." Once or twice, she might ask the children to point to the place on the page where she should start reading. As she comes to letters that have particular meaning for the children, she might lead a brief discussion of the letter (e.g., "Oh, look! There's the letter *S*! Sara, you have an *S* at the beginning of your name! Does anyone else have an *S* in their name?"). Throughout this discussion, the teacher would keep her finger under the letter *S* in the book or point to another *S* in the teaching space (perhaps on Sara's name card). To help the children better connect the name of the letter *S* with its visual representation, the teacher might also invite children to find and name the *S*'s on the *S* page and to say the letter name each time.

Also while reading, the teacher and children would enjoy the silliness of the book, such as the duck-dog that David Donald Doo dreamed about (pp. 12–13). To develop comprehension and advance general knowledge, the teacher might ask why the dog is called a duck-dog (because it has duck feet) and discuss why ducks have feet of that sort.

USING THE LESSON SHEET

As the group enjoys the book, the teacher might use the lesson sheet to jog her memory for the things she was planning to do with the book. The sheet would also be used to capture brief notes concerning the responses of the individual children. In particular, the teacher would note children's progress toward accomplishing listed objectives and/or other observations she makes about individuals, using the *beginning* (B), *developing* (D), and *proficient* (P) designations discussed in Chapter 1. For example, if Alex seems confident in directing the teacher to the uppermost and leftmost word on the page when asked where to start, the teacher might record a *D* or a *P* (depending upon her previous observations of Alex) in Alex's box under Print Concepts on the lesson sheet. The teacher might also use the Comments/Notes for Next Session space at the bottom of the page for additional note taking. The lesson sheet would be used in similar ways across subsequent components.

Small-Group Read-Aloud: After the Lesson

At some point after the lesson, the teacher would take a few minutes to reflect on the focus and pace of the lesson and the children's response to it and add any additional notes and comments that may help with planning upcoming lessons and that may be important for capturing on the group snapshots. In planning future lessons, the teacher would, once again, review the snapshots and look through the last couple of lessons for a particular group.

Rereading: Before the Lesson

CONSIDER THE CHILDREN

For children who are a bit further along, the first segment of the lesson would involve rereading one or more books that had been read in previous lessons. The purposes of rereading are to:

- Enable the children to read the text more fluently, which will, in turn, enable them to better comprehend it.
- Build children's confidence and sense of competence as readers.
- Reinforce children's ability to identify newly encountered high-frequency words.
- Provide children with practice in using decoding elements that occur in the text.
- Give children the opportunity to employ their developing word identification strategies with greater fluency and ease.

To reap the maximum benefit from the rereading segment, the teacher would give children some choice about which books they read; choice in reading materials is an important contributor to motivation. Also, ideally, each child would read a different book during this segment, or, if two children chose the same book, they would not read in unison. The point is to allow each child the opportunity to read an entire book and to do the thinking and problem solving that this entails. If children read a book in unison, some children may simply shadow their friends, saying each word just a split second after the other children. As a result, these children will not extend their word-solving skills or build their sight vocabulary as effectively.

SELECTING THE BOOKS

While book selection for rereading is limited to books previously read, the teacher would offer books that will help to reinforce particular skills or strategies that the children are learning. In general, books offered for rereading in the context of an intervention lesson should engage children in some strategic processing, as these books will provide more opportunity to guide the children's application of word-solving strategies. Books that the children read quite fluently are best utilized for free choice and/or take-home reading.

PREPARING THE LESSON SHEET

The names of the books to be offered for rereading would be listed in the *Title* (*and level*) box on the lesson sheet. The teacher may plan to review particular skills or strategies that are appropriate for the children in relation to each book that will be offered. For example, for children who are just beginning to read emergent-level texts, the teacher might plan to remind them of the *check-the-pictures* strategy and the *think-about-the-sounds* strategy. For children at this point in development the *think-about-the-sounds* strategy would be qualified (e.g., "Think about the sound of the first letter"). The teacher would note that plan on her record sheet by circling/highlighting *TS* (for *Think about the sounds*) and circling/highlighting the *F* (for *first sound*) and *PIC* (for *pictures*) in the Word Identification Strategy section. For a more advanced group of children, the teacher might plan to remind them of a word family that was previously taught and that appears in a given book. She would record that plan by writing in the phonogram in the Letter/Sound section in Segment 1 (Read-Aloud/Shared Reading or ReReading) of the lesson sheet.

Rereading: During the Lesson

READING THE BOOK(S)

Listening to children read provides the opportunity to observe their individual approaches to word solving and to guide the development of their strategic approach to reading. In a small-group context, the teacher can listen to one child read while the other children either read independently or take turns reading to one another. Alternatively, all (in our example, three) of the children in the group can be asked to read, but in a quiet voice or whisper, so that the teacher can "tune in" to each child on an as-needed basis (this usually means that the teacher is out of her chair and at the side of different children as they read). As the children read, the teacher should note such areas as the word identification strategies and decoding skills they use effectively and which skills and strategies need to be revisited. As always, there should be some brief discussion of the story or information encountered in the book before, during, and after the children read.

Rereading: After the Lesson

Once the lesson is completed, the teacher would make a determination about whether the book(s) that was used would be useful for another rereading in the small-group context. The teacher would also reflect on, and make note of, instructional priorities for future lessons for the group.

Segment 2: Phonological Awareness

In this segment the instruction is designed to help children become attuned to the phonemes in spoken language. The development of sensitivity to, and awareness of, the individual sound components in spoken words tends to follow a predictable pattern. As discussed in Chapter 5, familiarity with this progression enables teachers to identify where children are in the process of becoming phonemically aware and what they are ready to learn next. In early lessons with beginning kindergartners who have been identified as at risk for early reading difficulties, we suggest that teachers begin by focusing on the easiest phonological analysis skills and advancing through those skills as quickly as the children are able. For older and/or more advanced children, the teacher might consider using a dictated spelling assessment (e.g., the Primary Spelling Inventory provided by Bear et al., 2008) to gain initial insight into the parts of spoken words that the children are noticing and representing. Children who, in their attempted spellings, represent many of the sounds in spoken words probably do not need to receive instruction on isolated phonological analysis skills. For them, ongoing instruction around the alphabetic code will serve to further their ability to analyze spoken words at the level of the phoneme. For such children, the second segment (phonological awareness) of the lesson might be utilized only as an introductory step in teaching about some aspects of decoding. For example, in teaching about the long and the short sound of a vowel, the teacher might begin by having the children listen for the vowels sounds in spoken words and decide whether the targeted vowel sound comes at the beginning, in the middle, or at the end of spoken words.

The group snapshot for phonological skills provided in Chapter 5 (p. 106) is intended to help teachers keep the progression of skills in mind and to provide a way of documenting observations of students' skills. The first section of this snapshot would be used to record observations of the children's sensitivity to rhyme and alliteration in the context of read-alouds. The remainder is intended to be used during more isolated instructional activities, which are the focus of this second segment of the lesson.

Before the Lesson

CONSIDER THE CHILDREN

During the lesson planning phase, the teacher would review the group snapshot for phonological skills and her notes from prior lessons to determine the appropriate next steps for the children in the group.

• *Instruction for children at the earliest points in the development of phonological skills* would begin with activities that involve them in analyzing words at the level of onsets and rimes. The teacher might start with sound-sorting activities focused on either rhyming words or words with the same beginning sounds. When first introducing a particular sorting principle, the teacher would start with an odd-one-out procedure (e.g., choosing the one word in a set of four that doesn't rhyme with the rest of the words in the set). When children seem to understand the sorting principle, the teacher might use sorting boards (see Figure 5.5, p. 95). For sound-blending instruction, the teacher would begin with blending onsets and rimes and have the children select the picture that represents the blended word from a small set of pictures. For both beginning sound sorting and initial blending instruction, the teacher would use words with "stretchable" sounds in the onset (e.g., *net, fan, soup*) because it is easier to draw children's attention to sounds that can be elongated without distortion.

Children who are just beginning to attend to the sounds in words will not benefit from phoneme counting activities, so that type of instruction would be reserved for when they have made some progress in sound-sorting and -blending skills.

• *For children who are able to sort by beginning sound and rhyme and who can blend onsets and rimes,* instruction would focus their attention on all of the sounds in single-syllable words. The teacher might, for example, engage the children in sound blending with single phonemes by using a puppet. The first time this activity is initiated, the puppet would pronounce each phoneme in a word and the children would identify the word by choosing it from a small group of pictures. Words in which all of the consonant sounds are stretchable would be used in the earliest lesson(s). As the children progress, such restrictions are relaxed. When the children demonstrate the ability to easily select the correct picture, the level of challenge is adjusted by removing the pictures from view while the teacher articulates the sounds. Later still, the teacher would engage the children in doing the segmenting. Some children will pick up these skills quite readily. This segment of the lesson can be eliminated when the children are proficient with all of the skills listed in sections II through IV of the group snapshot for phonological awareness (see Figure 5.11, p. 106).

PREPARING THE LESSON SHEET

In any given lesson, the teacher would typically engage the children in only one or two phonological awareness activities. Three types of phonemic awareness activities are listed on the lesson sheet: sound sorting, sound blending, and sound counting/segmentation. For each type of activity, teachers choose different kinds of words and provide different supports, depending upon children's needs. In preparing the lesson sheet for the children at the earliest point in development, for example, the teacher might plan to teach them how to sort pictures by commonality in beginning sounds. This would be noted on the lesson sheet by circling/highlighting *BEG* in the *sound sorting* line. For at least the first sorting lesson, the teacher would use only words with stretchable beginning sounds. This would be noted by circling/highlighting the word *stretch*. The teacher would also note whether odd-one-out or sorting board activities will be used. For the group with more advanced phonological skills described above, the teacher would circle *Single Phonemes* and *w/Pics* (with *pictures*) on the lesson sheet.

During the Lesson

Instruction for the two groups of children under discussion would begin with explicit instruction on the relevant skills, including demonstration and modeling if the activity is new. For the first several items that the children sort or blend, the teacher would emphasize the portion of the words to which the children are to attend. For example, the word *sun* would be pronounced ssssssun for a beginning sound sort and sunnnnnn for an ending sound sort. However, as the children begin to demonstrate the ability to sort or blend, the teacher should gradually reduce the amount of stretching she does to the point where the words are articulated in a normal way. When children are able to analyze (i.e., sort, blend, segment) words that are articulated normally, they are ready to move on to the next skill in the sequence, which involves the same task but with words that do not have stretchable sounds.

In the context of small-group lessons, children will inevitably make gains at different rates. Therefore, the teacher will need to modify instruction during the lesson, based on the skills of individual children. For example, the teacher might do more word stretching for some children than for others. Or, in a blending activity, she might leave less time between word segments for some children and leave more time between segments for others.

Segment 3: Letters and Sounds, Alphabetic Mapping, Word Families, and Decoding

As noted in Chapters 6–9, children learn about individual letters in the alphabet in a predictable sequence. First they learn to recognize a letter, then to name it, then its most common sound, and ultimately they learn to use it in decoding (or sounding out) words. Most children who qualify for intervention in kindergarten need to learn the names of the letters (recognition and naming). Once they have learned a letter's name, they are ready to learn its sound and how to use it in reading and writing. As children begin to learn about the sounds of letters, the phonemic analysis and letter sounds segments of the lessons should be brought together so that they can more readily understand the purposes of both phonemic analysis and letter–sound instruction. As children progress in learning about the alphabetic code, they need to learn to process larger orthographic units (word families, prefixes, suffixes, etc.) to effectively and efficiently identify new words in text. Throughout this process the children need to learn to be flexible in their use of the code because many words in written English are only partially decodable. In this segment of the lesson, the focus is on helping the children (1) learn about the elements of the alphabetic code and how the code works, and (2) become automatic (fluent) in the use of a variety of phonologically based reading and spelling strategies.

Chapters 6–9 provide substantial detail on the development of skill with the alphabetic code. Each of these chapters also provides group snapshots, which are designed to help teachers think about the various components that comprise skill with the code and to document the skills of individual children. For children who are just beginning to learn about the alphabet, the group snapshots for alphabet knowledge and for alphabetic code—early development will be most useful. For more advanced students, the snapshots for alphabetic code—later development and for larger orthographic units will be most helpful.

As noted in Part II, instruction on new alphabetic skills should generally occur in preparation for reading a book in which a particular skill or skills can be applied. Once a skill has been taught, it should be revisited in subsequent lessons until children seem fairly secure in their ability to utilize the skill in isolation, and, most importantly, in their ability to rely on the skill when attempting to identify unfamiliar words encountered while reading.

Before the Lesson

CONSIDER THE CHILDREN AND THE BOOK THAT THEY WILL READ

The order in which given elements of the alphabetic code are taught is partly dependent on the instructional materials (i.e., the books in both intervention and classroom settings) that are available for the children to read and partly dependent on what the children are ready to learn. We address book selection a bit in discussing Segment 4 (Reading) of the lesson. Further discussion of that topic is presented in the Introduction to Part III, Word Learning (see pp. 189–195). Here it is important to point out that in our more recent intervention studies, we used a series of books that were designed to build decoding skills and sight vocabulary in a systematic way. In this series, the first book in which a particular element is addressed provides the children with multiple opportunities to practice decoding that element. In the next several books, that decoding element appears again, although not as frequently. These additional practice opportunities are intended to reinforce children's developing skills. While using such a series simplifies book selection a bit, for the children who struggled the most, it was often necessary for teachers to search for additional books to help reinforce particular decoding skills or books that focused more on other kinds of skills (e.g., high-frequency words). Clearly, no single set of instructional materials will meet the needs of all of the children all of the time.

Once the teacher has considered the skills of the students and has selected a book, instructional planning for this segment is fairly straightforward. For children who know little about the alphabet, developing letter-name knowledge would be the focus. Usually one or two letters would be introduced for specific attention but whole-alphabet activities would be used as well (see Chapter 6). In the next segment of the lesson, the children would read one or more emergent-level books in which the targeted letter(s) occurs frequently. After reading the book with the children, the teacher would focus their attention on the new letter(s) through letter hunts and similar playful activities.

For children who have learned some letter sounds and who are ready to learn more, the teacher might plan to specifically teach a letter–sound correspondence and the appropriate key word. Word building, word reading, and written spelling would be used to practice and reinforce the newly taught and previously taught correspondences. Children who know most letter–sound correspondences for consonants, and who can successfully engage in word-building, word-reading, and written-spelling exercises that require them to make changes at the beginnings and ends of words, are ready to learn the vowel sounds and to engage in practice activities that involve switching between the long and short sounds of each vowel. These children are also ready to learn to use phonograms and word families in their decoding and spelling attempts, and because they will also be encountering multisyllabic words in their reading, they will need guidance on how to puzzle through such words.

PREPARING THE LESSON SHEET

The teacher would note the skill(s) she is planning to work on with the children by circling/highlighting the type of activity and writing in the specific elements for Segment 3. For example, for a group that is going to be learning the name of the letter *M* and doing a whole-alphabet activity (e.g., singing an alphabet song and pointing to the letters as it is sung), on the Letter Names line the teacher would write in the *M* and might write "Alphabet Song." She would also circle/highlight REC (for *Recognize*), or NAM (for *Name*), or PR (for *Print*), depending on the purpose of her instruction. For children learning to be flexible with the long- and short-*a* sounds, the teacher would write in "*a* sounds" on the "Other Decoding Elements" line. If the teacher plans to use word-building, word-reading, and/or written-spelling activities, she would write in the words that she will use on the appropriate lines and be sure to have the moveable letters she needs to engage the children in these activities.

During the Lesson

The teacher would introduce and teach new skills explicitly, as detailed in Chapters 6 to 9. As the children engage in the practice activities, the teacher should carefully observe individual children and provide guidance and feedback as appropriate. The activities should allow each child in the group to engage in the intended thinking. Thus, each child would have his own set of letters to use for word-building activities and his own writing materials during written spelling.

Segment 4: Reading a New Book

As discussed in some detail in Chapter 1, reading really is a complicated process. Indeed, we've devoted pages and pages to detailing the multiple attitudes, subprocesses, knowledge sources, strategies, and skills that a proficient reader ultimately develops. The complexity of reading development becomes even more evident when one considers that the reader has to coordinate all of these components and, for the most part, do most of it in an automatic and unconscious way while attending primarily or exclusively to the information/story that the text conveys. Despite this complexity, there is one rather simple rule regarding reading development: The more reading a child does, the better reader he becomes (see Hiebert, 2009). Of course, it has to be engaged reading, meaning, the child needs to be thinking about what he is reading while reading. It also needs to be fairly accurate reading, meaning, the child needs to read the words that are on the page, not just supply words that fit the context fairly well but don't match the printed letters. Disengaged and inaccurate reading are common occurrences among young readers and older struggling readers. This occurs, in part, because the children do not really understand what they are supposed to be doing when they read. In small-group and one-to-one reading lessons, the new book segment of the ISA provides the opportunity to clarify what reading entails and to guide the children's thinking about the process.

In most lessons, the children should read at least one new book that is somewhat, but not too, challenging for them. Books that present some challenge give children the opportunity to apply what they are learning about the reading process and provide the teacher with the opportunity to coach the children in word-solving strategies. Because the teaching opportunities and the potential points of confusion vary considerably from one book to the next, all of the children should be reading the same book the first time a book is read in a small group context. The book should be discussed before, during, and after reading to maintain a focus on reading for meaning rather than simply for the purpose of accurate decoding.

The children should be explicitly prepared to read the new book through the teaching of one or more high-frequency words and/or through instruction on new decoding elements that will be encountered in the book. Instruction relating to the decoding elements was discussed in Segment 3 above. The high-frequency words selected for explicit teaching would be those that the children are unlikely to be able to read given their current decoding skills and the strength of the context in which the word appears. These words would be taught before the children begin to read. For each book, the teacher plans to focus on particular instructional objectives that are appropriate for the children. Furthermore, in each lesson the teacher might plan to pay particular attention to one child as the children read so that she can document that child's effectiveness in using word identification strategies either when specifically prompted or spontaneously while reading. As was discussed briefly for Segment 1, a variety of goals and specific objectives might be pursued in the context of preparing for and reading the new book. Greater emphasis is placed on strategic word solving in this segment, as there is generally more opportunity to be strategic on the first reading of a book than in a rereading.

One of the most important goals we hope to achieve in the course of reading instruction is to teach children to help themselves learn to read. By providing them with a variety of strategies to use in figuring out words and encouraging them to take responsibility for assuring that their reading makes sense, we increase the likelihood that the children will become successful, independent readers (see Chapter 10).

Before the Lesson

CONSIDER THE CHILDREN AND SELECT THE BOOK

Choosing an appropriate book for the children to read is an important first step. Books should be chosen such that they allow children to build upon what they already know and are able to do. Thus, if children are just beginning to learn the names of some of the letters, then predictable books with a repetitive pattern and strong picture support would be used. These books will help children learn about important print concepts and provide a vehicle for letter-recognition and letter-naming activities. For children who know several letter–sound correspondences and who have some basic print concepts established, the easiest strategy-promoting books would be a better match (see Part III, p. 194). The use of such books might be interspersed with books that focus on the development of high-frequency sight vocabulary (e.g., early sight word books, p. 192).

As the children grow as readers, they need increasingly challenging books. There is widespread agreement that, in supported reading settings, children should read books that are at their *instructional level*. This is sometimes defined as texts in which the child can accurately identify 95–98% of the words (Betts, 1946). However, in settings where children are provided with close support and where the goal is to help them learn effective word-solving strategies, we feel that texts that are somewhat more challenging (90–95% accuracy) can be appropriately employed. Of course, exactly how challenging a book will be for a given child or group of children will depend partially on the preparation they have for reading the book. Further, for beginning readers, the difficulty of a particular text will depend, to a great extent, on the children's instructional experiences prior to encountering the text. For example, young children who are in a program that emphasizes decoding are likely to find decodable texts easier to read than will children in programs that make heavy use of predictable texts and place comparatively little emphasis on teaching decoding strategies. Therefore, although teachers will certainly want to consider the designated level of difficulty for the books that their students read, it is most important to consider the challenges posed by the book for their students at their point of development and relative to the instructional experiences that the children have had. A review of the group's snapshots for listening and reading comprehension as well as for strategic word solving is particularly important when selecting the book and planning the instruction.[1]

PREPARING THE LESSON SHEET

The name of the book and the book's level (if it has one) should be recorded at the top of the reading segment of the lesson sheet. Prior to meeting with students, the teacher would consider the various goals and objectives listed on the lesson sheet for Segment 4. There should be a specific plan for addressing several of the major goals listed before, during, and/or after reading the book with the children. The Comprehension and Word Identification Strategies goals would be addressed every time children read a book. Therefore, these goals are at the top of the list. The teacher would circle the particular objectives she plans to address and (may) make brief notes about how this will be done. For example, the teacher would think about the comprehension challenges posed by the text and what she might need to do to prepare the children to make sense of the text by, perhaps, explaining the structure of the text (see the example for the book *Look Closer* [Logan, 1997] described below), identifying an appropriate schema for the text, or engaging the children in anticipating what will happen in the text based on the title and the picture on the cover. Sometimes, for books with particular challenges, a teacher would plan a more thorough book introduction. Similarly, for word identification strategies the teacher might plan to teach a new strategy before the children read, or to review all of the strategies that have already been taught. Also during this phase, the teacher would determine whether the children will encounter any new concepts or words for which they may not know the meaning. If so, she would prepare a brief, child-friendly explanation of the word and note it in the vocabulary section of the lesson sheet.

During the Lesson

The teacher would start by introducing the book and generating enthusiasm for reading it (e.g., "I think you are really going to like this book" or "We are going to learn a lot about whales in this book," or "I picked this book because I know how much you like cats"). She might then show the high-frequency words, name each one, and have children practice reading them a few times. To draw the children's attention to the internal structure of the words, the teacher might have them name their letters or write the words. Before moving into the book, the teacher might also teach a new word identification strategy and/or remind the children of strate-

---

[1]There are multiple leveling systems available (e.g., Fountas & Pinnell, 1996; Fry, 2002; Beaver, 2006) and ongoing concern about the reliability and validity of such systems (Pitcher & Zhihui, 2007).

gies that have already been discussed and practiced. She would then briefly discuss the content of the book. All of these introductory activities would take only a few minutes and might occur in any order.

Following the introductory activities, the children begin to read. Each would read the entire book individually and simultaneously—although not in unison. As the children read, the teacher would observe and provide guidance and support on the application of word-solving strategies and the use of resources (e.g., the word wall, the key-word chart, the word family display, and the strategies list) as scaffolding for independence. The teacher might move from child to child, or focus on an individual child, providing guidance and engaging in brief conversations to maintain a focus on the meaning of the text. The teacher would be attentive to the children's strategic word solving, making note of observable strategy use on the lesson sheet.

For the purpose of supporting strategic processing, the teacher will need to make multiple, on-the-spot decisions about how to respond to individual children's word-solving attempts. In doing so, the teacher would try to:

• Provide the child with enough time to think about the puzzling words—it takes time to be strategic.

• Consider whether or not to interrupt (or prompt) for minor miscues (errors) that do not disrupt the meaning of the text. If a miscue occurs on a high-frequency word that has been taught but that the child does not yet have in his sight vocabulary, the miscue may be important to address. If, however, a miscue occurs on a word that the child knows well, does not change the meaning of the texts, and simply reflects the child's focus on the meaning of the text, then there is no benefit in bringing the child's attention to the miscue.

• Encourage the child to look carefully at the words on the page when a highly repetitive text leads the child to overgeneralize or overpredict the contents. While errors of this type may not seriously disrupt the meaning of the text, overreliance on the repetitive refrain is a habit that is sometimes difficult for children to overcome. In these situations, it is helpful to remind children to be sure that their spoken words "match the words on the page."

• Avoid responding too quickly to meaning-disruptive miscues. The goal is for the child to realize that meaning has been disrupted and to self-correct. Therefore, the teacher needs to wait until the child has read far enough along to realize that he has made an error. (This often means allowing the child to read to the end of the sentence or perhaps further.) If, at this point, the child doesn't notice and/or attempt to correct the error, the teacher would ask whether what he read made sense or sounded right and provide him with some suggestions for fixing the error, if need be. (The teacher remembers to sometimes ask the "Did that make sense?" question when what the child read did, in fact, make sense because the goal is to help children learn to monitor their own reading.)

• Provide low-utility and low-frequency words such as unusual proper names or other words that the child is unlikely to encounter often in other contexts if he hesitates over them at early points in development. As his reading skills develop, the child should be expected to at least make an attempt at such words.

When children are finished reading, there should be a brief group discussion of/reaction to the book.

USING THE LESSON SHEET

As the children read, the teacher would use the lesson sheet to record observations regarding individual children. For example, in the comprehension section she might note whether the child draws the needed inferences to make sense of the text or whether he uses the picture cues (*PC*) to enhance understanding. Similarly, the teacher might use the letter codes for the word identification strategies to note the strategies that the child uses spontaneously (noting RP = Spon when she observes a child spontaneously reading past a puzzling word in efforts to identify it) or the strategies that the teacher needed to prompt (noting RP = prom when she needed to prompt a child to read past a puzzling word). The lesson sheet can also be used to note high-frequency words that children might need additional practice on, print concepts that do not appear to be firmly established, etc. At the bottom of the lesson sheet for Segment 4, the teacher would make more extensive notes to help her plan upcoming lessons.

Segment 5: Writing

In the context of a small-group-supported literacy lesson, writing is used to provide opportunities for children to learn to apply their developing alphabetic skills, including print concepts and phonemic analysis, and to emphasize the need to spell known high-frequency words conventionally. Because of this focus, the writing that the children do is often somewhat contrived and/or determined and dictated by the teacher. Although the objectives addressed in the writing component are generally focused on the mechanical aspects of writing rather than on the development of composition skills and story/text elements, this particular lens should not suggest that composition skills are unimportant for beginning and struggling readers. Rather, there is simply too little time in an intervention lesson to allow for a focus on composition. In whole-class contexts children should, of course, be given the opportunity to compose text for authentic purposes.

Before the Lesson

CONSIDER THE CHILDREN

As for reading, writing requires the orchestration of various types of knowledge and skill. To identify reasonable next steps for children in the writing segment of the lesson, the teacher might review the group snapshots for purposes and conventions of print, phonological skills, alphabet knowledge, early and/or later development of the alphabetic code, larger orthographic units, and the group's "Words We Know" chart (see Segment 6 below). For children who are just beginning to learn about print, the writing segment often involves shared writing (as discussed in Chapter 2), wherein the teacher emphasizes concepts and processes that are appropriate for the children with whom she is working. For more advanced children, less time would be spent on shared writing and more time would be devoted to having the children write. Thus, for example, the teacher might model a sentence she'd like the children to write and then ask them to write their own similar sentence. For children who are even further along, the writing in an intervention lesson would often be done in response to the book they read in the previous segment. For the sake of efficiency, the teacher might give the children a specific writing prompt related to the book so that most of the writing time can be devoted to guiding the children's thinking related to how to apply their developing knowledge of the writing system and how to use resources such as word walls and key-word charts. In writing a response to a book, the children would be encouraged to use the book as a resource to support conventional spelling.

PREPARING THE LESSON SHEET

The sentence or writing prompt that will be used during the writing segment should be noted on the lesson sheet prior to the lesson. The sentence/prompt should be constructed to elicit the skills that the children have been learning. Thus, the prompt should include recently taught high-frequency words and elements of the code (letters, word families, digraphs, etc.). In addition, the teacher should plan to observe how successfully the children handle various aspects of the process. For example, for the Letters/Sounds line of the writing segment, the teacher might circle *ES* (for ending sound) to remind herself to notice whether the children are using acceptable letters to represent the ending sounds in the words they write.

During the Lesson

As in other segments of the lesson, instruction should be as explicit as necessary to help children understand the processes and to learn to uses the resources. Shared writing should be used to introduce new skills and concepts (e.g., leaving spaces between words, adding a silent *e* on long vowel words, checking the word wall for the spelling of a high-frequency word). The teacher should model the thinking that she'd ultimately like the children to do by thinking aloud (e.g., "I need to leave a space before I start to write the next word").

When the children write, the teacher should move from one child to the next, offering assistance and guidance as needed, while being mindful of the goal of building independence. Thus, for example, when a child is puzzling over how to write a particular word, the teacher would need to decide whether to stretch the word for the child or to help him do the stretching. The latter approach contributes to the development of the child's ultimate independence as a writer.

After the Lesson

As for other segments, the teacher would reflect on what occurred in the lesson and make note of what should be addressed in upcoming lessons. Periodically she should update the group snapshots in order to document the children's progress relative to print concepts and skill with the alphabetic code (early and later development).

Segment 6: High-Frequency Words

This segment of the lesson is used primarily for practice activities with high-frequency words and to evaluate growth in sight vocabulary; it does not include initial explicit teaching (high-frequency words are taught in preparation for reading a book). Therefore, we do not discuss the before, during, and after phases of lesson planning for high-frequency words as we did for previous segments.

Recently taught high-frequency words and/or words that the children continue to confuse can be used in game-like activities during this segment. Words that are particularly troublesome for children should be practiced via writing them several times, as writing a word helps children attend to its internal features. Because there are several productive games that can be used to provide practice on high-frequency words, a teacher can periodically find time to assess individual children's knowledge in this area by having some of the children play sight word games (e.g., tic-tac-toe, parking lot) while she assesses one child. The Eeds's list presented in Figure 11.4, p. 240, might be used for this purpose. As an alternative to an explicit assessment, the teacher might engage one child in a Your Pile/My Pile game while other children in the group play sight word games. Periodically this segment of the lesson should be used to review all of the words on the group's "Words We Know" chart by reading the entire chart or sections of it and/or by administering spelling "tests" in which the children *get* to refer to the chart for conventional spellings.

A COMPLETE SMALL-GROUP LESSON

The discussion of the segments of a small-group lesson, above, was intended to cover various aspects of the thinking, planning, decision making, and record keeping that go into delivering effective and responsive small-group early literacy instruction. Because we attempted to represent children at various points along the developmental continuum, the discussion does not provide a sense of the flow and pacing of an actual lesson. Therefore, below we provide a description of an entire lesson provided by an intervention teacher for a group of kindergartners toward the end of the school year. Two of the children (Michaela and Alex) have been in the group since October. The third (Max) joined the group more recently, having moved to the school in March. All three have the same classroom teacher. Figure 14.5 presents the lesson sheet for the lesson that is described below. Cursive font is used to show what was written on the lesson sheet before the lesson began; things that the teacher wrote during and after the lesson appear as handwritten. (The codes provided in Figure 14.4 will aid in the interpretation of this lesson sheet. Also, note that the teacher uses the codes B, D, and P to indicate whether she perceives each child to be at a beginning, developing, or proficient level of performance.)

Segment 1: Read-Aloud/Shared Reading or Rereading

Earlier in the school year, Mrs. D used the first part of the lesson as a time for read-aloud or shared reading, often choosing an alphabet book or a book that featured rhyme or alliteration. More recently, she has begun to use this time for rereading emergent-level books from earlier lessons. Today she has chosen two emergent-level (*EM* on Figure 14.5) books, *My Bear* (Beech, 2003) and *go to* (Short Books, 1999), because they provide important opportunities for the children to practice a number of high-frequency words that have already been taught, and because the pictures, while supportive, are sometimes ambiguous and require the children to attend to the print in addition to being guided by context. For example, in *go to*, the children must attend to at least the first letter in the final word on the page to know if the sentence should read "I go to *bed*" or "I go to *sleep*."

As she prepares them for rereading, Mrs. D reminds the children to point carefully to the words as they read, and she reviews what they have learned to do when they come to a word they don't know: "You really have to look at the letters, think about the sounds, and match the pictures." She lets each child decide which book to read first, and then she moves about the group, listening to each student read. Her interactions with the children focus on enjoying and understanding the stories as well as reading the words correctly. Because later in the lesson she plans to teach the children how to use the ending sounds as well as the beginning sounds when puzzling through words, she uses this opportunity to begin to focus their attention on the letters at the end of words. For example, when Michaela reads the sentence, "My bear can read," Mrs. D asks her how she knows the word is *read*. Mrs. D extends Michaela's response of "because it says *r-e-a-d*" by commenting, "Great, and you heard the /d/ at the end, rea*d*, and the picture shows him reading!" She uses a similar approach with each of the students, guiding them to attend to the ending sound in a word they have just read as they confirm that the pictures and the letter sounds do indeed match.

(text continues on p. 335)

Lesson Sheet

Child 1 *Alex* _____ Child 2 *Michaela* _____ Child 3 *Max* _____

1. Read-Aloud/Shared Reading or Rereading		
Title (and Level): *My Bear (EM), go to (EM)*		
Text Comprehension: (GU) AE, RET (PC) CON		
D	P	D
Word Identification Strategy: *IS-L (notice final letter sound)* Code (TS) [F, (L) M], WP, DP, BW), Meaning (PIC) MS, RP, SA), interactive and confirmatory (IC)		
D	D	B
Letter/Sound: REC, NAM		
Print Concepts: *Track print while reading* *point while reading* LR, TB, CW, CL, COM, PUN (1-1)		
P	P	D
High-Frequency Words: *review: my, can, go* REC, ID		
P	P	P—my, can D—go
Phonological Awareness: CR, IR, IA		
Vocabulary		
Comments/Notes for Next Session: Max occasionally used picture and first letter in confirmatory way. Alex and Michaela—consistent in doing so.		

FIGURE 14.5. Completed lesson sheet for small-group instruction. Adapted from Anderson (2010). Copyright 2010 by the International Reading Association. Adapted by permission. *(page 1 of 4)*

Child 1 *Alex*   Child 2 *Michaela*   Child 3 *Max*

2. Phonological Awareness		
Sound Sorting RH, BEG, (END) MID STRETCH??		
Sound Blending Onset–Rime, Single Phonemes w/Pics, w/o Pics STRETCH??		
Sound Counting/Segmentation 2 Phonemes, 3 Phonemes STRETCH??		
P	P	B
Comments/Notes for Next Session:		
Very difficult for Max—have Alex and Michaela work to complete an ending sound sort with letters for column headers. Work w/ Max on ending sound sort with stretchables.		

3. Letters and Sounds, Alphabetic Mapping, Word Families, Decoding		
Letter Names: RE, NAM, PR Letter Sounds (LS,) CS-B, CS-E *Review LS for L* Other Decoding Elements		
Word Building		
Word Reading		
Written Spelling		
Comments/Notes for Next Session:		
Consonant substitution for beginning and ending sounds—have Max focus mostly on beginning sound.		

FIGURE 14.5. *(page 2 of 4)*

Child 1 *Alex* _____   Child 2 *Michaela* _____   Child 3 *Max* _____

4. Reading		
Title (and Level): *Look Closer (EM)*		
Text Comprehension: *Text Structure—opposing pages* GU, AE, RET, PC, CON *Concepts of photography and magnifying glass*		
Word Identification Strategy: *TS-L, I see the leaf demo* Code (TS)[F,(L)M], WP, DP, BW), Meaning (PIC, MS, RP, SA), interactive and confirmatory (IC)		
TS-L **& Pic-Spon**	**TS-**L**-Prom**	**Pic and TS-B Spon** **Pic and TS-**L**-Prom**
Letter/Sound: REC, NAM		
Print Concepts: *Exclamation point—Look, look, look!* LR, TB, CW, CL, COM, (PUN) 1-1		
D	**D Surprised by last page:** **"They're all the same!"**	**B**
High-Frequency Words: *New: look Review: at* REC (ID)		
look—**D** *at*—**P**	*Look*—**D** *at*—**P**	*look*—**B** *at*—**D**
Phonological Awareness: CR, IR, IA		
Vocabulary *photograph, magnify, vein* log—no one knew		
D	**D**	**D**
Comments/Notes for Next Session: Review meaning of log on reread. Excited about photographs—include more nonfiction. Max needs more modeling re use of key-word chart. Alex can't wait to get to the books! Independently checked ending sound.		

FIGURE 14.5. *(page 3 of 4)*

Child 1 *Alex*   Child 2 *Michaela*   Child 3 *Max*

5. Writing		
Writing Prompt or Dictated Sentence: *Look at the . . . —Model writing and then remove before the children write.*		
Letters/Sounds: *Sound spell word from book that starts with L* PR, LS, BS, ES, SV, L, VCe, DI, BL		
LEF	LDBG	LXO
Print Concepts: (LR, TB,) CW, CL, COM, PUN		
LR, TB-P	LR, TB-P	LR, TB-?
High-Frequency Words: *Remind re WWK chart ("Words We Know")* CP, CS		
used chart for MY		
Comments/Notes for Next Session: Alex and Michaela noticing beginning, middle, and end sounds—using key-word chart independently. Max attending to beginning sounds only: needs more work on Phonemic Analysis.		

6. High-Frequency Words		
Practice Plan: *Parking lot with HF words*		
Fast and accurate at finding words.	Loves this game; promised one for take home.	Needs to look at model to find words.

FIGURE 14.5. *(page 4 of 4)*

Segment 2: Phonological Analysis

Alex, Michaela, and Max have already spent time sorting pictures that rhyme and that have the same beginning sounds, and have done quite well with those activities. They are also able to use beginning sounds when figuring out printed words and when they attempt to write. At this point, Mrs. D's goal is to help them use the sounds at both the beginning and the end of words for these purposes. Today, she uses a quick picture-sorting activity as a way to help them attend to the ending sounds in words without having to also think about the letter that goes with that sound. She gives the children a purpose for what they are learning: "This is going to help us when we read. We've been looking at the beginning sounds and matching them with pictures, but sometimes we need to look all the way through to the end of the word to make sure that we know what the word is." Because these children already know most of the consonant sounds, Mrs. D will make the connection to letters in the next segment.

Segment 3: Letters and Sounds, Word Families, Alphabetic Mapping, Decoding

The picture sort done in the phonemic analysis segment of the lesson is followed by a brief review of the sound for the letter *L*, with Mrs. D modeling the use of the key-word chart to remind them that, if they need to, they can use the picture of the lamp to remember the sound for *L*. Mrs. D then tells the group: "When we read our new book today, there'll be a lot of words that start with *L*. So you'll need to use your *L* sound, /llll/, and check your picture, but you'll also need to check your ending sound too."

Because Mrs. D plans to focus more on letters and sounds, as well as phonemic analysis, in the writing portion of today's lesson, she uses the time prior to reading a new book to introduce a new decoding strategy. Therefore, this portion of the lesson is abbreviated to allow time for strategy discussion in preparation for the new book.

Segment 4: Reading a New Book

At this point, Alex and Michaela are consistently able to use the first letter in an unfamiliar word to help in word identification; Max is somewhat less consistent with this, but is showing progress. All three children are able to use pictures and contextual cues, and they have been learning to use these various cues in conjunction with one another. An important next step for them is to use both beginning and ending sounds for decoding, in conjunction with picture and contextual cues.

Before introducing a text in which she will assist the children in applying this new strategy, Mrs. D first teaches the strategy. She begins by reminding the children of what they already know how to do when they encounter a puzzling word ("You know you can look at the pictures, think about the beginning sound, and think of what would make sense"). She then explains: "Sometimes, you could try all of those things and you still won't be sure what the word is. So today we are going to learn another thing we can try. We're going to try looking at the ending sound in the puzzling word. Let me show you." The teacher displays a sentence strip with the sentence "I see the leaf." She knows that the first three words are part of the children's sight vocabularies. *Leaf* is the word that they will need to puzzle over. The group reads the sentence up to the word *leaf*, and the teacher says: "There are a lot of words that begin with *L*. So, to figure out a word, sometimes we need to think about the beginning sound *and* the ending sound. I have four pictures here of a lamp, a leaf, a lion, and a lamb. They all start with that /l/ sound. We need to decide which word comes at the end of this sentence. Could it be *lamp?* . . . *Leaf?* . . . *Lion?* . . . *Lamb?*" When the children decide that the puzzling word must be *leaf*, the teacher confirms and reflects with them on how knowing the ending sound "comes in handy" when they are figuring out words. This brief activity allows the teacher to keep the children's attention focused on the extension of the "think-about-the-sounds" strategy that, until now, only applied to the first sound for these children. Mrs. D uses these isolated activities, as needed, for introducing and extending word identification strategies, but her goal is to have the children apply what they learn about strategies within the context of books. She reminds the children that when they think about the sounds in words, they now know how to use the beginning sound and the ending sound and that they will get to do it in their new book today.

Mrs. D introduces the new book, *Look Closer* (Logan, 1997). This book features many words that begin with the letter *L* and will provide extra practice with this letter–sound association. Because so many of the words begin with the same letter, it also provides an opportunity for the children to begin using ending sounds as well as beginning sounds for figuring out words.

As part of her book introduction, Mrs. D introduces two new vocabulary words: *photograph* and *magnifying glass*. These words are not in the book, but they are useful in helping the children to understand how the book is designed. (Each set of opposing pages features a photograph of an object in nature, such as a leaf, and then a close-up view of the same object, as seen through a magnifying glass.) She also introduces the new high-frequency word *look* and reviews the words *at* and *the* on the word wall. Because there are only a few unfamiliar words in this book and because she thinks the pictures are sufficiently supportive, Mrs. D chooses not to do a picture walk; she wants to provide the children with the opportunity to use the strategies they are learning for figuring out the new words as they occur.

After the book introduction, Mrs. D gives each child a book and reminds them all to "use your finger" to point to the words as they read. All three children stop at the word *log* on the first page after reading "Look at the. . . . " The teacher asks them, "What are you going to do to figure that word out?" and then prompts with a specific strategy, "Why don't you make your beginning sound first."

When Alex says the word *land* instead of *log*, Mrs. D responds by first pointing out all the things he did right: "Does *land* begin with *l*?" and "Is the picture showing land?" Then she suggests that it might not be the right word, saying "What does *land* end with?" as she emphasizes the /d/ sound. "So, that was a good thought, but we want a word that ends with *g*. What does *g* say?" After a bit of time, it becomes clear that the children do not have the word *log* in their spoken vocabulary, so she tells them the word and then gives a child-friendly explanation of what a log is, being sure to have them repeat the word after her. Having established the label for the picture, she returns to her systematic means of having them think about the sounds in the word: "Does *log* begin with *l*? Does *log* end with *g*? And this is a picture of a *log*. . . . "

This back-and-forth between meaning and print is seen on several occasions, as Mrs. D explains how the magnifying camera works and compares the veins in the leaf to the veins in the children's own wrists. Importantly, she draws their attention to the sounds in the word even when they are correct, reinforcing the problem solving they have done. "Could that word be *ladybug*? How do you know?" When the children respond that *ladybug* "starts with l and ends with g," she encourages them to also think about the picture by asking, "And does that look like a ladybug?"

On the last page of the book, Mrs. D draws their attention to the exclamation mark at the end of the sentence and models reading "like you're excited." She also takes the opportunity provided by the photographs on the last page to remind the children of the meaning of the word *log*. As they find the picture of the log on the page, she describes it again: "It's that big piece of a tree that's fallen down in the woods."

Segment 5: Writing

Mrs. D has planned two separate but related writing activities for today. First she asks each of the children in the group to think of one thing that was photographed in the book they just read that begins with the letter *L* (using the word *photographed* purposefully to reinforce its meaning for the children). She asks the children to keep the word they are thinking a secret, and she gives each of them a sticky note on which to write their word, using sound spelling. She encourages them to think about beginning, middle, and ending sounds and tells them that she will use the clues from their sound spelling to figure out which word from the story they have written.

After figuring out the word each child wrote—LEF, *leaf*; LTBG, *ladybug*; and LXO *leaf*—Mrs. D shows each of the children the "book spelling" for their words. As she writes the book spelling on the sticky notes underneath the words the children have written, she is careful to point out the places where the two spellings match. It is important to note here that, on many occasions, Mrs. D would have figured out the children's words and complimented them on their sound spelling but would not have shown them the book spellings. However, she shows the book spelling on this occasion because she is going to have the children write the words in their personal alphabet books, and she wants these permanent representations of the words to be spelled conventionally.

Finally, Mrs. D models the sentence that they are going to write in their books, explicitly engaging the children in conversation about important print concepts (e.g., "I am going to start writing up in this corner of the paper"; "I don't have room to finish my sentence here—what should I do?"; "I need to be sure to put a period at the end of my sentence") and the use of instructional resources (e.g., "If I can't remember how to spell the word *the*, what can I do?"). Each sentence will begin the same—"Look at the . . . "—and end with the child's own word from the sticky note. Mrs. D then gives each of the children their personal alphabet book that they have been working on throughout the year. When they finish writing, each child chooses a picture that matches their *L* word and glues it on the page with the sentence. They will take this alphabet book home at the end of the school year and will be encouraged to share it with their families and to continue to add to it over the summer.

Segment 6: High-Frequency Words

In the last few minutes of the lesson, the children play a parking lot game that includes some of the high-frequency words they have learned so far. Most of the words are those that have recently been introduced, including the day's new word, *look*.

Reflection on the Group

As is evident in Figure 14.5, Max is at a different point in development than the other two children in the group. The intervention teacher and the classroom teacher are both concerned that he has not made the kind of accelerated progress needed to close the gap between himself and his classmates. Alex and Michaela, on the other hand, are beginning to demonstrate the skills and strategies that are expected of kindergartners in their school at the end of the year. Because the group is not currently well matched in terms of the instructional needs of the children, the teachers and administrators involved in the school's early intervention program plan to meet in the near future to consider the most reasonable course of action. Given that there are 6 weeks of school remaining, they will consider several possibilities. The first consideration will be to regroup the children, putting Alex and Michaela in a group with one or more children who have similar skills and Max in a different group with one or two other children who are at similar points in development. Ideally this group would have more sessions than the two per week currently offered, as there is a clear need to intensify instruction if Max and similar children are going to begin to approach end-of-the-year expectations. An alternative might be to discontinue Alex's and Michaela's involvement in Tier 2 thereby allowing the intervention teacher to provide Max with one-to-one intervention for the remainder of the year. The teachers will also work with Max's family to insure that he will attend the district's summer literacy program. Unless dramatic changes are noted during the rest of the school year or during the summer, Max will likely qualify for Tier 3 intervention in the fall.

INTENSIFYING INSTRUCTION: ONE-TO-ONE INTERVENTION

The goals and procedures described for small-group instruction are very similar to the goals and procedures utilized in a one-to-one instructional situation. The major difference between small-group and one-to-one is the intensity of the instruction and the degree to which the lesson can be responsive to the individual child. For ongoing record keeping the teacher might utilize the group snapshot forms, tracking only one child on that form. The Daily Lesson Sheet used in the ISA, however is a bit more detailed than the small group lesson sheet. Figure 14.6 provides a slightly revised version of the lesson sheet used for one-to-one instruction in our most recent intervention study. The segment numbers align with the segments as discussed for the small group lesson described above. The major differences between small group and one-to-one instruction related to lesson planning and documentation are described below. The most important difference for the child is, of course, that he has vastly increased opportunities to respond and to receive explicit guidance and feedback.

Segment 1: Rereading

The lesson sheet provides room for the teacher to plan and record observations for two books in both Segments 1 and 4. Although it is not always the case that two books would be read in each segment, it is often possible to do so, especially when the child is still reading emergent-level books that tend to be quite short. In the rereading segment, for each book there is space for the teacher to record what, if anything, she plans to review with the child before he rereads a book. The review could focus on one or more strategies, high-frequency words, decoding elements, aspects of story structure, etc. The strategies section in both Segments 1 and 4 provides space for the teacher to record her observations of the child's strategy use while reading. The codes for noting strategies are provided in the text box at the bottom of both Segments 1 and 4. Teachers are encouraged to note the strategies that the child uses spontaneously (e.g., DP-Spon) and the strategies that the teacher prompts (e.g., BW-Prom). Teachers are not expected to note strategies that the child

(text continues on p. 342)

LESSON SHEET

Name _____ Date _____ Session # _____

1. Rereading	
Text/Level:	Text/Level:
Review:	Review:
Strategies: Spontaneous (Spon)/Prompted (Prom)	Strategies: Spontaneous (Spon)/Prompted (Prom)
Important words missed:	Important words missed:
Fluency: WBW—word by word Phr—Phrasing Fl—fluent	Fluency: WBW—word by word Phr—Phrasing Fl—fluent
Comments/Notes for Next Session:	

TS—think sounds	WP—word part	CP—check pictures	SA—start again
DP—different pronunciation	BW—break word	MS—make sense	RP—read past

2. Phonological Awareness	
Sound Sorting RH, BEG, END, MID	STRETCH??
Sound Blending Onset–Rime, Single Phonemes w/Pics, w/o Pics	STRETCH??
Sound Counting/Segmentation 2 Phonemes, 3 Phonemes	STRETCH??
	Level of success:

3. Letters and Sounds, Alphabetic Mapping, Word Families, Decoding	
Letter Names: REC, NAM, PR Letter Sounds: CS-B, CS-E Other Decoding Elements	 Level of success:
Alphabetic Mapping: Units/Decoding Principles	
Word Building:	Level of Success:
Word Reading:	Level of Success:
Writing:	Level of Success:
Comments/Notes for Next Session:	
Level of Success: B—beginning D—developing P—proficient	

FIGURE 14.6. One-to-one daily lesson sheet. *(page 1 of 2)*

4. Reading				
Text/Level:			Text/Level:	
Prereading activities:			Prereading activities:	
High-Frequency Words:			High-Frequency Words:	
Word Identification Strategies	Comprehension		Word Identification Strategies	Comprehension
Planned focus:			Planned focus:	
Observed use:			Observed use:	
Important words missed:			Important words missed:	
Fluency: WBW—word by word Phr—Phrasing Fl—fluent			Fluency: WBW—word by word Phr—Phrasing Fl—fluent	
Reading Log Entry:			Reading Log Entry:	
Comments/Notes for Next Session:				

TS—think sounds	WP—word part	CP—check pictures	SA—start again
DP—different pronunciation	BW—break word	MS—make sense	RP—read past

5. Writing
Writing Prompt or Dictated Sentence(s)
Notes/Comments for Next Session:

6. High-Frequency Words
Practice Activity:
Words **added** to "Words I Know" chart:
Words **missed** on "Words I Know" chart:
Comments/Notes for Next Session:

FIGURE 14.6. *(page 2 of 2)*

routinely employs (as would be evident on his snapshot for word identification strategies). Rather, the teacher notes emerging and developing strategies. There is also a place for the teacher to note important words that the child misreads, so that she can consider addressing those words in either Segment 5 of the current lesson or in upcoming lessons. In this context an important word is a high-frequency word that the teacher thought was part of the child's sight vocabulary. There is also a section for noting the degree of fluency for each book. Fluency determinations are based primarily on consideration of prosody, which includes phrasing and intonation. Books that a child reads accurately and fluently (i.e., sounds like a storyteller) would not typically be offered for rereading in upcoming lessons because they offer no opportunity for teaching or supporting the child's developing skills and strategies. Few, if any, books should be read in a word-by-word fashion in the context of a one-to-one lesson, so this code is rarely used. However, it is left on the lesson sheet as a reminder to teachers that, if they use the code often, they need to make adjustments to the books they are offering and/or to the preparation they are doing for those books.

Segment 2: Phonological Awareness

Instruction and record keeping for this segment of the lesson are similar to what was described for the small group. The major difference, of course, is that what is done in this segment should fit the child's current skills fairly precisely.

Segment 3: Letters and Sounds, Alphabetic Mapping, Word Families, Decoding

For Segment 3, instruction and record keeping are quite similar to what was described for Segment 3 of the group lesson. New skills taught in this segment are skills that can be applied in the book(s) that will be read in the next segment. The new skills are practiced in combination with previously taught skills. Further, to provide more individualized support, a word family chart is developed for each child. Based on earlier instruction and practice, the chart contains the word families that the teacher expects the child to know and to be able to use effectively in his reading and writing (see Chapter 9).

Segment 4: Reading

This segment of the lesson sheet looks quite different from the parallel segment for the small-group lesson. The different look is due primarily to an effort to save paper rather than to any shift in focus. For the reading segment, the teacher would note plans for introducing and preparing the child to read each book. The prereading activities section would include notations concerning the book introduction and any words for which the child may not know the meaning. The high-frequency words section is used to record words that are taught in preparation for reading the book. The next section provides space for the teacher to note the word identification strategies she plans to teach and to note what she plans to do to support comprehension. Just below the *planned focus* area is a space for the teacher to record her observations related to strategy use and comprehension. The *important words missed* and *fluency* sections were described in Segment 1, above. The *reading log entry* section is an optional component that is used if the child seems motivated to keep a list of books that he has read and to make comments on those books. If this approach appeals to the child, the reading log entry is often used to fulfill the writing component of the lesson.

Segment 5: Writing

The writing segment has the same purposes in the one-to-one context as it does in the small-group context. However, because the teacher is focused exclusively on one child, she can more effectively identify and address the child's needs and interests. In particular, the teacher can be flexible with regard to the type of writing that the child does, based on his preferences. For example, some chatty children are eager to share out-of-school experiences with the teacher; the teacher might channel that energy by asking the child to write about the experience. Alternatively, the teacher might prompt the child to write about something that was discussed while reading the new book for the day. In order to ensure that what the child writes provides the desired opportunities to apply developing skills and strategies, the teacher should always be prepared with a writing prompt or a sentence to dictate. If a better and more motivating alternative emerges during the course of a lesson, teachers are encouraged to utilize it.

Segment 6: High-Frequency Words

This segment of a one-to-one lesson is used to both provide practice on high-frequency words that were previously introduced and to document the child's progress. Important words missed during the course of reading the day's books might be incorporated into practice activities. Various games are used to practice previously taught high-frequency words. The Your Pile/My Pile game (see Chapter 11, p. 244) is used to practice and assess the child's knowledge of high-frequency words and to make a determination of which words should be placed on the individual's "Words I Know" chart. Words on this chart are expected to be identified automatically when encountered in context and to be spelled conventionally when the child writes. Conventional spelling should be supported by reference to the chart or to the classroom word wall.

CHAPTER 15

A Proposed Model for Multi-Tiered Intervention

In this chapter we describe a proposed model for implementing RTI across classroom, small-group, and one-to-one settings. As becomes evident, the model we propose is not highly prescriptive. It leaves schools/districts with many decisions to make with regard to assessments, criteria for including children in the at-risk group, criteria for moving children between and among the tiers of intervention, when to begin various tiers of intervention, how long a child might remain at a given tier before her need for intervention is reconsidered, etc. We are vague on these issues largely because, to date, there is too little research on them to allow confident recommendations.

The model we propose begins early in the kindergarten year and follows children through the end of first grade, at least. One major reason for beginning intervention efforts in the early primary grades is to address the initial gaps in knowledge and skills while they are relatively small and more amenable to instructional interventions. Another major reason is that we hope to prevent children from identifying reading and writing as activities that are too challenging for them.

KINDERGARTEN

• *Identification of children who are at risk.* Beginning at kindergarten entry, children would be assessed on a measure of early literacy skill, and those who score below a designated benchmark or cut point would be identified as being at increased risk of experiencing literacy learning difficulties. In our research we have typically used a cutoff of the 25th or 30th percentile on a normative measure of early literacy skill to identify risk status and have found that the vast majority of children who eventually demonstrate reading difficulties are picked up using this criterion (Scanlon et al., 2008). In fact, when both enhanced classroom instruction and small-group intervention beyond the classroom are in place, we have found that this criterion picks up all but about 1% of the children who will qualify as poor readers in first grade (Scanlon et al., 2008). We used the Phonological Awareness Literacy Screening (PALS; Invernizzi, Meier, & Juel, 2003–2007) in our most recent study. However, we have no reason to believe that the PALS would be any more or less sensitive than other measures of early literacy skill that provide benchmarks or norms (e.g., Dynamic Indicators of Basic Early Literacy Skills [DIBELS]—Good, Kaminski, Smith, Laimon, & Dill, 2001; Texas Primary Reading Inventory [TPRI]—Foorman, Fletcher, & Francis, 2004). We would recommend, however, that more comprehensive measures such as the PALS or the TPRI be used because, in addition to providing information on which children should be considered to be at risk, they also provide more information on what the children can and cannot do and thus preliminarily guide instructional planning.

It is important to note that scoring below the cutoff and qualifying for the at-risk group *does not* mean that a child *will* have difficulty with literacy acquisition. Rather it simply means that she is more likely to experience some difficulty than is a child who scores above the cutoff. Indeed, for children below the cutoff, instruction plays a particularly powerful role in determining literacy outcomes (that is, after all, the whole point of RTI approaches). Thus, for children who qualify as at risk, efforts would be instituted to accelerate their progress (i.e., increase their rate of progress) and thus to prevent them from experiencing long-term reading difficulties.

Children who do not qualify as being at risk on screening measures administered at the beginning of kindergarten would be assessed at least twice more during their kindergarten year to ensure that they are making the needed progress to maintain their "not-at-risk" status.

• *Adjustment of instruction at the classroom level for all children but especially those at risk (Tier 1).* The intervention component of an RTI process begins with more focused instruction provided by the classroom teacher. Instructional modifications would be most evident for at-risk children during the small-group instruction that is provided in the classroom. When possible, small-group literacy instruction for these children should be provided in smaller instructional groups and/or more frequently than for the children who do not qualify as being at risk. For example, the classroom teacher might meet with at-risk children in a small-group context every day of the week, while meeting with groups who are not at risk somewhat less frequently. The focus in the small-group context should be on preparing the children to more readily profit from the classroom language arts curriculum. Thus, in our proposed model, intervention does not involve a distinctly different program. Rather, it involves the teacher in determining what knowledge and skills the children in the at-risk group need to acquire to meet grade-level expectations and providing instruction that will help them develop those skills.

• *Periodic assessment of literacy skills for the children in the at-risk group to facilitate decision making regarding adjustments in instruction.* Assessment and instruction are integrally related activities. In order for instruction to be optimally effective, at any level, the instructor first needs to identify what the students already know and then plan and deliver instruction with the children's current knowledge in mind. We encourage the use of both formal and informal assessment methods. In kindergarten and for children with very limited early literacy skills, formal measures involve specific assessments of foundational literacy skills, such as letter-name knowledge and skill in phonemic analysis. For more advanced readers, formal assessment would test the children's ability to accurately read and comprehend text. Informal assessments involve teacher observations that occur during the course of instruction. We encourage teachers to make note of children's skills, abilities, strategies, and attitudes through the use of checklists (e.g., the snapshots described in earlier chapters) and anecdotal notes. Teachers should use information gleaned from both formal and informal assessments, in combination with their knowledge of the curriculum in use in the classroom and the instructional goals detailed in previous chapters to formulate instructional plans that are appropriate for all children.

In addition, formal assessment data often play an important role in the context of RTI in guiding decisions about the intensity of instruction that the children in the at-risk group need in order to accelerate their progress. Thus, for example, a child who demonstrates limited improvement in early literacy skills needs additional instructional support (more intensive intervention), whereas a child who shows greater gains may be reasonably continued at the current level of support, and a child who shows dramatic gains may no longer need the extra support she is receiving. The last few sentences suggest that decision making relating to the need for intervention is fairly straightforward. However, making such decisions can be difficult and controversial. Reading is a complex process, and children react to instruction in very different ways. Assessments often do not sufficiently account for the complexity of the process or for the differences among children. Thus, there is considerable debate about which aspects of the reading process should be assessed in the context of RTI, what sort of growth might be expected, how much acceleration in reading skills is sufficient, and so forth. Further, there is substantial controversy over some of the assessment tools commonly recommended (see Paris, 2005; Pearson, 2006; Scanlon, 2010). In our research we have typically relied on more comprehensive measures, administering them three or four times per year, and have used more informal measures to guide instructional decision making and planning. However, many RTI models call for frequent progress monitoring using tools that are more standardized but less comprehensive. To date, there is no definitive research guidance on the advantages of conducting frequent, formal progress monitoring (Gersten et al., 2008). There is still a great deal that needs to be learned about how to make appropriate decisions regarding instructional intensity.

• *Adjustment in instructional intensity (Tier 2).* As noted above, children in the at-risk group who make limited gains when provided with Tier 1 intervention alone need additional support (i.e., a second tier of intervention). Ideally, Tier 2 intervention would be provided in a very small-group setting (no more than three or four children) and by a teacher who has expertise in early literacy intervention. In our proposed model, Tier 2 intervention, like intervention at Tier 1, should support children in their classroom curriculum. However, because the instructional group is smaller at Tier 2 and because the teacher providing the intervention should have a high level of expertise, it is assumed that the teacher would be able to tailor instruction to more effectively meet the needs of the children in the group. The combination of the simultaneous implementation of the two tiers of intervention and the better match between what is taught and what the children are ready to learn is intended to accelerate the progress of children who find learning to read difficult. As discussed in Chapter 14, in general, small-group instruction offered at Tiers 1 and 2 would look quite similar because intervention in both settings is driven by the same set of goals and is designed to respond to what the children know and are able to do. The main difference between the two tiers would be the level of intensity (group size) and, perhaps, the expertise of the teacher. Another consideration with regard to intensification is the number of Tier 2 intervention sessions that would be offered per week. Here again, no research speaks directly to this question. In our studies, Tier 2 intervention for kindergartners was offered twice per week, approximately 30 minutes each, beginning in mid-October and continuing through May. This program typically amounted to about 50 intervention sessions across the year. Thus, the children received approximately 25 hours of instruction beyond what they received in the classroom. With just this relatively limited intervention effort, we found that the number of children who qualified for intervention in first grade was reduced by approximately 50% (Scanlon et al., 2008). We do not know whether more sessions or more concentrated sessions (e.g., four or five per week for a shorter period of time) would have been more effective.

In the model we propose, most at-risk kindergartners would not move beyond the second tier of intervention during their kindergarten year. However, we have encountered a very small number of children who made such limited progress with a combination of Tier 1 and Tier 2 intervention that it was not possible to effectively include them in the small-group instructional context either in or beyond the classroom. They were not accelerating their learning at the same rate as the other group members and were not ready to learn what the other children in the classroom and intervention groups were prepared to learn. For such children, a more intensive (Tier 3) instructional setting is likely to be the most appropriate context for attempting to increase their rate of progress.

Timing the Tiers

In many RTI models children are provided with a period of Tier 1 only, with Tier 2 intervention initiated for those children who do not make accelerated gains with Tier 1 alone. As an alternative, both Tier 1 and Tier 2 interventions could be initiated early in the school year in hopes of closing the gap between the at-risk children and their peers more quickly. To our knowledge, there is no research that has systematically compared the relative value of simultaneous versus incremental initiation of the first two tiers of intervention. However, while the advice most often offered to schools advocates for a period of classroom instruction only (e.g., Brown-Chidsey & Steege, 2005; Mellard & Johnson, 2008), we are swayed by an argument recently made by Dorn and Shubert (2008) that "interventions should be grounded in a sense of urgency" (p. 31) because the sooner that children have the knowledge and skills that the classroom curriculum requires, the sooner they will be able to profit more fully from classroom instruction. In fact, this logic guided our thinking in our studies of the effects of kindergarten intervention, in which we provided small-group interventions for at-risk kindergartners in addition to their classroom language arts program, beginning approximately 6 weeks into their kindergarten year (Scanlon et al., 2005, 2008). Starting even earlier and/or providing Tier 2 interventions more frequently may have been even more effective. Clearly there is much yet to be learned about the costs and benefits of beginning interventions at different points in children's educational development.

FIRST GRADE

At the beginning of first grade, an assessment of early literacy skills would be administered to all children and, as is the case at the kindergarten level, children who score in the at-risk range would participate in the RTI process. Children in this group would be treated differently depending on their instructional history, as described below. Children who do not score in the at-risk range should be assessed at least two or three more times during the remainder of the school year to ensure that they are making the necessary progress to maintain their "not-at-risk" status. If they qualify as being at risk at any point in the school year, they would be included in at least the first tier of intervention.

   • *Children who participated in Tier 1 and Tier 2 intervention in kindergarten.* The purpose of providing interventions in kindergarten is to reduce the number of children who experience literacy learning difficulties. If instruction at Tiers 1 and 2 in kindergarten is effective, most children will show accelerated progress and may not need additional tiers of intervention. Some children will, however, continue to need support beyond what is typically offered at Tiers 1 and 2.

Ineffective Intervention

If many of the children who participated in both Tier 1 and Tier 2 intervention in kindergarten continue to score in the at-risk range at the end of kindergarten, it is likely that the interventions that were offered were not as effective as they need to be. To prevent a recurrence of such outcomes, efforts should be made to enhance the effectiveness of the intervention. A number of factors could account for the children's limited progress. Consideration should be given to improving the effectiveness of intervention through such areas as providing (more) professional development for the teachers who were unable to promote accelerated progress, selecting different instructional materials, adjusting schedules, and the like.

• *Children who demonstrated very limited progress in kindergarten, despite receiving intervention that was effective for most children.* In many RTI models, children who do not respond to a combination of Tier 1 and Tier 2 intervention would come under consideration for identification as learning disabled. However, we consider intensive one-to-one intervention to be a critical step *before* any consideration is given to possible classification because we have found that many children who do not show adequate progress in the context of Tiers 1 and 2 interventions do make strong gains when provided with more intensive intervention (Tier 3). In fact, many children who receive Tier 3 intervention go on to make adequate progress in literacy development in subsequent years of schooling (Vellutino, Scanlon, Zhang, & Schatschneider, 2008).[1] Tier 3 intervention has the potential to be more powerful than Tiers 1 and 2 because the teacher has the opportunity to plan instruction to meet the needs of the individual child. Further, because she is working with only one child at a time, the teacher is able to provide a great deal more explicit guidance and feedback and to more effectively attend to the child's strengths and points of confusion as instruction unfolds. Further, the child is likely to be a much more engaged participant. Tier 3 intervention should be as intensive as possible. Ideally, children at Tier 3 would received 30 minutes of one-to-one instruction *per day* from a teacher who has expertise in early literacy instruction. The duration of one-to-one instruction should be determined by the child's progress. Those who make rapids gains and attain average or better performance levels

---

[1] We found that children who met grade-level expectations when provided with intensive intervention but who then went on to make slow progress in subsequent grades tended to be concentrated in schools. Thus, in some schools, virtually all of the children who showed strong gains in intensive intervention continued to make adequate progress through third and fourth grades. In other schools, over half of the children lost ground after intervention was discontinued. Such a pattern clearly suggests that the instruction the children received in second grade and beyond was a determining factor in their postintervention progress. Unfortunately, because of the design of the study, we do not know whether the differences between schools are attributable to instruction offered in the classroom or in remedial settings.

would be discontinued from Tier 3 in order to open their slot for other students. However, the progress these children make should be closely monitored, and consideration should be given to including them in less intensive tiers of intervention until it is clear that they are able to maintain their growth without more intensive support.

• *Children who demonstrated progress with a combination of Tier 1 and Tier 2 interventions in kindergarten but who do not quite meet grade-level expectations at the beginning of first grade.* Children who demonstrated their ability to make gains in the context of Tier 1 and Tier 2 interventions in kindergarten but who nevertheless qualify as being at risk in first grade might be offered a period of Tier 1 plus Tier 2 interventions in first grade in hopes that such a level of intensity will be sufficient to help them catch up to the expected performance levels. If, however, staffing patterns and funding allow for these children to be served in the context of a Tier 3 intervention, it is likely that they would show greater acceleration and could ultimately move out of the at-risk group.

• *Children who were never considered to be at risk in kindergarten but who score in the at-risk range at the beginning of first grade.* For a variety of reasons, some children might fit this profile, including that they were always close to the boundary between qualifying and not qualifying, that their kindergarten literacy instruction was inadequate, that they had little or no engagement in literacy activities during the summer between kindergarten and first grade, and so on. Depending on their history, children who fit this description may be best served either by a period of Tier 1 only or by a combination of Tier 1 and Tier 2 interventions because it has not yet been demonstrated that these less intensive intervention efforts are ineffective for them.

• *Children who are new to the school and who score in the at-risk range at the beginning of first grade.* If the school has little knowledge of a child's instructional history and therefore cannot determine whether the child had adequate instruction and intervention in kindergarten, it may be most appropriate to begin by providing a combination of Tier 1 and Tier 2 interventions—unless, of course, staffing patterns allow for a more intensive form of intervention to be initiated at the beginning of the school year.

• *Movement through the tiers in first grade.* The general pattern depicted above for the children who qualify as at risk in first grade is that, if Tier 1 and Tier 2 interventions have already proven to be ineffective for them, then they should have high priority for access to Tier 3 (intensive one-to-one) instruction. Tier 3 instruction for these children should begin as soon as possible at the beginning of the first grade year. If, on the other hand, a child has been fairly responsive to either Tier 1 alone or to a combination of Tiers 1 and 2 in the past, continuing that child in that same format may be sufficient to accelerate her progress. Further, in the case of a child for whom the instructional history is unknown, beginning with less intensive forms of intervention may be the most appropriate first step—if, of course, the child has sufficient early literacy skills to work effectively in a small group. As the school year progresses, at-risk children who began in less intensive tiers of intervention should be offered more intensive levels of intervention if they make limited progress. Because many of the children who receive Tier 3 intervention at the beginning of first grade make enough progress that they no longer need such intensity by 10 or 15 weeks into the school year, the intervention "slots" that they occupied will become available for children who do not make sufficient progress at Tiers 1 and 2.

• *Ongoing assessment of progress for purposes of instructional planning and decision making in first grade.* As was true at the kindergarten level, ongoing progress monitoring, both formal and informal, should be continued for the children in the at-risk group throughout first grade for the purpose of planning instruction and determining what level of intervention the children need to support their progress toward meeting grade level expectations by the end of the school year.

SECOND GRADE AND BEYOND

While this book focuses primarily on a kindergarten and first-grade RTI process, there inevitably are children who reach second grade, or further, who have not had the benefit of effective interventions to help them overcome early literacy difficulties either because they were in schools that did not have intervention programs in place or because the interventions they received were not responsive and flexible enough to meet their needs. For children with this background, the sense of urgency to accelerate their literacy development deepens even further. A period of Tier 1 only or even Tier 1 plus Tier 2 intervention is probably *not* in the best interest of the child. Rather, intensive Tier 3 intervention, in combination with appropriate classroom intervention (Tier 1), is probably most appropriate. As noted earlier, in an effective RTI model, children are provided with effective interventions, at appropriate levels of intensity, before consideration is given to the possibility of identifying them as being in need of long-term instructional support in the form of special education. There is emerging evidence that intensive intervention for older struggling readers can lead to accelerated progress (e.g., Battacharya & Ehri, 2004; Gelzheiser et al., 2009; Lovett et al., 2008; Torgesen et al., 2001). It is important to note that, in these studies, intensive intervention was provided *after* the children were identified as being learning disabled. The fact that the students demonstrated accelerated growth when provided with intervention and that their instructional experiences generally predated the institution of RTI processes strongly suggests that most would have avoided the classification had an appropriately effective and intensive intervention been available to them early in their educational history.

• *Instruction for children who do not accelerate in the context of an RTI process.* The goal of instruction within an RTI process is to accelerate children's progress in such a way that they are able to meet or at least approach grade-level expectations. Proponents of RTI processes generally argue that, if a child has participated in several tiers of otherwise effective classroom and beyond-the-classroom intervention and does not demonstrate adequate progress, that child is likely to need longer-term instructional support than what is offered in the RTI process. Currently the only vehicle available for providing such long-term support in most American schools is the special education system. In our model of RTI, special education, which requires that the child be identified as learning disabled, would serve as a fourth tier of intervention. If the first three tiers of intervention are as effective as we believe they can be, very few children should need this additional tier. While children who are identified as learning disabled, particularly as they move up in grades, will likely require a variety of instructional supports in order to benefit from their classroom program, *acceleration* of their progress in the *acquisition* of literacy skills should remain an important goal of reading instruction.

A FINAL WORD ON ASSESSMENT

We have consciously skirted the "formal" assessment issue that looms so large in the minds of many who are involved in the planning and implementation of RTI procedures. Documenting student growth and change over time is considered to be a central issue in RTI because it is typically the basis upon which decisions are made concerning the amount and type of intervention a student should receive and whether or not a student should be discontinued from intervention or considered for special education classification. Because this text focuses on intervention and because, in our minds, there is a need for more research regarding the value and place of various assessment procedures in RTI implementations, we have elected to remain fairly silent on the issue. A discussion of concerns over assessment approaches can be found in Scanlon (in press).

References

Adams, M. J. (1990). *Beginning to read: Thinking and learning about print.* Cambridge, MA: MIT Press.

Adams, M. J., Foorman, B. R., Lundberg, I., & Beeler, T. (1998). *Phonemic awareness in young children.* Baltimore: Brookes.

Allington, R. L. (2009). *What really matters in response to intervention.* Boston: Pearson.

Almasi, J. F. (2003). *Teaching strategic processes in reading.* New York: Guilford Press.

American Heritage Children's Dictionary. (2003). New York: Houghton-Mifflin.

Anderson, K. L. (2009). *The effects of professional development on early reading skills: A comparison of two approaches.* (Doctoral dissertation). Retrieved from ProQuest (ATT 3365837)

Anderson, K. L. (2010). Spotlight on the Interactive Strategies Approach: The case of Roosevelt Elementary School. In M. Y. Lipson & K. K. Wixson (Eds.), *Models for Response to Intervention (RTI): Evidence-based frameworks for preventing reading difficulties.* International Reading Association.

Anderson, R. C. (1984). The role of readers' schema in comprehension, learning, and memory. In R. C. Anderson, J. Osbourne, & R. Tierney (Eds.), *Learning to read in American schools: Basal readers and content texts* (pp. 243–257). Hillsdale, NJ: Erlbaum.

Anderson, R. C., Chinn, C., Waggoner, M., & Nguyen, K. (1998). Intellectually stimulating story discussions. In J. Osborn & F. Lehr (Eds.), *Literacy for all: Issues in teaching and learning* (pp. 170–186). New York: Guilford Press.

Anderson, R. C., & Pearson, P. D. (1984). A schema-theoretic view of basic processes in reading. In P. D. Pearson (Ed.), *Handbook of reading research* (pp. 255–291). New York: Longman.

Baker, L., & Beall, L. C. (2009). Metacognitive processes and reading comprehension. In S. E. D. Israel (Ed.), *Handbook of research on reading comprehension* (pp. 373–388). New York: Routledge.

Ball, E., & Blachman, B. (1991). Does phoneme awareness training in kindergarten make a difference in early word recognition and developmental spelling? *Reading Research Quarterly, 26*(1), 49–66.

Bandura, A. (1997). *Self-efficacy: The exercise of control.* New York: Freeman.

Battacharya, A., & Ehri, L. C. (2004). Graphosyllabic analysis helps adolescent struggling readers read and spell words. *Journal of Learning Disabilities, 37*(4), 331–348.

Bear, D. R., Invernizzi, M., Templeton, S., & Johnston, F. (2008). *Words their way: Word study for phonics, vocabulary, and spelling instruction* (4th ed.). Upper Saddle River, NJ: Prentice-Hall.

Beaver, J. (2006). *Developmental Reading Assessment Resource Guide 2.* Glenview, IL: Celebration Press.

Beck, I. L., & McKeown, M. G. (2001). Text talk: Capturing the benefits of read-aloud experiences for young children. *The Reading Teacher, 55*, 10–20.

Beck, I. L., & McKeown, M. G. (2007). Increasing young low-income children's oral vocabulary repertoires through rich and focused instruction. *Elementary School Journal, 107*(3), 251–271.

Beck, I. L., McKeown, M. G., & Kucan, L. (2002). *Bringing words to life: Robust vocabulary instruction.* New York: Guilford Press.

Betts, E. A. (1946). *Foundations of reading instruction.* New York: American Books.

Biemiller, A. (2006). Vocabulary development and instruction: A prerequisite for school learning. In S. B. Neuman & D. K. Dickenson (Eds.), *Handbook of early literacy research* (Vol. 2, pp. 29–40). New York: Guilford Press.

Biemiller, A., & Boote, C. (2006). An effective method for building meaning vocabulary in primary grades. *Journal of Educational Psychology, 98*(1), 44–62.

Blachman, B. A. (1991). Early intervention for children's reading problems: Clinical applications of the research in phonological awareness. *Topics in Language Disorders, 12*, 51–65.

Blachman, B. A., Ball, E. W., Black, R., & Tangel, D. M. (1994). Kindergarten teachers develop phoneme awareness in low-income, inner-city classrooms: Does it make a difference? *Reading and Writing: An Interdisciplinary Journal, 6*, 1–18.

Block, C. C., & Mangieri, J. N. (2003). *Exemplary literacy teachers: Promoting success for all children in grades K–5.* New York: Guilford Press.

Bloom, P. (2000). *How children learn the meanings of words.* Cambridge, MA: MIT Press.

Bond, G. L., & Dykstra, R. (1967). The cooperative research program in first-grade reading instruction. *Reading Research Quarterly, 2*, 5–142.

Borman, G. D., Wong, K. K., Hedges, L. V., & D'Agostino, J. V. (2001). Coordinating categorical and regular programs: Effects on Title I students' educational opportunities and outcomes. In G. D. Borman, S. C. Stringfield & R. E. Slavin (Eds.), *Title I: Compensatory education at the crossroads* (pp. 79–116). Mahwah, NJ: Erlbaum.

Bradley, L., & Bryant, P. (1991). Phonological skills before and after learning to read. In S. A. Brady & D. P. Shankweiler (Eds.), *Phonological processes in literacy: A tribute to Isabelle Y. Liberman* (pp. 37–45). Hillsdale, NJ: Erlbaum.

Brady, S. A., Shankweiler, D., & Mann, V. (1983). Speech perception and memory coding in relation to reading ability. *Journal of Experimental Child Psychology, 35*, 346–367.

Bransford, J. D., & Johnson M. (1972). Contextual prerequisites for understanding: Some investigations of comprehension and recall. *Journal of Verbal Learning and Behavior, 11*(6), 717–726.

Brown, R., Pressley, M., Van Meter, P., & Schuder, T. (1996). A quasi-experimental validation of transactional strategies instruction with low-achieving second graders. *Journal of Educational Psychology, 88*, 18–37.

Brown, W., Denton, E., Kelly, L., Outhred, L., & McNaught, M. (1999). RRs effectiveness: A five-year success story in San Louis Coastal Unified School District. *ERS Spectrum, 11* 3–10.

Brown-Chidsey, R., & Steege, M. W. (2005). *Response to intervention: Principles and strategies for effective practice.* New York: Guilford Press.

Bryant, P. E., MacLean, M., Bradley, L. L., & Crossland, J. (1990). Rhyme and alliteration, phoneme detection, and learning to read. *Developmental Psychology, 26,* 429–438.

Burgess, S. R. (2006). The development of phonological sensitivity. In D. K. Dickinson & S. B. Neuman (Eds.), *Handbook of early literacy research* (Vol. 2, pp. 90–100). New York: Guilford Press.

Cain, K., & Oakhill, J. (1999). Inference ability and its relation to comprehension failure in young children. *Reading and Writing, 11,* 489–503.

Cain, K., Oakhill, J., Barnes, M., & Bryant, P. (2001). Comprehension skill, inference making ability, and their relation to knowledge. *Memory and Cognition, 29*(6), 850–860.

Cain, K., Oakhill, J., & Bryant, P. (2004). Children's reading comprehension ability: Concurrent prediction by working memory, verbal ability, and component skills. *Journal of Educational Psychology, 96,* 31–42.

Center, Y., Wheldall, K., Freeman, L., Outhred, L., & McNaught, M. (1995). An evaluation of Reading Recovery. *Reading Research Quarterly, 30,* 240–263.

Chall, Jeanne S. (1967). *Learning to read: The great debate.* New York: McGraw-Hill.

Chapman, J. W., & Tunmer, W. E. (1995). Development of young children's reading self-concepts: An examination of emerging subcomponents. *Journal of Educational Psychology, 87*(1), 154.

Chorzempa, B. F., & Graham, S. (2006). Primary-grade teachers' use of within-class ability grouping in reading. *Journal of Educational Psychology, 98*(3), 529–541.

Christian, K., Morrison, F. J., Frazier, J. A., & Massetti, G. (2000). Specificity in the nature and timing of cognitive growth in kindergarten and first grade. *Journal of Cognition and Development, 1*(4), 429–448.

Clay, M. M. (1985). *The early detection of reading difficulties.* Exeter, NH: Heinemann.

Clymer, T. (1963). The utility of phonic generalizations in the primary grades. *The Reading Teacher, 16,* 252–258.

Coyne, M. D., McCoach, D. B., Loftus, S., Zipoli, R., & Kapp, K. (2009). Direct vocabulary instruction in kindergarten: Teaching for breadth versus depth. *Elementary School Journal, 110*(1), 1–18.

Cunningham, A. E., & Stanovich, K. E. (1997). Early reading acquisition and its relation to reading experience and ability 10 years later. *Developmental Psychology, 33*(6), 934–945.

Dickinson, D. K. (2001). Patterns of book reading in preschool classrooms. In D. K. Dickinson & P. O. Tabors (Eds.), *Preparing for literacy at home and school: The critical role of language development in the preschool years.* Baltimore: Brookes.

Dickinson, D. K., McCabe, A., & Clark-Chiarelli, N. (2004). Preschool-based prevention of reading disability: Realities versus possibilities. In C. A. Stone, E. R. Silliman, B. J. Ehren, & K. Apel (Eds.), *Handbook of literacy and language: Development and disorders* (pp. 209–227). New York: Guilford Press.

Dickinson, D. K., McCabe, A., & Essex, M. J. (2006). A window of opportunity we must open to all: The case for preschool with high-quality language and literacy. In D. K. Dickinson & S. B. Neuman (Eds.), *Handbook of early literacy research* (Vol. 2, pp. 11–28). New York: Guilford Press.

Dickinson, D. K., & Smith, M. W. (1994). Long-term effects of preschool teachers' book readings on low-income children's vocabulary and story comprehension. *Reading Research Quarterly, 29,* 104–122.

Dickinson, D. K., & Tabors, P. O. (2001). *Preparing for literacy at home and school: The critical role of language development in the preschool years.* Baltimore: Brookes.

Dolch, E. W. (1936). A basic sight vocabulary. *Elementary School Journal, 36,* 456–460.

Dole, J. A., Nokes, J. D., & Drits, D. (2009). Cognitive strategy instruction. In S. E. Isreal & G. G. Duffy (Eds.), *Handbook of research on reading comprehension* (pp. 347–372). New York: Routledge.

Dorn, L., & Shubert, B. (2008). A comprehensive intervention model for preventing reading failure: A response to intervention process. *Journal of Reading Recovery, Spring,* 29–41.

Duffy, G. G. (2003). *Explaining reading: A resource for teaching concepts, skills, and strategies.* New York: Guilford Press.

Duffy, G. G., & Hoffman, J. V. (1999). In pursuit of an illusion: The flawed search for a perfect method. *Reading Teacher, 53*(1), 10.

Duke, N. K., & Bennett-Armistead, V. S. (2003). *Reading and writing informational text in the primary grades: Research-based practices.* New York: Scholastic.

Duke, N. K., & Pearson, P. D. (2002). Effective practices for developing reading comprehension. In A. E. Farstrup & S. J. Samuels (Eds.), *What research has to say about reading instruction* (pp. 205–242). Newark, DE: International Reading Association.

Durrell, D. D. (1963). *Phonograms in primary grade words.* Boston: Boston University Press.

Dweck, C. S., & Molden, D. C. (2005). Self-theories: Their impact on competence, motivation, and acquisition. In A. J. Elliot & C. S. Dweck (Eds.), *Handbook of competence and motivation* (pp. 122–140). New York: Guilford Press.

Eeds, M. (1985). Book words: Using a beginning word list of high-frequency words from children's literature: K–3. *The Reading Teacher, 38,* 418–423.

Ehri, L. C. (1998). Grapheme–phoneme knowledge is essential for learning to read words in English. In J. Metsala & L. C. Ehri (Eds.), *Word recognition in beginning literacy* (pp. 3–40). Mahwah, NJ: Erlbaum.

Ehri, L. C. (2005). Learning to read words: Theory, findings, and issues. *Scientific Studies of Reading, 9*(2), 167–188.

Ehri, L. C., Deffner, N. D., & Wilce, L. S. (1984). Pictorial mnemonics for phonics. *Journal of Educational Psychology, 76,* 880–893.

Ehri, L. C., Dreyer, L. G., Flugman, B., & Gross, A. (2007). Reading Rescue: An effective tutoring intervention model for language minority students who are struggling readers in first grade. *American Educational Research Journal, 44*(2), 414–448.

Elkonin, D. B. (1973). U.S.S.R. In J. Downing (Eds.), *Comparative reading* (pp. 551–579). New York: Macmillan.

Fisher, C. W., & Berliner, D. C. (1985). *Perspectives on instructional time.* New York: Longmans.

Fisher, D., Flood, J., Lapp, D., & Frey, N. (2004). Interactive read alouds: Is there a common set of implementation practices? *The Reading Teacher, 58,* 8–17.

Fletcher, J. M., Shaywitz, S. E., Shankweiler, D., Katz, I., Liberman, I., Steubing, K. K., et al. (1994). Cognitive profiles of reading disability: Comparisons of discrepancy and low achievement definitions. *Journal of Educational Psychology, 86,* 6–23.

Foorman, B. F., Fletcher, J. M., & Francis, D. (2004). *Texas Primary Reading Inventory.* Austin: Texas Educational Agency and the University of Texas System.

Fountas, I. C., & Pinnell, G. S. (1996). *Guided reading: Good first teaching for all children.* Portsmouth, NH: Heinemann.

Fox, B., & Routh, D. K. (1975). Analyzing spoken language into words, syllables, and phonemes: A developmental study. *Journal of Psycholinguist Research, 4,* 331–342.

Francis, D. J., Shaywitz, S., & Steubing, K. (1996). Developmental lag versus deficit models of reading disability: A longitudinal, individual growth curves analysis. *Journal of Educational Psychology, 88,* 3–17.

Fromkin, V., Rodman, R., & Hyams, N. (2003). *An introduction to language* (7th ed.). Boston: Wadsworth.

Fry, E. B. (2002). Readability versus leveling. *The Reading Teacher, 56,* 272–286.

Fry, E. B., Kress, J. E., & Fountoukidis, D. L. (1993). *The reading teacher's book of lists* (3rd ed.). Paramus, NY: Prentice-Hall.

Fuchs, D., & Fuchs, L. S. (2006). Introduction to response to intervention: What, why, and how valid is it? *Reading Research Quarterly, 41*(1), 93–98.

Fuchs, D., Fuchs, L. S., & Burish, P. (2000). Peer-assisted learning strategies: An evidence-based practice to promote reading achievement. *Learning Disabilities Research and Practice, 15,* 85–91.

Gallagher, A., Frith, U., & Snowling, M. J. (2000). Precursors of literacy delay among children at genetic risk of dyslexia. *Journal of Child Psychology and Psychiatry, 41,* 203–213.

Gelzheiser, L. M., Scanlon, D. M., Vellutino, F. R., & Hallgren-Flynn, L. (under review). Effects of the Interactive Strategies Approach-Extended, a responsive and comprehensive intervention for older struggling readers.

Gomez-Bellenge, F. X., Rogers, E., & Fullerton, S. K. (2003). *Reading Recovery and Descubriendo la Lectura national report 2001–2002.* Columbus: Reading Recovery National Data Evaluation Center, Ohio State University.

Good, R. H., Kaminski, R. A., Smith, S., Laimon, D., & Dill, S. (2001). *Dynamic indicators of basic early literacy skills* (5th ed.). Eugene: University of Oregon.

Goodman, K. S. (1967). Reading: A psycholinguistic guessing game. *Journal of the Reading Specialist, 6,* 126–135.

Gough, P., Juel, C., & Griffith, P. (1992). Reading, spelling, and the orthographic cipher. In P. Gough, L. C. Ehri, & R. Treiman (Eds.), *Reading acquisition* (pp. 35–48). Hillsdale, NJ: Erlbaum.

Graves, M. F. (2006). *The vocabulary book: Learning and instruction.* New York: Teachers College Press.

Graves, M. F., & Slater, W. (1987, April). *The development of reading vocabularies in rural disadvantaged students, inner-city disadvantaged students, and middle-class suburban students.* Paper presented at the annual meeting of the American Educational Research Association, Washington, DC.

Guthrie, J. T., Wigfield, A., Barbosa, P., Perencevich, K. C., Taboada, A., Davis, M. H., et al. (2004). Increasing reading comprehension and engagement through concept-oriented reading instruction. *Journal of Educational Psychology, 96*(3), 403–423.

Hart, B., & Risley, T. R. (1995). *Meaning differences in the everyday experience of young American children.* Baltimore: Brookes.

Harvey, S., & Goudvis, A. (2007). *Strategies that work: Teaching comprehension to enhance understanding* (2nd ed.). York, ME: Stenhouse.

Hickman, P., Pollard-Durodola, S., & Vaughn, S. (2004). Storybook reading: Improving vocabulary and comprehension for English-language learners. *The Reading Teacher, 57,* 720–730.

Hiebert, E. H. (Ed.). (2009). *Reading more, reading better.* New York: Guilford Press.

Hirsch, E. D. (2006). *The knowledge deficit: Closing the shocking educational gap for American children.* Boston: Houghton Mifflin.

Hirsch, E. D. J. (2003). Reading comprehension requires knowledge of words and the world: Scientific insights into the fourth grade slump and the nation's stagnant comprehension scores. *American Educator, 27*(1), 10–48.

Invernizzi, M. A., Meier, J., & Juel, C. (2003–2007). *PALS: Phonological Awareness Literacy Screening.* Charlottesville, VA: University of Virginia.

Johnston, P. H. (1997). *Knowing literacy: Constructive literacy assessment.* York, ME: Stenhouse.

Juel, C. (1988). Learning to read and write: A longitudinal study of 54 children from first through fourth grades. *Journal of Educational Psychology, 80,* 437–447.

Klingner, J., Vaughn, S., & Schumm, J. S. (1998). Collaborative strategic reading during social studies in herterogeneous fourth-grade classrooms. *Elementary School Journal, 99,* 3–22.

Lonigan, C., & Whitehurst, G. J. (1998). Efficacy of parent and teacher involvement in a shared-reading intervention for preschool children from low-income backgrounds. *Early Childhood Research Quarterly, 13,* 263–290.

Lovett, M. W., De Palma, M., Frijters, J., Steinbach, K., Temple, M., Benson, N., et al. (2008). Interventions for reading difficulties. *Journal of Learning Disabilities, 41*(4), 333–352.

Lovett, M. W., Lacerenza, L., Borden, S., Frijiters, J., Steinbach, K. A., & De Palma, M. (2000). Components of effective remediation for developmental reading disability: Combining phonological and strategy-based instruction to improve outcomes. *Journal of Educational Psychology, 92,* 263–283.

Lyman, F. T. (1981). The responsive classroom discussion: The inclusion of all students. In A. Anderson (Ed.), *Mainstreaming digest* (pp. 109–113). College Park: University of Maryland Press.

Marriott, S. (1995). *Read on: Using fiction in the primary school.* London: Paul Chapman.

Mathes, P. G., Denton, C. A., Fletcher, J. M., Anthony, J. L., Francis, D. J., & Schatschneider, C. (2005). The effects of theoretically different instruction and student characteristics on the skills of struggling readers. *Reading Research Quarterly, 40*(2), 148–182.

McGee, L. M., & Schickendanz, J. A. (2007). Repeated interactive read alouds in preschool and kindergarten. *The Reading Teacher, 60*(8), 742–751.

McKenna, M. C., Kear, D. J., & Ellsworth, R. A. (1995). Children's attitude towards reading: A national survey. *Reading Research Quarterly, 30,* 934–956.

McKeown, M. G., & Beck, I. L. (2006). Encouraging young children's language interactions with stories. In D. K. Dickinson & S. B. Neuman (Eds.), *Handbook of early literacy research* (Vol. 2, pp. 281–294). New York: Guilford Press.

McKeown, M. G., Beck, I. L., & Blake, R. G. K. (2009). Rethinking reading comprehension instruction: A comparison of instruction for strategies and content approaches. *Reading Research Quarterly, 44*(3), 218–253.

Mellard, D. F., & Johnson, E. (2008). *RTI: A practitioner's guide to implementing response to intervention.* Thousand Oaks, CA: Corwin Press.

Mesmer, H. A. E. (2008). *Tools for matching readers to texts: Research-based practices.* New York: Guilford Press.

Morgan, P. L., Fuchs, D., Compton, D. L., Cordray, D. S., & Fuchs, L. S. (2008). Does early reading failure decrease children's reading motivation? *Journal of Learning Disabilities, 41*(5), 387–404.

Morrow, L. M., & Gambrell, L. B. (2000). Literature-based reading instruction. In M. L. Kamil, P. B. Mosenthal, P. D. Pearson, & R. Barr (Eds.), *Handbook of reading research* (Vol. 3, pp. 563–586). Mahwah, NJ: Erlbaum.

Morrow, L. M., & Grambrell, L. B. (2001). Literature-based instruction in the early years. In S. B. Neuman & D. D. Dickinson (Eds.), *Handbook of early literacy research* (pp. 348–360). New York: Guilford Press.

Morrow, L. M., & Schickedanz, J. A. (2006). The relationships between sociodramatic play and literacy development. In D. K. Dickinson & S. B. Neuman (Eds.), *Handbook of early literacy research* (Vol. 2, pp. 269–280). New York: Guilford Press.

Muter, V., Hulme, C., Snowling, M. J., & Stevenson, J. (2004). Phonemes, rimes, vocabulary, and grammatical skills as foundations for early reading development: Evidence from a longitudinal study. *Developmental Psychology, 40,* 665–681.

Nagy, W. E., & Herman, P. A. (1987). Breadth and depth of vocabulary knowledge: Implications for acquisition and instruction. In M. G. McKeown & M. E. Curtis (Eds.), *The nature of vocabulary acquisition* (pp. 19–36). Hillside, NJ: Erlbaum.

National Association of State Directors of Special Education. (2005). *Response to intervention: Policy Considerations and Implementation.* Alexandria, VA: Author.

National Early Literacy Panel. (2008). *Developing early literacy.* Washington, DC: National Institute for Literacy.

National Reading Panel. (2000). *Teaching children to read: An evidence-based assessment of the scientific research literature on reading and its implications for reading instruction:*

Reports of subgroups. Washington, DC: National Institute of Child Health and Human Development.

Neuman, S. B. (2006). The knowledge gap: Implications for early education. In S. B. Neuman & D. K. Dickenson (Eds.), *Handbook of early literacy research* (Vol. 2, pp. 29–40). New York: Guilford Press.

Neuman, S. B., & Roskos, K. (1993). Access to print for children of poverty: Differential effects of adult mediation and literacy-enriched play settings on environmental and functional print tasks. *American Educational Research Journal, 30,* 95–122.

Nicholls, J. G. (1978). The development of the concepts of effort and ability, perception of academic attainment, and the understanding that difficult tasks require more than ability. *Child Development, 49,* 800–814.

Nicholls, J. G. (1990). What is ability and why are we mindful of it?: A developmental perspective. In R. Sternberg & J. Kolligian (Eds.), *Competence considered* (pp. 11–40). New Haven, CT: Yale University Press.

Nicholson, T. (1991). Do children read words better in context or in lists? A classic study revisited. *Journal of Educational Psychology, 83,* 444–450.

Niiya, Y., Crocker, J., & Bartmess, E. N. (2004). From vulnerability to resilience: Learning orientations buffer contingent self-esteem from failure. *Psychological Science, 15,* 801–805.

Nolen, S. B. (2001). Constructing literacy in the kindergarten: Task structure, collaboration, and motivation. *Cognition and Instruction, 19,* 95–142.

Nye, B., Konstantopolous, S., & Hedges, L. V. (2004). How large are teacher effects? *Educational Evaluation and Policy Analysis, 26*(3), 237–257.

Nystrand, M. (with Gamoran, A., Kachur, R., & Prendergast, C.). (1997). *Opening dialogue: Understanding the dynamics of language and learning in the English classroom.* New York: Teachers College Press.

O'Connor, R. E. (2000). Increasing the intensity of intervention in kindergarten and first grade. *Learning Disabilities Research and Practice, 15*(1), 43–54.

O'Connor, R. E., Harty, K. R., & Fulmer, D. (2005). Tiers of intervention in kindergarten through third grade. *Journal of Learning Disabilities, 38*(6), 532–538.

Ogle, D. (1986). K-W-L: A teaching model that develops action reading of expository text. *The Reading Teacher, 40,* 564–570

Ouellette, G. P. (2006). What's meaning got to do with it: The role of vocabulary in word reading and reading comprehension. *Journal of Educational Psychology, 98*(3), 554–566.

Paris, A. H., & Paris, S. G. (2007). Teaching narrative comprehension strategies to first graders. *Cognition and Instruction, 25*(1), 1–44.

Paris, S. G. (2005). Reinterpreting the development of reading skills. *Reading Research Quarterly, 40*(2), 184–202.

Paris, S. G., Lipson, M., & Wixson, K. K. (1983). Becoming a strategic reader. *Contemporary Educational Psychology, 8,* 293–216.

Pearson, P. D. (2006). Foreword. In K. S. Goodman (Ed.), *The truth about DIBELS: What it is, what it does* (pp. v–viii). Portsmouth, NH: Heinemann.

Pearson, P. D., & Gallagher, M. (1983). The instruction of reading comprehension. *Contemporary Educational Psychology, 8,* 317–344.

Perfetti, C. A., Landi, N., & Oakhill, J. (2005). The acquisition of reading comprehension skill. In M. J. Snowling & C. Hulme (Eds.), *The science of reading: A handbook* (pp. 227–247). Malden, MA: Blackwell.

Phillips, L. M., Norris, S. P., Osmond, W. C., & Maynard, A. M. (2002). Relative reading achievement: A longitudinal study of 187 children from first through sixth grades. *Journal of Educational Psychology, 94*(1), 3–13.

Pitcher, B., & Zhihui, F. (2007). Can we trust levelled texts? An examination of their reliability and quality from a linguistic perspective. *Literacy, 41*(1), 43–51.

Prawat, R. S. (1989). Promoting access to knowledge, strategy, and disposition in students: A research synthesis. *Review of Educational Research, 59*(1), 1–41.

Pressley, M. (2006). *Reading instruction that works: The case for balanced teaching* (3rd ed.). New York: Guilford Press.

Pressley, M., Wood, E., Woloshyn, V. E., Martin, V., King, A., & Menke, D. (1992). Encouraging mindful use of prior knowledge: Attempting to construct explanatory answers facilitates learning. *Educational Psychologist, 27*, 91–110.

Rayner, K., Foorman, B. R., Perfetti, C. A., Pesetsky, D., & Seidenberg, M. S. (2002). How should reading be taught? *Scientific American, 286*, 84–91.

Read, C. (1971). Preschool children's knowledge of English phonology. *Harvard Educational Review, 41*, 1–34.

Read, C., Zhang, Y. F., Nie, H. Y., & Ding, B. Q. (1986). The ability to manipulate speech sounds depends on knowing alphabetic writing. *Cognition, 24*, 270–292.

Roberts, K. L., & Duke, N. K. (2010). Comprehension in the elementary grades: The research base. In K. Ganske & D. Fisher (Eds.), *Comprehension across the curriculum: Perspectives and practices K–12* (pp. 23–45). New York: Guilford Press.

Roehler, I. R., & Duffy, G. G. (1984). Direct explanation of comprehension processes. In G. G. Duffy, I. R. Roehler, & J. Mason (Eds.), *Comprehension instruction: Perspectives and suggestions* (pp. 265–280). New York: Longman.

Santoro, L. E., Chard, D. J., Howard, L., & Baker, S. (2008). Making the very most of classroom read-alouds to promote comprehension and vocabulary. *The Reading Teacher, 61*(5), 396–408.

Saunders-Smith, G. (2003). *The ultimate guided reading how-to book: Building literacy through small-group instruction.* Tucson, AZ: Zephyr Press.

Scanlon, D. M. (2010). Response to intervention as an assessment: The role of assessment and instruction in the prevention and identification of reading disabilities. In R. Allington & A. McGill-Franzen (Eds.), *Handbook of reading disabilities research.* New York: Routledge.

Scanlon, D. M., & Anderson, K. L. (2010). Using the interactive strategies approach to preventing reading difficulties in an RTI context. In K. Wixson & M. Lipson (Eds.), *Approaches to response to intervention (RTI): Evidence-based frameworks for preventing reading difficulties.* Newark, DE: International Reading Association.

Scanlon, D. M., Gelzheiser, L. M., & Anderson, K. L., Vellutino, F. R., & Schatschneider (in preparation). *The effects of professional development based on the interactive strategies approach on instruction and learning in the early primary grades.*

Scanlon, D. M., Gelzheiser, L. M., Vellutino, F. R., Schatschneider, C., & Sweeny, J. M. (2008). Reducing the incidence of early reading difficulties: Professional development for classroom teachers versus direct interventions for children. *Learning and Individual Differences, 18*(3), 346–359.

Scanlon, D. M., & Sweeney, J. M. (2008). Response to intervention: An overview. *Educator's Voice, 1*, 16–29.

Scanlon, D. M., & Vellutino, F. R. (1996). Prerequisite skills, early instruction, and success in first-grade reading: Selected results from a longitudinal study. *Mental Retardation and Developmental Disabilities Research Reviews, 2*, 54–63.

Scanlon, D. M., & Vellutino, F. R. (1997). A comparison of the instructional backgrounds and cognitive profiles of poor, average, and good readers who were initially identified as at risk for reading failure. *Scientific Studies of Reading, 1*(3), 191–215.

Scanlon, D. M., Vellutino, F. R., Small, S. G., Fanuele, D. P., & Sweeny, J. M. (2005). Severe reading difficulties—can they be prevented?: A comparison of prevention and intervention approaches. *Exceptionality, 13*(4), 209–227.

Scarborough, H. S. (2001). Connecting early language and literacy to later reading (dis)abilities: Evidence, theory, and practice. In S. B. Neuman & D. K. Dickinson (Eds.), *Handbook of early literacy research* (Vol. 1, pp. 97–110). New York: Guilford Press.

Scarborough, H. S., & Dobrich, W. (1994). On the efficacy of reading to preschoolers. *Developmental Review, 14*, 245–302.

Scarborough, H. S. & Parker, J. D. (2003). Matthew Effects in children with learning disabilities: Development of reading, IQ, and psychosocial problems from grade 2 to grade 8. *Annals of Dyslexia, 53*, 47–71.

Schneider, W., Roth, E., & Ennemoser, M. (2000). Training phonological skills and letter knowledge in children at risk for dyslexia: A comparison of three kindergarten intervention programs. *Journal of Educational Psychology, 92*, 284–295.

Schultheiss, O. C., & Brunstein, J. C. (2005). An implicit motive perspective on competence. In A. J. Elliot & C. S. Dweck (Eds.), *Handbook of competence and motivation* (pp. 31–51). New York: Guilford Press.

Schunk, D. H., Pintrich, P. R., & Meece, J. L. (2008). *Motivation in education: Theory, research, and applications* (3rd ed.). Upper Saddle River, NJ: Pearson.

Scott, J. A., Jamieson-Noel, D., & Asselin, M. (2003). Vocabulary instruction throughout the day in twenty-three Canadian upper-elementary classrooms. *Elementary School Journal, 103*(3), 269–286.

Sénéchal, M., Ouellette, G., & Rodney, D. (2006). The misunderstood giant: On the predictive role of early vocabulary to future reading. In S. B. Neuman & D. D. Dickinson (Eds.), *Handbook of early literacy research* (Vol. 2, pp. 173–184). New York: Guilford Press.

Share, D. L. (1995). Phonological recoding and self-teaching: Sine qua non of reading acquisition. *Cognition, 55*, 151–218.

Silverman, R. (2007). A comparison of three methods of vocabulary instruction during read-alouds in kindergarten. *Elementary School Journal, 108*(2), 97–113.

Smith, A. E., Jussim, L., & Eccles, J. (1999). Do self-fulfilling prophecies accumulate, dissipate, or remain stable over time? *Journal of Personality and Social Psychology, 77*, 548–565.

Snow, C. E., Burns, M. S., & Griffin, P. (1998). *Preventing reading difficulties in young children*. Washington, DC: National Academy Press.

Stanovich, K. E. (1986). Matthew effects in reading: Some consequences of individual differences in the acquisition of literacy. *Reading Research Quarterly, 21*, 360–407.

Storch, S. A., & Whitehurst, G. J. (2002). Oral language and code-related precursors to reading: Evidence from a longitudinal structural model. *Developmental Psychology, 38*, 934–947.

Tangel, D. M., & Blachman, B. A. (1992). Effect of phoneme awareness instruction on kindergarten children's invented spelling. *Journal of Reading Behavior, 24*(2), 233–261.

Tangel, D. M., & Blachman, B. A. (1995). Effect of phoneme awareness instruction on the invented spelling of first-grade children. *Journal of Reading Behavior, 27*(2), 153–186.

Taylor, B. M., Pearson, P. D., Clark, K. M., & Walpole, S. (2000). Effective schools and accomplished teachers: Lessons about primary-grade reading instruction in low-income schools. *Elementary School Journal, 101*, 121–165.

Taylor, L., & Adelman, H. S. (1999). Personalizing classroom instruction to account for motivational and developmental differences. *Reading and Writing Quarterly, 15*, 255–276.

Tivnan, T., & Hemphill, L. (2005). Comparing four literacy reform models in high-poverty schools: Patterns of first-grade achievement. *Elementary School Journal, 105*(5), 419–441.

Toregesen, J. K., Alexander, A. W., Wagner, R. K., Rashotte, C. A., Voeller, K., & Conway, T. (2001). Intensive remedial instruction for students with severe reading disabilities: Immediate and long-term outcomes from two instructional approaches *Journal of Learning Disabilities, 34*, 33–58.

Torgesen, J. K., & Burgess, S. R. (1998). Consistency of reading-related phonological processes throughout early childhood: Evidence from longitudinal-correlational and instructional studies. In J. L. Metsala & L. C. Ehri (Eds.), *Word recognition in beginning literacy* (pp. 161–188). Mahwah, NJ: Erlbaum.

Toregesen, J. K., Wagner, R. K., & Rashotte, C. (1994). Longitudinal studies of phonological processing and reading. *Journal of Learning Disabilities, 27*, 276–286.

Treiman, R., Sotak, L., & Bowman, M. (2001). The role of letter names and letter sounds in connecting print to speech. *Memory and Cognition, 29*, 860–873.

Treiman, R., & Zukowski, A. (1996). Children's sensitivity to syllables, onsets, rimes, and phonemes. *Journal of Experimental Child Psychology, 61*, 193–215.

Tunmer, W. E., & Chapman, J. W. (1998). Language prediction skill, phonological recoding ability, and reading. In C. Hulme & R. M. Joshi (Eds.), *Reading and spelling: Development and disorders* (pp. 33–68). Mahwah, NJ: Erlbaum.

Tunmer, W. E., & Chapman, J. W. (2004). The use of context in learning to read. In T. Nunues & P. Bryant (Eds.), *Handbook of children's literacy* (pp. 199–212). Dordrecht, The Netherlands: Kluwer Academic.

Vaughn, S., Linan-Thompson, S., & Hickman, P. (2003). Response to treatment as a means of identifying students with reading/learning disabilities. *Exceptional Children, 69*(4), 391–409.

Vellutino, F. R. (1979). *Dyslexia: Theory and research.* Cambridge, MA: MIT Press.

Vellutino, F. R., Fletcher, J. M., Snowling, M. J., & Scanlon, D. M. (2004). Specific reading disability (dyslexia): What have we learned in the past four decades? *Journal of Child Psychology and Psychiatry, 45*(1), 2–40.

Vellutino, F. R., & Scanlon, D. M. (2002). The interactive strategies approach to reading intervention. *Contemporary Educational Psychology, 27*(4), 573–635.

Vellutino, F. R., Scanlon, D. M., Sipay, E. R., Small, S. G., Pratt, A., Chen, R., et al. (1996). Cognitive profiles of difficult-to-remediate and readily remediated poor readers: Early intervention as a vehicle for distinguishing between cognitive and experiential deficits as basic causes of specific reading disability. *Journal of Educational Psychology, 88*(4), 601–638.

Vellutino, F. R., Scanlon, D. M., Zhang, H., & Schatschneider, C. (2008). Using response to kindergarten and first-grade intervention to identify children at risk for long-term reading difficulties. *Reading and Writing, 21*, 437–480.

Venezky, R. L. (1998) An alternative perspective on Success for All. *Advances in Educational Policy, 4*, 145–165.

Vygotsky, L. S. (1978). *Mind in society: The development of higher psychological processes.* Cambridge, MA: Harvard University Press.

Wagner, R. K., Toregesen, J. K., & Rashotte, C. (1994). The development of reading related phonological processing abilities: New evidence of bidirectional causality from a latent variable longitudinal study. *Developmental Psychology, 30*, 73–78.

Wanzek, J., & Vaughn, S. (2008). Response to varying amounts of time in reading intervention for students with low response to intervention. *Journal of Learning Disabilities, 42*(2), 126–142.

Watts, S. (1995). Vocabulary instruction during reading lessons in six classrooms. *Journal of Reading Behavior, 27*(3), 399–424.

Wegerif, R., Mercer, N., & Dawes, L. (1999). From social interaction to individual reasoning: An empirical investigation of a possible socio-cultural model of cognitive development. *Learning and Instruction, 9*(6), 493–516.

Weinstein, C. F., & Mayer, R. F. (1986). The teaching of learning strategies. In M. C. Wittrock (Ed.), *Handbook of research on teaching* (pp. 315–327). New York: Macmillan.

Welsch, J. G. (2008). Playing within and beyond the story: Encouraging book-related pretend play. *The Reading Teacher, 62*(2), 138–147.

Whitehurst, G. J., Arnold, D. S., Epstein, J. N., Angell, A. L., Smith, M., & Fischel, J. E. (1994). A picture book reading intervention in day care and home for children from low-income families. *Developmental Psychology, 30*, 679–689.

Whitehurst, G. J., & Lonigan, C. J. (1998). Child development and emergent literacy. *Child Development, 68*, 848–872.

Wood, D., Bruner, J. S., & Ross, G. (1976). The role of tutoring in problem solving. *Journal of Child Psychology and Child Psychiatry, 17*(2), 89–100.

Yell, M. L., Shriner, J. G., & Katsiyannis, A. (2006). Individuals with Disabilities Education Improvement Act of 2004 and IDEA Regulations of 2006: Implications for educators, administrators, and teacher trainers. *Focus on Exceptional Children, 39*(1), 1–24.

Yopp, H. K. (1988). The validity and reliability of phonemic awareness tests. *Reading Research Quarterly, 23*, 159–199.

Yopp, H. K. (1995). Read-aloud books for developing phonemic awareness: An annotated bibliography. *The Reading Teacher, 48*(6), 538–542.

Yuill, N., & Oakhill, J. (1991). *Children's problems in text comprehension.* Cambridge, UK: Cambridge University Press.

CHILDREN'S BOOKS

Beech, L. W. (2003). *My bear.* New York: Scholastic.

Cameron, P. (1961). *"I can't," said the ant.* New York: Coward-McCann.

Carle, E. (1974). *All about Arthur (an absolutely absurd ape).* New York: Franklin-Watts.

Day, E. (1997). *Good dog Carl.* New York: Aladdin Paperbacks.

Dobeck, M. (1996). *Six fine fish* (Celebration Press Ready Readers). Parsippany, NJ: Modern Curriculum Press.

Gordon, J. (1991). *Six sleepy sheep.* New York: Puffin Books.

go to. (1999). Jenison, MI: Short Books.

Hague, K. (1984). *Alphabears: An ABC book.* New York: Holt.

Hillert, M. (1963) *The three little pigs* (Modern Curriculum Press Beginning to Read Series). Upper Saddle River, NJ: Pearson Education.

Lionni, L. (1963). *Swimmy.* New York: Knopf.

Logan, C. (1997). *Look closer.* Parsippany, NJ: Pearson Education.

Mark, A. (1997). *Monster mop* (Celebration Press Ready Readers). Parsippany, NJ: Modern Curriculum Press.

Minkoff, M. (1996). *Where is the Queen?* (Celebration Press Ready Readers). Parsippany, NJ: Modern Curriculum Press.

Pollock, P. (1996). *The turkey girl.* New York: Little, Brown.

Potter, B. (2002). *The tale of Peter Rabbit.* London: Penguin. (Original work published 1902)

Robinson, F. R. (1997). *Eggs!* (Celebration Press Ready Readers). Parsippany, NJ: Modern Curriculum Press.

Seuss, Dr. (1963). *ABC.* New York: Random House.

Seuss, Dr. (1974). *There's a wocket in my pocket.* New York: Random House.

Spevack, J. (1997). *My room* (Celebration Press Ready Readers). Parsippany, NJ: Modern Curriculum Press.

Williams, M. (1922). *The velveteen rabbit.* New York: Knopf.

Index